THE CHRIST WITHIN

The Church and New Age Seek Him

R.E. McMaster, Jr.

Copyright © 1995
R.E. McMaster, Jr.

ISBN 0-9643552-0-5

First Printing 1995

Cover design by Imperial Lithography & Dryography

Published by:
A.N. International, Inc.
P.O. Box 84901
Phoenix, Arizona 85071
(800) 528-0559

For My Father
Ralph E. McMaster, Sr.

Who Faithfully loved and cherished
my mother for over 55 years.

Who taught me manly traits
which have carried me through
life's trials and tribulations.

Who passed away the afternoon
I completed this book.

Books by

R.E. McMaster, Jr.

Cycles of War, The Next Six Years, 1977
The Trader's Notebook, 1978
The Trader's Notebook, 1979
The Trader's Notebook, 1980
Wealth for All, 1982
(Book 1 - Religion, Politics and War)
Wealth for All, 1982
(Book 2 - Economics)
No Time for Slaves, 1986
McMaster's Eight M's of Successful Investing, 1994
The Power of Total Perspective, 1994
The Christ Within, 1995
A Highlander's Passion (A Book of Poetry), 1996

Acknowledgment

I have spent seventeen years writing this book. Nevertheless, the completion of this work would not have been possible without the help of the following:

Michelle Arrendale - Rough editing
Katie Baker & Ron King - Indexing
Jane Cooper - Proofreading
Velda King - Coordinating of publishing
Nina Mourning - Grammatical proofreading and readability
Betty Riess - Formatting of manuscript
Lauretta J. Smith - Word processing and cleanup

A special thank you is extended to R. J. Rushdoony at Chalcedon for previously publishing some of these chapters, thus providing a forum for valuable feedback.

My appreciation is also expressed to Bob Jones, for his continual insight and encouragement during the past five years.

Where Scripture is quoted, it is from Thomas Nelson's The Open Bible Expanded Edition, The New King James Version of the Holy Bible.

PREFACE

The following chapters were written over a seventeen-year period. Each stands on its own. Yet, each has been carefully reviewed and revised, updated, and provided with a thread of continuity to tie the entire work together. Therefore, a reader may pick and choose a particular essay of interest. Or, in order to obtain a comprehensive holistic view, a reader may mentally journey through this work from start to finish. In either case, there are hopefully benefits to be obtained. At the very least, the work is unconventional in its attempt to tie government to religion and economics. It is also unique in its linking of the insight of the New Age with Christianity, in piecing together what it means for "the kingdom of God to be within." The kingdom must be within before it can be externalized.

First Light

by

R.E. McMaster, Jr.

I have always awakened at first light

It is the time of day I cherish most

A time when God awakens me to deliver

my daily marching orders

A time when my Father and I have

time alone just to be

A time when I can gently arouse the creatures

from their peaceful slumber

First light, when all is still and quiet

That state of eternal being

As darkness is progressively swept away and joy dawns.

October 18, 1995

Table of Contents

SECTION C: LOVE

SECTION D: GOD'S LAW

SECTION E: CHRISTIAN LEADERSHIP

SECTION F: CHRISTIAN GOVERNMENT

SECTION G: CHRISTIAN ECONOMICS

SECTION H: THE CREATION

SECTION I: CONCLUSIONS

SECTION A

LIGHT STAR WARS

RELIGION IN AMERICA: THE OUTER LIMITS

Promptly at 7:00 a.m. every morning, seven mystics sit on mats in a circle around a fire built in a pit. Accompanying them from a ground-level shelf is a collection of seven deities which also face the flames. The fire ceremony begins when a woman begins to sing in Sanskrit. Thus begins the ancient pre-Vedic ritual which is rooted in the Hindu faith.

A clear crystal is anointed with various substances. There is the passing of a candle flame which serves the purpose of "singing the praises of the Universal Mother." Grain is tossed into the fire along with fruits and flowers as an offering to the god. The candle ritual is followed by the throwing of a coconut, some apples and bananas into the fire.

What is all of this, anyway? Where is it? Some mystical Hindu religious service being held in the high Himalayas? Perhaps instead it is what remains of a cult of '60s hippies who are strung out and wasted on drugs. But neither is the case. Every morning, this ceremony takes place in the woods behind the Aspen Institute for Humanistic Studies in the Colorado Mountains! (Source: The High Valley Independent, Crestone, Colorado)

What happens at the Aspen Institute for Humanistic Studies affects us all. The Aspen Institute is one of the leading intellectual think tanks for the Eastern Establishment which runs this country politically and economically. It often links up with the left-leaning, legislation-drafting Brookings Institution. This confirms again that government is religion applied to economics. It is the Hindu religion which is primarily influential on the U.S. Establishment's governmental and economic policy. Just how far has Hinduism taken India economically?

Located high in the central Colorado Rocky Mountains lies the once-sleepy mountain town of Crestone, Colorado. Nestled in the shadow of the three 14,000-foot-plus Crestone peaks, what was once a nice, little all-American mountain town, has now become what some local residents call "just a cover for an elite group to control things throughout the world."

Let's gather around the fire and have a roll call of these "all-American types" who have now squatted at The Baca area in Crestone. Formerly this was the domain of all-American mountain men. We have the Lindisfarne Mountain Retreat and Chapel, the San Luis Valley Tibetan Project and Monastery, the Taoist Retreat, the Muslim/Sufi Learning Center, Dingo Khentse Rinpoche, the Tibetan Buddhist Monastery, the Zen Institute of Japanese Culture, Eiheja, Zen Buddhist Temple, the Carmelite Chapel and Retreat, the Carmelite Hermitage, the Lam Gampo, Tibetan Buddhist Retreat, the Babaji Ashram, Mother's Temple Shrine of Shiva, Sri Aurobindo and Savitri House Learning Center, the College of the Adepts along with the Library and Archives of Ancient Knowledge, the Suncircle Archaeological Site, the Center for Development Alternatives, the World Garden, Flowers and Herbs of World Religions, the Bistro Restaurant, the Native American Elders Council, the Shontu Arabian Farms, the Experimental Gardens, the Wisdom Education Center, the School of Hebraic Studies, the Sierra Blanca High Altitude School and Experimentation Farm, the Agricultural Center and Seed Bank, the Baca Wildlife Sanctuary for Indigenous and Endangered Species, the Rediscovery Four Corners Wilderness Camp, the Native American Center of Traditional Medicine, the Spiritual Life Institute, the Liberty Hermitage, the Essene School of Life, the Karma Triyana Dharmachakra, the Colorado State University Experimental Farm, and, oh yes, a Baptist church.

What? A Baptist church? What's a Baptist church doing here? "In over their heads?" Actually, the Baptist church was here first. Oh well, maybe they're meditating on James Jordan's book, "The Failure Of The American Baptist Culture."

Strange. I don't see any Puritan Development Center, NFL Showcase or John Wayne Center for Western Art named among this august list at Crestone. But this is not America today - or is it?

I talked to a young man at a Christ for the Nations gathering in Dallas, Texas about the summer he spent at Crestone on a religious retreat. He said strange people would regularly gather around their dormitory in Crestone at night and chant and cast spells.

Just what are all these alien religious groups up to here in the heartland of America? Not contemplating "In God We Trust," I wouldn't think. On July 5, 1987, ground-breaking ceremonies were held for the Temple to the Divine Universal Mother at the Haidakhandi Universal Harham. One could say it was a kind of late 4th of July celebration, Divine Universal Mother style. Of course, the Universal Mother's handmaidens, "the sun and moon were in very auspicious positions according to the Indian astrological calendar.

"The significance of the ground-breaking ceremony is to worship Mother Earth. Worship is also offered to the mineral kingdom, the animal kingdom and the plant kingdom. The beings that live in the underworld are offered prayers. Prayers are also offered to the protectors of the eight directions and all the planets of the zodiac.

"Ceremonies were made to Ananta, the king of snakes, who is considered master of the underworld, for protection of all beings on the site. A gold replica of a snake representing Ananta was made...

"An invocation was given to the Universal Mother, 'the Creatrix and Protectress of all Creation...'" (The High Valley Independent).

Undoubtedly, they've never considered that "Mother Earth," when left to her whims without the reconciliating and subduing efforts of dominion man, and man the steward, is nothing more than a cruel, parsimonious witch. Someone needs to tell them that the natural characteristics of "Mother Earth" include conflict, chance, cycles, poverty and death. Some mother! Men of the cloth would say these negative attributes of "Mother Earth" are pretty close to those of the Prince of Darkness, too.

It seems that anybody who is somebody in this world today knows about this little hot spot of international global religion in Colorado, with the exception, of course, of typical red-blooded Americans. But then again, how long has it been since typical red-blooded Americans knew what was really going on in their country? They've been duped and seduced since at least 1913.

A prince from Thailand, Suchart Kosolkitiwong, who calls himself the "World Peace Envoy," and who is president of the International Federation of Religions in association with the United Nations, made a trek to The Baca at Crestone. He was there July 1 and 2, 1987. (So, American Independence Day was surrounded by two non-American ceremonies.) Prince Suchart Kosolkitiwong, who is also with the World Constitution and Parliament Association, and who is prime director of the Religious Land Hooppa Sawan, is considering building a religious center at The Baca.

All this activity taking place in America makes sense when one observes that the U.S. is, of course, the headquarters for the United Nations, the symbol of the global political movement toward a New World Order. The Council on Foreign Relations and The Trilateral Commission, both located here, could vie for this One-World "honor," too. So, it should come as no surprise, given this internationalist economic and political reality, that the center for One-World religion should be established here in the United States as well.

Government is always religion applied to economics. (The U.S. Founding Fathers knew the importance of having different men run the church than those who ran the government.)

Speaking of economics, the United States is also the origin of the debt-based world reserve currency, the U.S. dollar. (The crescent, the circle and the truncated pyramid on the back of the U.S. one dollar bill is identical to that of the sign of "Tanit." "Tanit" was a consort of Baal Hammon to whom the Carthaginians offered child sacrifices for over 200 years. In the infrared range of the light spectrum, where frequency, form and substance are all interrelated, the symbol of "Tanit" and that which appears on the back of the U.S. one dollar bill attract and emit the same frequency. A continuity of evil? Abortion today is the equivalent of child sacrifice by the Carthaginians.)

Now, as you might suspect, this "Rocky Mountain High" area was not chosen whimsically. The Sangre de Cristos have long been a site of major religious significance for American Indians. Blanca Peak, located 40 miles south of Crestone, is one of the Hopi Indians' four sacred mountains. Considerable archaeological religious evidence has been unearthed there, too, including the discovery of ancient shrines, underground kivis, and burial grounds. Shamans used to make annual pilgrimages to "power points" located on these mountains in a quest for knowledge. For thousands of years this area was considered to be one of the holiest of holy places on earth. These transplanted people here now believe that Crestone is where "the preparation for the new world will take place."

By now it has probably occurred to many that this type of thing did not "evolve" naturally. A man by the name of Maurice Strong wove this web of religious internationalists together. Maurice Strong, who heads up The Baca project, is no 90-pound weakling. He has been called "Custodian of the Planet," "Anti-poverty Warrior," "Salesman for Relief" and "Mystic Millionaire." His entry in Who's Who is three inches long. He holds 26 honorary degrees from universities in the United States, Canada and Europe. He has linked together the twin carnal gods of money and power with his internationalism, couched in the religion of humanitarianism and environmentalism.

Canadian by birth (Oak Lake, Manitoba), Maurice Frederick Strong has served as Undersecretary General of the United Nations. As Undersecretary General of the UN, he was responsible for the World Conference on Environment held in Stockholm in 1972. Out of that arose the United Nations Environment Program. Strong sat with Michael Sweatman and Edmund de Rothschild at the World Conservation Bank Caucus where the plans were laid to capture one-third of the earth into a One-World land trust under the guise of environmentalism. He was also responsible for the infamous Earth Summit held in Rio in 1992.

Strong is the Director of Finance of the Lindisfarne Association, which relocated its headquarters from New York to The Baca in 1979. It was soon followed by the Aspen Institute. Strong donated 300 acres to the Aspen Institute. One of Strong's partners is William Ruckelshaus, a prominent Republican and former head of the EPA.

Under internationalist Canadian Prime Minister Pierre Trudeau, Strong organized the Canadian national energy agency - Petro-Canada. Petro-Canada is the most controversial, socialistic Crown corporation ever created in Canada.

Strong has made his mark (and his fortune) in private industry as well. He developed a graphite mine in Africa, along with a string of gas stations in Eastern Africa. (He learned to speak Swahili.) He made a fortune in Canadian mining stocks and was active in the early stages of the oil and gas development boom headquartered in Calgary, Alberta, Canada. A millionaire at age 30, his corporation was appropriately named "Power Corporation." (Who financed all this?)

Additionally, Strong is or has been a director of over 40 other corporations. He has served as the Canadian Deputy Minister for External Affairs, where he assumed responsibility for foreign aid as these issues came before the United Nations and the World Bank. He bought Prochemo, a Texas-based company, through which he was able to buy control of the Arizona Colorado Land and Cattle Company. Strong later merged AZL with TOSCO, the second largest independent oil refining company in the United States at that time. He now heads Hydro-Quebec, which has caught flak over its treatment of Canada's native peoples who are affected by the utility company's development projects.

Strong also headed up the Canada Development Investment Corporation which was the overall umbrella for many corporations owned by the government of Canada. CFR member and former U.S. Secretary of State George Schultz awarded Maurice Strong a humanitarian award as a result of his work with the UN Office for Emergency Operations in Africa. Says Strong, "I'm hoping to connect what I'm doing at Baca on a grass-roots level with the global level." So, if the "Strong man" has his way, the trend toward One-

World religion, government and economics will continue, based in the United States, backed unknowingly by the American people and their tax dollars.

(Credit for much of the research for this chapter goes to Reaper reader Mr. Donald R. Hood, the staff writers of The Valley Courier of Alamoso, Colorado and the staff writers of The High Valley Independent of Crestone, Colorado.)

* * *

The March 1, 1992 issue of Parade Magazine featured a full-color, three-page article by Carl Sagan entitled, "To Avert a Common Danger." Sagan talked about how religion and science, old antagonists, are now forging a new alliance. He stated, "And at each step, we have emphasized the local over the global, the short-term over the long. We have destroyed the forests, eroded the topsoil, changed the composition of the atmosphere, depleted the protective ozone layer, tampered with the climate, poisoned the air and the waters, and made the poorest people suffer most from the deteriorating environment. We have become predators on the biosphere - full of arrogant entitlement, always taking and never giving back. And so, we are now a danger to ourselves and the other beings with whom we share the planet.

"The wholesale attack on the global environment is not the fault only of profit-hungry industrialists or visionless and corrupt politicians. There is plenty of blame to share.

"The tribe of scientists has played a central role. Many of us didn't even bother to think about the long-term consequences of our inventions. We have been too ready to put devastating powers into the hands of the highest bidder and the officials of whichever nation we happen to be living in. In too many cases, we have lacked a moral compass. Science from its very beginnings has been eager, in the words of René Descartes, 'to make us masters and possessors of nature,' and to use science, as Francis Bacon said, to bend all of nature into 'the service of man.'...

"The religious tribe also has played a central role...The notion of 'us against Nature' is a legacy of our religious traditions. In the book of Genesis, God gives humans 'dominion...over every living thing,' and the 'fear' and 'dread' of us is to be upon 'every beast.' Man is urged to 'subdue' nature, and the word 'subdue' was translated from a Hebrew word with strong military connotations. There is much else in the Bible - and in the medieval Christian tradition out of which modern science emerged - along similar lines...

"True, there is nothing in the Judeo-Christian-Muslim tradition that approaches the cherishing of nature in the Hindu-Buddhist-Jain tradition or among Native Americans. Indeed, both Western religion and Western science have gone out of their way to assert that nature is just the setting and not the story, that nature should not be viewed as sacred...

"It has been my good fortune to participate in an extraordinary sequence of recent gatherings that have helped set the stage for the May meeting in Washington and other, similar meetings throughout the world: The leaders of our planet's religions have met with legislators from many nations, and with scientists, to try to deal with the rapidly worsening world environmental crisis...

"The interconnectedness of all human beings was a theme constantly stressed...

"Since the Oxford and Moscow meetings, many parliamentarians and environmentalists have worked to prepare for this June's 'Earth Summit' of national leaders in Brazil, which may lead to true international commitments to fix the global environment - or at least to slow the rate of its degradation...

"Religious leaders in many nations, including the United States, have moved into action...U.S. Sen. Al Gore (now Vice-President) is playing a central role...

"Cleaning up the environment and changing industrial practices that threaten it take money, of course..."

Next, Sagan, also in Parade, reprinted a text sent by scientists to religious leaders. Part of this text includes the following statements: "...We are close to committing - many would argue we are already committing - what in religious language is sometimes called Crimes against Creation...

"The environmental crisis requires radical changes not only in public policy, but also in individual behavior. The historical record makes clear that religious teaching, example and leadership are powerfully able to influence personal conduct and commitment.

"As scientists, many of us have had profound experiences of awe and reverence before the universe. We understand that what is regarded as sacred is more likely to be treated with care and respect. Our planetary home should be so regarded. Efforts to safeguard and cherish the environment need to be infused with a vision of the sacred...

"We believe the environmental crisis is intrinsically religious."

Isn't it interesting that the only attack Carl Sagan made against any religion was against the uniquely monotheistic Judeo-Christian-Muslim tradition. Sagan's remarks are revolutionary. The Hebrew-Christian heritage is the backbone of our political and economic structure. The environmental scare tactics have been widely publicized. Sagan's comments betray an underlying assumption that the problems that concern us today: war and the threat of war, world hunger and ecological devastation stem from the Christian world view of man as the focal point of creation with nature playing a subordinate role as man's servant. The logical result of the Christian paradigm, according to Sagan's thinking, is the attitude that we are in charge, hence we can do whatever we want with nature if it promotes our interests. Christians supposedly reason that since God gave us dominion over the earth, we can do with it as we please.

In reality, true environmental distress occurs in non-Christian, non-free market cultures, in the undeveloped Third World, and in statist countries such as the old U.S.S.R. In the Judeo-Christian-Muslim tradition, man is created by God to be a steward, exercising loving responsibility over the garden (nature), which He has given man to use and to safeguard. This is in sharp contrast to many other religions in which man is seen as an evolutionary part of nature who can become his own autonomous god.

* * *

The Earth Summit was held in Rio de Janeiro, Brazil on June 1-12, 1992. This was preceded by the World Wilderness Congress held in Denver, Colorado in 1987. The Earth Summit was officially called the United Nations Conference on Environment and Development. Representatives from 140 countries attended. All total, 6,000 government officials gathered in Rio.

This Earth Summit was the official global launching of the New World Order under the guise of environmentalism. It was an exercise by "watermelons," green on the outside but red on the inside. It was the fulfillment of the synthesis of the Hegelian dialectic; of the evolutionary, collective thesis of communism versus the evolutionary radical antithesis of individualism and debt capitalism into the synthesis of the New World Order as fascist mercantilism - One-World socialism. The Tower of Babel, Old Babylon, is rising.

Now the U.S. government has a series of global treaties set to be signed that will gut U.S. sovereignty and merge the U.S. into the New World Order: NAFTA and GATT are two. A treaty is the only document that supersedes the U.S. Constitution. All this, of course, will be accomplished in the name of "saving the planet." Look for a series of orchestrated articles and catastrophes to be used as catalysts to bring about this New World Order. (You have to break an egg to make an omelet, or so it is said.)

THE QUEST FOR SUPERNATURAL POWER

Man is made in the image of God (spiritual) and formed from the dust of the earth (physical). The "God is dead" movement of the 1960s logically gave way to the rampant materialism of the '70s and '80s when man, denying his spiritual nature, focused on his physical nature. It also made consistent the federal government's redistribution of wealth. With the absence of a Creator, the civil government assumes the role of Sovereign and thereby attempts to provide for the economic sustenance of its creatures.

The Christian spiritual void which accelerated in this country with Darwin and the War of Northern Aggression against the South, accelerated again in the 1890s during the era of the Robber Barons. It then picked up momentum in 1913, World War I, during the FDR era, World War II, Korea, and in the Vietnam decade of the '60s, coming to full fruition in the '90s. The New Age Movement, effectively high-tech neo-paganism, is man's concession that he in fact does have a spiritual nature. This time, it's clearly sans God and His authority, His law, but is rather man as god (individually and/or as civil government). For today's New Agers, everyone gets to be a god, except, of course, Jesus Christ, who is the only religious leader whose name is taken in vain.

The contemporary "human potential," "be all you can be," "do your own thing," politically correct, feminine, astrological and witchcraft-based New Age movement, which literally runs this country now through its influence in the White House, is Luciferian. Satan, as Lucifer, comes disguised as an angel of light. Some New Agers are now self-consciously meditating and going into the spirit world to bring back their "angels." Others, such as Vice President Al Gore, merely couch their neo-paganism in environmentalism, where man belongs to Mother Earth (feminine), rather than the created earth belonging to man (masculine).

It was Satan's first sin, the desire of his heart, to "be as God." The fallout of this pride was/is rebellion, conflict and lawlessness. Eve picked up on this naturally. Women are by creation ungrounded and open to the spiritual world. The feminine neo-paganism of today accordingly produces angry, roaring lions, seeking to kill, steal and destroy. Anyone who doubts the roots of this present-ruling, New Age, American neo-pagan religion just needs to go back and check the writings of last century's famous black arts magician, Aleister Crowley, the writings of Anton LaVey in "The Satanic Bible," or that of William James.

Is the idea of developing one's full potential an attractive one? Of course it is. The most dangerous lies are 95 percent true. It is gratifying to human pride to sing, "I did it my way," as opposed to submitting oneself unto the teaching of the Holy Spirit and the correction of God's Holy and character-building Living Word. When one does submit to this teaching, sin is replaced in one's life so that the heart and spirit are pure before God, holy and righteous. Then God can develop one's God-given calling, according to the purpose for which one was created, thus truly becoming in every way, naturally and supernaturally, temporally and eternally, all that one can and should be. It is a subtle, but very important difference, "doing it my way" versus God's way.

Make no mistake about it. We do have tremendous human potential. But God purposely created us with limits for our own good. By and large, the power of the spirit world is not intended for us. God has created us for a specific purpose, and even though we have self-willed potential which can be realized, as submitted creatures unto the Creator, we are obediently obliged to do nothing more than what He allows us and has called us to do. Supernatural power in a Christian sense, then, is dependent and predicated upon Scripture-based spiritual growth. In other words, it is earned. This is in sharp contrast to neo-pagan, lawless, New Age, Golden Dawn-based magic, which is unearned spiritual power. The work of the Holy Spirit builds on man's discipleship and obedience to God's Law-Word (the Sword of the Spirit is the Word of God), rather than the astrology and witchcraft-based techniques of the New Ager, who works to determine and predestine the thoughts, emotions and actions of fallen man. It boils down to God's promotion versus self-promotion.

Truly, the battle is for the heart (emotions), mind (thoughts), soul and body of man. As a man thinketh, so he is. A man's thoughts arise from his values which, from the perspective of the natural man, are controlled by the unbridled emotions of his heart, rather than the law of God. (If it feels good, do it.) In the Bible and in church history, God has consistently chosen His humble, pure of heart and obedient ones to perform His supernatural works. Moses was the most humble man on the face of the earth. David was a man after God's own heart who loved His law. The miracle-performing prophets of the Old Testament were pure of heart and obedient. Jesus, of course, was the capstone and cornerstone who perfectly kept the law. His disciples were "sold out" to God after His ascension.

Because we are creatures, not the Creator or co-creators with God, only adopted sons in Christ, Christians for the most part, are to stand still when it comes to the supernatural phenomena as the world knows it today, and as Hollywood depicts it. The battle is the Lord's. We walk by faith, not by sight. Not by might, not by power, but by His Spirit do we walk. Prayer and knowledge of the Scriptures are our basic weapons in the supernatural arena. It is only after we become more Christ-like and fully mature, manifesting the fruit of the Spirit, can God trust us with the gifts of the Spirit (supernatural power).

Consider our eyes, for example. Of all of God's created light spectrum, we only see five percent of it, from .4-.7 micrometers. Self-willed men who have sought to "maximize their human potential" have broadened their states of consciousness into altered states of consciousness, and expanded the realm of their vision through mind-altering drugs (in the '60s), and today through technology. They have been able to see outside of this limited sight range further into the infrared. And what have they seen? The spirit realm. There is only a thin veil which separates what we are able to see naturally (via God's creation) from the rest of the infrared realm of "dark light," (the colors of Halloween - orange and black), where spirits reside. If we could see it, we would have to deal with it. Then when we become old and our strength leaves us, we will be tormented by the spirits, like old Indian medicine men.

Our eye cameras have been given limits purposefully. We are not created to deal with this realm of the supernatural. We are created to live our lives in the Newtonian realm of matter and not see where energy becomes matter ($E=MC^2$), or view the personality of energy, the spirit realm, unless God has matured us to this point and specifically uses us. Normally this is only for a specific purpose for a short period of time, clearly guided by the Holy Spirit. Again, to the degree it is possible for God to use man supernaturally, man has to be grounded, rooted, established, obedient, righteous, holy, and pure of heart. This is not the essence of the quest for supernatural power by today's high tech neo-pagans, the contemporary New Agers, beginning with those in the White House. When the disguise is ripped away from what they think they see, and they are confronted with the harsh spiritual reality of evil, they will be horrified and hopefully repentant.

When we see a man who claims to move in supernatural power, what we want to see first and foremost is a man who is poor in spirit, meek, humble, who hungers and thirsts for righteousness, who is merciful, pure of heart, compassionate and a peacemaker. We want to see a man who is not vulnerable to money, sex or power. We look for a man whose character and works radiate love, joy, peace, goodness, kindness, gentleness, faithfulness, patience, long-suffering, humility and self-control - the fruit of the Spirit. We look for a man who is not rude, who is not self-seeking nor easily angered, who does not keep a record of wrongs, who does not delight in evil but rejoices in the truth, who bears all things, believes all things, hopes and trusts for all things and endures all things, whose love never fails, a man whose heart is thirsting for obedience to God's commandment so the Holy Spirit can use him supernaturally. After all, such a grounded, obedient, Hertzian-wave individual is the carrier wave for the non-Hertzian spiritual, supernatural wave of God. The Sword of the Spirit is the Word of God.

We know that the church always takes on the trappings of its culture, the heresy of its day. This is syncretism. We see it in the Arminian, humanistic free will gospel preached today (if the gospel is preached at all). We see it in the human potential movements which have swept the churches. We view it in culturally accepted church tradition. We also see it too often in the charismatic Christian community, where there are attempts to manifest the fruit without the root. Where is the discipline of every emotion, thought, word and deed being brought into obedience and captivity to the Lord Jesus Christ? Where is the servant's heart that looks to another's prosperity first? Where is the humility that leads to total obedience? Where is the perspective by which the church, the non-bloodline spiritual body and bride of the Lord Jesus Christ, places Jesus as the head of everything? Where is the mind that studies to prove all things and holds fast to that which is good, who searches God's word daily, incessantly, for His truth, and then works to bring His creation of facts under the umbrella of dominion and stewardship of His eternal truth? Where is the total reverence of the Lord's table, communion, in the body of Christ, and the recognition of its supernatural, spiritual significance? Where is the emphasis on prayer or fasting? On self-sacrifice?

Let's quickly look at the church in the areas of worship, communion and prayer from a supernatural perspective. After all, we are to forsake not the gathering of ourselves together. We are not autonomous. The church is the body and bride of Christ. There as iron sharpens iron, so does a man sharpen the countenance of a friend.

Most Bible-believing Christians clearly understand that the blood sacrifices performed by the priests of the Hebrews of the Old Testament foreshadowed what was to come: the real thing, the blood sacrifice of the Lord Jesus Christ. Blood sacrifice in the Old Testament was also required on the land where an unsolved murder had occurred. Physically, this was a restoration process, restoring harmony in the earth with the spiritual and supernatural realm, or to put it scientifically, restoring harmonious links between Newtonian, Einsteinian, quantum and chaotic physics. (What does this say about the millions of abortions performed in this nation? The shedding of innocent blood does not go unpunished.) The communion table symbolically identifies us as Christian believers with the body and blood of the Lord Jesus Christ. This spiritually puts us in Him. The spiritual ramifications are physical, as Scripture teaches us. If anyone eats or drinks unworthily of the Lord's table, they can become sick and die. Thus, we have to become pure of heart prior to taking communion and confess our sins, just as Jesus Christ remained pure of heart with no iniquity found in Him. Our hearts must be without iniquity, without guile, particularly prior to the communion worship service. This is consistently God's pattern for Christians to have His supernatural power: pure of heart, humble and broken hearts and spirits, spiritual identification with the Lord Jesus Christ as in communion, prayer and worship (grounded first in study of the Word of God), followed by action. We are to have faith, hope and love. Love leads to action. Love serves. Faith without works is dead. And we have hope, both in time and eternally.

When Old Testament Israel became self-willed (humanistic) and went out to battle on its own without God's approval and blessing, it was defeated. When Israel simply petitioned God and then did not go to fight, nothing happened. God's normal methodology is spiritual preparation followed by physical action, that action being determined by God, based upon the development of Jesus Christ's character in that individual or church, and His will. This being true, our identification with Jesus Christ in the communion worship service is a most serious, solemn and reverent act.

Just as significant is our prayer and worship service. Orbiting satellites have picked up light emanating from the earth on Caribbean islands where there should not have been such intense light. This light, as it turned out, emanated only at a certain time and on a certain day, during a Christian praise and worship service.

The supernatural power of prayer is not totally realized or appreciated by the Body of Christ today. In prayer, we know one can put a thousand to flight and two, ten thousand to flight. So, there is an exponential increase in the power of prayer by loving, obedient, pure-hearted, like-minded Christians gathering together. It has been said that all it takes is 27 united pure-hearted Christians, fervently praying, to put all of Satan's army to flight.

The counterfeit to communion, prayer and the Holy Spirit are respectively the occult blood sacrifices, the curses, spells and other black art matriculations of the New Age magicians, witches and warlocks (including their use of modern technology such as radionics), astrology, and calling down spirits. These occultists are frustrated by God's creation because they know that the human brain is the only thing that cannot be penetrated by ELF - extra low frequency. They can be thwarted.

We are fearfully and wonderfully made. God has created us with a left brain and right brain, connected by the corpus callosum, which makes us a perfect scalar interferometer (as scientist Tom Bearden would put it), two transmitters coming together with unified intent on the same point possessed with incredible power. The power of prayer activates the Sword of the Spirit which is the Word of God. The supernatural rides on the natural, just as a non-Hertzian feminine wave rides on a masculine Hertzian wave.

Why does Christian prayer have so much power that one can put a thousand to flight and two, ten thousand? Because mature Christians are grounded, rooted, and established. New Agers are not. Mature Christians are obedient, magnetically charged, law- and blood-based, grounded Hertzian carrier waves for the non-Hertzian, ungrounded, electrical, spiritual, supernatural wave. New Age occultists are not. It is beyond them. They cannot be grounded. They short circuit. They try to substitute their own animal and human blood sacrifices for Christ's blood; they try to ground out naturally in sexual orgies; they use curses, spells and incantations as counterfeits for prayer; they rely upon fickle astrology to offset the power of the Holy Spirit. But all this has limited power, is of limited duration, and requires incredible energy and resources. The 1992 occult thriller hit movie, "The Lawnmower Man," hit the bullseye in this regard. It is "That Hideous Strength," as C.S. Lewis stated it.

Jesus Christ is the historical, physical, spiritual, holographic, laser-like link which restored fellowship between heaven and earth. He achieved the total victory and all power resides in Him. Anything else is flawed, counterfeit. We are, accordingly, redeemed by the blood of the Lamb, which was shed for the remission of our sins (errors). His blood was spilled from His pure heart. Jesus Christ was the restored second Adam. His blood has a perfect electromagnetic charge, providing the perfect grounding.

(Incidentally, in churches, women should not serve the communion service or serve as ruling elders. These are blood- and law-related matters, respectively. They are grounded, rooted, and established, and are accordingly masculine. The way God has created man [the male] electromagnetically is in harmony with such functions. Men are naturally grounded [left brain, right side of the body]. The work of scientists Davis and Rawls has clearly established this, as has Anne Moir and David Jessel in their book, "Brain Sex." Women are electromagnetically ungrounded and thus must always be "covered" by a father, husband or pastor, preferably all three. By contrast, it is no accident that the "trust the heart," self-willed, humanistic, neo-pagan, lawless New Age uncovered women naturally have access to the fallen spiritual realm of Satan and his demons. It's no accident that so many cults are started by women who exhibit supernatural power. It's a throwback to Satan's natural access to Eve. The Golden Dawn is a major root to darkness. The church must not imitate the occult heresy.)

Let's focus some more on prayer. Just as a man thinketh mentally, so he is physically. This is what the relatively new medical field of psychoneuroimmunology is about. Just as when there is iniquity in man's heart prior to communion, he is subject to becoming sick and dying, just as faith is to be followed by works, so too is prayer the vital preparation for the church in its effort (work) to expand the eternal kingdom of God. The church's spiritual sequence is that of repentance, revival, restoration, reformation and reconstruction, leading to a return toward perfect environment by redeemed second Adams in Christ. There are many documented cases where Christian saints knew, absolutely knew, they had broken through in prayer in the spiritual realm, had defeated Satan's army, and so what they had to do next was walk out their victory in time in His created realm on earth. This is the godly example of God's chosen people in the Old Testament - Israel. It is the example of our Lord Jesus Christ. Before He did anything, He prayed. It is the example of the church in history, particularly in cases of revival. It should be the modus operandi of the church today.

Think of it. Think of the power of 27 loving, dedicated, pure-hearted Christian men and women, who with a clear and focused intent, love the Lord with all their hearts, all their souls, all their mind and all their strength, getting together in laser-like fashion and intensity, to pray for a specific clearcut act of God, an intervention in His creation, in accordance with His will, for the expansion of His kingdom on earth as it is in heaven. Think of the power of such prayer binding and loosening on earth, thus binding and loosening in heaven. If one can put a thousand to flight and two, ten thousand, how much power do 27 have? Could 27 put the whole of Satan's kingdom in retreat? What is the result of their faith, hope and courage to act? Remember Revelation 21:8 lists cowardice (lack of courage) as the lead sin, along with unbelief, the abominable, murderers, the sexually immoral, sorcerers, idolaters, and all liars who have their part in the lake of fire and brimstone which is the second death.

Some men and women do have a special supernatural call of God on their lives. While God may speak audibly or an angel appear and provide direction, this usually occurs in an extreme crisis situation, where often the occult supernatural is out of bounds. Then God intervenes. More times than not, God prefers His people to walk through His will in the creation in a normal and orderly way to victory, that victorious walk preceded by preparation and prayer. We walk by faith, not by sight, but events often occur that have a low probability of occurrence. The neo-pagan New Agers walk by sight. Their faith is in their own godhood, their own power.

Fasting also has a role in being more effective spiritually. Fasting is short term denial of earthly things for spiritual things. It cleanses the body, mind and spirit, as it accompanies and strengthens prayer. Physiologically, it also clears up the 12 organ systems of a balanced human body so that they can resonate to the same frequency (piezoelectric charge) as the 12 gemstones on the breastplate of the high priest of ancient Israel, the same 12 gemstones as are in the heavenly city of Revelation. Fasting helps clear the channel, so to speak. (Of course, Jesus Christ had such a perfectly operative system on earth.) New Agers know far more about the mechanics of this than Christians.

To complete the picture we look at the heart, which researchers at Loma Linda Hospital in California have demonstrated controls the endocrine system - the equivalent of what the Eastern religions call the chakras. The heart and mind are linked by the anti-gravitational (spiritual) cerebral spinal fluid called by ancient physicians the tears of Jesus. When the chakras line up in laser-like fashion in a pure-hearted Christian, whose 12 gemstones (organs) are all resonating with his heart and mind in unity, a literal vortex of laser-living-light energy as information, in prayer, is created in a company of like-minded Christian believers. (The vortex, like a whirlwind, is the integration of linear and cyclical reality, making straight the paths of the Lord.)

Such intense, concentrated prayer becomes reality, just as energy becomes matter when it's slowed down below the speed of light and sets up in a standing electromagnetic wave. Obviously, if Christians do not pray, then the counterfeit will fill the void, just as where Christians do not occupy, the troops of Satan's fallen realm will rule. There is no neutrality in supernatural or natural warfare. There is only advance or retreat.

Think also of prayer much like an architect who has a thought, creates the blueprints, and then builds a shopping center. Thought has become reality. Or, think of prayer as water vapor which then liquefies and becomes water, and then hardens and freezes as ice. Jesus spoke (energy/sound) and the world (matter) was created. We are commanded to think God's thoughts after Him, to pray with specific, intense focus.

The supernatural void of the "God is dead" era of the 1960s was filled by the neo-pagan, occult supernatural New Agers of the '90s. New Age women are now regularly involved in meditation groups that go out into the natural, fallen spiritual realm and redeem an animal spirit to protect them. When these women find themselves in danger on earth, they literally call upon their animal spirit (fallen angel) to manifest in the natural, Newtonian-created, physical realm and protect them. There are documented cases of this. In one case, a lady in New York had two burglars break into her apartment, and she called upon her animal spirit, a cougar, which manifested and literally drove the two potential burglars out of the apartment, leaving claw marks on their automobile. Such power has an attractive draw. New Age women love wolves, too, nature's most perfect killing machine. There's the death wish again, the wages of sin.

Satan does come disguised as an angel of light. How does the church, the body of born-again believers, the most important community on earth, the spiritual non-bloodline family, recognize and respond to this supernatural challenge? "First, by rightly dividing the Word of Truth and studying to show themselves approved unto God, workmen who need not be ashamed." - II Timothy 2:15. The church must bring every emotion, thought, word and deed into captivity to the obedience of the Lord Jesus Christ. This pure of heart, humble, service-oriented church must then unite in purpose, and with love and laser-like clarity, pray for specific victory, binding and loosening on earth so it is bound and loosened in heaven, holding with faith and hope in their hearts the purpose and victory which God has given them, then moving out with courage and action (works), fulfilling God's will on earth as it is in heaven. Because God is consistent and dependable, the Holy Spirit inescapably joins such grounded activity, and is not to be resisted, grieved or quenched. Will the gifts of the Spirit, such as healing, miracles and prophecy, follow? If God wills. This certainly is the grounded, rooted, established, foundational base upon which God acts supernaturally.

THE CRYSTAL CHRIST

It is important to explore the connection between the resurrection of Jesus Christ, relative to the gemstones worn on of the breastplate of Israel's High Priest of the Old Testament, and the same gemstones which appear in the New Jerusalem of Revelation in the New Testament, and how this relates to the human body.

In the Gospel of Mark, chapter 15, verse 33 we read, "Now when the sixth hour had come, there was darkness over the whole land until the ninth hour." ...How could it be otherwise? Jesus is the light of the world. The perfect truth and light of the Creator of the universe, the Lord God Jesus Christ, had become flesh in His creation, taking on all the errors/sins/mistakes that occurred in the past, present and future history of the earth, into His own body. Jesus, the light of the world, literally bore the darkness of the entire world for all of time for the benefit of His people.

We then read in verses 37 and 38, "And Jesus cried out with a loud voice, and breathed His last. Then the veil of the temple was torn in two from top to bottom." When the veil of the temple was ripped, the connection between heaven and earth was restored.

Until Jesus Christ completed His work on earth and restored the rift between Himself as supernatural with the fallen natural world, there was no salvation, no victory. Repairing the rift in time/space which began with Adam, Jesus Christ became the transitional bridge, unifying the kingdom of earth with the kingdom of heaven, and returning the closed system of the Newtonian natural, fallen creation to spiritual harmony with the open system of God's heavenly kingdom. Accordingly, it is no surprise, as Matthew discusses in chapter 27, verses 50-53, that when Jesus cried out with a loud voice and yielded up His spirit, the veil of the temple was torn in two from top to bottom, the earth quaked, and rocks were split. Even the graves were opened and many bodies of the saints who had fallen asleep (died) were raised. This was a sign that death (the ultimate result of the Second Law of Thermodynamics - entropy) had been defeated and that life eternal had been restored by the Creator to His own creation.

Heretofore, the temple, where the High Priest of Israel went into the holy of holies, wearing the breastplate containing 12 gemstones, was the transitional bridge, the link between heaven and earth, between God and man. Such was human action in ritualistic symbolism, which provided the means by which God could interface with

His fallen creation. The animal blood sacrifices in the temple were the substitute, the foreshadowing, fulfilled by the perfect blood sacrifice of the Lamb of God, the Lord God Jesus Christ upon the cross as He hung between heaven and earth, connected to both, providing the link up, the reconnection, the propitiation, the restoration of all things. The Roman centurion who stood opposite Jesus Christ when He cried out and breathed His last intuitively knew this ultimate historic truth when he commented, "Truly this man was the Son of God!" - Mark 15:39.

The Lord God Jesus Christ was in the grave three days. But the grave is death, and there is no death inherent or by human action in the spirit, mentality, or emotion of the Lord Jesus Christ. He only took the death (sins) of the world upon Himself in His body, as The Sacrificial Lamb. He substituted Himself, made the sacrifice, and was the propitiation for the death which resulted from sin (error). This was the ultimate act of love. The grave could not hold him, and after three days, He arose.

Jesus Christ was apparently in the grave exactly three days. From Gleason Archer's book, "Difficulties In The Bible," we read, "Seventy-two hours later, exactly three days and three nights, at the beginning of the first day of the week (Saturday at sunset), He arose again from the grave. When the women visited the tomb just before dawn the next morning, they found the grave already empty." This source goes on to comment, "Three days and three nights His body was dead and lay in a sepulchre. While His body lay dead, He Himself being quickened in the spirit (I Peter 3:18) went into the heart of the earth and preached unto the spirits which were in prison (I Peter 3:19). Jesus was crucified at sunset on Wednesday just as Thursday was beginning. Saturday at sunset is really the first day of the week, which is Sunday. In 30 A.D., the year of the crucifixion of Jesus Christ, the Passover was kept on Thursday, April 6, the moon being full that day. Jesus was crucified not on the Passover day, but on the preparation of the Passover, that would be Wednesday, exactly three days and three nights in the grave, seventy-two hours."

The fact that Jesus Christ was most probably in the grave exactly 72 hours, three days and three nights, is very significant. It takes precisely that long scientifically for a perfect spirit, which Jesus Christ is, to requicken his flesh. There is a nine octave wave of the elements, which is the basis for the perfect transmutation of elements, which in the case of Jesus Christ, was His resurrection. As the book, "A New Concept Of The Universe" (pp. 115, 119), discusses, "every completed idea in nature is expressed in nine efforts -

or stages - which are eight octave waves plus the matured centering amplitude wave of the whole nine octave cycle." In other words, 8 x 9 = 72 for the completion of perfection in nature; the Perfect Jesus Christ having assumed our sin, to again become Perfect. Moreover, each hour is 360 degrees, or a cyclical completion. Seventy-two hours, the 8 x 9 completed expression, was necessary to return perfection to that which rightfully is perfect and without flaw and blemish, the Lord God Jesus Christ in His resurrection body.

Are there any other clues in science that help us understand how the resurrection of the Lord God Jesus Christ was accomplished? Put differently, since religion and science are different sides of the same coin, one spirit (living energy), one matter (frozen energy), one unseen, one seen, one at one end of the spectrum and one at the other end of the spectrum of God's creation, are there any scientific clues that help us understand the essence of this marvelous event, the resurrection of the Lord God Jesus Christ, which restored the "all in all?"

To catch a glimpse of this miraculous scientific/religious reality, the resurrection of the Lord God Jesus Christ, let's begin by looking at the 12 gemstones which were worn on the breastplate of the High Priest of Israel. These gemstones, as discussed in Exodus 28:15-21, are exactly the same 12 gemstones which appear in the New Jerusalem in Revelation 21:19-20. Of course, these gemstones also represented the 12 tribes of Israel: Reuben, Simon, Levi, Judah, Dan, Naphtali, Gad, Asher, Issachar, Zebulun, Joseph, and Benjamin. Jesus, too, had 12 disciples: Matthew, Mark, Luke, John, etc.

(The number $12^2 = 144$. The number 144 is the first Fibonacci number - named after the Italian mathematician Fibonacci - which is a square. This is very significant because it integrates linear time with cyclical time, the two aspects of time. Moreover, the Fibonacci ratio is the everpresent evidence of God's handiwork which permeates all of His creation in the natural order, in deer antlers, seashells and the like. Additionally, the Fibonacci ratio was basic in the Egyptian construction of the pyramids, and as we shall see, is significant in Scripture.)

The breastplate worn by the High Priest of Israel allowed man to stand in the presence of God, so God could reveal His divine will to His chosen people. The 12 gemstones on the breastplate are the sardius, topaz, carbuncle, emerald, sapphire, diamond, ligure, agate, amethyst, beryl, onyx, and jasper. Let's think a minute about what a gemstone is. A gemstone is a crystal. It accordingly carries a piezo-electric charge (like man's organs, skull and skin), which is activated

when put under pressure. This is because the molecules of a gemstone are aligned like a laser. Plus, each gemstone has a specific
primary color (frequency). Moreover, each gemstone is made up of
minerals, basic elements of the Periodic Table. Physicians in the ancient world, in fact, used gemstones to heal. Gemstones were literally crushed up and taken internally by sick patients. William T.
Ferne, M.D., in his 1973 book, "The Occult and Creative Power Of
Precious Stones," discusses this ancient medical practice in detail.
One important sidelight: the emerald has long been worn by royalty
because it reputedly kills serpents, and sends evil spirits off howling
into the abyss. Is it any accident that around the throne of God, in
Revelation 4, there is a rainbow which appears like an emerald?
What devil could stay in the presence of the throne of the Lord God
Jesus Christ?

There is more significance to the breastplate and its 12 gemstones. The number 12 completes the cycle of the year, 12 months
of the year. There are 12 signs in the zodiac. The heavens speak of
the handiwork of God. The zodiac with its 12 signs, rightfully interpreted, are the story of the Lord God Jesus Christ as E.W. Bullinger
so carefully documented in his book, "The Witness Of The Stars,"
written in 1893. The arrangement of the gemstones, in the 3 x 4
matrix in which they appeared on the breastplate, was also important.
Look at it this way. It takes four 90 degree turns (linear) to complete
a 360 degree circle (a complete cycle). Each of these four turns corresponds to the Hebrew Old Testament's rendering of God: YHVH
(YOD, HEH, VAU, HEH). From the zero point on the circle, the
first 90 degree turn is 3^0, which is equal to 1C - the speed of light, or
the speed at which matter oscillates on the physical plane. Two turns
take us to 180 degrees, or 3^1 (3C) - three times the speed of light,
where the human mind resides. This, in Scripture, is also the second
heaven, where Satan reigns. This is why the gospel comes by hearing - and hearing by the Word of God, if man's mind is to be recaptured from Satan's realm. All men are naturally fallen, and begin life
in Satan's camp. Their minds and hearts have to be redeemed. The
Word of God has to be heard by the mind of man so that his heart
can be transformed, so, in turn, his thinking and emotions change,
with his behavior and body ultimately changing as well. With emotions oscillating closely at 2.5C, it's no wonder Satan has such a hold
on man. Man operates naturally in the same plane at the same frequency as Satan with his mind and emotions.

Turning a third time takes us to 270 degrees, which is 3^2, or 9C,
nine times the speed of light, which is the spiritual realm in which

Jesus Christ created the earth. A fourth turn brings us to 360 degrees - the starting point, which is 3^3, or 27C, God's heaven of heavens. Thus, we know that the breastplate in and of itself, by its format (3 x 4), and its 12 gemstones, was an integrated picture of God's all-in-all, of a unified heaven and earth.

The breastplate, when worn by the High Priest of Israel, was suspended from his shoulders by means of two gold chains, hung from gold rings on the uppermost corners of the breastplate. The 12 gemstones of the breastplate were set in gold in their enclosings. Josephus (A.D. 37-95) stated that the stones "were extraordinary in largeness and beauty, and were an ornament not to be purchased by men because of their immense value." This breastplate was worn over the heart when the high priest Aaron went into the most Holy Place, literally the presence of God. In other words, the breastplate of the High Priest of Israel was a protection, the means by which man was able to enter the presence of a perfect God and survive. Ordinary sinful man could not stand in the presence of a perfect superconductive God otherwise.

Recall that God is light. Perfect light contains all colors. There are 12 colors in the spectrum, a basic seven of the rainbow plus five others. Each of the 12 gemstones in the breastplate gave off primarily one of these 12 primary colors, the color itself corresponding to a specific degree in the 360 degree circle: red - 0 degrees; orange - 30 degrees; yellow - 60 degrees; lime - 90 degrees; green - 120 degrees; turquoise - 150 degrees; blue - 180 degrees; indigo - 210 degrees; violet - 240 degrees; purple - 270 degrees; magenta - 300 degrees; and scarlet - 330 degrees. Notice the colors at each of the 90 degree turns in the circle. Red at 0 degrees is the color of blood. Jesus Christ became the ultimate blood sacrifice. Lime at 90 degrees is a food for man, which as lime water aids not only in digestion, but also in detoxifying the human body (which oscillates at 1C, the speed of light, at 90 degrees). At 180 degrees, there is blue, which moves us into the heavens, and at 270 degrees the color purple, the color of royalty. Specifically, with regard to the 12 colors, each of the 12 gemstones contained the color (frequency) to support (or heal) a particular system of the human body, of which there are basically 12 systems. Each gemstone's resonant frequency (color) and elemental makeup was geared uniquely to support one of the 12 specific body systems. No wonder Israel's High Priest needed to wear the 12 gemstones in God's presence. He needed the organ support.

There are 12 primary systems in the human body, just as there are 12 primary acupuncture meridians corresponding to these systems. The Easterners say there are 12 chakras, or 12 nerve conflu-ences in the human body. Moreover, the human body's living tissue is of a crystalline nature, just like a gemstone. The crystalline nature of the human connective tissue arises because of the way the compo-nent collagen molecules organize themselves into very regular paral-lel arrays. These human collagen crystals are piezoelectric, just like a gemstone. Thus, every compression or stretching of the body's fabric generates an electric field that travels through the matrix, just like when a gemstone is compressed. So, the molecularly aligned laser crystal color of each of the 12 gemstones, each carrying the piezoelectric charge of a particular body organ system, when worn by the High Priest of Israel in the presence of God, effectively served, in a crutchlike manner, to give the High Priest a pure totally online superconductive body, which corresponded as closely as pos-sible to the perfect sinless, superconductive body of the Lord Jesus Christ. Small wonder then the Bible calls man a living stone, liter-ally a living crystal.

Let's look at just one color, lime, which occurs at the first 90 degree turn where the body of man oscillates at 1C - the speed of light. Lime is a thymus activator. The thymus gland is the gland of the endocrine system which is most closely associated with the heart. It also plays a big part in regulating the entire endocrine system. Which gemstone manifested this color and frequency? And the other 11? Recall also that sound is a frequency, just like color is a fre-quency. Christian monks in the Middle Ages in Europe used specific tuned notes strummed on a stringed instrument 24 hours a day to help heal an ailing monk afflicted with a particular disease.

In addition to color and its therapeutic effect on the 12 body or-gan systems and acupuncture meridians of man, the gemstones also contained minerals and/or elements, which are used in healing vari-ous diseases. The basic minerals and elements of each gemstone were system specific. Additionally, each of the 12 gemstones also contained primarily one of the 12 mineral salts (or tissue salts) which make up the body of man: 1) sodium chloride, 2) silicone (silica), 3) chloride of potash, 4) fluoride of lime, 5) sulfate of lime, 6) sulfate of potash, 7) phosphate of potash, 8) phosphate of magnesia, 9) phosphate of iron, 10) phosphate of lime, 11) sulphate of soda, and 12) phosphate of soda. So, when the High Priest wore the breastplate into the holy of holies and stood in the presence of God, he was able to reach into heaven, was grounded to the earth, being complete through these 12 gemstones in light (color), in fre-quency, in each of the 12 tissue salts, and in the basic elements which compose the physical body. This made him complete in energy and matter, spirit and flesh, feminine and masculine, yin and yang - all complete in this crystal torroid, which when resting over his human heart, allowed the High Priest to effectively be perfect in his body, his body's 12 basic systems and 12 acupuncture meridians, in the presence of The Perfect God.

There are six yin and six yang (six feminine and six masculine), body systems and accompanying meridians for a total of 12: 1) spleen - pancreas (yin), 2) lung (yin), 3) liver (yin), 4) circulatory (yin), 5) kidneys (yin), 6) heart channel (yin); 1) stomach (yang), 2) large intestine (yang), 3) gall bladder (yang), 4) triple warmer (yang), 5) bladder (yang), and 6) small intestine (yang).

The human body is truly made in the image of God when, in perfection, it is a perfect spiral or vortex, half masculine, half feminine, working perfectly together, balanced, compressing and decompressing, explosive and implosive, clockwise and counterclockwise, a vector and a matrix, light and dark, electric and magnetic, the individual united into one.

One has to speculate since sinful E-motion (energy-in-motion) leads to dis-ease, whether the 12 gemstones on the breastplate did also keep the 12 key E-motions which cause dis-ease at bay. These 12 negative E-motions are, according to Dr. M.L. Rees: 1) suspicion; 2) disorganization; 3) hate; 4) misjudgment; 5) misunderstanding; 6) despair; 7) destructiveness; 8) antagonism; 9) a critical spirit; 10) being lethargic; 11) hesitation; and 12) procrastination.

In Revelation 21, the New Jerusalem has 12 gates with the names of the 12 tribes written on the 12 gates just as they were written on the 12 gemstones. It is laid out with three gates on the east, three gates on the north, three gates on the south, and three gates on the west. Here again is a picture of the four 90 degree turns of 3^0, 3^1, 3^2, and 3^3 (1C, 3C, 9C, 27C). The wall of the city has 12 foundations on which are written the names of the 12 apostles of the Lamb (Jesus Christ). The city is laid out as a square, actually a cube, 12,000 furlongs, its length, breadth and height all being equal. One wall is 144 cubits, again 144 being the first Fibonacci number which is also a square. Each of the 12 foundations of the wall contains the 12 gemstones, the same 12 gemstones which are in the breastplate of the High Priest. Additionally, in each of the 12 gates are 12 pearls. As Matthew 13:45-56 states, "The kingdom of heaven is like a merchant seeking beautiful pearls, who, when he had found one pearl of great price, went and sold all that he had and bought it." Is there any pearl equal to the value of the Lord God Jesus Christ? He is the pearl of unequaled price.

Now, with all this background data, let's return to the resurrection of the Lord Jesus Christ. We know that Jesus was in the earth (grave) for 72 hours, three full days, because that's how long it took for a perfect body - which because of its perfect spirit, mentality, and emotion, had no inherent sin - to regenerate itself. We know that energy creates matter. Matter is frozen energy. Jesus Christ spoke (righteous, living energy with personality, purpose and information) and matter was created. In Genesis, God said, "Let there be light," and there was light. God said, "Let there be a firmament," and there was a firmament. Even after Jesus took on the sins of the world in His body, there remained perfection in His spirit, mentality and emotion. Again, spirit (living energy with personality, purpose and information) creates matter. It is very significant when the Bible speaks in John 19:36 that none of Jesus Christ's bones were broken. "For these things were done that the Scripture should be fulfilled, 'Not one of His bones shall be broken.'" - Psalms 34:20. Why was this important? Because the physical frame, the skeleton of Jesus, had to remain perfectly intact to reconstitute His perfect resurrection body. The Bible teaches that 666 is the number of man. Scientifically, 666 is also the radionic number for the human skeletal system. Jesus Christ's perfect skeleton, with no broken bones, maintained its perfect infrared frequency, as well as all of the undisturbed basic elements and 12 tissue salts (corresponding to the 12 gemstones), interacting for over 72 hours with His perfect Holy Spirit, mentality and emotion, perfectly reconstituted His new supernatural, superconductive resurrection body, containing 12 superconductive organ systems, corresponding to the 12 acupuncture meridians. Thus, the Prince of Peace, the God-man, Jesus, perfectly at ease with no disease, arose from the grave. The grave, death, could not hold Him because there was no death (sin) in Him. This is indeed Good News, the Gospel, that in Jesus Christ all our sins, errors, mistakes, were paid for and forgiven. He took our place and paid our ransom. We are cleansed and washed in His perfect blood, and in Him death is defeated and we have life eternal.

That perfect living energy with personality, purpose and information (spirit) should create perfect living matter (in this case, the Holy Spirit reconstituting His perfect body) is consistent with the observations of modern science regarding the nature of man. Let's review. Dr. Robert O. Becker, M.D., in his books, "The Body Electric" and "Cross Currents," has confirmed that the electrical field of man is the determinant of what occurs in the physical body. Dr. Harold Saxton Burr, M.D., in his 1972 book, "Blueprint For Immortality," established that the L-field, the electrodynamic field, reveals the physical and mental conditions of the body and makes it possible for M.D.'s to diagnose illnesses before the usual symptoms develop and are manifest in the physical body itself. Dr. Burr, for 43 years a faculty member of the Yale University School of Medicine as professor of anatomy and neuro-anatomy, compiled 40 years of documentation to confirm that all living things - plants, animals and humans - are controlled by an electrodynamic field, which can be measured and mapped with standard modern volt-meters. The SQUID (superconducting quantum interference device) is an extremely sensitive magnetometer capable of measuring the biomagnetic field produced by a single heartbeat, muscle twitch, or pattern of neural brain activity. With SQUID, the body's energy fields are mapped with great precision by scientists.

From another perspective, Stanley Keleman, in his book, "Your Body Speaks Its Mind," establishes the same thing. The physical human body is a reflection of its mental and E-motional processes. A chiropractor in California, Dr. Lowell Ward, and his son, working with Loma Linda Hospital, have over 30 years of documentation, in conjunction with German physicians, in mapping out with computers how the body reflects what is going on in the mind and E-motions. Two X-rays taken from the back, one standing, one sitting, and two more taken from the side, the results run through a computer with mathematical and geometric analyses, confirm what E-motional software programming an individual brought into this world from his forefathers. Dr. Lowell Ward has effectively demonstrated that the errors (sins) of the father (and mother) are passed onto the sons and daughters for at least four generations behaviorally and physically. Ward's work was once featured on early morning CBS television.

In France, physicians have over 800,000 documented cases, gathered over a 12-year period, showing that with Kirlian photographic pattern recognition, the energy field of the body can actually predict what dis-ease will appear in the body three, six, nine, 12 months or more down the road. Dr. Samuel C. West, a Utah naturopath, has demonstrated that the 12 +2 acupuncture meridian systems of the human body and the lymphatic system are effectively identical. Both the meridian system and the lymphatic system are electrical. This means that we are effectively spiritual living energy - light men! The lymphatic system has a greater fluid content than blood in the body. The lymphatic system is the key to health. So, what all this means is that, as a man thinks, so he is physically.

Louise L. Hay's book, "Heal Your Body," lists the supposed E-motional basis of dis-ease. Dr. Valerie V. Hunt, formerly of UCLA, has successfully demonstrated that the human mind is an energy-information field and is the true source of all health problems.

In conclusion, why do men reject and rebel against the Lord God Jesus Christ and His life-bringing open system? They are deceived - along with pride, humanism, rebellion, the devil within them, so to speak. Men want to do their own thing, to do it their way, and to be their own god, just like Satan with his offer to Eve, to which Adam acquiesced. Because men love darkness more than light, they love evil more than good, and thus, they also return evil for good. There-fore, the world is at enmity, at war, with God and with His provision, Jesus Christ, who turned death into life. All those who war against God wrong their own souls; all those who hate God love death, Prov-erbs 8:36 teaches. The pain of losing face and admitting error (sin), plus the painful E-motional clearing necessary to become Christ-like, is just too much for most men. Thus, narrow is the gate into the kingdom of God. As Sarah Rossbach wrote in her book, "Feng Shui," "The most potent fear, an old Feng Shui carryover, is death-oriented symbolism. In Hong Kong, modern housing complexes glisten with woks and mirrors that residents place outside their win-dows to ward off the bad luck of church crosses. A Chinese minister explained: 'They think it is the cross of death and we believe it is the cross of love.'

"This philosophy was the bane of Western missionaries in China. In the 19th century, the missionary-scholar Reverend Edkins de-scribed Feng Shui as 'one of the great obstacles to the progress of civilization,' which, he wrote, 'checks the efforts of missionary zeal.' In the 19th century, missionaries were forced to remove the earth-impaling crosses from their churches."

So, there we have it, Jesus Christ, His work on the cross, and His resurrection as the central vital turning point in history, linked to the breastplate of Israel's High Priest, linked to the New Jerusalem of Revelation, and linked to the human body. We are made in the im-age of God. We are the temple of the Holy Spirit. The kingdom of God is within us. It must be within us before it can be externalized. This is what the New Age is attempting to counterfeit, a perfect su-perconductive human body, a humanistic superman, minus the Holy Spirit-produced righteousness of God in us. The battle is joined. Is it then no small wonder that the issue on which life literally and physically hangs is, "What think you of Christ?" - Matthew 22:42.

Once an individual is "born again" from the dark, death-based closed system of the natural earth, into the light, life-based open system of God's supernatural, the challenge for an individual Christian is to clear all the sin (error) out of his spirit, his mind, his E-motions, and his body to become integrated and superconductive. He does this in pursuing his God-given calling and sacrificial service opportunities which are presented to him during his time on earth, as he is obedient to God's Law-Word. This way all his organ systems and meridians can come online, and become living gemstones, like Jesus Christ's, which will enable a Christian to walk victoriously on the earth, hear clearly the Holy Spirit as He accesses our minds' theta and alpha rhythms and networks with our autonomic nervous systems, victoriously achieve God's will for his life which is consistent with his calling and talents, and literally become a complete son of God. Will Christians in such an elevated spiritual status, then be able to accomplish what Jesus Christ promised, that is, to do greater things than He did? The creation groans, awaiting the revelation of the sons of God. This is the fullness of Christ in us, as crystal christs. Then we may be able to fully manifest the gifts of the Holy Spirit.

BEING CHRIST-LIKE

Newly born-again Christians' lifestyles are effectively no different than those of the unbeliever. For a Christian to really become a new man and truly Christ-like, literally a new creature in Christ, the following must occur: the Holy Spirit must give him/her faith and awaken (quicken) the human spirit to the reality that God has saved him/her eternally through the work of the Lord Jesus Christ and has now called him/her to service in time, to fulfill his/her calling, while in the process of becoming increasingly Christ-like. This spiritual awakening, literally becoming born again, enables man to truly hear the music as it were, the Word of God, and apply it to his/her life. The grounding male vector of the Law-Word of the Lord Jesus Christ which is "alive and powerful, sharper than any two-edged sword, piercing even to the dividing asunder of the joints of the marrow and is the critic of thoughts and intents of the heart," begins its work. It is a grounding vector in the mind, seeking to link up and integrate with the law which is written on the heart of God's elect. They are man's head and heart, consciously and subconsciously, mentally and emotionally, becoming totally integrated to the obedience of the Lord Jesus Christ. The new man, the new creature in Christ, the mature Christian who is truly Christ-like, becomes literally a "light man" when his body becomes superconductive, with light moving in the body at the speed of sound. This is the closest that man, "made in the image of God," but "formed from the dust of the earth," can become to being God-like. "God is light" is perfect, living, righteous energy with personality.

As the Holy Spirit of God penetrates and transforms the human spirit of man through God's Law-Word, this frequency at 9C - nine times the speed of light - moves down to the human mentality at 3C - three times the speed of light, having met the challenge of first cycling through the emotion of man at 2.5C - 2.5 times the speed of light. As the human spirit is transformed, the mentality is changed, the emotion is altered, and as the emotion is finally transformed, then the physical body heals. The physical body is matter, which is simply light energy of electromagnetic waves, slowed down to below the speed of light, held together by an electromagnetic field.

For example, when a Christian who is obedient to God's authority learns that there should be no root of bitterness in him/her, and that to prevent this he/she must repent and forgive, the open-minded, humble-hearted and contrite human spirit of the man/woman allows the Holy Spirit to quicken this in him/her. This establishes a new value in his/her mind, in turn changing the emotional response of his/her heart, resulting in a change of behavior. Because man is an infrared antenna, who literally gets back what he/she gives off (reaps what he/she sows), this change in spirit, thinking, and emotion, will inescapably bring up a challenge to see if the new behavior pattern is established. This is painful emotionally. But once the new behavior pattern has been walked through and the circumstance has been handled differently from old behavior patterns, as in this example, the individual is then able to forgive those who have trespassed against him/her, he/she starts to literally see things differently with his/her spirit eyes and ears as it were. Next time, because of the spiritual change, his/her mental, emotional and behavioral response will be easier when he/she is called upon to forgive those who have wronged him/her. The new pattern has been grounded, established in the earth. If he/she has the nutritional support and can feel the emotional pain of the sin of bitterness in his/her diaphragm and solar plexus when this challenge to his/her new change of behavior is taking place, and if he/she can breathe through it, fully feel it, and release it in the name of the Lord Jesus Christ, through the power of His precious, holy and redeeming blood, and the enabling work of the Holy Spirit, then there will be a transformation in his/her physical body as well. After all, the organ systems, the 12 gemstones of the human body, not only store physical dis-ease, they also store emotional disease at a higher frequency, which is what dysfunctional E-motion (energy in motion) is, being not at ease but at dis-ease. When this is released, because of the change and new harmony spiritually, mentally, and emotionally, the physical body then will change. Therefore, except for possibly multi-generational sin leading to genetic defects, accidents, or environmental-caused illnesses, for the most part, Christians should be the healthiest people around.

It is a common observation that we see other people's faults more easily than we recognize our own. In other words, we are not as "conscious" of our own faults as other folks are conscious of our faults. This means we are, for the most part "unconscious" when it comes to our own sins/faults/weaknesses. But if we welcome criticisms and fault-finding of other caring, insightful people, and take it to heart, we have a golden opportunity to link up our conscious (masculine) with our subconscious (feminine), so we can become better integrated, more clear, and more full of light. We become accordingly more Christ-like. Jesus Christ was totally integrated spiritually, mentally, emotionally and physically. His conscious and subconscious were one. His brain's beta, alpha, theta and delta rhythms were all in harmony. Is this what the early church in Acts was involved with - clearing, integrating their conscious and subconscious when they rebuked each other, so that everyone could become more Christ-like in the holy supernatural vortex of the Holy Spirit?

On an individual basis, mature Christians (Christ-like) will be obedient to God's Law-Word (masculine), manifest the fruit of the Spirit (feminine), and exhibit such behavior as taking full responsibility for personal sin, never defending oneself, never taking credit for achievements but instead giving the credit to God and others, never owning anything (in spirit) but being the steward of everything, never passing on anything bad about anyone else, never fearing, and being full of forgiveness and compassion. In such a Christ-like person the gifts of the Spirit may be manifested.

THE LIGHT OF THE WORLD

As recorded in John 8:12, Jesus said, "I am the light of the world. He who follows Me shall not walk in darkness, but have the light of life." Jesus' statement is a mirror image of John 1:4, "In Him was life, and the life was the light of men." Small wonder then that Jesus said in Matthew 5:14, "You are the light of the world." Elsewhere in Scripture we are told that His word is a lamp unto our feet, and a light unto our path, that the light is sweet, that we are to walk in the light, that we are to let our light so shine, that the lamp of the body is the eye, and if the eye is good, the whole body is full of light, that we are sons of light, that we are to walk as children of light, that God is light. The countenance (aura/electromagnetic field) of the Lord is like lightning.

When the apostle Paul was bitten by the poisonous viper and shook it off without harm (Acts 28), the natives thought he was a god. Paul's countenance was strong because his spirit unto God was strong, and as a result, most probably his immune system was strong and loaded with B vitamins which neutralized the protein-based venom of the viper. Paul must have had one fabulous countenance, full of light.

How do we become like Jesus, the light of the world? How do we work out our salvation with fear and trembling? We know that the lust of the eye, the lust of the flesh, and the pride of life will destroy us. These are the same things as money, sex, and power, or gold, gals and glory. They are to be offset spiritually on the femi-nine/magnetic end of the spectrum by faith, hope and love. Faith is the currency of God's supernatural realm, defeating the lust of the eye/money/gold. Hope overcomes the pride of life/power/glory. Love defeats the lust of the flesh/sex/gals. Of course, the greatest of these three is love, because love is the umbrella over both ends of the electromagnetic spectrum, over spirit and law. Jesus Christ said "If you love Me, you will keep My commandments." - John 14:15. This is the masculine/electrical/light, blood/law end of the spectrum, which emphasizes the sovereignty of God and commands obedience. The fear of the Lord is the beginning of wisdom. It is also true, at the other end of the spectrum, that love is patient; love is kind; it does not envy; it does not boast; it is not proud; it is not rude; it is not self-seeking; it is not easily angered; it does not keep a record of wrongs. "Love does not rejoice with evil but delights in the truth. Love believes all things, bears all things, hopes and trusts for all things, and endures all things. Love never fails," - I Corinthians 13:4-8. This is clearly the ungrounded feminine magnetic end of the spectrum. But for such to be complete, it has to be grounded in the masculine end of the spectrum. A non-Hertzian wave needs a grounded Hertzian carrier wave, as it were. Quantum physics has to be grounded through Einsteinian physics in Newtonian physics.

Light was in the heavens when Jesus was born, and the glory of the Lord shone all around the angels as they appeared to the shepherds in the fields. And so as God became man in the person of the Lord Jesus Christ, He reestablished the connection between heaven and earth by obedience to the Father in perfectly keeping God's law, by shedding His own blood on the cross, by dying, being resurrected from the dead and ascending to heaven, completing the loop as it were, as He now sits at the right hand of the Father. He has been given dominion over all things in heaven and on earth, with the earth as His footstool. His heavenly city needs no light, for the glory of God illuminates it and the Lamb is its light. All the nations of those who are saved walk in its light as well. New Agers know we are light beings, spirits, made in the image of God. The Bible teaches how we are illuminated.

Individually, as we think, so we are. It's absolutely critical we bring every thought, emotion, word and deed into captivity to the obedience of the Lord Jesus Christ. "His Word is a lamp unto our feet and a light to our path." - Psalm 119:105. His Word keeps us grounded. Jesus Christ searches our minds and hearts and judges us accordingly. He gives to each of us according to our works (Revelation 2:23). Whatever things are true, honest, just, pure, lovely, of good report, virtuous and praiseworthy - such should be the focus of our thoughts (Philippians 4:8). Our thoughts interact with the emotions of our hearts. The lamp of the body is the eye, and if the eye is good, the entire body is full of light (Matthew 6:22). Light enters the eye, refracts off the retina and feeds the pineal and pituitary glands and the hypothalamus. The heart then controls the endocrine system and its hormones, which in turn helps determine the status of the 12 primary organ systems, which in turn determines the way our muscles operate, which in turn determines how structurally correct our skeletal system is - all of which determines the light in our countenance/electromagnetic field/aura - which is an expression of the light of God which is within us. It obviously follows that being anxious about nothing, working faithfully in our calling, being obedient to God, being supportive and loving with our families, friends and church, being a Good Samaritan, and manifesting the fruit of the

Spirit are vital to our light. Getting plenty of rest, exercising and watching what we eat are also important.

The New Agers try to make these natural "creature" things of primary importance because they can't change their hearts. Even by attempting to do so, they're at war with themselves, which speaks of their need for a supernatural savior from outside the natural created realm of so-called "Mother Earth." No house at war against itself can stand.

Our faith/light has to be grounded and expressed in good works. In Matthew 5:14-16, Jesus stated so in no uncertain terms: "You are the light of the world. A city that is set on a hill cannot be hidden. Nor do they light a lamp and put it under a basket, but on a lampstand, and it gives light to all who are in the house. Let your light so shine before men, that they may see your good works and glorify your Father in heaven." (In places in Scripture, God uses the words "light" and "lamp" interchangeably.)

Equal consideration must be given to the body of believers (the church) in order to maintain the balance between the one (the collective) and the many (individuals). The collective manifestation of light, believers in the local church, is no better expressed than in Revelation 1-3, in the letters to the seven churches. Revelation 1 tells us there are seven spirits (lamps) before His throne, and seven golden lampstands, and in the midst of them One like the Son of Man. The seven lampstands are the seven churches. So what are the positives and negatives of the seven churches from Jesus Christ's point of view? What error (sin) inhibits light in the local church? What action increases light?

1. To the church at Ephesus, "I know your works, your labor, your patience, and that you cannot bear those who are evil." This church tested those who said they were apostles and found them liars. This church persevered, had patience, labored for Jesus' name sake and did not become weary. Ephesus did indeed hate the deeds of the Nicolaitans, an early Christian sect that taught moral looseness. But, the church left its first love and needed to repent and to do the first works.

2. To the church at Smyrna, Jesus knew their works, tribulation and poverty and the blasphemy of those who said they were Jews but were not, but instead were a synagogue of Satan. Faithfulness unto death was required. The challenge was to overcome.

3. To the church at Pergamos, "I know your works and where you dwell, where Satan's throne is. And you hold fast to My name,

and did not deny My faith," ...even to martyrdom. But the church at Pergamos also listened to false prophets who taught the doctrine of Balaam, having to do with eating things sacrificed to idols and committing sexual immorality, thus holding to the doctrine of the Nicolaitans. Repentance was required. The challenge was to overcome. Here again, obedience to God's law was required for the stability of the lampstand.

4. To the church in Thyatira, "I know your works, love, service, faith and your patience; and as for your works, the last are more than the first." But a false prophetess, Jezebel, was teaching and beguiling Jesus' servants to commit sexual immorality and to eat things sacrificed to idols. Here again, repentance was required. Holding fast and overcoming were required, keeping Christ's works unto the end.

5. To the church at Sardis, "I know your works, that you have a name, that you are alive, but you are dead." Their works were not perfect before God. The commandment was to hold fast and repent. If not, judgment comes. The challenge was to overcome.

6. To the church at Philadelphia, again, "I know your works...you have a little strength, have kept My word and have not denied My name...you have kept My commandment to persevere." The challenge was to hold fast and overcome.

7. To the church at Laodicea - this lukewarm church was spewed out because it was neither hot nor cold. It became rich, wealthy in a worldly sense, and as a result thought it had need of nothing. It did not see that it was in reality wretched, miserable, poor, blind and naked. It was challenged to be zealous and repent, and to overcome.

These messages to the seven churches, the seven lampstands, were given to the angels of each of the churches via the Spirit. So this was a "light" event. The challenge to "light" is both individual and collective, to the one (the collective - the church) and to the many (individuals).

A chain is no stronger than its weakest link. The individuals in the collective churches in this day and age as never before need to become lights, lamps on lampstands, that are the light of the world, that give light to all who are in the house, that shine before men, and by their individual and collective good works glorify our Father in heaven. Christ's praise and criticism of the seven churches in Revelation provide us with the standard by which we can evaluate the collective light or darkness in our own churches. By praying, fasting, worshiping, fellowshiping, eating together, studying the Word, rebuking one another, strengthening one another, keeping the sacraments and ordinances, manifesting the fruit and gifts of the Holy Spirit, etc., we can become the light of the world. "To him who overcomes I will grant to sit with Me on My throne, as I also overcame and sat down with My Father on His throne."

Make no mistake about it, Satan has his counterfeit. Just as there are seven spirits (lamps) before the throne of God, and seven stars which are the angels of the seven churches, and seven golden lampstands which are the seven churches, so too, every morning at 7:00 a.m., in Crestone, Colorado, the religious center of the New World Order, located in the Sangre de Cristo ("blood of Christ") mountains, seven mystics faithfully sit on mats in a circle around a fire built in a pit with a collection of seven deities which also face the flames. The Hindu ceremony rolls on.

The seven "dark light" principalities of Satan's realm which we war against are: 1) An unnamed principality that blasphemes God and Christianity in movies, music and the like; 2) the principality, Pan, whose modus operandi is instilling panic, shattering nerves, causing fear and pandemonium; 3) the principality, Bacchus, the power behind addiction; 4) the principality, Rege, who heads up occultism, including divination, astrology, fortune telling, magic, witchcraft, mind control, and all forms of deception; 5) the principality, Larz, who operates in the realm of sexual lust, promiscuity, fornication, adultery, perversion, and homosexuality; 6) the principality, Medit, whose mission is to stir up anarchy, riots, chaos and rebellion; and 7) the principality, Set, whose purpose is to bring about depression, bloodshed, death and suicide.

To offset these principalities, we need to armor up in accordance with Ephesians 6, "For we wrestle not against flesh and blood but against principalities, against powers, against the rulers of darkness of this world, against spiritual wickedness in heavenly places."

The seven spirits (lamps) of God are working on our behalf: The Spirit of the Lord, of wisdom and understanding, of counsel and might, of knowledge and of the fear of the Lord (Isaiah 11:2). We can call on the Lord of Hosts, the King of Kings, the Lord of Lords, our Husband, Jesus Christ. Jehovah Nissi is our Victor; Jehovah M'Kaddesh, our Sanctifier; Jehovah Rohi, our Shepherd; Jehovah Rophe, our Healer; Jehovah Jireh, our Provider; Jehovah Jsidkenu, our Righteousness; Jehovah Shammah, the Presence of God; and Jehovah Shalom, our Peace.

The New Age dawning effective March 21, 1995, is the Age of Aquarius, with its lawlessness of the unrestrained human heart, and totally integrated knowledge, manifesting autonomous supernatural power. A Jesus Christ-blaspheming "Beast," a creature-worshiping New World Order, which cuts itself off from God's heaven and attempts to ground itself out in a lawless "Mother Earth," is coming to fruition. The United Nations Conference on Environment and Development, the Earth Summit, held in Rio de Janeiro June 1-12, 1992, was attended by many heads of state and thousands of government officials. The political economics of this lawless environmentalism has its spiritual roots in Wicca - witchcraft. It is intent on effectively establishing global socialism/fascism, the end target of communism, by destroying individual freedom, industrial society, and killing millions of members of the human race. Most of all, it hates the light of Christianity. It is darkness personified. God makes it abundantly clear in Revelation 8 and 9 that His reason for judging the earth environmentally is due to the worship of demons and idols by man, plus man's sorceries (witchcraft), sexual immorality, murders and thefts. The best hope for the environment is a redeemed, light-filled Christian world. It is time for Christians, the light of the world, to arise.

LIGHT MAN

On June 12, 1991, a large solar flare hit Planet Earth. The National Oceanic and Atmospheric Administration (NOAA) reported that the geomagnetic field was mostly active due to this solar flare, and that storm conditions occurred.

On June 8, 1991, Mount Unzen exploded in Japan, and Mount Pinatubo blew its top in the Philippines. These two volcanoes became active for the first time in 200 years and 600 years, respectively. Mount Pinatubo shot sulfur dioxide gas into the stratosphere 21 miles high. Volcanic debris in the upper atmosphere in significant amounts blocks sunlight and plays havoc with crop production. An El Niño resulted, and 1992 saw roaring bull markets in "protein gold" (corn, wheat, soybeans) and a coffee freeze in Brazil. The California drought ended. The occurrence of 5.0 or greater Richter scale earthquakes recently is 15 times more frequent than in the 1950s.

The heavens are churning. Graviton waves, put out by nova stars, are numerous. A full solar eclipse occurred July 11, 1991. The full moon of July 26, 1991 recorded a lunar eclipse. The bright planets of Venus, Jupiter and Mars appeared to rendezvous in the evening sky on the summer solstice of June 21, 1991. Love and war were at it. These three planets were within three degrees of each other. The last time they were this close was December 23, 1769, when the American colonists were arguing with King George over taxes. This massing of planets again found Americans grim-faced over taxes. The hit movie was, "Robin Hood: Prince of Thieves." Robin Hood stole from the government to give to the people. Globally, governments everywhere are under stress.

Upset in the heavens causes turmoil in the earth and distress among the nations. After all, the earth is just a big electromagnet that creates an energy grid around itself. Peter Kelly of Interdimensional Sciences reports that the last time the earth's magnetic field went through such a radical shift was during the lifetime of Jesus Christ. History records that during such times supernatural manifestations proliferate. Given Hollywood's emphasis in this area, we should expect such an outbreak. Hollywood's films have increasingly dealt with the supernatural.

In a sense, we human beings are living electromagnetic units. Medically, we are measured with an EEG (electrically) and an EMG (magnetically). We say that some folks have their heads in the clouds, where others have their feet on the ground. Some people are called "airheads," others are well-grounded. Some are upset, some are settled down. If someone is "losing ground," he is in trouble. These sayings speak to this electromagnetic continuum, as well.

Kirlian photography measures the energy field/countenance/aura emanating from the human body. This field is still intact even if a physical limb, such as a hand, is missing. Light is taken in through the human eye and is processed through the retina to the optic nerve from whence it feeds the pineal, pituitary and hypothalamus. On the other end of the electromagnetic spectrum, African tribes partially bury men in paramagnetically-charged, iron-rich red earth to cure them of skin disease and other illnesses. Stateside, a famous major medical school has used the work of Albert Davis and Walter Rawls, Jr. and effected a 90 percent cure rate of cancer using magnets (north pole, I suspect). Human blood carries a magnetic charge. Human lymph carries an electrical charge. Magnetic therapy is in wide-spread use in India and France. Healing results. Electrical therapy is used in the West.

As human beings we are holographic, compressed energy patterns, slowed down below the speed of light, and held together by an electromagnetic field. We are human photocells, frozen, compressed light. This is why physicians of various specialties around the world can analyze a particular part of the human body and from it obtain a picture of the whole. We are holographic; each part reflects the whole. A reflexologist can analyze a foot to ascertain the health of the whole body. Lines in the hands or in the face also provide clues to the system's health. An acupuncturist can evaluate an ear. An Indian doctor can analyze the urine and a birth chart; a medical doctor, the tongue or the blood; an iridologist, the eye; and so it goes. Each holographic part contains within it the picture of the entire living, holographic, electromagnetic whole. So, it should come as no surprise that as the heavens go, so goes the earth and mankind, individually and collectively.

Leading physicians today state that at least 80 percent of all disease has an emotional base. When we fail to handle the challenges of life properly, our emotions slow down below the speed of light and become living dark crystals in our bodies. These living dark crystals or biological resistors impede light/energy flow, shutting down geometric and holographic electromagnetic connections, which vent and feed from the heavens through the head down to the feet, grounding in the earth, or feed from the earth up through our feet. The greater our number of bio-resistors, the less functional we are.

Of course, we all come into this world with excess baggage, bio-resistors already built in, which have been passed down to us genetically via our ancestors' RNA/DNA. Then we have our own creations as well. The more dark crystals/biological resistors, the darker the shadow we cast, the less light there is in our bio-system. If our ancestral and personal error/sin creates too many biological resistors, particularly where they start to shut down the holographic circuitry in the 695 key acupuncture points of intense luminosity, then we are really headed for trouble. (This is confirmed by Kirlian photography.) We start to get sick in many ways, perhaps emotionally, mentally, and/or physically, and we make increasingly poor judgments. We are literally in bondage.

The heart is the key in all this as it not only pumps life (oxygen, cellular food), but also controls the endocrine system which affects everything else. Plus, the heart is the spiritual/mental/emotional/physical integration organ between the conscious and subconscious.

Yes, the likes of homeopathy, Rolfing, stressology, point holding, colonics, massage, reflexology and chiropractic can clear some of the circuits short term. But unless the spirit, heart, soul, mental and emotional software programming is changed, particularly down into the delta, theta, and alpha regions of the subconscious, the same old patterns will reemerge, maybe worse, perhaps seven times worse.

Old Adam had it good (perfect environment) before ambitious Eve was deceived into playing god, and Adam let his woman dominate him. All of Adam's circuits were originally on line. He was perfectly electromagnetically connected, both supernaturally and naturally, in touch with both heaven and earth. All 12 of his key organ systems manifest through his skin and cranium the perfect piezoelectric charge, carried there without resistance along the 12 acupuncture meridians, handled superconductively by the central and governing meridians. Adam's entire system was superconductive before his self-will entered a bio-resistor/dark crystal into the system and began shutting him down.

Later on, Moses, the most humble man on the face of the earth, had to ground out by taking his shoes off in the presence of the Burning Bush. Whoever touched the Ark of the Covenant (in part a capacitor) in ancient Israel was electrocuted. The high priest of ancient Israel was required to wear the breastplate of 12 gemstones, representing not only the 12 tribes of Israel, but also the 12 organ systems in his own body, when he entered the presence of God.

These 12 gemstones provided each of the high priest's 12 individual key organs with a piezoelectric, colored-crystal crutch, as it were, so that he could come on line electromagnetically, superconductively and directly access the throne room of God from earth.

When God, in the fullness of His historic chosen time, became matter through the personalized energetic work of the Holy Spirit, He created the earthly representative of Himself in the person of Jesus Christ. Because, according to God's Newtonian-realm law, the sins of the father are visited upon the sons, Jesus Christ had to avoid the grounded inherited baggage and biological resistors/dark crystals which come down the pike for all the rest of us. He escaped the blown circuits by way of the immaculate conception. None of the rest of us had the Holy Spirit working for us on behalf of God the Father. So Jesus Christ came in clean, with all systems go, all 12 acupuncture meridians perfectly on line, superconductive, central and governing meridians a go, perfectly pH balanced, fully mineralized, complete enzymes, perfect electrolytes, and void of any biological sin/error resistors. The 695 key acupuncture points were operating at maximum luminosity, with all the rest of the points operational, too. The total holographic light network was intact, integrated and on line.

As God and man, Jesus could operate both supernaturally and naturally, in the quantum realm and in the Newtonian realm, crossing the Einsteinian relativity bridge without a problem. He had perfect access to both extremes (and everything in between) of the electromagnetic spectrum. He was Alpha and Omega. He was the second Adam. Jesus was on earth humanly as Adam was initially - before the first Adam violated God's law and set into play the downward dark death spiral, as biological resistors/dark crystals entered his system. But there was still a catch. Jesus had to walk through his entire life on earth without making a mistake (sin). It was only by perfectly keeping God's law that He could keep from introducing error/sin/biological resistors/dark crystals into His own system, and thereby prevent the short-circuiting of His perfect electromagnetic connection.

If we possessed perfect electromagnetic connections, or perhaps even partially good ones, strengthening faith, even the equivalent of a mustard seed, we'd be able to say to a mulberry tree, "Be uprooted and planted in the ocean," and it would happen. Christ said, "Greater things than I have done you shall do."

As Creator, Law-giver, and godly establisher of religious protocol, Jesus Christ was the personalization of government as religion applied to economics, the $E=MC^2$ of human action. Thus, it was no accident that Satan's three Gospel-recorded temptations of Jesus were governmental (offering Him the kingdoms of the world), religious (cast yourself down) and economic (turning stones into bread). Because God is basically covenantal (Old Covenant/New Covenant), to keep the faith and restore the rift in the heaven/earth electromagnetic connection, Jesus Christ made the voluntary decision to take on all the world's error/sin/biological resistors/dark crystals on the cross. He thereby laid the covenantal basis for His people to clear their systems in time on earth. The eternal connection was first reestablished by the work of Christ Himself. How could the grave hold someone who had no personal or ancestral death in His system? The Father of Lights would not permit it. Justice prevailed.

The proof of the eternal connection for saved man was to be manifest in time through his works on the earth as he progressively moved from darkness to light, clearing his system of darkness, increasingly filling it with light through obedience to God's commandments until physical death. This "magnetic" activity was joined on the "living electrical" end of the spectrum, by faith and the work of the Holy Spirit.

Biblically, man, by attaching through God-given faith to His perfect holographic model, Jesus Christ, and the laser plumb line of His blood, through the power of the Holy Spirit, establishes himself spiritually in both the electrical and magnetic ends of the spectrum, heaven and earth, the supernatural and the natural, quantum and Newtonian. By walking out his life on earth in faith through increasingly perfect obedience to God's moral law and supernatural guidance, man further clears, grounds, and establishes both the electrical and magnetic ends of the spectrum within himself. He becomes harmless as a dove yet cunning as a serpent, manifesting the fruit of the Spirit and obeying the law of God, in spirit and truth, by faith and works. In time he becomes what he had already established by faith abstractly and conceptually in the spiritual realm eternally. Man is required to ground out what he believes to be true eternally, to prove all things, and complete the connection. (The kingdom of God is within before it can be externalized.) In such a fashion, the electromagnetic and magnetoelectric scalar interferometry is established. The ultimate goal is an integrated, holographic, electromagnetic, linear and cyclical, personal and spiritual, supernatural and natural, energetic and physical, perfect living photocell. The creation groans, eagerly awaiting the revealing of the sons of God.

Signs in the heavens, geophysical upset on earth, and turmoil among mankind is joined by war in the spirit realm. (Planetary angles in the infrared emit frequencies which affect specific human organ systems and trigger emotional responses in the natural man.) And true enough, some people don't believe what they can't see. But they might consider what historical evidence has confirmed with regard to the spiritual realm, and what we can now measure with advanced instrumentation, Ghostbusters-style. After all, we humans only see five percent of the entire light spectrum, from 0.4-0.7 micrometers. Yet we live at 10 micrometers in the infrared range. Therefore, all demons/ghosts/spirits have to do is move in and out of this narrow light spectrum to be seen or unseen by our extremely limited eye cameras. Those medicine men, shamans, hippies who worked around with drugs like LSD and moved outside of this limited 0.4-0.7 micrometer light spectrum, along with those researchers and religious leaders who have delved into exploring the infrared range (the arena of dark light), know all too well of the existence of the demonic. New Agers have used modern brain wave technology to reach altered states of consciousness.

With the earth's magnetic field weakening, the humanistic crowd wants to be lawless by being their own gods and doing what is right in their own eyes. They are emotionally based, stripping their protective grounding flesh from their souls, getting out of their bodies, free of the bounds of earth, so they can manifest ungodly, ungrounded, quantum realm supernatural power which sure as hellfire will burn them out.

A seminal work that further discusses this issue of light and the human being is Bruce L. Cathie's "The Energy Grid: Harmonic 695: The Pulse Of The Universe" (American West Publishers, P.O. Box 6451, Tehachapi, CA 93582, $13.95, ISBN 0-922356-20-3, Phone (805) 822-9655). Chapter 17 of Cathie's book is entitled, "The Harmonics of Humans." Cathie writes, "The unified equations tell us that the whole universe is manifested by the harmonic geometric matrix of light itself. The whole of reality is light. Therefore, it follows, that we as human beings must consist of nothing more than a geometric collection of the harmonic wave-forms of light - guided by intelligence...

"As each day forms a part of our geometric time cycle it seems reasonable to assume that perfection would be more likely to result from a gestation period of: 269.44 days.

"This would tune the body directly with the harmonic value derived from the unified equation: 26944...

"I would predict that the temperature at which the human body performs most efficiently, both physically and mentally, is 98.80412 degrees F.

"98.80412 degrees fahrenheit - 37.1134 degrees centigrade - The harmonic reciprocal of 371134 = 269444.

"If the unified harmonic is built into the body at birth, then the temperature at which it functions appears to be at a level which would set up the harmonic reciprocal, causing a reaction, and life.

"A third clue is evident in the nodal points in the human body where our bio-energetic processes are most prevalent. These are the major points used in the science of acupuncture...

"At Alma-Ata, the Leningrad surgeon, Dr. M.K. Geykin, was experimenting with Kirlian Photography. He had spent some time in China, where he worked on acupuncture. Fascinated by Kirlian's method, he decided to visit him in Krasnodar and induce him to build a gadget that could help physicians find the points of acupuncture on the human body. Kirlian listened to him with great interest. He had already discovered long before that the 695 points on the human body considered to be the points for acupuncture coincided with the points of intense luminosity brought out by Kirlian Photography.

"The number of acupuncture points: 695 - the reciprocal harmonic of the speed of light at the Earth's surface. Again it appears that the body's bio-energy system is tuned to react to the harmonic of light."...

Man was created in the image of the Father of Lights.

Now, let's turn our attention to the earth's electromagnetic grid system, the earth's energy grid. The earth as a big spinning electromagnet, winds energy lines around it, called ley lines, much in the same manner a baseball is constructed with the strands crisscrossing each other.

The technology exists to tap this earth energy, providing the world with an endless supply of free energy. Nikola Tesla, America's greatest scientist in the field of electromagnetism (International Tesla Society; Colorado Springs, Colorado, Phone 719-475-0918) proved this in New York earlier in this century. Also, when the earth's magnetic field weakens and/or solar storms rage, these grid-lines weaken, allowing more earthquakes and volcanic eruptions. Additionally, during times of ley line distortions the dividing line between the natural and the supernatural blurs. Spirit crossover increases.

Nearly all of the early churches in Europe, England, Ireland and North America were located at "power points" on these ley lines, vortexes and the like. Map readers in Japan, China (Feng Shui), and in Egypt, dating back to the pyramids considered the electromagnetic "ley of the land" in computing where and how to place buildings. Present day petroleum geology, utility companies and water dowsers are bringing this work into the modern scientific world. Research at Utah State University has advanced and confirmed the science, as well.

The June, 1989, East-West Magazine featured an article by Richard Leviton entitled, "Can the Earth's Stress Spots Make You Sick?" The answer is yes. The beds of people who died from cancer were found to be consistently located above noxious radiation emanating from the earth's faults in Vilsbiburg, a small Bavarian community in southern Germany.

In the town of Stettin, the homes of 5,438 people who died of cancer over 21 years were found to have a subterranean water vein under the house in each case. This research was accomplished by Baron Gustav Freiherr von Pohl's colleague, Dr. Hager, back in the 1920's. Later, in the 1940s, a German physician, Manfred Curry, M.D., discovered the Curry Network Screen, a grid which girds the planet. German born Ernest Hartmann, M.D., director of the Research Circle for Geobiology, formulated the Hartmann Grid. It runs diagonally to the Curry Grid. The intersections of these grids are found to be harmful to plants, animals and humans, particularly the intersection of grid lines of similar electrical charge.

In 1972, Kathe Vachler, a mathematics teacher in Austria commissioned by the Pedagogical Institute in Salzburg, found 95 percent of slow-learners' beds were situated on either water veins or Curry Grid crossings.

Ludger Mersmann, M.D. contends that the cause of geopathic stress is localized magnetic anomalies that upset human health. It is Mersmann who invented the Geo-Magnetometer and Data Logger which can take precise readings in a suspected geopathic zone and get a three-dimensional computer graphic of the disturbed field. Says Mersmann, "Geopathic stress consists of several factors, but the main factor is a disturbed magnetic field. Here the natural homogeneous magnetic field meets with or turns into a nonhomogeneous field, resulting in a disturbed zone."

The earth oscillates at the resonant frequency of 7.83 Hertz, or cycles per second. The earth's natural magnetic field usually averages about 0.5 gauss. However, regularly occurring anomalies and sudden field shifts often range up to three times as high. So with all the solar, geophysical and geomagnetic field upset we are experiencing presently, we should expect people to increasingly become ill, and for there to be more outbreaks of supernatural phenomena. Says Leviton, "For two decades scientists have been gathering evidence of the deleterious effects on humans of extremely weak magnetic fields, and it all supports Mersmann's hypothesis. The human body has composite and individual organ fields as low as 1×10^{-9} gauss, or about one-billionth of the earth's field. Recent studies in New York and Colorado have linked exposure to low-frequency, weak electromagnetic fields - for example, from high voltage power lines - and cancer, particularly childhood leukemia."

Helmut Ziehe, president of the International Institute of Baubiologie and Ecology in Clearwater, Florida, has found a dozen physiological changes scientists have observed in people who live within geopathic zones. These include electrocardiogram and pulse changes, changes in blood sedimentation, pH, electrical cell polarity, and alterations in immune function. Dr. Hans Nieper of the Sibersee Hospital in Hanover, Germany maintains that 75 percent of his multiple sclerosis patients "spend too much time in a geopathogenic zone," and at least 92 percent of all his cancer patients have remained for long periods in geopathogenic zones.

Underground water and magnetic field anomalies are consistently the main problems. In Germany, approximately 50 percent of all physicians are aware of the geopathic factor. How many U.S. M.D.s are conscious of it? However, there is some emerging consciousness in the United States. In Seattle, Washington, a group of architects, artists and others, called the Geo Group, have mapped the ley lines of Seattle.

In understanding how these subtle earth energies cause illness, it is helpful to remember that we are well when we are at "ease," when all our bodies' systems are oscillating at their correct resonant frequencies. When we are emotionally upset, ungrounded, not settled down, or under stress, we are "dis-eased." This is also why we are to think on whatever things are true, noble, just, pure, lovely and of good report. As a man thinketh so he is. We should ground out by eating fresh, live, non-toxic foods, drinking plenty of pure water, breathing correctly, exercising appropriately, and being anxious about nothing while being full of faith, hope and love.

There is another interesting aspect to these ley lines or energy grid lines of the earth. They have long been the tracks on which the purported UFOs have run. Flying saucers, or anti-gravity devices, are well documented. The Nazis had flying saucers. The U.S. had them as early as 1942, as reported by the April 7, 1950, U.S. News & World Report. Press reports on UFOs went underground in the mid-1950s, following a North Carolina confab.

Studies at Michigan State University have confirmed the connection between magnetism, levitation and gyroscopic motion.

The July/August 1989 issue of The Journal of Borderland Research featured an article by Michael Potter entitled, "UFOs: We have the Technology." Wrote Potter, "UFOs are aerodynamic...This half-lens shape - like a frisbee - is an aerofoil and when flown it will create life.

"However, unlike a frisbee, the UFO glider does not need to be spun to fly. UFOs have never been observed to spin, although energy has been seen spinning around them...

Circular aircraft are certainly not new. Before the 1947 UFO flap there was a round airplane called a 'U.S. Flying Flapjack' and the Russians experimented with a similar craft. What was different about these airplanes is that they had propellers, tails and elevators...

"A UFO glider's center of gravity - the coin - is its means of guidance. The saucer 'follows' the weight of the falling coin. If the coin is shifted to the center of the lower dome the UFO glider will descend vertically.

"Now a magnet replaces the rim coin with an internal mechanical ballast. In fact, a shifting ballast is a method blimps use to navigate. However, unlike a blimp, any part of the saucer's rim can be a front. If the ballast is quickly moved around the saucer's rim 90 degrees, the gliding saucer will execute a right-angle turn as it follows the falling ballast...

"The elliptical-hull airship designed by the Spacial Company in Mexico is a circular rigid blimp. This helium aircraft comes very close to fulfilling our UFO theory...

"Now imagine a saucer that combines the asymmetrical lenticular shape of the UFO glider, the structural strength of the Spacial airship and the hot air lift of a Cameron airship. Here we have an entirely new aircraft capable of vertical takeoff and landing, rapid horizontal flight and right-angle turns."

If gravity is a wave, if the wave of gravity is offset through the correct harmonic frequency, then a saucer could literally fall into a vacuum in any direction also.

On Page 58 of the book, "Anti-Gravity And The World Grid," edited by David Hatcher Childress, it is mentioned that Australia has a permanent diamagnetic levitation vortex at Alice Springs. Alice Springs is located in the middle of Australia. It is where an infamous, longtime, U.S. super-secret military installation is located, known as Pine Gap. Pine Gap is as hush-hush as Area 51 in Nevada. Nevada? UFO sightings are common in an area known as S-4, located about 7 miles south of the western border of Area 51. This region is also known as "Dreamland."

I suspect by 2001, and for sure by 2010, all this technology that has been with us since at least the early 1950s, will be sprung on us in an attempt to "wow" mankind into accepting a New World Order, complete with a One-world government, a One-world currency, a One-world central bank, and a One-world religion. But, it won't be anything new. I have personally visited with many of the men who have developed this fascinating technology. Put differently, there is not a natural problem I know of we face on this earth, which has not already been solved technologically if the present Establishment would get out of the way politically, financially, religiously, legally, and special interests be damned.

Finally, pages 55-57 of the book "Anti-Gravity And The World Grid," presents an interesting section subtitled, "Human Diamagnetism Gravity Antenna Levitation." This section shows how any group of people, anywhere, as a party activity, can levitate anyone else. The step-by-step directions, along with the easy-to-understand theory, is all presented there.

Levitation is not necessarily magic or an occult activity. It is more times than not, technology which has been hidden from us. The ancients had it. Bruce Cathie documented how Tibetan monks used sound waves to create an anti-gravitational effect - offsetting the frequency of gravity - to levitate stones. This was confirmed by Dr. Jarl, a Swedish doctor who studied at Oxford, on behalf of the English Scientific Society. One wonders if this is one of the reasons why the Red Chinese have shut off Tibet from the rest of the world, perhaps at the behest of the proponents of the New World Order. Could they not want all of this fantastic knowledge released just yet? These Tibetan monks functionally understood the laws governing the structure of matter. And the TM meditators, with their "soft landing" pillow? Their chanted mantras reach the point where they harmonically oscillate all their body's cells at a frequency which offsets gravity. And in nature? Water moves up the trunk of a tree. Antigravity!

All of the above, while possibly somewhat shocking to some of you, and undoubtedly mind-blowing to the American general public and most Christians, has become over time matter-of-fact to this writer. It is pretty much demonstrable, verifiable, and repeatable. Among the global scientists, it is all taken for granted as common working knowledge. But then again, the federal government persecutes the independent avant garde global scientists the same way it does the Franklin Sanders-type honest moneychangers, and the American patriot tax protestor/honest money movement and fundamental Christians. The Dark Ages did not occur in the Middle Ages. The Dark Ages are now. There needs to be light in light men on the earth. Christians have their work and challenge cut out for them.

BRUCE CATHIE VISITED

Everything new is first laughed at, then attacked by the Establishment. Finally, people wonder why this wonderful "new thing" wasn't with us all along. Ignaz Semmelweiss, in Vienna in the 19th century, had the audacity to suggest that physicians should wash up after handling cadavers before delivering babies. He was labeled a kook and an occultist and driven out of Austria. Columbus was called demon-possessed and told he would sail off the edge of the earth. Pasteur's concept of germs was initially labeled "satanic." The controversy between Ptolemy and Copernicus was first a question of theological heresy. The telephone, airplane and computer were all labeled to be "of the devil" by various churchmen of their day. Two years after the first motorized flight of the Wright brothers in December 1903, Scientific American (1905) reported that the flight was a hoax and a prank contrary to the on-site observation of approximately 500 witnesses. Meanwhile, the less religious and more secular members of the general public just dismissed the geniuses of their times as "kooks" and "nuts." Never mind that it is such "kooks" and "nuts" who bring us the quantum advances and scientific leaps forward that make a better world for the average man. It never pays to be too far out in front. Too many arrows wind up in the back.

A quick word to my theologically inclined readers: The word "occult" means "secret, hidden knowledge." Power, mysteries and magic which cannot be repeated by anyone or explained openly may indeed be occult, of demonic origin, as a theologian would put it. However, all things were originally created good. And so it seems that both men and nature are supposed to be recaptured theologically and scientifically from the cursed natural order of conflict, chance, cycles, poverty and death to harmony, dominion, love, light, life, law, liberty, laughter and long-term view. This includes the "occult." The foregoing was the basis upon which valid Christian science was built.

How often have pagans labeled technology and science that we easily understand as "magic"? The American Indians once thought that what made corn pop were little demons inside. Could it be that "magic" may in some cases be technology and science which we do not yet understand, that needs to be recaptured? Chemistry came out of alchemy. Albert Einstein astutely wrote, "Science without religion is lame, religion without science is blind." Certainly, the history of new science and the human response to it would suggest that Einstein was correct.

For Christian working purposes, I describe the occult as: 1) anything that God specifically defines as occult; 2) anything that is elevated from the created natural realm to God's eternal realm, which is not directly linked to the sacrificial provision of Jesus Christ; and 3) anything from the natural order, man or creation, which is not recaptured from the curse of the earth to the peace of the kingdom.

In late 1985, I was in New Zealand and arranged an interview with Bruce Cathie. What was expected to be a casual two-hour chat turned into an intense 11-hour discussion of point and counterpoint, followed by illustration, demonstration and documentation. My pressing question is: Is Bruce Cathie to "insider" Establishment modern science and technology what Dr. Antony Sutton is to "insider" Establishment history and geo-political affairs?

Dr. Antony Sutton, of course, formerly a researcher at the Hoover War Institute at Stanford University, has carefully documented the occult nature of The Order, a One-world political, socialistic conspiracy, into which George Bush was initiated at Yale. Dr. Sutton has also documented the fact that the former Soviet Union and the United States are effectively working together. An alarming 95 percent of the technology the former Soviet Union had procured, was given to it, sold to it, or financed by the West. Bruce Cathie, in like manner, discovered a possible occult, geometric, scientific link between the United States and the former Soviet Union. Such confirms the observations of authors and philosophers Gore Vidal and Norman Mailer. These two men declared that in an overall historical context, the U.S. and the former U.S.S.R. are natural allies. This strongly suggests a One-world socialistic, scientific conspiracy - a master collective being formed from the top down. Furthermore, this is in keeping with the Hegelian dialectic of thesis versus antithesis equals synthesis. The thesis - the individualistic extreme of monopolistic, evolutionary, debt capitalism - versus the antithesis - the collectivist extreme of communism - form a synthesis between the many and the one, respectively, in a One-world socialist/fascist state - a New World Order.

Communism obviously failed. Communists, both in the former Soviet Union and Red China, loosened up and allowed "capitalism" in order to survive. Debt capitalism is also failing in the West. How could it do otherwise? The words "debt" and "capitalism" are incompatible long term. Putting the two words together is in fact Orwellian. "Debt" is borrowing from the future by mortgaging the past to consume in the present. "Capitalism" requires savings from the past through the present for investment in the future. So the "debt capitalism" of today is present oriented, while "capitalism" itself is future oriented. Thus, debt capitalism collapses into top down bureaucratic socialism/fascism. The synthesis comes easily with the bureaucratic Soviet Union which, after all, was the Union of Soviet "Socialist" Republics. Amerika is symbolized by Russian cosmonauts and U.S. astronauts joining together in the Russian space station MIR, as they did in mid-year 1995...Back to Cathie.

Bruce Cathie pretty much fits the stereotype of a research scientist. He is of average height, on the thin side, somewhat frail, bespectacled, and mentally sharp as a tack. A voracious reader, surrounded by his computers and calculators, Bruce Cathie is a meticulous perfectionist when it comes to his calculations, a man who refuses to compromise the integrity of what he is doing for money or publicity. In short, while I don't agree with him in some matters, I found him to be dedicated to a search for truth. His home, while nice, was not extravagant nor sumptuously furnished. It fit in with the neighborhood and with the lifestyle of other New Zealanders. His family exhibited the hallmarks of a tightly knit, mutually supportive group, which has been harassed, questioned and haunted by global intelligence agents.

Bruce Cathie is no lightweight when it comes to science and technology. He was educated at Otahuhu Technical College. He was an engineering apprentice prior to joining the Royal New Zealand Air Force, where he became a pilot. In March of 1977, he became a qualified Boeing 737 pilot for Air New Zealand. Cathie commented that present day airliners have been obsolete for at least 20 years. It was back in 1952, when Captain Bruce Cathie was a pilot with National Airways Corporation, that he and a group of friends made a prolonged evening sighting of a UFO at Mangere, Auckland.

Cathie's first book, "Harmonic 33," presented the theory that the whole world is crisscrossed by an electromagnetic grid system. His second book, "Harmonic 695" contained evidence that this grid system is known to our scientists and is being used for secret experimentation, particularly by the nations involved in atomic bomb tests. Cathie's third book, "The Pulse Of The Universe, Harmonic 288," provided formulations of a series of unified field equations. In his last book, "The Bridge To Infinity, Harmonic 371244," Cathie demonstrated the harmonic nature of physical reality, and that today's scientists have at their command a fantastic store of knowledge with which they could dramatically advance the welfare of the human race. This knowledge, however, is being carefully guarded.

One cannot help but wonder, if at some time in the future, during a created and controlled crisis, the global Establishment (New World Order) might drop on us the reappearance of flying saucers and other advanced technology with "wealth for all" type solutions to our problems, in order to centralize government totalitarian power. Perhaps, free energy like that discovered by Nikola Tesla, Joseph Newman and Bruce Cathie, and consistent medical healing, such as that which existed before 1930 in hospitals in this country using the multiwave oscillator invented by George Lakhovsky. (The multiwave oscillator healed at the frequency [energy] level rather than the matter level, by electrically energizing the body's cells.)

Most of us deal with the dimensions - length, breadth, height and time. However, Cathie related that 10 to 15 years ago New Zealand scientists commented that they were working in 15 dimensions. A dimension can be jumped, according to Cathie. It has to do with the idea that each of the eight spaces for electrons in the shell of an atom is first "filled."

I watched with a critical and somewhat skeptical eye as Cathie pulled out three full three-ring binders of letters documenting the military and intelligence officials he had worked with in the United States and New Zealand. There was a September 18, 1968 letter in which New Zealand Prime Minister Holyoake referred to the "facets" that scientists in New Zealand used in two-way communication with UFOs. There were also letters from Colonel Burnett and Colonel Lewis H. Walker of Wright-Patterson Air Force Base in the United States, our UFO center. There was correspondence with leading U.S. scientists, and documentation of how Bruce Cathie was taken to Seattle to interview for a job with Boeing. But when Cathie refused to sign away his New Zealand citizenship and a form pledging total secrecy, the job offer was withdrawn.

There were letters from New Zealand intelligence officials who provide Bruce Cathie with protection now, as has been the case for several years, as he provides the New Zealand government with the results of his latest work. There were also copious files obtained through the Freedom of Information Act that the U.S. intelligence community had accumulated on Bruce Cathie. And on and on it went.

Question: Why would the clandestine upper level "insider" Establishment military intelligence and scientific community be interested in Bruce Cathie's work if it wasn't valid? Cathie's work is very similar in theory to that of Joseph Newman in Lucedale, Mississippi, inventor of the free energy machine. Joseph Newman discussed principles of physics and his invention on nationwide TV on NBC's Johnny Carson's "The Tonight Show" (February 27, 1986). Newman has received patents in Spain and South Africa.

Cathie had never heard of Newman. The history of science is the history of the simultaneous discovery of like principles at various places around the world. One may be overcome with the sneaky suspicion that the "insider" Establishment is withholding important information in physics and basic science, just as it has mislead us in political theory, economics and theology.

For his free energy machine, Joseph Newman's theory proposes gyroscopic motion at the speed of light, spinning at the speed of light and moving forward at the speed of light. Centrifugal force is manifest. Bruce Cathie demonstrated that the harmonic wave-form which creates an atom of matter and antimatter in alternate pulses also has three simultaneous movements - directional, spinning and rotation. But again, Bruce Cathie has never heard of the work of Joseph Newman, and I suspect that Newman has never heard of Cathie.

This Cathie theory harmonizes with part of quantum theory, that life (matter) exists in pulses. We view matter/life as we view a motion picture. There are separate frames of still photographs sped up to make motion appear evident. Cathie postulates this is the matter/antimatter sequence. This in turn links to jumping into a new dimension. To quote Cathie, "Matter and antimatter are formed by the same wave motions in space. The waves travel through space in a spiraling motion, and alternately pass through positive and negative stages. Matter is formed through the positive stage, or pulse, and antimatter through the negative pulse.

"Every spiral of 360 degrees forms a single pulse. The circular motion of an electron about the nucleus of an atom is therefore an illusion. The relative motion of the nucleus and electrons through space gives the illusion of circular motion. The period during the formation of antimatter is completely undetectable, since obviously all physical matter is manifesting at the same pulse rate, including any instruments or detectors used to probe atomic structures.

"The period or frequency rate between each pulse of physical matter creates the measurement which we call time, as well as the speed of light, at the particular position in space of which we are aware, at any given moment.

"If the frequency rate of positive and negative pulses is either increased or decreased, then time and the speed of light vary in direct proportion.

"This concept would explain time as a geometric, as Einstein theorized it to be.

"A rough analogy of physical existence can be made by reference to a strip of motion picture film. Each frame or static picture on the film strip may be likened to a single pulse of physical existence. The division between one frame and the next represents a frame of antimatter. When viewed as a complete strip, each frame would be seen as a static picture - say, one at either end of the strip - then the past and the future could be viewed simultaneously. However, when the film is fed through a projector, we obtain the illusion of motion and the passage of time. The divisions between the static pictures are not detected by our senses because of the frequency or speed of each projection on the movie screen. But by speeding up or slowing down the projector, we can alter the apparent time rate of the action shown by the film...

"The theory outlined above explains why life has been described as being caused by both a wave motion and a pulse. Both explanations are correct."

The harmonic of the circle is determined by multiplying the radius of the circle times two to get the diameter. The diameter is multiplied times pi to obtain the circumference, which is then divided by eight and then divided by six. Increasing divisions, or multiples of six, provide new harmonics according to Cathie (666). It is Cathie's firm conviction that the unified field equation expressed in terms of light is pure electromagnetic wave form, the key to the universe, and that the whole of existence has been known for some time. As Cathie states it, "All of creation is light." Interesting. God is light.

Joseph Newman stated on February 27, 1986, on "The Tonight Show" with Johnny Carson, "I just set out to figure out the how, why and what of things. To prove to myself that this energy was the real energy, I had to come up with the unified field theory mechanically explaining gravity, electricity, magnetism, inertia, planetary motion and a new source of energy. It took me over 15 years to do that."

When a couple of U.S. intelligence agents visited Cathie, he opened up to them and explained how his unified field theory applied to the gravitational fields, making possible the antigravity flotation of discs, as well as the geometrics of the atomic bomb. He said one of the agents became drunk during their discussions and kept saying over and over again, "How could a common man like you uncover this? How could a man like you find out about this?" Cathie related that the gentleman was quite frustrated that this "secret" had gotten out.

Once Cathie presented it, the concepts of antigravity and anti-gravitational discs in motion became quite simple. "The earth is simply a huge magnet, a dynamo, wound with magnetic lines of force as it coils, telescopically counted to be 1257 to the square centimeter in one direction and 1850 to the square centimeter in the other direction (eddy currents), indicates that natural law (sic) has placed these lines as close together as the hairs on one's head." Interestingly, the Bible speaks of how the very hairs on our head are numbered.

"A spectroscope shows that there is an enormous magnetic field around the sun. And it is the present conclusion of the best minds that magnetic lines of force from the sun envelope this earth and extend to the moon, and that everything, no matter what its form on this planet, exists by reason, by magnetic lines of force." Again, interesting. The Old Testament particularly refers to the sun, moon and earth in what could be regarded as in harmony with Cathie's statement.

Cathie believes that the magnetic lines of force enter the earth at the poles and then carry out a loop path through the body of the earth before passing out of the opposite poles.

"The flow is not in one pole and out the other, but in both poles and out both poles, although the field intensity both ways is unbalanced. It is imbalance that creates gravity. The lines of force of the magnetic field form a lattice, or a grid pattern due to the spin of the earth. This is just like a machine-wound ball of string. The length of string has taken on the form of a ball, and at the same time has formed a crisscross pattern. A small vortex is created at the trillions of points where the lines of force cross each other in the lattice pattern. Each vortex manifests as an atomic structure and creates within itself what we term a gravitational field. The gravitational field is nothing more than the effect of relative motion in space. Matter is drawn toward a gravitational field just as a piece of wood floating on water is drawn toward a whirlpool. So matter is effectively the slowing down of light at the intersections of these lines of force."

Cathie states, "...my belief that as a harmonic of light is fractionally decreased, the energy which is released is converted to form physical matter." This is what Joseph Newman has said about his free energy machine, which he has demonstrated and had verified by some scientists. Both Cathie and Newman's work confirm Einstein's declaration that physical matter is nothing more than a concentrated field of force.

Now let's carry this discussion over into antigravitational discs. The difference in the force fields going into the earth as opposed to those coming out of the earth is equal to 3928.371. Again, this excess of energy flowing into the earth as opposed to energy coming out of the earth (through vortices) is what creates gravity. Stated differently, there are more lines of force (vortices) penetrating the earth than there are coming out of the earth. The resultant difference between the two creates gravity. Or, the lines of force weaken after having worked their way through the earth's resistance, thereby permitting gravity. All an antigravity disc has to do then is to be tuned to a frequency to balance out the difference of 3928.371 to get it to float or become antigravitational. Then, only the pulse rate has to be increased or decreased, which decreases or increases time, to cause movement. It is rather simple. There is really not all that much to what we mistakenly call a UFO.

Cathie further provided me with a December, 1956, Establishment paper entitled, "The Gravitics Situation." This work was produced by Gravity Rand Ltd., of 66 Sloane Street, London, S.W.1. Now, as you read direct quotes from this paper, remember it was written nearly forty years ago. How far have we come since then?

"Electrostatic disks can provide lift without speed over a flat surface. This can be an important advance over all forms of airfoil which require induced flow; and lift without airflow is the development that deserves to be followed up in its own right and one that for military purposes is already envisioned by the users as applicable to all three services. This point has been appreciated in the United States and a program in hand may now ensure that development of large-size disks will be continued."

The word "continued" tells us that we had these floating antigravity disks over forty years ago. In fact, Dr. Townsend Brown has a patent on them. Project Winterhaven recommended major efforts be concentrated on electrogravitics, based upon the principle of Brown's disks.

We are a movie projector in a sense. We can expand or contract the "T" (time) factor. Angular velocity is the same while linear motion changes. With the speed of light, angular velocity is constant while linear velocity is variable. This gives us our spiral, or our combination of linear and cyclical time.

Imagine if you will a spinning bicycle wheel with a bug crawling up the same spoke at the same speed. The bug is moving at the same speed angularly, but at a faster speed linearly the farther out he gets from the hub. All this links to temperature as well, because at absolute zero we hit antimatter. So to change matter, we use both frequency and temperature.

In Einstein's equation, $E=MC^2$, E is energy, M is mass, and C is the speed of light. "Einstein declared that physical matter was nothing more than a concentrated field of force. What we term a physical substance is in reality an intangible concentration of wave-forms. Different combinations of structural patterns of waves unite to form the myriad chemicals and elements, which in turn react to one another to form physical substances. Different wave-forms of matter appear to us to be solid because we are constituted of similar wave-forms, which resonate within a clearly defined range of frequencies - and which control the physical processes of our limited world.

"Einstein believed that M, the value for mass in the equation, could eventually be removed and a value substituted that would express the physical in the form of pure energy. In other words, by substituting for M a unified field equation should result, which would express in mathematical terms the whole of existence - including this universe and everything in it." What Cathie explores in "The Bridge To Infinity" are harmonic unified equations 1, 2 and 3.

I asked Cathie about Tesla's free energy work. He said it was incredibly simple. The earth is covered with static electricity. All you have to do is oscillate this electricity and you can use it. For example, every time a raindrop hits the earth, a static charge is set up. This provides us with an unlimited amount of potential electricity if we can just find a way to oscillate it, which is what Tesla did. Interesting. This is exactly what John Bedini's Free Energy Generator does. It captures and utilizes a static charge.

Regular waves that we use every day flow from the atmosphere to an antenna, to a radio (or TV) and then to earth (ground) in terms of the signals we receive. Tesla discovered how to reverse the process - from the earth (ground), to the radio, to the antenna and into the atmosphere. Thus, we literally have the potential to electrify the entire earth - or the atmosphere as Tom Bearden claims the Soviets were doing with scalar waves. All some poor peasant would have to do in Brazil, for example, is to put a probe in the ground and presto - instant power, once we resonate the whole earth. At the crossover points of the ley lines, the intersection of the earth's energy acupuncture meridians (much like the nerve intersections of the chakras of the human body), are points where energy can be generated or used (matter created?). Through the earth's own network this energy could be transferred all over the globe and put to good use. Remember, the earth is simply a huge magnet, a dynamo, with magnetic lines of force. A recent underground nuclear test was conducted at one of these earth energy intersections, and the result was a huge crater and radiation readings popping up out of the earth, all over the earth.

Finally, Cathie has confirmed fascinating harmonic relationships in Washington, D.C. involving the geometric placement of the Pentagon and the CIA. The bottom line of this work is that he believes there is some type of unseen, below the surface, controlling, all-powerful government which has knowledge and use of this secret harmonic geometric power to manipulate the apparent economic and political powers of today's world. This brings us full circle back to Dr. Antony Sutton and his work in a different field (using different evidence), which has strongly documented that the same thing is true. It further lines up with the possibility that the world's central banks are in cahoots also. Money runs the world. And it confirms the Hegelian dialectic. C.S. Lewis' "That Hideous Strength" is alive and well.

* * *

Antigravity is evident throughout creation. Water rises through evaporation (antigravity). Trees grow (antigravity). Hurricanes and tornadoes through vortex mechanics lift objects (antigravity). We need to recognize that the other side of heat/explosion physics is cold/implosion physics. Newton should have focused on how the apple got up there in the first place, before it fell due to gravity.

* * *

One type of UFO, an antigravity disk, probably operates like a gyroscope. If the antigravity disk, the UFO, is gyroscopic in nature, when pressure is exerted on it from the top down, it rises. If pressure is applied from the bottom up, it falls. A gyroscopic antigravity disk (UFO) moves opposite to the direction in which force is applied. So, once the gravitational lines of force are offset, allowing the antigravitational gyroscopic disk to float, then the appropriately applied pressure determines the direction of movement.

* * *

The Searl effect was discovered by an English electronic technician named John Searl in 1949. He noticed a small EMF or voltage was induced in rotating metal objects. The negative charge was on the outside, and the positive charge was around the center of rotation. He reasoned that free electrons were thrown outward by centrifugal force, leaving a positive charge in the central portion. It followed that an electrical generator might be built utilizing this principle.

He constructed his first generator in 1952, and tested it outdoors. Its performance and behavior far exceeded his expectations. The armature was rotated by a small engine. It produced a powerful electrostatic effect on nearby objects, accompanied by crackling sounds and the smell of ozone. Beyond a critical rotational speed, the armature continued to accelerate without the aid of the engine. The generator finally lifted off the ground, while still accelerating, and rose about 50 feet, breaking the connection between it and the engine. It remained at this height for a brief period, while still increasing its rotational velocity, at which stage it rapidly gained altitude and disappeared.

Since 1952, Searl and others have constructed numerous generators of varying sizes from three to 30 feet in diameter. Some of them have been lost in a similar manner. They claim to have developed a means of controlling them in the process. Source: "The Awesome Life Source."

* * *

The following is quoted from a late 1985 West German publication, "Vertrauliche Mitteilungen":

"On the 14th of November the 'Vertrauliche' reported (No. 2590, Para. 11), in connection with the theme 'Free Energy', about the CASIMIR-EFFECT, with the help of which zero-point-radiation in space may be changed into usable energy. On the same day, on which you received that issue (namely 15th Nov.) there was entered in the Berlin office of the German Patent Office the patent report of the 'Inventors Association For Energy'. Categorization:

"'Directions or procedure to produce a varying Casimir-analog force and release of usable energy.'

"Now we will see if the Patent Office can free itself from a dogmatic defense of the current theories. Physicists hold their breath! More: Casimir is a Dutch physicist, who worked in the Phillips research labs and in 1948 demonstrated that there are electromagnetic fields in a vacuum.

"The motor of the Berliner 'Inventors Association For Energy' is a young physicist, Sven Mielordt, whose introductory book, 'Tachyonenergy/Hyperenergy/Antigravitation,' you will find on our book list enclosed today. 'Vertrauliche' has with Herr Mielordt promised that everyone who orders the book will receive gratis a copy of the patent report.

"To fill things out further: In the October 1985 issue of 'Spectrum of Science,' the American physicist/professor Timothy H. Boyer of the City University of New York published the noteworthy article entitled, 'The Vacuum in Modern View.' Quintessence: In spite of its characterization, the vacuum is no way 'empty.' Each space-area which is free from matter and heat radiation remains filled with a fluctuating electromagnetic field."

* * *

"I do believe that at least one nation other than the Soviet Union has weapons and devices based on scalar electromagnetics. I have very good data to lead me to make that statement. I do believe that a very, very small part of the UFO phenomena is indeed ships made right here on this world by that nation and by the Soviet Union...The work that was being done in electrogravitics simply went under classification...." - Physicist Tom Bearden in The Moneychanger, August 1985.

The bottom line: There is significant evidence to support the contention that UFOs have been with us for some time, that they may very well involve a spirit-energy connection; and there is high technology, including free energy, available for the taking. Could, in an upcoming crisis, mankind be offered high tech salvation in return for taking a "mark of the beast," such as an invisible laser tattoo on his hand or forehead? Such today is definitely within the realm of possibility, particularly in a top-down, bureaucratic, New World Order.

THE SPACE-TIME QUESTION

If it's true we now have knowledge and utilization of the unified field theory, and UFOs are able to manipulate space-time, then is history threatened? Time is history, as the super linear aspect of time and the subordinate cyclical aspect of time move forward in a progressive spiral. If time can be altered, history can be changed.

The time manipulation of history has long been a goal of man. Who of us is not at least vaguely familiar with H.G. Wells', "The Time Machine"? Many box office hit movies have dealt with the manipulation of time/history. Arnold Schwarzenegger's "Terminator" movies dealt with a successful attempt to go back in time, but an unsuccessful attempt to manipulate history. Steven Spielberg's smash hits, "Back To The Future," focused on going back in time for the achieved purpose of successfully manipulating the future. The space-time question was also the focus of the flick, "Peggy Sue Got Married." From these early successes, movies concerning time travel have proliferated.

If this was all sci-fi, we wouldn't give it a second thought. But remember, science fiction all too often precedes scientific reality. Literature and art (movies) project the future accurately often enough to make us seriously consider this particular space-time question. What if men with a lust for power, inclined toward evil, were truly able to get a handle on space-time? What if men could literally go back in time and, assuming they were strong supporters of the British Empire, were able to eliminate Paul Revere, Benjamin Franklin, John Adams, James Madison, Thomas Jefferson, Patrick Henry, and George Washington? What if these Founding Fathers were eliminated (terminated) when they were children? Where would we be today? What if some Luciferian and occultist with the money, power and inclination went back in time and eliminated King David, or Solomon, or Mary or Joseph? Then Jesus would never have come on the scene and the lineages of Matthew 1 and Luke 3 would not be history.

Sounds crazy, doesn't it? And yet, we're actually dealing with the space-time question with the application of the scientific thinking of two of the greatest scientists of all time - Albert Einstein and Nikola Tesla.

Einstein's search for the unified field theory as well as his "theory of relativity" are well known. Less known, but probably just as important, if not more important, was the work of Nikola Tesla (1857-1943). Nikola Tesla invented the first electric clock, the first computer circuit designs, the first X-rays, the first fluorescent light, the first system to harness alternating current (AC), the first radio (two years before Marconi), conceived the first VTOL aircraft (Vertical Takeoff and Landing Aircraft), the automobile speedometer, the bladeless turbine, and on and on. In fact, Thomas Edison received credit for most of the inventions which really belonged to Nikola Tesla. J.P. Morgan, George Westinghouse and Thomas Edison fought over Tesla for his time and the rights to his inventions (Freedom Magazine, March 1986). Tesla, with the financing of J.P. Morgan, built a tower in New York that would have provided the world with free energy. It was only under the persuasion of oil baron John D. Rockefeller that J.P. Morgan jerked the financial rug out from under Tesla and left him adrift, unable to complete the project.

The essence of Bruce Cathie's book, "The Bridge To Infinity," is that by manipulating time, man can literally bridge the limits and boundaries of time and become infinite. Let's get down to brass tacks: What we're talking about here is man playing and/or becoming god. Furthermore, one does not have to be too well read to be troubled by the fact that all this "time jumping" involves the 666 harmonic.

The Russians have been involved with the physics of Einstein and Tesla since the advent of the atomic bomb. American physicist Tom Bearden in a speech delivered in 1984 declared, "We've gone through...a one-way door. This is the final technology. You can engineer physical reality itself, with the full implications eventually as the technology develops. We must quickly develop counters to the...weapons so that they might not decide to move when they could use them. I should point out one other disadvantage of these weapons. They have a limit of how much you can use because they shake space/time. Can you imagine what happens if you cause time to oscillate, and time in half cycles is running backwards?

"Suppose you were shot in the breast and blown apart in such an oscillation in positive time. And then time backs up in the negative half cycle and you sit there and blow apart, come back together and restore your life, blow apart and die, come back together and restore your life. That's possible. That's real.

"Do you know what gravity is in negative space/time? It's a repulsion, not an attraction, so all the...buildings sit there and jump up and down and so do you. You go flying up and crashing down. You see what I mean? You can only use these things on a limited scale or you'll blow your own leg off. But the ability to engineer things like that is now in our hands, as ill-prepared as we are. So the first thing is, we must buy some time, counter the Russian weapons that are already sitting there... and have been. They've been developing them for 30 something years."

Downright mind blowing, isn't it? I haven't met many fools in my life. Every man who knows something and puts it to good use has a handle on some truth, in some form, shape or fashion. On the other hand, I've met deceivers, liars, and men who have been deceived or lied to, but where there's smoke there's usually fire. And there's been entirely too much smoke over the past 45 years in this UFO space-time area, and too much money, too many high-powered Establishment brains, and insider Establishment support, to cause this writer to just dismiss it all as science fiction. Beyond question, when we're dealing with manipulating space/time/history, we're dealing with the supernatural as well as the normal science of the created realm. The two are integrated like nothing else when it comes to space/time/history. Religion and science are becoming one.

Now, we all have presuppositions (assumptions) about the ultimate nature of reality. This is inescapable because all of us have limited time, limited knowledge and limited minds. My ultimate presupposition is that there is a sovereign God. This being the case, it follows logically that there are limits to man's capability of manipulating time, if in fact this purported space-time manipulation is not an illusion (or man is being deluded). Jesus said to His disciples in Acts Chapter 1, verse 7, "It is not for you to know times or seasons which the Father has put in His own authority." To me this means that just like matter and energy, in the manipulation of time, the buck stops with a sovereign God. But there is no question that man is fooling around with it. If I had to put my money on the line, my best guess is that there will be some hair-raising events in this area openly manifest before the year 2012. (Remember the movies "2001" and "2010"?)

What we can't do is shrink from our responsibility to investigate and exercise dominion and stewardship over this area - time. Because we have not been judicious and responsible in exercising our dominion and stewardship in the areas of economics and finance, we now have the Babylonian occult, freedom-stealing, debt (death) money system running this world again. As we have shrunk from our governmental responsibilities (primarily self-government and local government, the government of the local school, job, family, and church), we are now back to the establishment of vertical pyramids, structured bureaucratic pagan empires. It's the tower of Babel all over again. And these government/gods, like all gods, demand tributes and sacrifices, human sacrifices. So we are becoming poor through debt, inflation and/or high taxation, while becoming more enslaved by administrative, bureaucratic law by edict. This means we cannot leave the scientific arena unchallenged either, particularly in the area of space-time. To do so is to further guarantee the loss of our freedom, peace and prosperity.

* * *

"Relativity is presently regarded as a theory or a statement about fundamental physical reality. In fact, it is only a statement about FIRST ORDER reality - the reality that emerges from the vector interaction of electromagnetic energy with matter. When we break down the vectors into scalars, shadow vectors or hypervectors, we immediately enter a vastly different, far more fundamental reality. In this reality, superluminal velocity, multiple universes travel back and forth in time, higher dimensions, variation of all 'fundamental constants' of nature, materialization and dematerialization and the violation of the 'conservation of energy' are all involved." - T.E. Bearden, "Comments on the New Tesla Electromagnetics," 1982.

* * *

"Presently, gravitational field and electrical field are considered mutually exclusive. Actually, this is also untrue. In 1974, for example, Santilly proved that electrical field and gravitational field indeed are not mutually exclusive. In that case, one is left with two possibilities: (a) They are totally the same thing; or (b) They are partially the same thing... With the new Tesla electromagnetics, pure scalar waves in time itself can be produced electrically, and electrostatics (when the charge has been separated from the mass) becomes a 'magic tool' capable of directly affecting and altering anything that exists in time - including gravitational field. Anti-gravity and the inertial drive are immediate and direct consequences of the new electromagnetics." Ibid.

* * *

"Then Joshua spoke to the Lord in the day when the Lord delivered up the Amorites before the children of Israel, and he said in the sight of Israel:

'Sun, stand still over Gibeon;
and Moon, in the Valley of Ajalon.'
So the sun stood still,
And the moon stopped,
till the people had revenge
upon their enemies.

"Is this not written in the Book of Joshua? So the sun stood still in the midst of heaven, and did not hasten to go down for about a whole day." (Time-space was altered, in this case stopped.) - Joshua 10:12-13.

* * *

"'Behold, I will bring the shadow on the sundial, which has gone down with the sun on the sundial of Ahaz, ten degrees backward.' So the sun returned ten degrees on the dial by which it had gone down." (Time-space was reversed.) - Isaiah 38:8.

Some computer retracements of time-history have confirmed both Joshua 10:12-13 and Isaiah 38:8.

* * *

The following is taken from C.S. Lewis' 1971 book, "The Screwtape Letters." A letter is written from a senior demon (Screwtape) to a junior temptor (Wormwood).

"Our policy, for the moment, is to conceal ourselves. Of course this has not always been so. We are really faced with a cruel dilemma. When the humans disbelieve in our existence we lose all the pleasing results of direct terrorism, and we make no magicians. On the other hand, when they believe in us, we cannot make them materialists and skeptics. At least, not yet. I have great hopes that we shall learn in due time how to emotionalize and mythologize their science to such an extent that what is, in effect, a belief in us (though not under that name) will creep in while the human mind remains closed to belief in the Enemy. The 'Life Force,' the worship of sex, and some aspects of psychoanalysis may here prove useful. If once we can produce our perfect work - the Materialistic Magician, the man, not using, but veritably worshipping, what he vaguely calls 'Forces' while denying the existence of 'spirits' - then the end of the war will be in sight. But in the meantime we must obey our orders. I do not think you will have much difficulty in keeping the patient in the dark. The fact that 'devils' are predominantly comic figures in the modern imagination will help you. If any faint suspicion of your existence begins to arise in his mind, suggest to him a picture of something in red tights, and persuade him that since he cannot believe in that (it is an old textbook method of confusing them) he therefore cannot believe in you." ...In the movie, "Star Wars," the vital power was the Force: "May The Force Be With You."

* * *

"Witchcraft is flourishing because of its positive benefits to participants and the entire planet. Most rituals have some focus or concern for healing our ravaged Mother Earth. Women are especially drawn to it because of the emphasis on a female divinity which has been denied us in all formal Western religions."

"...Most feel Satan is a figment of the medieval church's collective imagination used to coerce people into becoming tithe-giving churchgoers." - Brigid Beth Kelly - Tempe, Arizona - Source: Insight Magazine - Letters to the Editor, 7/13/87

* * *

Emerging science, linked to religion today belongs to the New Agers. They have in their grasp the proven beneficial technology to: 1) clean up the environment; 2) heal the sick - including cancer and AIDS; 3) recapture the earth from a wasteland to a garden; 4) make it rain and stabilize the weather at will any place on the earth; 5) provide free energy; 6) and neutralize radioactivity. And that's just for starters!

Much of this marvelous science and technology is repeatable, verifiable, and can be done by almost anyone. The New Agers literally have the technical tools to create widespread peace and prosperity on earth. And this technological explosion is surfacing. In other words, the New Agers have achieved what was the church's dominion responsibility.

"God is dead" and the New Agers are the evolutionary result of the revolutionary 1960s "me generation." Into their spiritual void has come feminine (yin) Eastern collective mystical humanism, every man as his own reincarnated god, every man with his own "spirit guide" or "entity." Are these nice names for demons? In Western civilization, bloody occultism is not in the open as it is in the Philippines and Haiti.

Since the New Age technology is operative in the frequency range where demons comfortably operate (outside of normal human sight), and because these New Agers have no frame of reference for demons, they are right at home in linking their science and technology with natural occult religions and these alien "spirit guides" and "entities." Here then is the successful coup about which C.S. Lewis warned us in "The Screwtape Letters."

* * *

"...it is appointed for men to die once, but after this the judgment." - Hebrews 9:27.

TWO SHIFTS IN CONSCIOUSNESS

Both the individual (yang) and collective (yin) levels of aware-
ness are dependent upon how people subjectively interpret objective
phenomena. In other words, all of us interpret the objective world
subjectively based upon our beliefs, values, attitudes, vocabularies,
categories of understanding, frames of references and experiences.
One of the overwhelming influences of technology is that technology
establishes, indeed dictates, the way in which people generally interpret their world.   For example, we are living at the end of the
Mechanistic Age, brought on by the advent of the automobile. Industrial nomenclature, the verbiage of the factory, is still the primary
mindset the majority uses to describe its political and economic processes. It permeates our contemporary news. Even our schools still
maintain the design and methodology of the industrial factory. But a
shift is most definitely and definitively taking place. The shift is
from a mechanistic (mechanical) world view to that of a computerized world view, and more specifically, a bio-computerized, virtual
reality world view.

The explosive growth and widespread use of computer technology, filtering into the mindset of the general public over the past two
and a half decades, has led to this change in perception of the world
in which we live and the way it works. Couple that with the fax
machine, fiber optics, Internet, cyberspace, and holographic reality,
and the result is we are now beginning to "see" the world differently. But these shifts take place slowly, and normally take at least a
generation (40 years) to become primary. When the shift reaches the
explosive exponential point of mass human consciousness, a significant alteration will take place in all our institutions. We are ap-
proaching such a threshold, as the Information Age expands.

One of the painful fallouts of this massive adjustment/readjust-
ment is that the synergy between computers and mechanization is
eliminating jobs, permanently. People, workers, are becoming increasingly unnecessary. Until the "Nasty Nineties," it was widely
held to be true that the level of a person's income and status in life
was dependent upon his level of education (and experience on the
job). Education was the economic god, so to speak. This god has
now been slain. The plague of the "Nasty Nineties" is chronic unemployment. We are learning what the Argentineans learned by economic fire in the 1980s, that it is the demand of the marketplace in a
chaotic (feminine) economy that determines economic wherewithal,
not formal, factorylike, status-based education. Who makes it eco-

nomically in today's world? Those who have demand-side, hands-on education, avant-garde education, and experience in providing the goods and services demanded by the marketplace. Today's world of speed-of-light communication goes to those who are visionaries, entrepreneurs, risk-takers, those on the cutting edge who deliver the demanded goods and services, as well as those who are long-term and service oriented, who supply the basics of life in a state-of-the-art way. This "new world disorder" in which we live, requires - nay, even demands - a yang and yin, positive/negative, acid/alkaline, clockwise/counterclockwise, masculine/feminine balance. It requires an integrated linear vector and a cycle, vortices - spirals if you will - to achieve the demands of the age in a balanced way. The pre-creation void, the black hole of space, the energy-rich, charged potential of the womb, so to speak, needs the directional, life-bringing masculine linear vector to frame it with laws, give it direction, and anchor its creativity so it can be productive and progressive. In a world struggling to find balance between the one and the many, between the collective and the individual, between the feminine and the masculine, recognition of this truism is vital. Without the horizontal balance and the simultaneous vertical hierarchy of authority, chaos and anarchy reign. Why? Because we are already too close to the edge of the dark abyss of total chaos (feminine). It takes a real juggling act today to maintain balance, direction, and creativity in life.

Few can conceive of the importance of the Eastern yin/yang balance and of the simultaneous Western directional/hierarchical/masculine lead vector. It is the emphasis on diversity and individuality - a masculine impulse - which leads to risk-taking, the multiplicity of richness in the marketplace, progress, and eventually unity in society. Yes, diversity produces unity because the diversity of specialization in the division of labor yields to cooperation in the exchange of goods and services, which results in harmony. The many voluntarily become the one, from the bottom up. At the same time, without the gentle, kind and collective, chaotic, feminine impulse to balance, the marketplace becomes cutthroat and warlike, legalistic and harsh, destroying itself. Thus, the acid legalism of the masculine impulse, by itself, kills. It needs the alkaline feminine offset.

While this overemphasis on masculinity has been a primary issue in earlier Western civilization, it is not the primary issue today. Today, the pendulum has swung too far the other way - toward the collective, the democratic, the feminine - where the focus is on security, acceptance/approval and control. These natural, basic, biological instincts, when not held in check and given direction, destroy the very essence of themselves, resulting in chaos and anarchy - a dark empty economic womb, if you will. Tragically, this is where we are rapidly moving today, at a time when the effort to stop time, tinker with time, call an end to history, kill progress, establish total control, security, and politically correct approval, is at its height. We would expect as much, with lesbian-based witchcraft - the extreme of the feminine, democratic, collective principle - running the nation today.

The ruling, natural, occult sequence is to cycle from order to chaos in the fulfillment of the Hegelian dialectic of thesis, antithesis, synthesis. But cycles are, by definition, non-progressive. Thus, out of the emerging chaos and anarchy we should expect to arise, in the natural order of things, a compensating hyper-masculine figure - our version of a pharaoh if you will. It will be an ugly synthesis for the freedom-loving, but then again, freedom is an open system, and the primary mindset paradigms in operation today remain Newtonian, closed system.

This brings us to the second major shift of consciousness which is just emerging among those who think, live and work at the cutting edge. This perspective has not yet begun to dawn on the mass consciousness. It is this: It is a now-proven spiritual, scientific, economic reality that the "field," electromagnetic phenomenon, not only influences but determines - is prior to - physical Newtonian reality. Living energy, energy as information with personality, determines matter.

I am convinced that the reason the likes of honest money, true free markets, free energy machines, and alternative medicine are brutally persecuted and shut down by the closed system-loving Establishment is because such would bring about a radical transformation in the conceptual thinking of the mass mind - literally a paradigm shift. If open system thinking became widespread and generally accepted in mass human consciousness, it would shortly render the Establishment powerless. The Establishment, after all, depends on a comprehensive, expensive campaign of ongoing deception through public education and the mass media to maintain power. The New World Order Establishment can maintain its control, its elitism, and get filthy rich as long as the public is trapped in the lie of an exclusive Newtonian closed system, with its Second Law of Thermodynamics, entropy, and its modus operandi of conflict, chance, cycles, poverty, and death. After all, if the masses remain convinced that we live in a world of scarcity, of conflict, of chance, etc., then the ruling elite can justify its existence by being referees (in a token way), and doling out in some inequitable fashion, so-called scarce resources. There is never enough to go around in a closed system. Therefore, someone has to referee the conflict. That's the Establishment, the New World Order government, the global parasite.

On the other hand, with a massive shift in consciousness from a closed to an open system, from death to life, from a dark spiral down to a plentiful open-ended light spiral up, the Newtonian closed system philosophy of conflict, chance, cycles, poverty, and death, wilts. Time and time again, in brief flashes of history, where the open system methodology of freedom (free markets, free energy machines, energetic health, honest, free market money in a system of self-governing [supernatural] law) is allowed to manifest, mankind flourishes with the parasitic, bureaucratic government and ruling elite diminishing accordingly. This is what is emerging presently. It is all the insider Establishment can do to keep the lid on it presently. There either has to be total control now - a comprehensive suffocating, bureaucratic New World Order - or the international banking system and its ilk which has plagued us for nearly 500 years, and its ruling elite, are dead in the water. Thus, the urgency of the New World Order. It is a race against time, against the computerization and dissemination of knowledge and information, bringing about understanding and wisdom of the many ways in which man can better himself through the open system's abstract and following concrete reality. In other words, God's light kingdom is pressing the kingdom of darkness.

The primary contradiction (so designed) of the New Age, with its emphasis on the natural, earth-based religions of Mother Earth and environmentalism, is that it focuses in large part on open system technology, while maintaining a closed system (natural) philosophy of government, religion and economics. Again, this is not accidental. It is deliberate and purposeful. For example, "Hillary the Hippie," as she was known in the '60s, established her values in the radically chaotic 1960s when God was officially pronounced dead. This spiritual void was attempted to be filled in the '70s, and especially in the '80s, by materialism. Thus, the egregious expansion of debt (death) occurred in the 1980s. This orgy of materialism - debt-based death - proved to be unsatisfying and empty to the human spirit and so the pendulum has now swung back toward spiritualism. But this time, since the Christian God is officially dead, it is a neo-pagan spiritualism - a return to the "natural" Newtonian, earth-based religions with their fallen spirits of antiquity. It is the religion of empire, of Babylon, of ancient Egypt.

In this neo-pagan framework, one is either in the elite or part of the ruling bureaucracy, or one loses. It is as simple as that. Power accrues at the top of the pyramid. Thus, the strategy of the New World Order Luciferian banksters is to bring about global crises, resulting in chaos, from which the New World Order can emerge, with a world central bank, a world court, effectively a world parliament, a global religion, a One-world military, and all the rest of it, arising like a phoenix from the ashes. Once in total control - probably aided and abetted by a high-tech sound and light show of UFOs - the ruling elite of the New World Order can take the lid off all of this quantum, open system-based reality and give the masses free energy, open system energetic medicine, gold-based money, and so on. Paradoxically, they would seek to totally control, but only after the global population had first been dramatically reduced by at least two billion, and pledged its allegiance to the NWO. After all, in a world of computerized technology, what in the world are we going to do with all these useless people? "Mother Earth" must be cleansed in a closed, dark system.

In this New Age of Dark Enlightenment, since "God is dead," who gets to rule religiously? The biblical concept that "God is light" has also been replaced by the New World Order elitists. It is about to be resurrected in a new form, by a new god. Who indeed but a substitute "light bearer" will fill the bill? A natural, created angel of light? The logical candidate to fill this "light" void is Lucifer. It is thus no accident that for the past several centuries, Luciferianism has been the guiding religion of what has now "evolved" into fascist New World Order elitism. With the breakdown of the earth's magnetic field, and the resultant boundary between open and closed systems, between the natural and the supernatural, becoming increasingly indistinct, expect New Age magicians to shortly begin "wowing" the masses in preparation for the neo-pagan spiritualistic New World Order. The old paradigm, which is dead at the cutting edge, is the old theory of evolution, as we were taught it - the concept that we all evolved meaninglessly by chance out of the primordial mud and slime. The new reality is that the spiritual/energetic "field" created the physical Newtonian world in which we live. We're back to spirit preceding matter, minus our Creator.

GETTING GROUNDED IN AN OPEN SYSTEM

If there is one perspective that captures the essence of these times, it is this: All of our established institutions operate via the closed system of conflict, chance, cycles, shortages, poverty and death. These institutions are dying. They are locked into a trend which is topping out. By contrast, the abstract, philosophical and scientific basis for institutions founded upon an open system of love, life, light, liberty, law, laughter and a long-term view is emerging in the new uptrend. We are caught up in the throes of this transition.

The old ways - the established institutions - are doing everything they can to prevent this new emergence. Hence, we are experiencing Gestapo-like tactics: the oppression and persecution of independent human life, of mavericks, of freedom, of true creativity, free energy, non-drug-based free market medicine, honest money, self-government, supernatural law, free enterprise, nuclear heterosexual families, decentralization, local government, free choice in education, an armed militia, an open and free media, the U.S. Constitution, common law, and on and on.

A social order is either formed by bottom up self-government which voluntarily forms collectives, or a police state instituted from the top down that uses coercion to form collectives. A social order is either operating with a win-win-win-win bottom-up system anchored in supernatural law (yang/masculine/individual), or it is moving toward philosophical bankruptcy in a statist, top-down natural system (yin/feminine/collective). The United States is clearly moving toward the latter: a fascist, occult, Nazi-type, top-down police state. Waco and Oklahoma City are two prime examples. The uncovered/ungrounded, New Age feministic spirit which is "guiding" these chaotic times will most probably find its ultimate grounding in a bureaucratic masculine compensation. This is precisely what happened in Nazi Germany. The feministic New Age spirit there found its grounding in Hitler who with his SS bureaucracy, was eventually worse than the feministic, ungrounded extreme at the other end of the spectrum. There was no feminine-masculine balance in pre-Hitler Germany, no male grounding authority. Nor is there one in the United States today.

Civil government is eventually the ultimate power in every natural, closed earth-based system. Government is in reality a parasite, a religious and economic parasite. It draws its ideas for its laws from the religious realm of right and wrong, good and evil, and morality. It draws its economic sustenance from taxes extracted from its subjects. But today the parasite, the civil government, is rapidly consuming the host. It has wrapped itself up like a cat in a ball of twine with excessive laws which have rendered the system not only noncompetitive, ineffective and cumbersome, but unintelligible, irrational, and gridlocked. On the economic end of the spectrum, by the early 21st century, the federal government will have drained so much economic sustenance from its subjects, that the compounding effect of the interest on the debt alone will consume the host, "we the people."

The civil government has destroyed its former religious base, primarily the Ten Commandments and English common law, the Founding Fathers' Constitution, and courageous individuals like George Washington and Christopher Columbus. It has also consumed its economic base, having destroyed the U.S. dollar, first by removing its gold and silver backing, and now removing what little confidence remains in a fiat currency that has been depreciated 95 percent since the turn of the century.

True to the death spiral that exists in outmoded institutions (also true in individuals), the federal government is doing exactly the wrong thing at the wrong time by biting off more than it can chew, thus ensuring its destruction. It should be backing off. It is exhausted and bankrupt, spiritually and economically. Getting U.S. troops involved in wars all over the world, telling Japan what to do to get its house in order, attempting to regulate all areas of life stateside, propagating endless domestic programs is suicidal. Even reformers in Congress have trouble making truly meaningful progress.

Moneychanger writer Franklin Sanders states that there are three questions that cannot be asked openly in this country any more, particularly in court. They are: "1) If we have a constitutional right to gold and silver money, why are we using the notes of a private corporation, i.e., the Federal Reserve System? 2) What statute makes any individual liable for an income tax? 3) If we have a constitutional republic, why is an oligarchy running it?" And I would add one other: "How can there truly be equal rights in a country if minorities have special privileges, and our elected representatives are immune from the laws they pass?" A dark, closed, death-based system has to oppress and persecute an open living system. A lit candle illuminates a dark room.

These are clearly revolutionary times. Ideally, there would be a peaceful, nonviolent repentance, revival, renewal, reformation, restoration and reconstruction in this country to turn things around. But the history of a natural order, government in a closed system such as ours argues, sadly, for violence. (There is always that blood sacrifice and the operative Second Law of Thermodynamics.) There is something very sinister about the fact that over 500 gang members from all around the country met in Kansas City, Missouri on April 29, 1993, just prior to the high day of witchcraft, May 1, the anniversary of the birth of both the Illuminati and the Bolshevik revolution, under the guise of the National Urban Peace and Justice Summit. You get the sense that earth changes and social changes are about to break wide open.

"Man" and the "earth" are the two basic parts of the economic equation. People who adhere to the tenets of natural order in a closed, dark, death-based system - one of the "natural man" - inescapably are environmentally influenced. As the earth goes, so goes such a man. This is the case in the United States today. (The EPA has been promoted to the Cabinet level.) By contrast, what used to exist in the early history of this nation, at least up until the War of Northern Aggression (called the U.S. Civil War by modern historians), was a faith based in an open system of law, which came supernaturally (the Ten Commandments, etc.). This gave man an abstract base to withstand natural earth changes. Thus, as man went, so went the earth in early American history to a degree. Man had dominion over the earth rather than being a slave to it. Where the U.S. missed the philosophical boat was by not building on the masculine foundation of God's supernatural biblical law, so that legalism and materialism could have been overcome by a masculine-based stewardship, kinder and gentler in nature, love-based, satisfying to the feminine gender, where men are more "response-able" (responsible). Once dominion (masculine) was established, stewardship (feminine) should have followed, led by gentle men.

Scientifically, man is tied to the earth, given the connecting commonality of his piezoelectric charge and his carbon/mineralized base. But mankind is also inescapably religious. Therefore, he will either posit his faith increasingly in the creation, the earth, and see it as sacred, which locks him into the Second Law of Thermodynamics and the death spiral of a closed system, or he will posit it in a source from outside of nature, a supernatural God and His laws, which provides the faith and following institutions for an open system with all the hope that brings. Today, faith has clearly been placed in the creature/creation (the earth) versus the Creator, rabidly so by the ruling elite. Thus, it is no accident that Mother Earth, witchcraft-based environmentalism has moved to control food and farming, establish wetlands, and eliminate hunting and grazing on all public lands. Agriculture is seen as the primary pollutant of U.S. rivers. Public lands are viewed as a wilderness, not a potential garden. The masses have been deceived into buying the idea that civil government can solve all of man's problems and can clean up the earth, despite the dismal history of the U.S. and the former U.S.S.R. in this area.

We are told that people are the problem. None other than a U.S. Nobel Prize winner in economics, Milton Friedman, has described this issue clearly: "So long as the attitude in society is that people are responsible for themselves, but that nature inevitably will limit what we can have, there is a chance that the discontent people feel will be directed at nature. But when we take the attitude that government is all-powerful, that it's only because somebody didn't pass the right law that we're in a bad way, the discontent will be directed at people." There you have it, the contrast in philosophies. Dr. Friedman makes apparent that personal responsibility (yang/masculine) focuses on redeeming a niggardly earth, while a focus on civil government (yin/feminine) results in godlike demands.

The federal government today wrongfully views itself as an unrestrained god/goddess, locking up and prohibiting man's access to Mother Earth, which is viewed as the sacred source of life. This is, again, in sharp contrast to our Western Hebrew-Christian heritage which sees the earth as under man's dominion (masculine), over which he had stewardship (feminine). This is an irreconcilable conflict in philosophies. Man's thinking will inescapably stem ultimately from one of these two faiths, an evolutionary one or a creationist one, and the results of this faith will work out over time.

Recall in American history a phrase which long existed regarding our law: "Ignorance of the law is no excuse." This phrase stemmed from the fact that up until early in this century, everyone knew the law of God, the Ten Commandments. They were posted on the walls of the public schools and taught to the children.

What I have found truly incredible is that even now, after nearly a century of conditioning - and in keeping with the "80-20 rule" of stability - Time magazine reluctantly admitted that 80 percent of Americans in the 46-64 age group agree that the Bible is the "totally accurate" word of God. In the younger 25-45 age bracket, Time found that 73 percent agree that the Bible is the "totally accurate" word of God.

We must have laws that come from outside of a closed, earth-based system - supernatural laws - in order to have true self-government and freedom. After all, the source of law is the god of any society because laws are legislated, religious ideas which frame the arena of human action (economics). Only ruling supernatural law can relegate the civil government to the status of an institution like any other - the family, the church, the school, business, the military, etc. The federal government has a limited function when supernatural law is the basis of a society, because the civil government cannot play the role of god. Can the American people really trust the federal government with all the high-tech power it is accumulating, particularly at a time when the earth is changing?

The Century III Foundation of Oak Brook, Illinois has held numerous seminars made up of people of all races, religions, age groups, and from all economic strata. The participants of these seminars had logically and rationally formulated a series of laws to govern society on which they could agree. Remarkably, there was over 80 percent consensus among these seminar attendees that the Ten Commandments met their criteria for justice, equality and uniformity in society. How's that for grounding and an open system governmental opportunity?

One of the world's leading scientists, Peter M. Rothschild, M.D., stated in his book entitled, "The Scientific Background Of The Ten Commandments," "As Quantum Physics, the most advanced discipline, demonstrated beyond the slightest doubt - the ultimate mechanisms of the Universe cannot be explained without this concept of God, or whatever the term you care to use to refer to a supreme Maker.

"Unquestionably, the complex laws that govern the behavior of all forms of energy and their interactions with all matter - which are but expressions of energies - necessarily had to precede the material processes of Creation, which we describe as our Universe.

"Creation is an ever-open process. And so is, for that matter, intelligence." There it is, the open system. Dr. Rothschild continues, "...Recent discoveries made in Quantum Physics - the stoutest pillar of modern science - reveal that indeed everything that exists stems from a central source, God, without whose acts the entire Creation would not have occurred."

Dr. Rothschild concluded, "Love is the most essential ingredient in the entire Creation. It is love that secures the delicate balance of opposing forces - good and bad; positive and negative - and ensures the stability of the Universe. The Ten Commandments contain the complete formula of love. The first Ten Commandments are the original vectors which began all the energies necessary to generate and perceive the magnificence of love."

Our death-based, closed system-based, federal government has ruled the Ten Commandments not only out of court, but out of our schools, and out of our lives. No wonder there is so little love in our society; no wonder there are over 40 wars on the planet today. We logically and consistently have a death wish in our closed system. No wonder the U.S. is the world's leading debtor (death) nation, the world's leading arms exporter (death), the world's financier of the global drug trade (death), the U.N.'s military strong arm (death), the leader in abortion (death), allowing those infected with AIDS, TB and hepatitis to roam freely (death), and the leading exporter of violence billed as entertainment (death), and the nation responsible for introducing the rest of the world to fast food (death).

Particularly fascinating are Dr. Rothschild's comments concerning the Fourth Commandment: the keeping of the Sabbath day, taking one day out of seven for rest. Such used to be standard practice in this nation. Dr. Rothschild writes, "The six-plus-one day concept is perfectly compatible with the postulates of Quantum Physics for the simple notion that reveals that nothing can progress as long as its existence is subject to an unvaried, uninterrupted routine. The 6:1 proposition is one of the most dynamic factors in the progressive processes of the Universe. Without periodic interruptions, harmonics deteriorate, progress comes to a standstill, and after a brief period of stagnation, the Universe reverts to chaos. The ideal rhythm to interrupt harmonics in order to prevent there becoming a routine is represented by the proposition 6:1. Indeed, Quantum Physics establishes beyond doubt that none of the energies that exist in the Cosmos are generated in continuous emissions, but in variable packets, that is, partial transmissions.

"Remarkably, the time-lapse required for the transmission of a quantum is exactly six times longer than the intervals that separate each transmission from the next one."

Where is our Sabbath rest today? Where is the 6:1 break that allows us to progress? Where is the supernatural grounding of God's law (masculine/yang) which holds in check chaos (feminine/yin).

Where instead is routine worshipped? Where is initiative, creativity, and innovation thwarted? In the brain-dead big bureaucracies. There is the open versus the closed system in a nutshell, life versus death, freedom versus slavery, prosperity versus poverty, peace versus conflict, creativity versus bureaucratic rules and regulations, and so on. In Proverbs we read, "He who keeps the commandments keeps his soul, but he who is careless of his ways will die." Also, "But he who sins against me wrongs his own soul; all those who hate me love death." - Proverbs 19:16 and 8:36.

We must keep our perspective. We are spiritual beings, having a physical experience, biochemically activated and emotionally charged. We are made in the image of God, but formed from the dust of the earth. At a time when the earth is losing its magnetic charge and everything is becoming ungrounded, when the line between the natural and supernatural is being blurred, where fearsome high-tech weapons exist, the compensation for man is that scalar energy (left brain/right brain interaction across the corpus callosum) is becoming more powerful. Therefore, it is critical now as never before that we control all of our thoughts and E-motions to keep us "at ease" so that we don't become "dis-eased." But for this to occur, our thoughts and E-motions have to be grounded in eternal values and principles, such as the Ten Commandments and the Second Great Commandment. Moreover, in the positive-negative, masculine-feminine balanced perspective, we must think on whatever things are true, just and noble (masculine/yang), and whatever things are pure, lovely and of good report (feminine/yin). We must think, too, primarily of those things which are praiseworthy and virtuous. This must be the focus of our balanced meditations.

In addition to our spiritual grounding, we must ground ourselves physically, with a good nutritional base, rest, and exercise. For example, in Corpus Christi, Texas, the staff of the Lester Roloff school for wayward girls stated that regardless what was done with these girls, regardless of what they were taught, how they were disciplined, how much they were loved, worked, exercised and rested, nothing worked and nothing stuck, until these girls first received the right nutritional grounding physically so that the psychological, emotional, mental and spiritual change desired could be anchored, take root and flourish. We need physical backbone to have spiritual backbone, so to speak. Over 70 percent of "dis-ease," according to Dr. Robert Kaplan, can be traced to nutritional deficiencies.

Compounding poor nutrition in the U.S. today is the fact that 70-80 percent of "dis-ease" is also traced to emotional problems, as confirmed by the new Establishment medical field of psy-choneuroimmunology. (A related book on the subject of E-motion and "dis-ease" is Louise L. Hay's "Heal Your Body.") Negative E-motion burns up the nutritional grounding. We can therefore conclude that if we are emotionally and nutritionally correct, that is spiritually and physically correct, we stand a good chance of being "at ease," rather than "dis-eased." If we are not grounded nutritionally and E-motionally, the odds are very low we will be grounded spiritually. God intends for us to be life-based and integrated at every level - spiritually, mentally, emotionally and physically. We all want to soar, to be mentally alert, E-motionally at ease, loving personally, grounded physically, and obedient spiritually. By doing so, we can be in good health and prosper long-term, and be more "response-able" (responsible), disciplined and discipled.

SECTION B
GROUNDED CHRISTIANITY

MAN'S FOUR BASIC CONFLICTS

Man has four basic conflicts in this life: 1) conflict with God; 2) conflict with his fellow man; 3) conflict within himself; and 4) conflict with nature (God's cursed creation). Most of our literature, theater, movie and television dramas include at least one of these four conflicts. Only when all four are resolved does man enjoy peace and prosperity on earth.

Our conflict with God is fundamentally resolved through the life, death and resurrection of Jesus Christ. Our proper response to the gift of salvation offered through Christ Jesus is to give back to God. Yet since God is the source of everything, and literally the Creator of man and matter, there is nothing material (economic) that man can give to God. Man can only praise and worship God. Even the tithes and offerings man gives to God are in effect intended to be used to support, serve and help his fellow man. This dramatically cuts down on the cost of civil government welfare. Therefore, it comes as no small surprise that the primary way God tells us to serve Him is by serving our fellow man (Matthew 5:23-24, 22:39). This is economics, works, human action. It is "better to give than to receive." For when we first give and serve before we receive, we resolve the conflict between an individual and his fellow man, and also bring about peace and prosperity on earth which pleases God. Additionally, it builds our self-worth.

"Give, and it will be given to you: good measure, pressed down, shaken together, and running over will be put into your bosom. For with the same measure that you use, it will be measured back to you" - Luke 6:38. This is Christ's statement on how the honest, moral, free market works. When we give to and serve our fellow man, the rewards which come back to us as God's blessings literally cover us up. So man's first problem is resolved, his conflict with God. Man serves God by serving his fellow man. The difference between being religious and a true Christian in the parable of the Good Samaritan supports this analysis of service to God by serving our fellow man.

Service to our fellow man demands humility, empathy, responsibility and duty. These are the basic Christian virtues with regard to self and others. Humility and empathy are internal; responsibility and duty are external. Humility and responsibility are personal; empathy and duty are others directed. With these virtues, God's requirements are fulfilled. Furthermore, God expects us to obey Him for our own good. This is why Jesus said, "But seek ye first the kingdom of God and His righteousness and all these things shall be added unto you." - Matthew 6:33. We are deceived in thinking anything other than God's laws are in our best interest. Religion does come down to economics (human actions) since faith without works is dead (James 2). The character of the self-governing, covenanting/contracting man is the key to both love and prosperity, the key to how Christian self-government is supernatural religion applied to peace and prosperity, bringing sound, workable economics.

Beyond taking by being a parasite or a predator, which produces conflict with both God and other men - and beyond covenanting and contracting, which produces peace and prosperity on earth and solves the problem of the one and the many - comes giving with no expectation of return. The latter is the deposit in one's divine bank account. Covenanting/contracting and giving unreservedly are the main ways man serves God. Man can have no idol, no other god, or law higher than God's law, in the process of serving Him.

Man is born into this world effectively as a slave. He is dependent and is a taker. Babies are dependent upon their parents. They are not free. They take. Babies' relationships are vertical, not horizontal (contractual). As a child becomes older, he can remain a taker by staying dependent upon others, or by becoming aggressively evil. Instead of remaining a parasite, he can become a predator, the worst form of taker. He can prey upon other people. He can take unfair advantage of the efforts (production) and money produced by his fellow man.

Mankind does have another choice, however. He can become a giver rather than a taker. He can learn to covenant and contract for his needs, instead of preying or depending upon someone else to provide for him. This is what being an adult is really all about - moving from slave-like vertical to freedom-loving horizontal, contractual relationships. By contracting with one's fellow man horizontally, by serving before receiving, man resolves the conflict between his fellow man and himself. Thus, one of man's four basic problems is solved via the mechanism of the contract. When the individual, underlying virtues which support the contract are humility, empathy, responsibility and duty, it's a home run for mankind.

It follows from correctly serving God and one's fellow man, that one's internal conflicts are more readily resolved. Each of us as individuals has two basic needs. These two needs can be summarized as a need for "love" and "money." These represent our "spiritual" and "economic" needs respectively. They reflect the fact that we are "made in the image of God" and "formed from the dust of the earth."

Man's internal problems, created by his basic economic needs, his safety and security needs, his love, social and belonging needs, and his self-esteem and self-fulfillment needs, are met and resolved when man is both at peace with God and his fellow man. In summary, this is only achieved through the spiritual and economic application of Christ's Second Great Commandment to "Love thy neighbor as thyself."

Men who are at peace with God, their fellow man and themselves, literally become individuals who volunteer for a collective army, assembled for the purpose of recapturing the last frontier - nature. The final battle is for the earth. The religious battle therefore comes down to economics. We don't have to ask where the battle is. Satan's army will always show us the front line. The battle is for people (evangelism) and their production (reconstruction) in the earth. This is economics. This was what Marx's atheistic "dialectic materialism" was all about, the satanic counterfeit to the Christian answer.

Not only man, but nature, too, needs our help. Nature (God's cursed creation), in fact, groans for our help. Nature is trapped by the curse of the Second Law of Thermodynamics. The First Law of Thermodynamics states that energy is neither created nor destroyed. Energy can only be transferred, but in the transferring process, there is a loss and deterioration of useful energy. The trend is therefore toward death (The Second Law). Nature trends toward death. This is entropy. So, when mankind develops a redeemed, overcoming, long-term cooperative view, his purpose on earth is to restore nature, to bring it back, to save it from erosion and death, to make it fruitful, to turn the earth into a garden. This is the way men finally overcome. After men have overcome themselves, individually and collectively, they can overcome nature. They can rule over the natural system and can get ahead. Men can make real progress in the earth over time. There can be re-creation. There can be peace and plenty for all - wealth for all! Each man can live under his own vine and fig tree. The natural spiral down toward death can be stopped and reversed. (It should be obvious at this point that the religious concept of natural evolution is a lie since nature's natural trend is not toward life, but rather in the other direction, toward death, in accordance with the Second Law of Thermodynamics.) So, the fourth of mankind's four major problems is resolved.

As stated earlier, all problems are ultimately human problems, because men create, use, abuse and destroy things. We have in essence resolved all four: man's conflict with God, man's conflict with his fellow man, man's conflict within himself, and man's conflict with nature. There is one final catch, however. The key to all four solutions rests upon the development of the individual man. If an individual man (yang - masculine) is to be able long-term to achieve all things through voluntary cooperation with his fellow man, then individual man must have a way to overcome his own nature. But, man himself is part of nature. He is "formed from the dust of the earth." And nature's primary trend is toward death.

Five primary characteristics of nature are conflict, chance, cycles, poverty and death. So, when the natural man, marked by pride and conflict, reigns supreme, not only are conflict, chance and cycles primarily active within him, but he is also captured by the inevitable subsequent trends of shortages/poverty and death.

Man by his own efforts cannot overcome himself without putting himself in conflict with himself. How can man war with himself and achieve victory? He cannot! A house divided against itself cannot stand. Individual man (and therefore collective man) cannot overcome the death spiral of his own biorhythms, his own biological cycles, which culminate in aging and death. Nor can man discipline himself mentally, emotionally, or physically without pain. Pain is conflict. Did you ever see a proud self-made, self-disciplined man who was not captured by pride, and whose internal tension was significant? Such men radiate their conflict and tension.

The human body is a spiritual/biological computer. Memory is stored in the organs and muscle tissues (and fat cells) of the body just as in the mind. This is why, for example, the Bible so often refers to the heart when it speaks of the emotions of man. So man, by man's efforts, attempting to overcome himself, experiences mental/emotional/physical pain for the purpose of inducing change. This change, even when intended to be constructive, puts man in a no-win situation, in irreconcilable conflict with his natural self. Man is still at war with himself even when he brings about forced change for the good.

Finally, because all men have limited time on this earth and imperfect knowledge, men are inescapably slaves to chance and probabilities in their decision making. On our own, we cannot perfectly know or execute with absolute excellence or certainty. Thus, the conflict, chance and cycles of nature inherent in man himself preclude the possibility of man playing god either individually (libertarianism) or collectively (socialism/communism/fascism/democracy). Man has limitations which he cannot on his own overcome, which trap him in a natural death spiral.

This is why, logically, a supernatural God, a Savior and His law are necessary for mankind. They provide the vital initial spark, the road map, the rules (laws) and methodology enabling man to rise above and overcome nature - both eternally and in time on earth. In other words, without a God, a Savior, His laws, and His Holy Spirit coming from above and outside of nature (supernaturally), man himself is trapped in the natural spiral down toward death by the conflict, chance and cycles, poverty and death of nature, of which he is a part.

Because all problems are, at their base, human problems, initially there had to be an outside solution provided for mankind before all the other problems could be addressed and resolved. So when Jesus Christ said, "I am the way, the truth, and the life. No one comes to the Father except through Me," He was making a logical statement. He was declaring that He had solved the basic covenantal problem of mankind, who was trapped in nature (God's cursed creation). Jesus Christ, as the spiritual Creator of the economic universe, as the Law-giver, and as the personal and collective Savior eternally and temporally for mankind, is both the initial and ultimate source of the solutions to man's four basic problems: man's conflict with God, with his fellow man, with himself and with nature.

SAVING SOULS?

In modern Christendom, there are two perspectives on the Gospel, the Good News. The first, often called the Calvinistic Gospel, rests on God's sovereignty, by focusing upon His election, calling, predestination and foreknowledge of men who are chosen by God to be saved eternally. The second perspective, the Arminian perspective, centers on man, and man's so-called "free will." The Arminian viewpoint in effect declares that man has the option of choosing or not choosing Jesus Christ as his personal savior, and thus determining for himself his eternal destiny. This makes man effectively sovereign. By far, The Arminian view is the most widely held.

The Arminian perspective puts Jesus Christ, the God-man, in the awkward position of having walked victoriously through life on earth in the flesh without sinning, fending off all of Satan's temptations, going to the cross, taking on the sins of the world, dying, defeating Satan and all his demons of hell, rising from the grave, ascending, sitting at the right hand of God the Father, and now having to wait and hope that sinning man chooses Him. What about the fact that all power is given to Jesus Christ on heaven and earth? This Arminian perspective makes Jesus Christ not unlike a dog waiting for a pat on the head from his master. Who is the master, Christ or man? The Scriptures clearly teach that faith is a gift given by God. Faith is not something that arises automatically from within the human heart, mind and soul of naturally fallen, imperfect, sinful man.

A problem that has historically developed from the Calvinistic perspective is that an elitist attitude tends to emerge from the understanding that the sovereign God chooses whomever He will save (the doctrine of election). Along with this elitist attitude is a lack of emphasis on evangelism: "After all, if God is sovereign, He'll take care of saving His elect," is too often the viewpoint of the Calvinists. By contrast, the Arminian free will perspective, which de facto has man as sovereign, is openly and aggressively evangelistic. After all, from this Arminian perspective, if Christians don't get out there and witness and evangelize, they won't save souls and people will go to hell, lost forever. There is a sense of urgency to the Arminian viewpoint.

Like so many principles in Scripture - rather than its being a case of either/or - the truth lies in a harmonious "both," with the authority relationship differentiating. Just as Jesus Christ is the bridegroom while the church is the bride, and the husband is head of the wife in a biblical covenantal marriage, the sovereignty of God in eternal salvation is superior to man's perspective of having chosen God.

Look at it this way, because God is sovereign, which makes Him God, He has in fact elected, chosen, predestined, called and foreordained His elect to the reality of his eternal salvation during their time here on earth. That's the purpose of the Gospel, the Great Awakening. God, the Holy Spirit, during some point of time in an elected man's life, will move on him, probably when he hears the Gospel. Then faith is given, his human spirit is quickened, and one of God's chosen/elect believes in the reality of his eternal salvation through Christ Jesus. This man has, from his humanistic perspective, chosen Jesus Christ. He has made a decision to respond positively to the Gospel. But, in eternal salvation, as with so many other things man does, man must be careful not to put himself first, not to put the cart before the horse, so to speak. God must come first.

From God's primary and sovereign perspective, the Gospel is the Good News announcing (past tense) that Jesus Christ - through His sinless life's work, perfect keeping of the law, death on the cross, burial, resurrection, ascension, and seating at the right hand of the Father - has saved His people eternally. He has also called his elect to discipleship in time here on earth to do the work and fulfill the calling for which purpose they were created, thus working out their temporal (time on earth) salvation with fear and trembling. So, the Gospel of Jesus Christ, when presented, awakens God's people to the reality of their gift of eternal salvation through the work of Jesus Christ (via the Holy Spirit). They can then grow to maturity, move from milk to meat, armor up and fight as soldiers in God's army, fully equipped according to Ephesians 6, working out their temporal salvation in their time on earth. Thus, salvation, rightfully seen biblically, has both an eternal and temporal aspect. After man is awakened to the realization of his eternal salvation, he then grows in Christ to become more Christlike in his remaining time left on earth. After all, faith without works is dead. But the initial quickening from the presentation of the Gospel speaks of a past tense historical fact in that even before a person acknowledges his justified position before God, it is an accomplished fact. From then on, it's merely the working out of temporal salvation, beginning with the Holy Spirit's awakening of an individual to the realization of their eternal salvation.

The Arminian gospel, the present tense gospel, standing on its own, is incomplete in that it presupposes that an individual suddenly acquires salvation when he makes a "decision for Christ" by "accepting Jesus as his Savior." It is humanistic because it assumes that man is the instrument and the ultimate determinant of his and others' eternal salvation. Such would effectively make man God, as in evolution, which also has man saving himself.

Looking at this from the perspective of the heathen, if the Arminian Gospel is true - if man is responsible for saving other men's souls eternally - what happens to the heathen who never hears the Gospel? There are only two options. The heathen who never hears the Gospel is either: 1) eternally saved, or 2) eternally damned. If the heathen who never hears the Gospel is eternally saved, then we are better off never taking him the Gospel, ever. Why? Because if the heathen who never hears the Gospel is eternally saved, and we take him the Gospel and he rejects it, he becomes eternally damned. Thus, the Gospel becomes the "Bad News." This is obviously incorrect.

What about the heathen who never hears the Gospel and therefore is eternally damned? If the heathen is eternally damned unless he hears the Gospel and accepts it, how can a just and loving God bless us rich American Christians, when we have nice homes, cars, savings accounts, and sit on our duffs watching NFL football, while millions of our fellow man, dying to hear the Gospel, are going to be lost? How is a just and loving God going to bless us when we don't give every cent we have to missions and evangelism for the spreading of the Gospel? Clearly, throughout Scripture, God promises to bless His obedient saints with good health, peace and prosperity. Obviously, this perspective violates the character of God and is contrary to His Word and His relationship with His saints.

Neither option is viable with the Arminian Gospel. The Arminian perspective that the Gospel is present tense and that the Gospel/man is the instrument of salvation - that man is responsible for saving other men's souls eternally or else they are eternally damned or are eternally saved - is an erroneous one. Men are not necessary to save other men's souls eternally. Free will is not primary. Neither man nor the Gospel is the present tense instrument of salvation. The Gospel is the Good News announcing that the work of Jesus Christ has saved man eternally (past tense). The biblical Gospel thus focuses on the historical work of Jesus Christ as opposed to the pervasive modern day Gospel which is clearly humanistic and present tense.

It is a blessing that God saved any of us, not that He didn't save all of us, even though it is His desire that all are saved. God built the entire eternal salvation bridge. God did not build half of the bridge through the work of Christ, and then require man to build the other half in order to be saved eternally.

Missionaries to the bush have consistently discovered, more times than not to their surprise, that primitives who have never seen or heard the Gospel presented by a man before, already have "eternity in their hearts." Jesus Christ, the Holy Spirit, and His angelic realm have already revealed themselves to these primitives before a missionary ever brought them the Gospel. They have been "saved" eternally and quickened. This is clearly recorded in missionary history.

So why take men the Gospel at all? When we present the Gospel, God the Holy Spirit uses it to awaken His elect/chosen/foreordained/called/predestined to the reality of their eternal salvation (past tense) so they can then become active in God's army in time on earth (present tense), producing fruit and good works. This perspective should set Calvinists on fire preaching the Gospel and keep Arminians active.

We never know whom God has elected, so we preach the Gospel to all. We should be preaching the Gospel to everyone so that God the Holy Spirit can quicken an eternally redeemed human spirit in time here on earth, so he/she can join us for the work that God has created and called us to do. After all, the more workers, the larger the army, the greater the fellowship, the greater the fruit. Also, the greater the individual and corporate peace and prosperity across the earth, commensurate with the spreading and application of the Gospel, as the kingdom of God advances.

Secular and religious economic studies have demonstrated that the per capita income of Protestant cultures is six to seven times greater than that of Catholic cultures, and that the per capita income of the Christian community overall versus that of the non-Christian community is a slam dunk win for the Christians! Religion does come down to economics, as faith comes down to works.

One final thought on Christian evangelism. We know that the wages of sin are death. Therefore, over time, those who consistently sin (and their offspring) will die, both in time and eternally. The darkness in them does them in. We have seen this historically, such as during the time of "The Great Sacrilege" when Henry VIII and his knights, nobles and co-conspirators seized the church's lands and properties, putting the orphans, indigents, widows and the poor out in the streets. Less than 150 years later, all of the descendants of the perpetrators of this sacrilege were dead. Their lines were cut off. This applies today to homosexuals, who die, on average, at age 41. This means, logically, the longer history continues, the more elect there are running around to be awakened. The sinful have died or are dying.

We are going through a time in human history when God clearly is separating the wheat from the chaff, the sheep from the goats (and wolves), the saved from the unsaved. And while the evil rule for a season, they are becoming a dwindling, dying minority. Perhaps this is their last gasp. This means the fields are ripe to be harvested. It's time for (Calvinist) Christians to become evangelistic reapers! The Christian army is ready to be awakened to a call to spiritual arms. By presenting the Gospel, Christians may serve as the catalyst by which God the Holy Spirit quickens/awakens members of His elect to the reality of their salvation so they can join God's army. Thereby, the numbers increase for the purpose of producing more fruit (good works).

The kingdom of God is built from the bottom up, beginning with the evangelism of the individual, then the family, then building the local church, the schools, the community, the state, the nation, and finally occupying in the world. Basically, as the individual human heart goes, eventually so goes the world. (Christianity on earth is bottom up. Paganism is top down.) Moving out with the balanced perspective of masculine dominion and feminine stewardship, Christians thereby subdue the earth. What a tremendous basis of hope. What an incredible call to action. God is a God of power and absolute victory.

What are men left with if they reject the Gospel of Jesus Christ? They have to deny the historical reality of Jesus Christ, claim that He was insane, allege that He was a con artist or that His disciples were insane or con artists. These are all very weak arguments. All these tenuous positions, though, help us understand why the unbelieving world that denies the Gospel is hostile to Jesus Christ. It is accordingly no coincidence that Jesus Christ is the only religious leader whose name is a cuss word in the modern era, and the only person in the New Age who is denied the status of being a god. Why? Because He is The God, His work is the issue, and His rulership and judgment are the central point of history. Therefore, the key question which remains in each man's life is, "What think ye of Jesus Christ?"

PRIESTS OR PAGANS?

Material blessing in time is a by-product of Christian obedience and dominion (III John 2; Deuteronomy 28:2). Christians are to work in all areas of life (Psalms 33:5). The result is inevitably prosperity. There is no way to create prosperity without work. By contrast, pagans, who emphasize leisure, have all the time in the world. They are accordingly poor, maybe apparently rich, but debt poor. The very nature of work incorporates the long-term perspective which automatically and immediately alienates it from the pagan world view to eat, drink, and be merry since death ends it all. The decision to work requires a "selecting against" present preferences in favor of long-term goals. When we're tired, but roll out of bed in the morning to go to work, we have selected against our short-term personal preference of staying in the sack in favor of the long-term rewards reaped as a by-product of going to work. So, it becomes apparent that a man's Christian calling, work, resulting prosperity, and the Christian long-term view of stewardship are inseparable. In truth, this is the documented philosophy which built this country, once the greatest Christian nation on the face of the earth. The Protestant work ethic was to earn all you can, so you can save all you can, so you can give all you can. This perspective is a far cry from the emotional gush, legalism, tradition, and pietistic escapism which dominates today in the so-called Christian community, and the "devil may care" attitude among the New Age Neo-Pagans.

Adam Smith, the great economist, who wrote "The Wealth Of Nations," observed key differences between the development of North America and South America, as did Irving Kristol, esteemed writer for The Wall Street Journal. South America had more natural resources and a more aristocratic population than did North America. It was, however, Adam Smith's view at that time, that North America would prosper while South America would languish. Why? Because the development of North America was based upon a better idea, the idea of work, the idea that men were responsible in time before God, a masculine (yang) bottom up concept, the idea that men had a sin nature and, therefore, institutions had to be decentralized for the protection of men, the idea that the earth was to be recaptured to the glory of God - in a word, Protestantism. By contrast, South America was built upon the classic pagan idea of a pyramid-type, top-down centralization of power (feminine - yin), reflected by the Catholic church and a landed hierarchy supported by the military, with a few very rich and many poor. South America today still has not caught up, particularly Brazil. The tragedy is that as America has given up its true Christian applied faith, it too has slipped into the South American "banana republic" syndrome. Today, only 2-3 percent of Americans have enough income to be self-sufficient at retirement age, and 95 percent of the privately-owned land in the nation is owned by only 3 percent of the people.

We are becoming poverty-stricken, as the historic substitute god, civil government, an economic parasite, is filling the vacuum formerly filled by responsible Christian men and women. The church has adopted the heresy of its day, as has been the tendency of the church down through time. Today, the civil government as god is performing the church's duties. If Christians don't provide the health, education and welfare needs of the people, the civil government will, for at least four times the cost. Government involvement in economics (work) creates conflict and brings about poverty long-term. Just look at what the federal government has done to the American Indians and inner-city Blacks. Only a dime of every dollar received by the Bureau of Indian Affairs ever reached the Indians.

God's mandate to His people in time has not changed. God gave Adam the Garden of Eden to groom and husband. He gave the Hebrews the nation of Israel, the land, to groom and husband. When Christ completed His work, the church became the agency of evangelism with economic dominion and stewardship following. But unlike Adam who was limited to the Garden of Eden, and the Hebrews who were limited to the nation of Israel, the church's responsibility now encompasses the entire world.

Christian missionaries have historically seen this multipurpose vision - to evangelize, and then apply that evangelism in the culture, bringing about a better life and God's blessing to all people on earth in time. The Bible is God's rulebook for reforming all cultures to the glory of God, bringing about harmony and prosperity.

This is the challenge today for American escapist Christians. After all, we are held accountable to God for how we spend our time on this earth (Matthew 24:46). When we stand before His throne, we stand alone. We don't want Him to say to us, "I never knew you; depart from me..." - Matthew 7:23. We will not be able to use the alibi, as The Beatles sang, that we got "by with a little help from our friends." We are called to be priests, not pagans.

Church historians have documented that less than five percent of England's population, Puritans and Presbyterians, reformed that country. Today, in the United States, we have some 55 million Americans who claim to be active born-again believers in Jesus Christ. This is approximately one-fourth of our population. Why has there not been a reformation? Plus, fully 88 percent of the U.S. population claims to be a Christian of some variety.

The answer to this reformation question is not so difficult. The corporate church today has simply slipped into the cultural heresy of its day; it has become a "top-down" (collective/yin/feminine) religion which escapes within, rather than a "bottom-up" (individual/yang/masculine) congregation which reaches out to serve. So, the question for Christians today is no different than the question believers have faced throughout the ages: Will we be active priests or withdrawn pagans? Will we be pietistic pagans or involved priests? Wearing the facade of biblical Christianity is not enough. It is the requirement of putting on the whole armor of God (Ephesians 6:11), of reforming the culture to the Biblical perspective, rather than letting the church slip further into cultural heresy, so much so that it again persecutes Christians.

Today, when we are beset by troubles all around, the cultural tendency has clearly been to escape. It was drugs and sex in the '60s and '70s, money in the '80s. Today, it is more infatuation with spectator sports, television, occultism, and self-indulgence. The average American will spend 15 years of his life in slavery to television. The emphasis on TV is upon leisure, upon escapism from reality, upon sex and violence, upon materialism and occultism. TV spurns God's law. And yet, in stark contrast to leisure, the Bible calls us to stewardship, to responsibility in time, to work! In fact, the Bible provides the death penalty for not working - If a man doesn't work, he doesn't eat (II Thessalonians 3:10). If he doesn't eat, he dies. When television shows men working, it often shows them playing at work. The federal government gives men food stamps for not working. No wonder the church has degenerated into a Sunday religious social club.

Again, a clear delineation between Christian priesthood cultures and pagan cultures is that Christian cultures emphasize work, man's responsibility to God by way of service to his fellow man. By contrast, pagan cultures emphasize leisure and escapism. The Gospel of Jesus Christ did not call man to be born-again so he could just squat like a vegetable until he dies. Rather, man is called to service in time, to occupy and fulfill his calling (Luke 19:13). It is in this broad area of Christianity - of comprehensive service, dominion, and stewardship - where the modern church has failed, with the possible exception of evangelism. But even the end product of evangelism is works, the maturing of the believer in time to holy stewardship and service. "Thy kingdom come. Thy will be done on earth as it is in heaven." - Matthew 6:10.

From the Christian perspective then, the primary purpose of life is work, not play. Man is commanded to work six days (Exodus 20:9). The emphasis of life in our culture on the pursuit of leisure is a classic and clearly pagan idea. Even if this is "the late great planet earth," there is no commandment scripturally to be an Eastern mystic and sit on a hilltop or in a cave contemplating the end of the world, waiting to cash in an eternal life and fire insurance policy and be raptured out of this world. Rather, the faith of Christianity always has an object - work! James 2 makes it abundantly clear that man's spiritual faith has application in God's created realm. His faith results in action - works! It is not faith or works. It's not an either/or situation. It is both. We are called to be "doers of the Word, not hearers only..." - James 1:22. This brings man's nature into complete harmony, a spiritual being with a physical nature.

Man is made in the image of God, clearly identifying his spiritual nature (Genesis 1:26). Man is also formed from the dust of the earth, thus tying his roots to the soil and the natural kingdom (Genesis 2:7). The essence of the Christian philosophy is the subduing of the natural man (man's fallen nature), by having his spiritual nature conform to God's laws and applying them in time in His creation. Martin Luther commented, "Christianity that isn't relevant isn't Christianity." How relevant is Christianity today to science, economics, and civil government and courts?

Christians are never to be weary in well-doing (Galatians 6:9). They are to take the long-term view. All of biblical principles, flipped into the realm of time, require a long-term view. Christians reap what they sow, both in time and eternally (Galatians 6:7). Christians, both in their spiritual development and in their calling on the earth, are required to undergo short-term pain for long-term gain. This is disciplined discipleship. This is the essence of Christian priesthood, of overcoming, of being a true ambassador for Christ. Pagans, by contrast, opt consistently for the short-term gain, reaping long-term pain. They are lost eternally. This pagan methodology is the way of death, the end product of a dying nature which cycles downward.

MAN'S GREATEST
NATURAL TENDENCY

The Bible clearly teaches that man's greatest natural tendency is to self-destruct, to move toward sin (error) and death. The scientific complement of this spiritual truth is the Second Law of Thermodynamics - entropy. Because we are made from the dust of the earth, we are tied into the physics of the Newtonian closed system where everything winds down toward death.

Now, when do people demonstrate the greatest tendency to self-destruct? When they are under pressure. One of the greatest sorrows we will ever experience is allowing people the freedom to self-destruct. This, by the way, is why there is sin, pain, suffering and death in this world. God, rather than being a tyrant, is a gentleman. He allows us the freedom to self-destruct. In other words, our freedom to choose and to make mistakes to our own detriment is more important than His dictatorial tyranny. God wants us to be responsible, to develop from the bottom up. Shouldn't the federal government learn this lesson also?

There are three primary manifestations of this tendency to self-destruct. These characteristics are:

1) <u>Making matters worse by taking on more activities and/or projects, by responding to the tyranny of the urgent rather than doing the important things, and by cutting back on quiet reflective time</u>. (This is the "chicken running around with its head cut off" syndrome.)

2) <u>Attacking people who are in the support system</u>. When a person is under pressure they are hurting. They are stressed, and tend to be irritable. They want to share their pain and thus they lash out at those who work for them, are under their authority, and/or close loved ones, if not clients, friends and acquaintances. This is exactly the wrong thing to do at precisely the wrong time. It drives the personal support system away at a time when it is needed the most. And aren't other people our greatest resource? Of course! They are our greatest treasure. Instead, the correct thing to do is to nurture and reach out for the support system (be kinder and gentler to) so it can help alleviate the pressure. Avoiding wild emotional outbursts is critical.

3) <u>Activating self-destructive behavior</u> such as over-indulging in alcohol, drugs, food, sex and entertainment; self-pity; working faster;

eating dead foods; not getting enough sleep or exercise; etc. This, too, is precisely the wrong thing at the wrong time. When under pressure and the tendency to self-destruct is strongest, the individual needs most to live a clean life, eat right (stay with live foods), get plenty of rest and exercise, and avoid escaping to pain-numbing activities such as alcohol, drugs, sex and entertainment. After all, we only grow when we squarely face the trials of life, walk with faith and courage through them, pray a lot, and breathe through the emotional pain in a relaxed and calm manner. We either grow or die. Truth kills those who hide from it! At all costs, we must avoid the tendency to revert to the womb-based needs of security (money), approval (sex), and control (power), and their concomitant emotional impulses. We must overcome our fear of chaos, loud noises, abandonment and rejection.

The test of the character of a person is how they respond under pressure, particularly when this pressure triggers the natural tendency to self-destruct. The remedy - take personal responsibility. Solid values, correct thinking, accurate emotional programming, carefully chosen words, staying focused and organized, taking important rather than urgent action, and a calm, cool, collected and kind disposition are the hallmarks of those who persevere and overcome, rather than self-destruct. Aren't those who overcome biblically those who are saved? Of course. Isn't this the true test of being a disciple (disciplined)? Of course.

What can we do for those we care about who are under pressure and self-destructing? Pray for them, and love them, and help them. "Do unto others as you would have them do unto you"...The Golden Rule... We reap what we sow.

REBELLION

While Satan's first mental attitude sin was pride, his first overt sin was rebellion against God. He wanted to be like The Most High. This is one reason God considers rebellion the equivalent of the sin of witchcraft. It accordingly comes as no surprise that of the seven satanic principalities which rule over the earth, the lead principality is Medit, whose purpose is to spread rebellion, riots and chaos among mankind.

An easy target for Medit to instill the spirit of rebellion is women - or men who operate primarily out of the feminine matrix. For this reason, God put women under men's authority/covering, for their protection. Unless women are covered by the authority of their fathers, pastors and/or husbands, Medit and his demonic army have direct access to them. Why? Women are by their very nature - their electromagnetic wiring - ungrounded, and thus always in the spirit. By nature, their ungrounded, chaotic right brain makes their mentalities and emotions subject to demonic attack. Therefore, it is no surprise that as the barrier between the natural and the supernatural breaks down during these times of significant ungrounded earth changes, the respected physicist Dr. Henry Montieff would warn women to be careful, because more and more of them are being increasingly indwelt by "animal spirits" - demons.

In addition to being covered, it is important for women to line up in obedience not only to their men, but to the principles of God's Word so that they can escape the onslaught on their feminine mentality and emotions by Medit and his demonic hosts.

Let's look closer at the nature of rebellion. The opposites of pride and rebellion are humility and obedience. In Proverbs, humility is considered to be the foremost of virtues - "a humble spirit." Obedience to God's Word is proof that we love Him. "If you love Me, keep My commandments." Women must also realize that in a temporal sense, the blessings from God arise from their humility and godly obedience to their husbands. A woman who in humility can say to her man, "I'm wrong, I'm sorry, I apologize, forgive me," and who honors him, has a heart to please him, and rejoices in being obedient under his authority - well, a good Christian "gentleman" will go to the end of the earth for such a woman. What a blessing! Her humble obedience is returned to her many fold. By contrast, when a good Christian "gentleman" is dealing with a proud and rebellious woman, usually an angry woman, he will leave. Better to sit out in a storm or in the desert than under the same roof with an uptight, bossy, angry woman. Ungodly men, when faced with rebellious women, will either turn into wimps or macho abusers. Women lose in all three cases when they are rebellious.

As the book of Esther clearly teaches, rebellion by a wife against her husband is grounds for divorce. In Esther Chapter 2, King Ahasuerus divorced Queen Vashti for her rebellion when she refused to come to him at the king's command, paving the way for Esther to become queen.

It's much easier for women to be obedient to men with whom they have a lot in common - spiritually, mentally, emotionally and physically, and in terms of work, hobbies, and recreational interests. In such a case, a woman's obedience comes more naturally because she and her husband's mutual interests are aligned.

Forget romantic love, Hollywood-style. It is a myth that destroys. It steals the soul. Make sure instead that the soul has fellowship with God, and that fellowship between husband and wife is based on commitment, friendship, appreciation, support, companionship, mutual respect, shared values and interests.

It is important that we remember with regard to God that we are all feminine. That is to say, we all are to be humble and obedient to His authority, not rebellious. Jesus Christ is the bridegroom, and as members of His church, we are His bride. The hierarchy is God the Son, husband, wife, children. The church, of course, also has authority over the Christian family, as does a godly state. The point is, all of us, all the time, are under authority. Our rebellion brings us only misery and death.

When it comes to men leading their wives, it is critical to recognize the difference between control and leadership. Christian men are commanded to lead by example, by service, caring, and love. There are two kinds of love. Covenantal love, being law based, tends to be more masculine in nature. Men understand it. Women, however, find it much easier to obey when their men operate out of the feminine, out of unconditional love toward them. It's not either/or, it's both, covenantal and unconditional love. In other words, unconditional love has boundaries. What will ensure the rebellion of a woman is harsh, legalistic, covenantal love, where a self-centered man exercises control and dominance in a tyrannical, authoritarian and/or abusive fashion. Women are receiving vessels. They must be filled before they can give back.

Rather than men ordering their women around and telling them what to do in a harsh and critical manner, men are much better served by speaking the truth in love, kindly and gently to their women, manifesting the fruit of the spirit (love, joy, peace, goodness, kindness, gentleness, faithfulness, patience, long-suffering, humility, self-control), and making suggestions or asking questions when they would like something done by their wives. No one likes to be ordered around, particularly women. Remember, women's natural inclination is to rebel and to become dominant. Thus, making requests or offering suggestions in a gentle manner goes a long way with a lady. By the same token, women need to realize when they argue, interrupt, are inconsiderate, or talk harshly or angrily to their husbands they are in rebellion and are undercutting his authority in the home, as well as setting a bad example for the children. Such women are like horses possessed of tremendous potential that never reach it because they always buck, and end up going to the canner for dog food. Having a heart to please, setting a priority for him in her use of time, sharing his interests in life, nurturing and supporting him, and holding her man first in her heart in all things ensures a woman that she will keep him. Men need honor and respect. To be responsible, they need to be appreciated.

In addition to the hierarchal authority relationship in a marriage, both husband and wife need to realize there is a horizontal or equitable relationship, much like that between a junior and a senior partner in a law firm. Each party in the marriage covenant needs to surrender to each other. This is in keeping with what Jesus said about having to die to live, to give before receiving, to lose yourself to find yourself, to become one. The beautiful irony of God's Word is that we get back multi-fold what we give. It is only when we lose ourselves to someone else, husbands to wives, and wives to husbands, that we find ourselves in terms of our true identity. Our sense of self-worth only comes from our being lovingly obedient to God and then giving/serving our fellow man. Thus, it is simple cause and effect that in our selfish, self-oriented, do your own thing, be all you can be culture, so many men and women are lost and angry, have low self-worth, and have no idea who they are. They are in rebellion to the Creator's law, which is designed for their own good.

Finally, it is important that we recognize that rebellion is often fomented by the desire of an individual to be totally free. However, total autonomous freedom is a myth. My freedom ends, for example, where your nose begins. Freedom always has boundaries because the law/boundaries are necessary to define the rights of the one and the many, the collective and the individual. What we need to realize is that God's law provides the maximum boundaries for individual freedom. Obedience to His loving laws is therefore in our best interest long-term. By contrast, when we slip into rebellion, when we fall victim to the natural, fallen realm of Satan, we fall victim to the conflict, chance, cycles, poverty and death of this realm, which strictly limits freedom and increases control, fear and insecurity. Moreover, when we are rebellious against God, the state (civil government) fills the vacuum of unbelief and disobedience, strictly limiting the arena of freedom available to us with the state widely expanding its control. The state effectively says, "We only allow you to do this, a very little. Everything else is either prohibited, regulated and/or controlled." By contrast, God says, "These few things you must not do ('Thou shalt not'). Everything else is allowed under My perfect law of liberty and love." The state has no concept of a law of liberty or a law of love. Thus, rebellion against God, which strictly limits our freedom and places us under the harsh chains of Satan's tyranny, is a death wish.

Here's an example of rebellion.... A rebellious woman is a scheduled passenger on an airline which has an excellent safety record; the particular aircraft is piloted by a gentle-man who has years of experience with the equipment and an impeccable safety record. The airline, the aircraft, and the pilot are proven worthy. The rebellious woman boards the plane. She snorts and complains to the flight attendants. She balks at putting on her seat belt. She resists putting her tray table up or her seat in the upright position prior to take-off. She demands to see the safety record of the aircraft and the pilot. Next, she demands to see the pilot personally and approve every decision he makes during the flight. For example, she instructs him not to leave the gate until she tells him; she instructs him exactly as to what speed to taxi and where to taxi. She demands to listen to all communications with the tower, ground control, departure control, ATC, and approach control. She wants to set the flying speed and altitude flown. She demands she have first choice of all drinks and magazines to read.

What's going to be the command pilot's and flight attendants' response to all this rebellion and dominance? They are going to kick her off the aircraft! The pilot, the captain in charge, has the authority to do so because he's in command.

In like manner, just as in the book of Esther, a husband has a right to divorce a wife who is rebellious, when for no good reason she stubbornly refuses to submit to his responsible leadership and plan to execute their family's journey through life. She lost her chance to be a team member and rest on both the flight and the journey through life. She left herself uncovered, unprotected and alone. She lost a good man to command their airship. Sure, she may get some wimpy little pilot to do her bidding for awhile. But, that's dangerous, because she's not equipped to command or fly. They will eventually crash. Or, she may find some abusive pilot that beats the tar out of her and makes her shape up short-term in order to accomplish his mission. Either way, she loses. And, when she's old, what then? Or injured? Or sick? Or needs assistance? Rebellion makes no sense and is terribly self-destructive. When men lovingly rule their homes and churches, and women support their efforts, there will not be rebellion elsewhere in society.

A RIGHT TO OUR FEELINGS?

How many times during a conversation have we heard someone say, "I have a right to my feelings!" As Christians, none of us have a so-called "right" to our feelings. As Christians we are bought with a price; we are not our own. Daily we are to become living sacrifices unto our Lord and King, Jesus Christ. This means we have to bring every thought, emotion, word and deed into captivity and obedience to the Lord Jesus Christ. This means that everything that we do in our mental and emotional processes, as well as our resulting words and actions, have to line up with His Law-Word. After all, He glorified His Word above His Name. And His Word is truth, alive and powerful, sharper than any two-edged sword, piercing even to the dividing asunder of the soul and the spirit and of the joints and the marrow, and is the critic of the thoughts and intents of the heart.

Think of our mental and emotional processes as akin to the workings of a computer. In a computer, the software program determines the output on the display terminal and printer. In like manner, our emotions, thoughts, words and deeds are reflections of the software programming of our subconscious, our hearts and minds. If there is iniquity found in our hearts, then the outward manifestation is that we will sin, err, miss the mark. Because our natural hearts are desperately wicked from the genetic programming passed down from our ancestors, from our time and place of birth, from our culture particularly during the formative first 10-12 years when our brain's delta, theta, and alpha rhythms are being imprinted, and from the environment, we have to reprogram. We must hide His Word in our hearts so that we do not sin against Him. We must renew our minds daily. We must be humble. We must obey. We must not resist, grieve or quench the Holy Spirit. We must pray.

Just what does it mean to have a "change of heart"? It first means that we must have a change in thinking, stemming from a change in values. Salvation comes by hearing - and hearing by the Word of God. After hearing the Word of God, which in turn through the power of the Holy Spirit changes our thinking, our values then change. As a result of our value change, the emotions which spring forth from our hearts are altered - thus, a "change of heart." Next, our behavior changes as a consequence of true repentance. We only have love, peace, joy, and the rest of the fruit of the Spirit when we line up totally under His authority, under His Law, which is written upon the hearts of His elect.

Emotions particularly are to be the appreciator of the soul, not the determiner of values. Emotions, which are the feminine (yin) side of the mind and heart, are to be anchored by the masculine (yang) side, God's Law-Word. This is 180 degrees opposite of what comes naturally. Fallen, unredeemed man by and large allows the emotions of his heart to dictate his thoughts, words and deeds. This is why the Bible says the heart is desperately wicked.

No wonder evil grows exponentially in our nation as so many subjectively base nearly everything upon their feelings. Moreover, in this day and age, when everything is becoming ungrounded, including the geomagnetic field itself, iniquity rises to the surface and manifests itself in sin unless the individual is grounded by the Law-Word of God. The importance of being grounded, rooted and established, as in the parable of the sower and soils (Luke 8), has never before been more vital. We cannot be physically grounded, unless we are first spiritually, mentally and emotionally grounded.

Is this biblical model a model for success in the real world? Absolutely! People who keep their emotions under control and stay "cool, calm and collected" are respected by others. They are rational. They "keep their feet on the ground." No one needs to tell them to "settle down" or "cool off." Such is characteristic of true leadership.

Leading psychiatrists consistently tell their patients that if they want to change the way they feel about things, and thus their behavior, they must first change their thinking. This is right in line with biblical doctrine. It takes a change of heart or emotion for there to be a change in behavior. This comes from a change in thinking, which proceeds from the Christian perspective of the Holy Spirit in working with the human spirit in applying the Word of God to the heart and mind of the individual. Anything else is lawless and proud, two abominations in God's eyes.

Psychiatrist Dr. Willard Gaylin, although not a Christian, in his book, "The Rage Within," points out that anger and fear are emotional reactions that occur in anticipation of danger, and prepare animals mentally and physically for the response of "fight or flight." But are we evolutionary animals, or are we created in the image of God? Dr. Gaylin, an evolutionist, goes on to point out that unlike other animals, human beings are not limited to "fight or flight" in their range of responses. A human being can exercise dominion, a rational, unemotional act, by eliminating the threat or correcting the threatening circumstances. In other words, man has the capability of shaping, molding and recreating his environment when his natural emotions are under control.

It's important to recognize that our emotional responses do not depend on what actually happens in reality, but on our perceptions and interpretations of reality. Psychologist Nathaniel Branden's definition of an emotion is: "the psychosomatic form in which man experiences his estimate of the beneficial or harmful relationships of some aspect of reality to himself." In other words, emotions are a spiritual/physical response to the perception of reality. The mental/emotional process is one of subjective evaluation, which means that we make a judgment as to whether something is beneficial or harmful - for us or against us. How do we decide? What is our basis of evaluation? If we are not anchored in the Word of God, we are not established; instead, we are like children, tossed to and fro and carried about with every wind of doctrine, by the trickery of men, in the cunning craftiness by which they lie in wait to deceive (Ephesians 4:14). So, if we don't anchor our hearts and emotions in God, and the rules and values He gives up, we are really vulnerable. We are, instead, subject to being victim to the anger, guilt, bitterness and resentment of the past; the pain and sorrow of the present; and the fear, anxiety and worry of the future.

We are instructed in the Bible that if we judge ourselves, we will not be judged. This is God's Law-Word applied to our lives. This certainly has primary application to our emotions. What we feel depends upon our standard of value. Are our values biblical or are they the values of a dying world? The values which take a peaceful, loving, gentle, serving, long-term view end up being almost inescapably biblical in nature, since the closest we can come to being Christ-like is to take a long-term view. (Christ is eternal.) Isn't this a key to success in the world, too? Of course. The long-term view has always been the characteristic of the upper class in any society. It is usually only the upper class, possessed of a long-term view, who are willing to discipline themselves, sacrifice, plan, save and invest for the future. This results in peace and prosperity long term. Those who plan and successfully execute, win. Short-term pain for long-term gain is God's way. This is just the opposite of Satan's way of doing things, of self-indulgence short term, of eat, drink and be merry for tomorrow we shall die. Satan, after all, has no long term, like all things natural and fallen. It is no accident that the lower class is consistently emotional and undisciplined.

Granted, some emotions/feelings are deep-seated, particularly those of the culture and family. But day by day, moment by moment, as God in us begins to bring about a change in response to a nonbiblical emotion/feeling, and thus short-circuit it and ground it out through our behavior, we change. We walk out the Christian life in our time on earth. After a while, a new biblical habit replaces an old nonbiblical one; iniquity is replaced by a heart unto God, and our emotions/feelings fall in line. This takes discipline, commitment and humility to grow and change. But after all, aren't we disciples of Jesus? If we're not disciples, we're really not followers of the King of Kings and Lord of Lords.

In summary, do we have a "right" to our natural, unredeemed feelings? No! They simply reveal the iniquity in our hearts before both God and man. Are our redeemed feelings important? Absolutely! They are the overt expression of the Sword of the Spirit which is the Word of God! As members of the Bride of Christ we find our emotions are the feminine expression of God's masculine Law-Word. Again, even in God's created science, we find an ungrounded, non-Hertzian wave (feminine) requires a grounded Hertzian wave (masculine) to be a carrier for expression.

May our redeemed feelings/emotions fully express compassion. May we judge not, condemn not, and may we forgive. May we bless, pray for, love and do good to our enemies. May our feelings/emotions fully express the fruit of the Spirit - love, joy, peace, goodness, kindness, gentleness, faithfulness, patience, long-suffering, humility and self-control. As Christians, we must take personal responsibility for our feelings and emotions, and make sure that they stem from biblical values in our hearts, based in biblical thinking from God's Holy Word. We are so held accountable unto God.

THE GREAT E-MOTION

As Dr. Gary Martin, Ph.D., of the Biological Immunity Research Institute of Scottsdale, Arizona puts it, man is a spiritual being, having a physical experience, being biochemically activated and emotionally charged. Just think what this world would be like if we became more interested primarily in our spiritual development than in our physical acquisitions, in open systems rather than in closed ones. After all, we are eternal. We'd all be healthier, happier and wealthier. We're not wealthy unless we're healthy, physically and E-motionally. It is the highly charged issue of E-motion, Energy-In-Motion, that I want to deal with here. E-motional stability is basic to being grounded, and having health and prosperity. Disciplined E-motions are as important as a disciplined mind and body.

E-motions, like fire, are fearful masters but wonderful servants. E-motions, properly handled, are a choice, not a reaction. Harnessing E-motion and staying grounded with values stemming from faith, allows one to remain calm, cool and collected under all circumstances in life. This is critical now as never before because life is becoming increasingly ungrounded. As the earth loses its magnetic charge, the compensating power is flowing to the mind of a man by way of scalar energy. This means the left-brain/right-brain scalar transmitters, pulsating simultaneously opposite each other across the corpus callosum, are increasing in strength. As man's mind becomes more powerful, chaotic E-motion (energy in motion) chews up nutritional grounding regardless of how solid it may be. Moreover, the human mind extends to all its bodily satellite stations wherein memory is stored, in the organ systems and every cell of the body. If this mind field, this energy field, is not rooted in godly, solid, eternal, grounded, quantum, supernatural values that bring forth a faith, mentality, and E-motion which enable an individual to constructively handle the circumstances of life, he will self-destruct. The essence of our age is self-destruction and madness. Thus, with all this energy flowing upward, it will take much more conscious effort to stay grounded. Positive E-motions arise from values which are positively reinforced, and negative E-motions arise from values which are violated. Therefore, our values must be grounded on godly reality.

What this means practically is that the New Agers, and too many charismatic Christians, have it 180 degrees out of phase. Too many are E-motionally out of control, angry, power hungry, insecure, fearful, ungrounded. Some attempt to get grounded by focusing selfishly on their bodies, and being self-absorbed about getting in shape and eating right. But spirit is more important than flesh, indeed it determines flesh. Spirit and energy precede flesh. To paraphrase Jesus, it's not what a man eats that is most important, but what comes out of his mouth (his heart/his mind), that is significant.

If we stop and think about it, we know that over 80 percent of dis-ease these days is caused by stress, by not processing life correctly E-motionally. In other words, over 80 percent of dis-ease these days stems from E-motion (energy in motion) dysfunction - negative energy. Three key words are: dis-ease, E-motion, response-ability. If we are able to process our E-motion constructively, we will be at ease and thus not be as subject to dis-ease. We will then be better equipped to process life, be better able to respond to life, or be "response-able" (responsible). People who are able to respond to life, to be "response-able," are free. Freedom and responsibility run hand in hand.

Again, E-motion, both positive and negative, stems from values - and their following thoughts - which have either been confirmed or violated, respectively. To be comprehensively healthy, we need a godly value system, which is supernatural/quantum (eternal) if we are to stay steady and grounded in our Newtonian and ever-changing natural world of flux which is subject to the Second Law of Thermodynamics - to entropy and death. We want to choose an open godly system rather than a closed one in establishing our value base. This is why the supernaturally given Ten Commandments and the Second Great Commandment (effectively the Golden Rule) are so important. Their implementation on earth has resulted in freedom and unequaled prosperity wherever they were applied historically.

This E-motionally correct value system is a supernatural/eternal/quantum-based open system producing light, life, love, liberty, law, laughter and a long-term view which consistently governs our lives. This brings into balance the masculine and feminine, the linear and cyclical, the yang and the yin, the many and the one, in a structured, holographic, authority relationship. We also need to learn the techniques necessary to process negative E-motions, and particularly clean up the chaotic and destructive E-motion in our subconscious, bringing it up to the level of consciousness where we can deal with it and release it, so it is no longer destructive to our system. We want to be integrated, consciously and subconsciously, mentally and E-motionally, naturally and spiritually.

There are only three things we can do with negative E-motion: 1) express it; 2) suppress it; or 3) confess it/release it. We always want to do the latter, confess/release it. When we express negative E-motion, we do harm to others which results in the need for damage control later on. When we suppress negative E-motion, we do damage to ourselves, mentally and physically. What we need to do instead is to confess, to forgive and forget in order to release it. Dr. Michael Ryce's work has been helpful in this area.

We all know that life is breath. Every time we experience a negative E-motion we literally shorten our breath and therefore effectively shorten our lives. We lock the memory and destructive force of that negative E-motion into our bodies' systems. It continues to work below the level of consciousness to our detriment. Thus, we always want to breathe deeply, under all circumstances, particularly through negative E-motional experiences. Hale Dwoskin of The Sedona Institute in Phoenix, Arizona places primary emphasis on feeling the negative E-motions in the diaphragm/solar plexus area, where the breath is shortened, then using an effective release technique, allowing the release of apathy, grief, fear, anger, lust, pride and all their negative sub-categories which are stored up in the body. When I release E-motion, I ask myself, "Could I, would I let it go?" I answer "yes." "When?" "Now." "How?" "By the power of the Holy Spirit." Then I take a deep breath and feel the E-motional pain in my solar plexus and diaphragm and then blow it out.

If we go back to our initial human experience, our consciousness in the womb, we find it is the closest natural thing on earth we will experience to a perfect environment. So, we naturally in life keep attempting to recreate our womb experience. There, in the womb, most of us felt secure, loved (approved of), and in control. In addition to our primal need for control, approval and security, we have our ego's (pride's) need to be "right." If we don't get these, we tend to lash out.

If we live to satisfy these primal natural E-motional needs, we err. This is why as Christians, if we are to move from milk to meat, from immaturity to maturity, eventually we have to become grounded and move from the ungrounded feminine womb-based needs to the grounded masculine hierarchial perspective, while simultaneously maintaining a balance between the masculine and the feminine. Ideally both the feminine (yin) and the masculine (yang) need to be held in a dialectic co-equal balance, but the authority relationship is simultaneously that of a masculine covering which grounds the feminine - justice tempered with mercy, if you will.

If, in order to obtain security, we look to establish security (feminine) as a primary motive, drive and goal, we will most likely fail in our efforts. In life, we often have to do the opposite to reach our desired end. For example, good leaders serve. We have to take risks if we want to be secure. Risk assumption is primarily a masculine trait. Many risk-averse investors have lost fortunes by playing it safe and secure. There is profit only when risk is taken. If we want approval (feminine), we have to give to others what they want first, both in the tangible and intangible realms (Golden Rule/Second Great Commandment). This means our own E-motion has to be sub-ordinated first for us to be empathetic with the needs of others. We have to possess the humility to recognize and align with the highest and best in others, and be response-able to meet their needs empathically and with a sense of duty. Finally, if we seek control (feminine) in life, it inevitably eludes us. People do not like being controlled.

The natural tendency is for men to be response-unable and women to be dominant. This goes back to Adam and Eve. We all have limited time, limited resources, limited knowledge, limited ability, limited power, limited mobility and limited energy. About the only thing we can control somewhat successfully is ourselves. We are only invulnerable where we are without defenses.

We all know that as we get older, life - energy in motion (E-motion) - takes its toll on our bodies if we don't handle it correctly. We want to be E-motionally correct. As we get older, we either get bitter or we get better. Stated differently, as we grow older, we either live more by faith (masculine) or by fear (feminine). Faith is risk-based (masculine) because it involves hope in something which does not yet exist in the tangible world, but instead exists in the mind and heart of man and in the spirit. Faith is sightless. It is also futuristic. Faith is thus the essence of growth and progress and the antithesis of uniform control, retrenching fear, security craving, and group approval, which lead to stagnation, decay and death. How many football teams have we seen attempt to sit on (control) a lead only to blow it? Fear, security, control, being comfortable with approval - all lead to failure. Life is dynamic. It is never stagnant. Any time we're coasting, we're going downhill, and we do that naturally, according to Newtonian physics and the Second Law of Thermodynamics - the law of decay and death.

We've already established the importance of grounding ourselves in values arising from godly supernatural law, so that our own natural E-motion and chaotically flawed values, stemming from our ancestry and culture, don't lead us into error. But what about what it takes to confess/release the negative E-motion which is locked up in our genetic pool (which can and does change), and in our subconscious? Well, for approximately 90 percent of us, the belief system exists to establish such a release. Our biblical heritage teaches us to be anxious about nothing, to bring every thought into captivity to obedience to Christ and to give thanks in all things. It further teaches us to renew our minds, that all things work together for good, that we're to overcome evil with good, that we're to bless, do good for, love, and pray for our enemies, that we're to think on whatever things are good, noble, and just (masculine), and whatever things are pure, lovely, and of good report (feminine), and to meditate on whatever things are praiseworthy and virtuous. As we do this and grow in grace (power), our E-motions become increasingly still, quiet, at peace. Joy takes over. We are better able to live in the present moment, to be fully conscious in the "now," and then be "response-able" (responsible). The intangible characteristics such as love, freedom, and health become more manifest in our being. We become more relaxed, more "at ease." We become more "thought-full" (thoughtful) as we become more "faith-full" (faithful) and less "fear-full" (fearful). The more feminine traits of compassion, kindness, gentleness and mercy become manifest. Overall, we become more loving. And love is the primary characteristic of the supernatural Law-Giver, covering both ends of life's spectrum. Love is the base which establishes the foundation/grounding which makes life-giving E-motion possible. After all, The Most High God is the great eternal E-MOTION (ENERGY IN MOTION).

To feel is both physical and E-motional. This is a basic psychosomatic connection. Accordingly, over the past few years I have worked through three different systems, all of which have proven beneficial. I have used the following three constructive techniques to begin cleaning out and reintegrating at the conscious and subconscious levels, the head and the heart, negative and destructive E-motion (energy in motion). I recommend all three of these courses on E-motional processing, from children on up. My preference is the following order:

1. First we put our heads on straight in order to understand. Dr. Michael Ryce's series, "Why Is This Happening to Me...Again?!" is great for this. Dr. Ryce teaches us why the same things happen to us over and over again, and why we react the same way over and over again, and how to clear out and change things for good. (Order from Robert Fridenstine, New Horizons Trust, (800) 755-6360, 53166 St. Rt. 681, Reedsville, OH 45772).

2. Next, to link the heart and E-motions up with breath, the body, and the subconscious, the Sedona Institute's Sedona Method is

a long-standing, highly appreciated technique. The Sedona Method includes eight videotapes, a master E-motion chart (invaluable), five workbooks to use with the videotapes, including three special workbooks on your appearance, health and well-being, your relationships, and your financial freedom. Phone (602) 553-3770; fax (602) 553-3790; or write 2701 E. Camelback Rd., #500, Phoenix, AZ 85016.

3. For detailed, specific and precise scientific integration of the E-motional with the physical, Dr. Gary Martin's Biological Immunity Research Institute is on the cutting edge. Dr. Martin works with the "dragons" within each of us which emit chaotic negative E-motion, literally destructive radiation, which attracts our repeating problems and frustrate our life's purpose. We get back what we give off. We reap what we sow. Dr. Martin confirms negative E-motion on the biochemical end with saliva and urine tests, leading to the suggested nutritional support. It's incredible to watch how an individual's saliva and urine test results change once their E-motional pattern changes and they become more calm and at peace. For counseling on literally slaying your own "dragons," contact Dr. Gary Martin at Biological Immunity Research Institute. Phone 800-654-3734; fax (602) 948-8150; or write to 13402 N. Scottsdale Rd., Suite B-170, Scottsdale, AZ 85254.

Regarding E-motion, for the exclusively investment-oriented among you, I want you to know that this emotional training has made a substantial beneficial contribution to my personal investment and trading efforts. Why? Because in today's society, money is inescapably tied directly to E-motion. Money is the means to the end of physical survival in our social order. Specifically, I have noticed the following benefits: Investing in the markets is less stressful because I do not have the E-motional tie-in that I had previously, either by way of fear or greed, or by way of exhilaration or remorse. This has made me more objective, with the by-product being increased psychological reserves, the ability to carry more positions simultaneously, and an enhanced, keener and broader perception of the markets than what previously existed. The above-discussed E-motional training has made me a better investor because I have become more astute, more aware, more in tune, more relaxed, and have gleaned more insight because my own E-motional issues no longer get in the way. I am stronger and more grounded. I see more clearly, and I act more readily. This was the delightful, unexpected by-product to all this E-motional work. It was worth it. Prosperity is a by-product of godliness.

We all go through a good part of our lives perceiving life subjectively - primarily one way and responding accordingly - based upon our genetic programming, and our parental, social, and peer group subconscious programming up until we are 12-years-old. But now, these E-motional processing techniques open up an entirely new way of perceiving and dealing with the world in which we live. The result is new, varied and more productive options in thinking, feeling and behavioral responses to opportunities and challenges as they present themselves.

Let me conclude with one of my favorite verses from the Old Testament of the Bible. It speaks to the importance of the mind/E-motion energy field (the aura or countenance) which surrounds the body. "The Lord bless you and keep you; the Lord make His face shine upon you, and be gracious unto you; the Lord lift up this countenance upon you, and give you peace."

TOWARD THE HEART OF THE MATTER

"Beloved, if our heart does not condemn us, we have confidence toward God." - I John 3:21.

"As for My people, children are their oppressors,

And women rule over them.

O My people! Those who lead you cause you to err,

And destroy the way of your paths." - Isaiah 3:12.

"The rod and rebuke give wisdom, but a child left to himself brings shame to his mother." - Proverbs 29:15.

"Foolishness is bound up in the heart of a child,

"The rod of correction will drive it far from him." - Proverbs 22:15.

The Lord God makes it very clear throughout His Word that He is effectively a heart surgeon. Jeremiah 17:9-10 makes this point: "The heart is deceitful above all things, and desperately wicked; who can know it? I, the Lord, search the heart, I test the mind. Even to every man according to his ways, and according to the fruit of his doings."

He wants to make us both righteous and tenderhearted. Our sovereign God writes His laws upon the hearts of His elect, in our spirit. Then by studying to show ourselves approved unto God - by learning His Law-Word - we establish His thinking, replacing our own in our minds/hearts. Then by faith, we take this learned spiritual reality and effectively establish a holographic concept which we walk out by works in our lives as our faith is tested, grounding out this reality. This reconnects our spiritual head with our spiritual heart which God has given us and cleans out the garbage in both. Thus, we become new creatures in Christ in time on earth as we already are eternally in Christ Jesus. We progressively establish His Word and Will in the subconscious software programming of our minds/hearts, replacing that of our old sinful nature which we received from Father Adam, from our birth, from our families and from our culture up until approximately age 12. Beyond age 12, most "new" sin is consciously established.

Obviously, a Christian family which repetitively teaches its children God's truth in love, by word and example, which provides a Christian education in a Christian school (home or otherwise), and lives in a Christian culture is a blessing for children. Such a situation works to minimize the multi-generational genetic impact of the old sinful nature naturally working in the heart of man. In other words, train up a child in the way he should go, and when he is old, he will not depart from it.

This software programming of the child is effectively completed by age 13. Under age 13, children are still operating primarily in the alpha, theta and delta ranges of the brain, below 13-14 hertz (cycles per second), the frequencies where automatic behavior (habits) are deeply established. Up until ages 8-12, the brain responds to physical punishment, and evil can literally be driven out with constructive reproof - physically with the rod. The old saying, "The rod of instruction should be applied to the seat of learning," is verified by modern science with children of this age, before they begin operating primarily in the beta frequencies of the human mind, of 13-30 hertz, the thinking realm, usually at ages 10-12.

Babies from birth to 2-3 years spend most of their time sleeping. This is the delta range of the brain, from 1 to 3-4 hertz (cycles per second). The Bible over and over again interchangeably uses the word "sleep" for "death." This is where man, while he is physically on earth, is closest naturally to the spirit realm. (Sleep in its various manifestations runs up to 14 hertz.) Delta is the equivalent of the ultraviolet range of the light spectrum, north pole magnetically, with very concentrated energy in an alkaline state which is oxygen rich. At 1 hertz, man (and a baby, particularly) is basically operating in the "universal news" with 186,000 miles equaling one cycle.

Next up the frequency range of the brain is theta. Theta is 3-7 hertz. Theta begins the all-important region of the subconscious, where the spirits that pull our strings in the dark operate. This is the software programming realm. It is primarily operative between 2-3 years old to 7-8 years old. It equates again to the colors on the electrical (spiritual) end of the spectrum, the blues to ultraviolet. Theta is the equivalent of the "global news." At 5 hertz, a cycle is 48,000 miles long.

From ages 8-12 years old, children operate primarily in the alpha frequency, which is 7-12 hertz. This is the range of the autonomic nervous system, the maintenance system of the body. It is linked to the endocrine system, which has to do with prayer, meditation, and green colors. The alpha frequency is effectively the "regional news," where 28,000 miles long equals one cycle a second. It is the largest region of the subconscious. The subconscious makes up 90 percent of our mind and is 100 times more powerful than the conscious mind. This is the last chance for parents to "automatically" train up a child in the way he should go in terms of subconscious software programming. For beyond then, beginning at the latest at age 13, a child operates nearly exclusively in the active conscious state in the thinking portion of the brain - the beta frequency of 13-30 hertz. This is the red energy area of the brain, the most acidic and the least oxygenated. It is equivalent to south pole magnetic energy and its frequency colors are primarily red, yellow and orange. The thinking beta frequency is effectively the "local news," which at one cycle per second is 19,000 miles long at 15 hertz.

The human mind has more interconnections than the estimated total number of atoms in the universe. And up to 80 percent of these connections in turn interconnect to the visual system. (Naturally, we walk by sight.) The left brain is primarily our external sensory information processor. The right brain interprets subjectively what the senses have "seen." The left brain is negative and deals with logic, reason, analysis and law. The right brain is positive and deals with creativity, intuition, tone, and love. Obviously, it's easier to instill faith in a child before age 13, when he is more receptive to walking by faith rather than by sight.

The brain's first level of memory is nerve fibers/spinal cord. That's dubbed the pre-amphibian mind and brain, the relay circuit. The brain stem is the so-called amphibian mind and life support system. Next comes the basal ganglia, the sensory motor relay system, called the reptilian brain. Then comes the limbic system, and finally the cerebrum. The reptilian brain controls the majority of the body's autonomic functions (breathing, digestion, heart regulation). The limbic brain deals with emotional feelings that guide reflex behavior. The cortex or neo-cortex, the thinking brain, deals with our conscious and subconscious minds.

It is no accident that many academic scholars, such as college professors, have far poorer health statistically than most men their own age. Their excessive time reading and thinking not only draws energy from the other key organs and lower energy centers of their body, but also the acidic and oxygen-using nature of such continuous mental activity depletes them if they're not careful to balance it out with physical activity, quiet time, rest, prayer and meditation. Too many college professors literally become acid heads.

Modern statist education, emphasizing nearly exclusively the left brain activity and ignoring/stifling the balancing creativity of the spiritual right brain, is turning out children who are effectively "acid heads" as well. They lack balance. It is a contributing reason why many of our youth are drawn into drugs these days. In our busy world, we need to take time to be quiet, to stand still, and to know that God is there. We need to be quiet every day. In other words, we need to get down daily into the alpha frequency of 7-13 hertz. Spiritually, this means time for prayer and meditation. This alpha region is the area of the endocrine system - and for our purposes, it is important to note that the heart controls the endocrine system. Thus, as a man thinketh in his heart, so he is, not only in his external works, but also in his physical body. It's holistic and holographic, where one part is reflected throughout the whole and the whole can be found in one part. Because the heart controls the endocrine system, it also controls the reflected, light-fed, crystal pineal gland, the pituitary gland (ciliary ganglion), the thyroid gland (superior cervical ganglion), the thymus gland (inferior cervical ganglion), the breathing area of man in the solar plexus and adrenal gland (celiac plexus and celiac ganglion), then the spleen, pancreas and liver (inferior mesenteric ganglion), and finally the bowels (as the Bible calls them), where the prostate gland and reproductive organs (gonads) are located (pelvic plexus and pelvic nerve).

Christians need to correctly see man as a spiritual, energetic, mental, emotional and physical creation, holographically all in one, made in the image of God, but formed from the dust of the earth and spanning the links from quantum to Newtonian physics - from supernatural to natural. It's not either/or, it's both. It's a created spectrum - a spiritual, electromagnetic, and physical spectrum. We are "living stones," vibrating biological crystals. It is not spiritual warfare or quantum energy and electromagnetic physics or Newtonian physical works and activity. It's always all three simultaneously, throughout the entire electromagnetic spectrum of life. This is expressed by one of the latest fields in medicine - psychoneuroimmunology - that takes into account how spirit, energy and body all interact and impact each other. It's the grounding, red, magnetic energy of the blood of Christ, the law of God and the fear of the Lord running all the way through the spectrum to lightning and the delicate comfort of the Holy Spirit. It's both the kindness and the severity of the Lord. Where there is spiritual warfare, it is manifest in the unseen dynamics of the manipulation of energy (Extra low frequency/Extra high frequency - ELF/EHF) spiritually by prayer; scientifically by using such instruments as radionics and psychotronics; physiologically, by such methods as homeopathy; and in the occult, using the witchcraft methodologies involved with the infrared range of the light spectrum. This manipulation of energy is simultaneously being manifest in the physically created world of Newtonian physics which we visually see, the range of our eye camera being only from .4-.7 micrometers in the infrared. This is only five percent of the created light spectrum. We had better walk by faith; we see very little.

Revelation 4 makes it apparent that Jesus Christ is the Ultimate Healer, the Great Physician, because the rainbow countenance (aura, electromagnetic field) of his throne is emerald green. Emerald green is the color of the heart - which controls the endocrine system - and is the point of balance between love and law. Green is both the color of the heart and of law. The frequency for emerald green, as manifest in Jesus Christ's (or a person's) countenance (aura, electromagnetic field) is 7.83 hertz. The frequency 7.83 hertz is the Schumann resonant frequency of the earth and, according to Dr. Bob Beckman of Stanford University, the frequency at which all healers heal. The frequency 7.8 hertz corresponds to the parasympathetic (relaxing) nervous system. The psychobiology of mind-body healing involves the limbic system, pineal, hypothalamus, and pituitary glands as they feed hormones to various parts of the body: TSH to the thyroid; ACTH to the adrenals; PRL, FSH, and LH to the ovaries; and FSH and LH to the testes. Selye's General Adaptation Syndrome emphasizes the mind-modulating role of the limbic-hypothalamic system on the autonomic, endocrine and immune systems. Thus, as a man thinks and feels, so he is physically.

In ancient times, rulers wore emeralds because it was thought emeralds sent evil spirits howling away in distress into the dark abyss. (The ancient Egyptians, who used angles [infrared] in their healing arts, knew that 38 degrees equaled the heart, which when converted to radians equaled 666. This corresponded also to their sacred cubit.) In Revelation 4:3, the emerald rainbow surrounding Christ's throne says volumes regarding His nature, His perfect heart, as perfectly balanced between law and love, between yang and yin, as the Victor over Satan, as well as the Great Physician and the complete Second Adam, restoring to God and His heaven His fallen creation.

Most of us in Western civilization spend most of our time in the thinking beta range of 14-30 hertz, the yellow range of our countenance. This is particularly true around universities. (Incidentally, yellow is the least popular color in the world.) But when we become quiet in our hearts/minds, and move down toward the emerald green alpha range of 7.83 hertz, the quiet time of prayer and meditation between 7 and 14 hertz, we are closer to both the spiritual and physical essence of our creation, harmonizing with the healing resonant frequency of the earth at 7.83 hertz, which is simultaneously the emerald green rainbow of Christ's throne in heaven. There, we can be spiritually and physically healed. Modern medicine has just started to become open to the beneficial properties of meditation in relation to our health. In fact, within the health care community, meditation is often being recommended to combat stress. Prayer has been documented in hospital studies to have aided the healing of patients.

When we drop down into theta, effectively from 3-7 hertz, we are in the mental state in which geniuses of the past have had their most creative moments. Creativity is a right brain activity, in contrast to the left brain-based beta activity which takes place from 14 to 30 hertz.

Ideally, our left brain and right brain will be balanced and work together, with the left brain providing the anchor (grounding) for the right brain across the corpus callosum. The "tears of Jesus," the spiritual, antigravitational cerebral spinal fluid, which moves down the spine to bathe the pericardium of the heart, unites the head and heart. The heart is the organ biblically associated with the head. The heart provides the biofeedback to the head. This brings us to the created differences between men and women.

It has been well established scientifically that men generally are more left-brain (intellectual/scientific/law/engineering) oriented and women are more right-brain (emotional/arts) oriented. Further, it is established that the left side of the brain controls the right side of the body, and the right side of the brain controls the left side of the body. Because the left side of the body has a negative polarity, particularly where the feet interface with the earth and the left hand with the atmosphere, and because women are primarily right-brain oriented, they are naturally, always "out there," exposed and uncovered in the spiritual realm. Women are by creation ungrounded and unprotected spiritually. This is why women naturally have an inclination toward religion. It is why women have been the founders of so many cults, and why ancient pagan empires had key goddesses which ruled (Ashtar, Isis, Diana, Tanit, Aphrodite). But the problem is, and this is a key point, ungrounded religion - religion which does not run the spectrum from faith to works, from the law and blood of Jesus Christ to the Holy Spirit - is satanic religion, the religion of the devil. This is why women, "empty vessels," were/are biblically always to be covered by a grounded man - whether it be a father, pastor/priest, or husband, and preferably two out of the three all of the time. This covering was for the woman's spiritual protection from the un-grounded spiritual realm of Satan to which she is naturally open.

Christianity is uniquely a grounded, full-spectrum religion. The very magnetic nature of red blood was basic to the animal sacrifices of the Old Testament which were symbolic of the Real Thing - the shed blood of the Lord Jesus Christ on the cross as the Messiah, the God-Man, who took the spiritual reality of God and grounded (recon-nected) it to the reality of His physical creation. (The Christian com-munion is an expression of our identity with Christ's work.) In other words, the Second Adam, Jesus Christ, through the emanations of His perfectly balanced law/love heart, restored the integrity of the perfect link-up between God and man in his grounding activity on the earth. To express it yet another way, the spiritual, electromag-netic and physical spectrum (heaven with earth) was reestablished through the work of the Lord Jesus Christ. A transcendent God oversaw it all.

The above also helps explain why Eve was tempted. Eve was, by her very created nature, "out there." The spiritual, energetic, un-grounded nature of the fallen spiritual world of Satan's kingdom had automatic access to Eve (and any other woman such as Jezebel, Deli-lah, Herod's wife and her daughter). So Eve could be tempted. It also explains why women naturally gravitate toward the running of churches, and the more they do so, the more religious and feminine (collective) the churches become and the less biblical - the less grounded in Christ's law and blood (masculine individual).

God's clear establishment of men as elders to rule the church and both teach and govern in terms of His Law-Word was established not only for the spiritual protection of the church, but also was an ex-pression of the way He created man. Men are by design primarily left-brain oriented, which is the negative/law/acidic/red energy side of the brain, which controls the right side of the body, and runs down through the gall bladder, the organ of government and judgment, into the grounding right side output of the positive polarity of the right hand and the right foot. (The earth itself [dialectic] carries a negative polarity.) The law of God is primarily negative - "Thou shalt not..." (This negativity of law maximizes man's area of freedom.) The beta frequency, law-oriented, thinking, male dominant, left side of the brain as a red energy region is, therefore, also associated with blood (red and magnetic). Thus, it is incorrect and blasphemous - actually an abomination to God, by both God's creation and dictates - for there to be women elders, particularly when they teach God's Law-Word to men, govern the local church, and, horror of horrors, serve communion at the Lord's table. For more reading on the scientific differences between men and women, see Anne Moir and David Jessel's recent book, "Brain Sex." Also helpful is Ann Douglas' book, "The Feminization of American Culture," and Steven Goldberg's book, "Why Men Rule."

Hopefully, this explanation will go a long way in helping Christians understand why the nation was strong when only men were elders in churches as per Titus 1:6, and men voted representing the leadership of the united male/female household. This was grounded in the spiritual, electromagnetic, practical, and physical sense. Men have a root in themselves - grounded.

Historians have long established that the time of the U.S. Civil War was the key time frame when the United States broke with its grounded Christian tradition. Northern armies destroyed the culture of the Calvinistic South (Primitive Baptists, Presbyterians, etc.). After the war, "The Ladies" began "A Feminization of American Culture," as Dr. Ann Douglas wrote so discerningly.

Dr. Glen Rein, formerly of Harvard and director of the Quantum Biology Research Lab at Cotati Research Institute, Palo Alto, California, confirms Scripture when he reports that the delicate nature of a non-hertzian scaler frequency (feminine) requires a grounded hertzian (masculine) wave to serve as a carrier wave. By analogy, at least, and consistent with the way God supernaturally works through His creation, this suggests that the delicate nature of the Holy Spirit uses a big magnetic base of the grounded Word of God - established in the heart by the blood of Jesus Christ - to establish God's purpose on earth.

A transcendent God of law and order can and does enter His spiritual/energetic/physical creation and accomplishes things miraculously. But more times than not, He prefers to work and manifest His essence and presence through the law and order of His creation, again reflecting His essence. So whether ancient or modern history is studied; whether spiritual or political kingdoms are analyzed (effectively one is a reflection of the other); where women rule church (and often state); we find ungodly, occult, devilish, satanic, pagan systems.

Satan wanted to give up his creaturehood and become as God. Eve, who was by God's design naturally ungrounded, also wanted to become as God - knowing both good and evil and determining for herself her own laws. The ancient empires, such as the Egyptians and Babylonians, with their goddesses, attempted to ground themselves out through the masculine phallic symbol. The Mayan culture in the Americas attempted to ground itself out with endless human blood sacrifices. Most of the occult religions of the Third World have substitute blood sacrifices (such as chickens in voodoo ceremonies). It seems there has to be a substitute blood sacrifice for the perfect law keeping masculine blood of Christ Jesus which was shed on the cross. Religion, after all, is always attempting to find a way to ground itself by getting around the blood of the Lord God Jesus Christ and obedience to His Law-Word.

It is no accident that historians (such as Amaury de Riencourt), who have studied countless civilizations, observe that when women begin to dominate, as in Rome, it is just prior to a fall. The ungrounded nature of women ruling is a reflection of the ungrounded nature of a civilization which has lost its roots, its anchor, and is therefore ready to topple. It often also occurs commensurate with a weakening/alteration in the earth's magnetic field. It is no accident that the United States was strong from 1620 to approximately 1830, for over 200 years, prior to the rise of a slew of women-led religious cults. The decline accelerated after the Civil War with the revival of ancient evolution, continuing in the twentieth century with the increase in women's rights as the demise of the patriarchal culture led to the rise of the matriarchal culture.

All of the foregoing is necessary background information to bring us to the point where we can now understand why the "Mother" Earth environmental movement and the feminists' political agenda is working to establish itself religiously in witchcraft. It is further working in line with its security need to install a New World Order (global fascism) under the guise of environmentalism. Government is always religion applied to economics. The pagan matriarchal model which has subverted and effectively emasculated the biblical patriarchal model in family, church and state today in the West is an expression of Satan's work at his finest. Too many men are no longer men anymore, since very few children receive the primary balanced training in a love/law-based family, school, or church, where men rule gently and kindly with biblical authority. All three of these primary institutions (family, church, school) are governed and run primarily by women today.

In 1991, less than 27 percent of U.S. women who conceived out of wedlock were marrying; more than two-thirds of teenagers who had babies were unmarried. Only 10 percent of black teenage mothers were married. Further, more U.S. marriages now end in divorce than in death, according to the American Bar Association. Only one of six single-parent households is headed by a man. This means that women are raising the children of the U.S. Today's children literally have few male patriarchal models, no grounding. Fully 40 percent of the members of the National Organization for Women (NOW) have admitted that they are lesbians since their leader, Patricia Ireland, confessed her sexual preference. Regarding this state of affairs, the World News Digest of December 27, 1991, commented, "Father may not always have known best, but now that the feminist quest for 'equality' has effectively knocked down the patriarchal society, it should be no surprise that men are shrinking from responsibility." Societies self-destruct when men become irresponsible and women become dominant.

The naturally sinful thing for women to do is to rebel against their male covering, to abandon the nurturing and creative nature of their right-brain activity - as well as their good business sense - and, instead, attempt to obtain power and dominance through manipulation in religion and politics. The overwhelming secular evidence is that women do not like to work for other women because they are too tough, showing no mercy. Women gangs are less merciful than male gangs. Divorce lawyers consistently state that women are less merciful. Men, by contrast, like Father Adam, tend in their sinful state to become irresponsible. This means men naturally understand justice tempered with mercy more than women, which is another reason God put man in charge of the law duties of both church and state.

It follows that the modern feministic perspective in child rearing would also be anti-God in its methodology. In Germany, a "child-friendly" law has been proposed, barring parents from spanking, boxing ears, withholding affection, constant nagging, or threatening children with the "bogeyman." In other words, no reproof, and spare the rod. Will this train a child in the way he ought to go from a biblical perspective (Proverbs 22:6)? No way. This child-rearing method is the godless, goddess antithesis to the biblical mandate. Dr. Elizabeth Sue Bowman, assistant professor of psychiatry at the Indiana University School of Medicine, told an assembly of pastoral ministers that fundamentalist (biblical) families have a high incidence of child abuse. Addressing a regional conference in Milwaukee, the theme of which was "When Theology Leads to Abuse," Dr. Bowman claimed that a 1989 study found significant links between child abuse and religious affiliation. Said Dr. Bowman, "Fundamentalists and child abusers share 'a low view of humanity', which includes the idea that children are 'bad and selfish'. Once subjugating the child's evil nature 'has become a divinely commissioned task', it is easier to rationalize the use of any means to bring this about.

"A view of God as punitive and humanity as worthless might make it hard for parents to have much self-esteem or to project feelings of self-worth onto the child." (Source: Secular Humanist Bulletin, 9/91) Dr. Bowman apparently takes issue with God's Word and not so subtly attacks biblical Christian families who raise their children according to God's written Word as "abusers."

Now, any Christian parent worth his "salt" knows that abuse has no place in the delicate working of the Holy Spirit in the application of God's Law-Word to the life of a child. But whom the Lord loves He does discipline. Contrary to Dr. Elizabeth Sue Bowman, the Bible does teach that man is not naturally good, that man's heart is desperately wicked, that he has a devilish sinful nature, and that it is the parent's divinely commissioned task to break the self-willed pride of the child to the humility and obedience of God's Word for the child's own good long term. Man biblically is not his own god, but is under authority. If men are not ruled by God, they are ruled by government tyrants. Of course, man is made in the image of God, and was created as the epitome of God's creation. Thus, he is far from being "worthless." But his fall requires repentance, a renewal of spirit, revival, reformation and personal reconstruction for him to move toward being restored, to becoming Christ-like while on earth, and toward being all he was created to be.

The academic and legal basis presently being established to accuse parents who raise their children according to the biblical standard is to label them as "child abusers," subjecting parents to the removal of their children from their homes, and possibly other legal action, such as fines and imprisonment. As we know, this has already been the case in too many court cases across the land. But Dr. Elizabeth Sue Bowman is incorrect that Christian families can "use any means to bring this about." Christian parents are clearly instructed biblically to love their children and to teach them God's truth in love, with kindness and gentleness. Moreover, a Christian husband is to see his wife as an extension of himself, literally as his own flesh (one flesh together). But, because God disciplines those He loves for their own good long term, and therefore is punitive, parents, too, have the responsibility to discipline, including appropriate physical discipline up through age 12. Physical discipline does not mean either God or a Christian parent views mankind or a child as "worthless." "No pain, no gain" is a loving lesson often taught by life. By contrast, the unbeliever generally, readily and naturally takes the path of least resistance. Furthermore, child psychologists have observed that when sympathy and comfort is given to a child who is under discipline, before that child has learned the necessary lesson, the child is destroyed because his rebellion is rewarded. Rebellion is the essence of both Satan's and Eve's first reaction (sin against) to God.

It is true that man does not naturally have any self-esteem or acceptable self-worth from a biblical perspective. Why else would he need a saviour? Any sense of personal worth man has biblically is first found in the God-man, in the Lord Jesus Christ. Then, as a result of his service to his fellow man in his calling - according to the Second Great Commandment - through man's application of his talents to his fellow man in humility, responsibility, empathy and duty, he develops a sense of personal worth. Also, as a man clears personally, internally and applies a Godly heart toward those close to him, he develops his self-worth. So-called true self-esteem and true self-worth can only be a result of grounded biblical training resulting in good works.

An issue of New Age magazine had on its cover John Bradshaw, a former alcoholic and drug abuser, who has hosted a series of tax-payer-financed PBS programs entitled, "Healing the Child Within." John Bradshaw is the "inner child" guru. His theology on child training and the family has swept the country, and is antagonistic at its core to biblical fundamental Christianity. The Bible teaches basi-cally that man's nature is sinful (wrong, evil) and that he needs a saviour and redemption. Thus, the birth, work, death and resurrec-tion of Jesus Christ was necessary. Reviewing John Bradshaw's work, the Austin American-Statesman of January 3, 1992, stated, "Bradshaw is talking about a patriarchal family model he says teaches damaging, unspoken rules: 'blind obedience, repressing emotions, crushing a person's will at an early age.'" Here we see clearly the direct attack upon the biblical, male-based patriarchal family, an assault on obedience to God's Law-Word, condemning the repression of the natural emotions of the heart which are desperately wicked, and advocating that children be self-willed - their own little gods and goddesses so to speak.

Throughout the New Age feministic goddess community today, the basic precept taught is to "trust your heart." This devilish idea that the heart of man is basically good and can be trusted is 180 degrees removed from the Bible. The concept explained is that man-kind can trust his own emotions which erupt from the heart because the heart is basically good. Further underlying this is the belief that a man/woman is his/her own god/goddess, and thus can make his/her own law, determining for himself/herself good and evil. This is the essence of what the Bible calls pride, one of the worst of sins. It was

Satan's first mental attitude sin (error). The biblical model is that a person's pride is to be broken to authority, unto the obedience of God's Law-Word, since man's heart/mind cannot be trusted. Biblically, emotions - right-brain and feminine in nature - are to be responders; governed, anchored and grounded by obedience to God's Law-Word and expressions thereof - a left-brain activity. Emotions, rightfully grounded, are appreciators of the soul.

If we stop and think about it, emotions are nothing more than the expression of values. Values are concepts of right or wrong, good and evil, which form the basis of law. In other words, when a person is emotionally upset, it is because something in his value (law) system has been violated. Therefore, we must ask, "What are the sources of those values? Are they biblical? Are they from ungodly family training, from the pagan culture? Did they arise from some genetic sinful predisposition that was passed down ancestrally by way of subconscious programming?" In this sense, man is predestined by the natural fallen world. Predestination is always either by God or Satan. Man is not autonomous, ever. The more we learn scientifically and psychologically, the closer we come back to predestination.

How much better to reestablish man's values consistently with those of a God of balanced law and love, who loves and cares for man, so that he can best serve God, serve his fellow man, and simultaneously meet his own spiritual and physical needs here on earth in a win-win arrangement. How much better that man's emotions be an expression of these godly Christian values/laws, rather than of the lawlessness of a desperately wicked heart, and of the fallen, death-oriented creation which is ruled by Satan. Where is our society today? John Bradshaw's book, "Homecoming: Reclaiming and Championing Your Inner Child," was on The New York Times Bestseller List for 52 weeks, and the number one book for 23 weeks. Based upon this, the nation is far astray.

We are going to have a homecoming all right. Mankind will stand before the Great White Throne and be held accountable! The "inner child" of John Bradshaw has no need of a saviour. It is the counterfeit to biblically "becoming as little children." Tell Jesus Christ when He returns that you "championed your inner child." This is the coming, ruling Jesus Christ who takes no prisoners! Better instead to have a heart unto God.

Giving the devil his due so to speak, when John Bradshaw says, "If our vulnerable child was hurt or abandoned, shamed or neglected, that child's pain, grief and anger live on within us," he is talking correctly about the basic improper programming of the subconscious up until age 12, down primarily in the alpha and theta regions, which man carries naturally with him through life. So, there is considerable merit to a Christian-based inner healing ministry. The Word of God is alive and powerful. But even though Bradshaw's analysis is correct, his solution is in error when he effectively says that man as his own god can go within himself and change himself with a new humanistic program which is clearly not in line with God's Law-Word. Such an effort puts man at war within himself. A house divided against itself cannot stand.

Bradshaw has certainly profited from his humanistic work. He has treatment centers in Los Angeles and Houston, travels incessantly, earns over a million dollars a year, owns a home in Houston and a ranch in Montana, and plays golf in Palm Springs. Said the Austin American-Statesman, "Bradshaw's inner child has led him down a path he says he never dreamed of - a road to fame and fortune strewn with the emotional wreckage of thousands of weeping workshop participants." Where's the biblical joy? The peace?

Where is all this leading us? What conclusions can we draw? Basically, we are on the verge of a cultural and civilizational abyss. We are descending very rapidly into chaotic   darkness, the essence of yin (feminine). Cyclically, from the collective, fallen human action progression, we know we are at the end of a 510-year civilization cycle, at a time of slavery. Scientifically, we know that the electromagnetic field of the earth is becoming ungrounded and is in flux. The National Oceanic and Atmospheric Administration (NOAA) has reported that the solar-charged magnetic particles have been intense and jolt the earth. We also know that the signs of impending judgment are with us, unless our merciful God intervenes. We know that women, who are by their very nature ungrounded and vulnerable naturally to the influence of Satan's kingdom, are effectively ruling today - in family, church and state, either directly, and/or indirectly through monetary means or by manipulation/influence/seduction. We know overall this present-day matriarchal malaise is ungrounded, lawless, and emotionally expresses its values of its unredeemed heart in an unbiblical, feministic way which is increasingly rooted in witchcraft. It has no root in itself. It is not established. We know the next generation coming up will be even worse off than the present one, unless God intervenes. Our youth have no substantial patriarchal model. Finally, we know that the massive pain and suffering resulting from the inevitable bloodshed stemming from such upcoming rebellion, anarchy, lawlessness, and/or oppressive statism is

God's judgment. The flip side of the coin is that we will be reaping what we have sown because in our hearts we have not grounded and established ourselves as loving disciples in obedience to His Law-Word with the new heart He has given us. We are without excuse, for in our hearts, we know He's right. May God have mercy, which He might if we're tenderhearted, and repentant, far less likely if we're hardhearted. When we process God-given values from our heads through our hearts, we can be more fully alive, more integrated, response-able (masculine/yang) and responsive (feminine/yin).

SELF-WORTH

There are volumes and volumes being written today on self-worth and self-esteem. We even see talking heads on television endlessly discussing how all of our emotional problems stem from having low self-worth and self-esteem. What about a fallen, inherited sinful nature?

Clearly both the Bible and honest psychological research demonstrate that self-worth/self-esteem stem from three sources: 1) knowing who one is in God; 2) making a sacrificial contribution to those who are close, like family and church, and making a contribution to one's fellow man arising from the development of one's unique gifting/calling; and 3) clearing the sin (dark crystals) out of one's being so one is integrated consciously and subconsciously, spiritually, mentally, emotionally and physically.

The present "me" generation is the most selfish one in this country's history. The love of money/greed/selfishness is the root of all evil. Thus, evil is widespread today because everyone is so selfish. Accordingly, it is no accident that self-worth and self-esteem are lacking and that the self-esteem movement focuses on the individual and how he or she can, in some god- or goddess-like fashion, achieve on his/her own, a high degree of self-worth/self-esteem. This, like all of Satan's lies, is deceptive and leads to failure. It is man again, humanistically on his own, attempting to be as God.

Let's look at self-worth/self-esteem from God's perspective. All of us have limited time, limited information, limited money, limited energy and limited capabilities on this earth. We have boundaries, limits. Therefore, we're capable of only one thing perfectly - error, or in the Bible's word, sin. Therefore, unless God communicates to us who He is, and who we are uniquely in Him, and who He has created us to be, we will never know who we truly are. Therefore, it is important that we first seek the kingdom of God and His righteousness for all these other things to be added to us, such as self-worth/self-esteem.

Sigmund Freud and Carl Jung both confirmed the biblical truth that when men and women live according to The Golden Rule and The Second Great Commandment, they develop a sense of self-esteem/self-worth. Men and women must develop their unique God-given talents and callings for the purpose of serving their fellow man. It is their fellow man's purchase/appreciation of a unique good or service, coupled with their approval given for the goods and/or services rendered, that builds up the self-worth or self-esteem of an individual. Nothing else lasts.

Religious Christians miss this point by a mile. They mouth some religious mush and tell their fellow man whatever they're doing (any and everything) is for the service of God. The way we serve and love God (fulfilling The First Commandment) is by living according to The Second Great Commandment/Golden Rule. In other words, in order for us to fulfill Commandment #1, see Commandment #2. This is what Jesus' parable of The Good Samaritan is all about.

Look at it this way, in a sense we are all like the apostle Paul - we are all salesmen. (Paul "sold" the Gospel.) We have to have something to offer in the free marketplace of life, or of what use are we? A businessman must offer viable goods or service if he is to stay in business. A teacher must be able to explain and teach the subject matter to the students for them to be able to learn or the teacher is of no value. A doctor must be able to heal his patients or the practice is in vain. A worker must be able to provide valuable labor to an employer if he/she is to maintain a job. A man or woman must submit their surrendered will unto God or what use are they to God? They are wood, hay and stubble to be burned up - not precious stones that can withstand the test of fire.

We must offer something to others; we have to give before we receive, if we are to have any value or use in life. Otherwise, we are parasites and/or predators on our fellow man. There is certainly no sense of self-esteem or self-worth that comes from being a predator or a parasite, a selfish user of people. Take, take, take, manipulate, deceive, intimidate, seduce, use - all lead to emptiness, anger, pain, suffering, bitterness, physical distress and no self-worth or self-esteem. Question: How can a government bureaucrat develop self-worth or self-esteem?

What about in our personal relationships? Let's say a man or woman is single. What does each of them have to offer the other in a potential relationship? Do they have character? Are they honest, trustworthy, loyal, organized, kind and gentle, giving, possessed of a servant's heart, loving, caring, sharing, thoughtful, considerate, helpful, hard-working, diligent, truthful, joyful, faithful, humble, self-controlled, slow to anger? If either the single man or woman are void of these values and character traits, what good are they to a prospective mate? None. They are useless. They are just another selfish human animal parading on the stage of life, looking for someone on whom to prey or suck on like a parasite. There is no basis for self-worth/self-esteem in a predator or parasite.

Have the man and woman developed their calling? Do they have a skill that will contribute to the general welfare of their mate in a marriage? Do they have assets rather than debt to bring to the relationship? If not, what use are they? Do they have shared interests? Do they have the capability of being supportive? If not, what good are they in a team relationship? What do they have to offer, to give? What do they bring to the table of life? Do they have the ability to love? God's perspective is that the greatest demonstration of love is when an individual sacrifices his own life for a friend. An individual crosses the bridge from darkness to light, from sickness to health, from death to life when he/she loves sacrificially. At this point, self-worth and self-esteem soars, when more joy comes from bringing joy to others than from receiving.

If void of these godly attributes, such a man or woman consistently runs head-long into failure in relationships in life, and instead enters the dark death spiral down of low self-worth/self-esteem. It is sad, but it is what dominates the pale human landscape of America today. It takes hard work to develop both character and calling, both professionally and personally, in putting others' needs first in all things. We have to die to self in order to live. But it is in this process that we clear personally and become Christ-like - integrated consciously and subconsciously, spiritually, mentally, emotionally and physically.

We simply don't move from death to life, from darkness to light, from sickness to health, from sorrow to joy, from rejection to acceptance, and from loneliness to love, clear abandonment and chaos, to a strong sense of self-worth and self-esteem, until we first learn to serve and then love it! Until it feels better to serve our fellow man than it does to receive, we will not have passed over the threshold from Satan's dark, closed, deathly, fallen, natural, earthly realm into God's open, light-filled supernatural kingdom of life. It is by meeting the needs of others in a godly self-sacrificing, kind and gentle way, obedient unto God, that our self-worth/self-esteem is established.

TENDER HEARTS/HARD HEARTS

The Bible describes the enemies of God as being "hardhearted," while those who draw near to God are characterized as "tender-hearted." The dividing line between the hardhearted and the tender-hearted is not only disobedience versus obedience to God's com-mands, but is also manifested in attitude and behavior toward other human beings. The status of the heart also determines an individ-ual's self-worth. The hardhearted have a low sense of self-worth, the tenderhearted have a high sense of self-worth. In other words, there is consistency and unity in God, the Great All in All. Those tender-hearted who line up with God's righteousness have joy and peace and a healthy sense of self-worth on all levels - spiritually, mentally and emotionally. They are also physically healthier.

What are the differences between the tenderhearted and hard-hearted? First, there is an inherited curse or a blessing toward the hardhearted or tenderhearted, back in an individual's ancestry at least four generations (30 ancestral possibilities). The genetic code handed down provides a spiritual/psychological/biochemical/men-tal/emotional/behavioral blueprint toward being either hardhearted or tenderhearted. In Biblical terms, the sins (errors) of the fathers and, more accurately, the mothers, are visited upon the sons and daugh-ters. (Much more genetic information is passed down through the mother than through the father.) There is also evidence that the time and place of birth, and the concomitant frequencies given off by planetary angles, programs the pineal gland of an individual, electro-magnetically establishing a behavioral predisposition.

Next, the way a child is raised (plus environmental influences - TV, movies, radio, peer groups, etc.) in his/her first 10-12 years, also establishes the "natural" thinking/feeling/behavioral pattern for that child throughout life. The logic centers of a child do not really kick in until ages 10-12 (12-14 Hz/cycles per second). Before then, the physical/natural senses are primary - sight, sound, taste, touch and smell. The child is literally absorbing information, soaking it in sen-sually like a sponge and programming his/her delta, theta and alpha brain rhythms - the spiritual/subconscious zone. (Delta is 1-3/4 Hz/cycles per second; theta is 3/4-6/7 Hz/cycles per second; and al-pha is 6/7-12/14 Hz/cycles per second.) This is why the Roman Catholic Church has long said if it is given a child for the first six years, and preferably the first 12 years (through the 6th grade), it will own him/her for life. Research indicates only two percent of people actually change their behavioral patterns significantly (reprogram their subconscious) as they go through life. The gate of change is indeed narrow. Thus, how important is the biblical training up of a child in his formative first 12 years? It is critical! How much more important is being "born again" for a change of heart? It is vital! Ninety-eight percent of the people would rather suffer and stay with what is familiar to them (fear of the unknown), even if it is physically and/or emotionally painful, rather than go through the excruciating emotional pain of growth that leads to altered beliefs, attitudes, opinions and behavioral change. To truly mature, one must walk through the change of behavior, however painful, in order to cancel the old subconscious software programming and establish the new. When values, thinking and behavior alters, emotions will follow suit. Works are proof of faith.

Information that we take into our minds, 85 percent of which comes through our sight, is first subjectively interpreted through our brain's emotional center before being processed by our logic. Few indeed are those who ever really ground out (narrow is the gate) to discipline (disciple) themselves to be obedient to God's Law/Word (values and subsequent thoughts), and then use such as a basis for emotional perception, discernment and behavioral response.

Emotion rules nearly all individuals. Dr. Glen Rein of the Heart Math Institute has established how the head and heart interrelate psychologically and physiologically. Emotions arise out of either reinforced spiritual values (positive emotions), or violated spiritual values (negative emotions). For the undiscipled (undisciplined) individual - young believer or unbeliever - emotions not only color, but determine thoughts and actions. For the most part, such folks are like robots, repeating the genetic patterns of their ancestry, birth pineal programming and their early training. If there are no godly established values, then such an individual is like a reed floating on the water, blown to and fro by the whims of the wind, by the circumstances of life. He/she has no grounding, no anchor, no godly yang male vector that provides direction, law, and linear cause and effect, in which the feminine matrix of emotions (like meaning and beauty) can be tempered, attached and grounded.

We want to build on the solid rock of Jesus Christ, on God's Word, rather than on shifting sand. The righteousness of the mature Christian provides the basis for the Holy Spirit to bring peace, joy and a tender heart. People seek the love, light, life, liberty and laughter (joy) of God, which is available to the tenderhearted, but the only way to obtain these qualities is to first have a foundation established in His Law/Word. This requires a sacrificial long-term view. Only through godly obedience do the tenderhearted enjoy love, joy, peace, goodness, kindness, gentleness, faithfulness, patience, longsuffering, humility and self-control - the complete fruit of the Spirit.

For the tenderhearted, in terms of their relationships with their fellow man, it comes down to living experientially day to day, according to the Second Great Commandment ("Love thy neighbor as thyself") - the restatement of the Golden Rule ("Do unto others as you would have them do unto you"). It is only by treating our fellow man in a godly way that we show evidence of loving God, thereby fulfilling the First Great Commandment. It comes down to selflessness of the tenderhearted versus selfishness of the hardhearted. Remember, it is the love of money/greed/basically selfishness that is the root of all evil. This selfishness of pride and autonomy is the first manifestation of rebellion against God. It leads to the hardhearted acting and reacting out of fear, rather than faith. How can it be otherwise? The hardhearted are at war with God. Anger often disguises this fear and hurt. In anger, the hardhearted emulate Satan, who is angry like a roaring lion, prowling around and seeking those he can devour. The hardhearted use (consume) other people. They intimidate and seduce, rather than negotiate. They are envious, jealous, scheming, often consciously cruel, and often wrongfully hurt others by taking advantage of the naive, trusting and innocent.

Selfishness, pride, lawlessness, rebellion, fear, anger, lying, addiction to natural sensations (self-indulgence) are all part of the sin (error) cluster of the hardhearted, whose spiritual eyes are closed as they follow Satan to death. "The wages of sin are death." As such the hardhearted should heed the warnings of Proverbs 8:26: "All those who war against Me wrong their own souls. All those who hate Me love death."

As made very clear in the book of James, we know people by their works. Therefore, we observe the behavior of the hardhearted versus the tenderhearted. The hardhearted are autonomous, lawless, discontent, contentious and selfish - doing their own thing regardless of who it hurts. They are takers and users, predators and parasites. By contrast, the tenderhearted are content to be under authority, to live lawfully, to give before receiving, often unconditionally giving, are merciful, humble and peacemakers.

The tenderhearted cross the bridge into the "peace that passes all understanding" where the Holy Spirit can operate fully in his/her life without being resisted, grieved or quenched. When a Christian reaches this place, then it truly feels better to give than receive, to bring joy to other people than for other people to bring joy to them. It is a wonderful way, the only way, to live in God's open system, the kingdom of heaven on earth.

The sense of self-worth that comes to the mature, tenderhearted Christian, is unknown and unfathomable to the unconscious hard-hearted person. Sadly, very little of this full heart joy is known in the professing Christian community. After all, this is true love - sacrificial service. It follows the example of the Lord Jesus Christ when He died on the cross sacrificially for us. Next, Jesus was glorified in heaven. In a sense, God's tenderhearted share that glory too in their high sense of self-worth on earth by living according to God's purpose for their lives and in harmony with their fellow man and God's creation.

Such a tenderhearted individual negotiates his/her differences with others, rather than using the power/fear of intimidation or the seduction of guilt. The tenderhearted seek cooperation instead of competition that mark the hardhearted. The tenderhearted are peacemakers, with the use of contracts and the keeping of covenants being paramount. Being indwelt by the Holy Spirit, the tenderhearted can experience the unification of their conscious and subconscious (the conscious beta and the subconscious alpha, theta and delta rhythms), by way of prayer and meditation. This leads to joy and a righteous peace, which is the epitome of the Christian life. Here one can give thanks for all things, where holiness and compassion walk hand in hand.

Only the tenderhearted have the ability to truly love in an intimate relationship. Love is based on sacrificial service to another, the ongoing conscious, thoughtful, heartfelt desire to please a loved one in both word and deed. Only from these strong roots can true affection and passion grow. Passion arises from compassion. The hardhearted never know love or how to love. Love as sacrificial service is an alien, ridiculous concept to them. So, in their mindless striving, they self-destruct in the darkness of their downward spiral of selfishness, the root of all evil. By contrast, desiring peace and harmony rather than conflict, it is easy for the tenderhearted to gently say such things as: "I'm responsible." "I was wrong." "Forgive me." "I want to grow." "Let me help you." "I want to forgive and forget." In such a state, God's tenderhearted are full, open, complete, living in the joy of the present moment which is the only place joy exists, while "forgetting those things which are behind." The hardhearted are enslaved in their own closed-down state, being insecure, incomplete, fearful, angry, jealous, envious, striving ruthlessly for what they know not. They are unfulfilled and unsatisfied by the sensual pleasures of "the lust of the eye, the lust of the flesh, and the pride of life" - always seeking, but never finding that unattainable security, control and approval which may have existed in the mother's womb. For the hardhearted, it is a pitiful and pathetic state where there is never enough money, sex, power or pleasure.

There is also a sexual difference between men and women when it comes to being tenderhearted versus hardhearted. If men and women miss their God-given roles by the time they reach age 40, particularly in Western culture, they often move into accelerated self-destruction. They become bitter rather than better. Women usually lock into a rage, and men into self-induced, closed-in bitter isolation. God designed man to be the initiator and woman to be the responder. Man is yang/light; woman is yin/dark. Man is the vector; woman is the matrix. If they are tenderhearted, together they can harmoniously make a beautiful spiral up - building spiritually, mentally, emotionally and physically (in that order). Equitably, because man is the initiator, the giver, he inescapably has authority (covering) over the woman in order for her to receive and feel cherished. Then she can give positive feedback. This is even manifest as basic truth in the physical/sexual differences between a man and a woman - man the initiator and giver, woman the receiver and, biblically, an empty vessel. Man is active, wo-man is re-active. A man must give and cherish his woman on at least a 2:1 basis, and the woman, in return, must fulfill and respect her man, giving back on at least a 1:2 basis.

It follows that the greatest sin for a man and a woman, going back to Adam and Eve, is for a man to rebel against God and become hardhearted, leading to irresponsibility (response-unable), and for a woman to rebel against God and become hardhearted, leading to dominance. In such sinful (erroneous) states, they destroy themselves. A man must do good to feel good. In other words, a man must be responsible (response-able) to have a positive sense of self-worth. When a man manifests his primary sin of becoming irresponsible, he is not only in rebellion against God, he also ends up with a low sense of self-worth. In a similar manner, a woman who does not allow herself to be cherished so she can be filled up and feel good to do good, and instead, in a rebellious hardhearted way, seeks to dominate, use and destroy her man, destroys herself. He is her ground. Being dominant is a masculine, active, aggressive act. In this state, a woman is not receptive. She cannot be cherished. And yet, she must be receptive/cherished if she is to be able to be sustained because she is by design an empty vessel - a receiving unit. So, a woman who manifests her primary sin of being dominant self-destructs and has a low sense of self-worth also. She does not feel good so she cannot do good. Dis-ease is a naturally following byproduct of low self-worth.

In conclusion, as Scripture teaches, it is better to give than receive. Moreover, when we lose ourselves, we find ourselves in Him. There is no more fulfilling and joyful life than being tenderhearted, as there is no more unfulfilling and joyless life than being hardhearted. The cutting difference between the tenderhearted and the hardhearted ultimately comes down to first fearing and loving, and therefore keeping, God's Law/Word, so that the Holy Spirit can work in an individual's life to bring about the fruit of the Spirit and a tender heart. In this righteous tenderheartedness comes completeness, peace, joy, and the unity that an individual enjoys with God, his fellow man, and God's creation. It is an upward spiral for those who have first sought the kingdom of God, the open system, and His righteousness, so that God can add unto them everything else. Literally, to him who has, more is given. By contrast, for the hardhearted, to him who has not, it is taken away, in the death downward spiral. In the death spiral, the unclean spirits (demons) feed on Satan's characteristics of murder, selfishness, lying, self-indulgence, wicked imaginations, mischief, lust, jealousy, envy, discontent, cruelty, anger, fear, rebellion and pride. No one is more unhappy than the hardhearted unbeliever who is at war with God. He/she above all men/women is to be most pitied.

THE GOOD SAMARITAN REVISITED

Jesus, in Luke 10, using the parable of the good Samaritan, drew the dividing line between self-righteous religious types and true Christians. Jesus made the point abundantly clear that he who shows compassion, mercy, and sacrificially serves his fellow man is a true child of God.

To review the parable, a man who was traveling from Jerusalem to Jericho had the misfortune of being stripped by thieves, wounded and left half-dead. In his helpless state, he was passed over by the religious types - a priest and a Levite. The religious types were too busy doing what they wanted to do, too preoccupied (under the guise of doing the Lord's work) to help a man in need. But a Samaritan, a non-religious type, had compassion and helped the unfortunate victim. This was a true act of Christian charity.

Religion may talk a good talk, put on a good show, and make an impressive pious appearance, but it is basically selfish, has its own agenda, and is marked by a lack of humble, personal, sacrificial service to mankind.

From this parable, we also learn that true Christian stewardship and service many times occur outside of organized religion. In other words, all of us are in full time Christian service all of the time. And from this good Samaritan (whom the Jewish religious leaders despised), we glean a great deal regarding what wise Christian stewardship is all about.

First of all, we learn that the good Samaritan was compassionate. For how many of us does compassion begin our Christian perspective on other people? Isn't compassion the opposite of judgment? Isn't the first inclination of most people, including religious Christians, to judge? Aren't we instead commanded, "Judge not, lest ye be judged"? There is a fine line between discerning with righteous judgment and condemning with judgment.

Next, obviously the good Samaritan had not taken a vow of poverty, thank God! Nor was he foolish enough to go on a dangerous journey with only the naive mystical concept that "God will take care of me." No, sir! The good Samaritan planned ahead. He knew what provisions he would require for such a perilous journey. He took his savings (note that he had some savings) and purchased appropriate provisions - bandages, oil, and wine. For the journey this

Samaritan brought the tools necessary for the task at hand. Because of savings, wise purchases and planning, he was able to execute his stewardship duties.

It's obvious this good Samaritan's animal was well trained, too. This beast of burden carried the poor man (who had fallen among thieves) without incident. Further, the good Samaritan took the poor fellow to an inn where they stayed the night. And the Samaritan picked up the tab. But what is really impressive was this Samaritan's business dealings with the innkeeper, and how he went the extra mile to assist a helpless stranger.

First of all, the good Samaritan did not consider extracting from the unfortunate traveler the cost of his room and board at the inn, much less the cost of the spent provisions. Nor did he lay a guilt trip or "Chamber of Commerce line" on the innkeeper to try to get a cheaper rate or entice the innkeeper into keeping the unfortunate soul at no charge. Instead, the good Samaritan took the responsibility on himself (to whom much is given, much is expected), and paid the innkeeper cash for his services. Obviously the good Samaritan was not broke or tapped out with debt as are far too many religious Christians today.

The good Samaritan's word, his verbal contract, carried tremendous integrity and clout. This is evident from the fact that the innkeeper did not challenge the good Samaritan's promise to pay for the care of the poor fellow when he returned.

How many Christians have this type of financial rapport with members of their community? How many people do we know, who think so highly of our integrity, word, covenant and contract, that we could tell them flat out to take care of someone for us regardless of cost, that we will pay them the next time we see them?

And, of course, the final and obvious point in this parable - who among us as Christians can say we have fulfilled the Second Great Commandment as well as did the good Samaritan, who truly loved his neighbor as himself? Loving our neighbor as ourself obviously involves much more than some verbal, maudlin, "I will pray for you, brother," phrase. As the parable of the good Samaritan clearly shows, truly loving our neighbor as ourselves entails careful planning, saving, provision, sacrifice of time and money on the behalf of others, compassion, skill, a good credit record, and the integrity of our word, covenants and contracts. The good Samaritan also had excellent first aid training. Otherwise, he would not have been able to save a man who was already half-dead.

Do we see this quality of Christian stewardship evident in Christian leaders and laymen today? Sadly, not often enough. No wonder the church and the nation are in such sad shape. Being a good Samaritan - helping others - requires much, much more than just tradition, singing hymns, praying, having fellowship, eating together, listening to preaching, Bible study, or going to church, as important as these things are. It's hard work, demanding comprehensive preparation and action, to be a good Samaritan like the one Jesus extolled.

THE WORST SINNER?

One of the best known of Jesus' parables is the story of the prodigal son. In Luke 15, Jesus discusses how the younger of a father's two sons secured his inheritance, traveled afar, squandered his wealth on harlots, ended up with the pigs, repented and then went home with the intent of working for his father as a servant. The father, excited to see his wayward son return, had compassion on him. The younger son repented. The father put fine garments on his returned prodigal son, killed the fatted calf and threw a party.

All this special attention given to the returning younger son angered the older son, who felt slighted. The elder son had served his father faithfully, without exception, and yet the father had never thrown a party for him. The father reminded the oldest son that he (the elder son) was with him always, and that everything the father had was his. The father, in other words, kept his law-word covenant with his older son. The younger son got nothing, no more inheritance. But the father felt it was the right thing to do to make merry and be glad because the younger son who was dead was now alive again, and who was lost was now found. The father showed compassion for his repentant prodigal son.

So much for a quick summary of this well-known parable. Now, stop and ask yourself a question: Whose sin was the worst, that of the elder son or that of the younger prodigal son? Be honest. In your opinion, whose sin was the worst, that of the older son who felt slighted because he had served his father faithfully and resented never having had a party thrown on his behalf? Or, was the sin of the younger prodigal son the worst of the two because he deserted his family and squandered his wealth with harlots?

Okay, now that you've made your choice as to whose sin was the most despicable - surprise, surprise! This little exercise tells you a great deal about yourself and how your personal attitudes measure up regarding God's Law-Word.

Two basic characteristics of God are His love and His law. The New Testament focuses primarily on His love, the Old Testament on His law. Of course, both work together simultaneously, in harmony. If we love God, we keep His law - His commandments. God gave us His law out of love, for our blessing. We find love emphasized in I Corinthians 13, while law is the focus of Deuteronomy 8 and 28. The point is, they both coexist and work together for good simultaneously.

Inevitably, over and over again, when I have given this test to Christians, Christians whose personal bias is toward the law say that the younger prodigal son's sin was the worst. By contrast, Christians whose inclination is toward God's love say the older son's sin was the most despicable. Political conservatives, in like manner, consistently say the younger son's sin was the more evil of the two, while political liberals declare that the older brother's behavior was the most reprehensible. Men tend to side with the law and declare the younger brother's sin was the worst, while women tend to side with love and declare the older brother's sin the worst.

All of these responses are unbalanced and therefore incorrect. Besides, it's not given to us to judge. Further, Christ paid the price for all sin on the cross, and any sin, without the covering blood of Christ, is a basis for God's wrath and judgment against mankind. Therefore, what this little test tells us is which side of God's equation we lean too heavily toward, which side we need to work on to develop a more godly balance in our lives, and whether we are given to being judgmental. We are taught that mercy is better than judgment, and so the father's response to his younger son's return was correct.

There is an interesting adjunct to this exercise. In Revelation 4, Jesus Christ's countenance, as it emanates from around his throne, appears like an emerald rainbow. So the color green is primary. Green is the color of balance, the mid-point in the red, orange, yellow, GREEN, blue, indigo, and violet seven-color spectrum. Also, Dr. Kate Baldwin, chief of surgery at Women's Hospital in Philadelphia for 20 years, worked with color healing and therapy. She confirmed ancient medical wisdom which states that green is the color of the heart. Well, we associate the heart with love. But green is also the color of the law in ancient writings. The Bible begins with the green Garden of Eden and ends with the green leaves of the tree of life healing the nations. And the very countenance of Jesus Christ's throne is emerald green, the perfect integration of love and law! From this perspective, the unified biblical harmony of Old Testament law and New Testament love, Western civilization has derived its legal doctrine of "justice tempered with mercy." This perspective then, at minimum, should help us as growing Christians to resist confining God's Word to the area of our own personal preference and natural strength. After all, unless love and law both coexist in harmony, we don't have the "all clear" spiritual green light to go.

THE IGNORED SIN

Chapter 21, verse 8 of Revelation reads, "But the...unbelieving, abominable, murderers, sexually immoral, sorcerers, idolaters, and all liars shall have their part in the lake which burns with fire and brimstone, which is the second death."

Now, most Bible-believing Christians in the neo-pagan United States today - few though they may be - would whole-heartedly agree that, consistent with the justice of God, such unredeemed sinners who practice the acts listed above from Revelation 21:8 have their part in the lake of fire and brimstone, the second death. Unbelief, abominations, murder, sexual immorality, sorcery, idolatry, lying - all are sins that are readily recognized and acknowledged by the Bible-believing Christian body. But wait, there is one more sin listed in Revelation 21:8, one that is included at the first of this verse. It is a sin that most everyone has forgotten and ignored. It is a sin that makes the modern body of Christian believers uncomfortable. It causes shudders in the nod-to-God, Sunday social clubs. It is a sin that challenges the Christian body to take on the political, financial, scientific and economic occult Establishment. It is a sin that requires a yang (masculine) response. It is the first sin listed among all of these widely recognized sins in Revelation 21:8. It is the sin of COWARDICE! For Revelation 21:8 begins, "But the cowardly,..."

That's right, dear Christian brothers and sisters, cowardice is listed right up there as the lead sin followed by unbelief, abominations, murder, sexual immorality, sorcery, idolatry and lying! And, yet, if there is anything that has widely characterized effeminate Christian leadership in the United States over recent decades, it has been cowardice! We never hear about "cowardly women," only "cowardly men." Cowardice is a man thing.

Who in the non-Christian and Christian community alike would characterize Christian leadership today as generally bold and courageous in assaulting the gates of hell? Where is the Christian leadership that leads with the courage of faith that characterized the prophets of the Old Testament, the apostles of the New Testament, and our Christian Founding Fathers?

Are our prayers not being heard or answered? Have we cited our sin of cowardice? Have we truly repented and become bold and courageous? The next time we are laundry-listing sins, and we tend to get self-righteous because we're not unbelievers, murderers, sexually immoral, sorcerers, idolaters or liars, we must first look hard at the first sin listed in this verse, the sin of being cowardly. For if Christians are indeed "cowardly," they are listed right up there at the front of the pack with unbelievers, the abominable, murderers, the sexually immoral, sorcerers, idolaters and liars - all of whom have their place in the lake of fire and brimstone which is the second death.

SUPERNATURAL DISCERNMENT

The professional world, men who run this world, are by and large contemptuous of Christians. They say Christians are religious escapists who have no judgment. Unfortunately, this is a bad tasting morsel which too often we must swallow. This observation is accurate today in far too many cases.

While it is true that the children of darkness are wiser than the children of light (Luke 16:8), we are nevertheless called out of this undesirable, unwise state and commanded to be wise as serpents and harmless as doves (Matthew 10:16). This requires judgment/discernment.

Where the word "judgment" appears in the Bible, it may refer to God's effectively saying, "Enough is enough! I will pour out my wrath upon these people (or this person)." Thus, the word "judgment," as used in the Bible for God's action, is different from our modern usage of the word. When today we say that someone has poor judgment, we are saying that a person has poor discernment and poor decision-making skills.

Throughout the book of Proverbs, which provides us with practical applications of God's law, we are told to seek wisdom, knowledge, understanding, instruction and discernment. A well-ordered mind, which can think categorically and logically, work inductively and deductively, with both abstract principles and concrete facts, is more valuable than gold, silver and precious stones according to the Proverbs. Why? Simply put, because everything in this world is not black and white. There are many shades of gray. Leaders are often required to make lose-lose judgments and win-lose decisions. While God's Law-Word never changes, we are constantly discovering new facts and applications of those facts to God's creation. In turn, these facts shade, alter and sometimes uproot our previous understanding of Scripture. We take the principles of God's Word to the facts of His creation, and then the facts of His creation back to His Word. It's not an either/or process. It is both, simultaneously. The Word of God is a rule book of life, an outline, a blueprint. Where the Bible speaks, it speaks with absolute truth, but it does not speak exhaustively when it comes to all the facts of God's creation. We do not, for example, find in the Bible the assembly manual for an automobile, or an explanation for how gravity works, or how to trigger nuclear fission or fusion. We glean such from the facts of God's world.

The key to maturing - moving from "milk to meat" - as a believer, is taking the wisdom, knowledge and understanding gleaned from God's Word and from the facts of His creation and then applying them with discernment, day by day, moment by moment. This is why the Bible offsets principle with principle. We have to know the context, circumstances and situation where each particular principle applies. This requires discernment on our part, what we call good judgment. This is also why a principle of Scripture made absolutely autonomously true often becomes no longer true. Unequivocal truth not balanced by other biblical truth becomes heresy. Throughout church history, heresies are often nothing more than a good word (principle) taken to an extreme, such as discipleship.

We find examples that require this kind of discernment over and over again throughout the Bible. For instance, in Proverbs 26:4 we read, "Do not answer a fool according to his folly, Lest you also be like him." Then the very next verse of Proverbs 26 reads, "Answer a fool according to his folly, Lest he be wise in his own eyes." So what do we do? In verse 4 we are told not to answer a fool, but then in verse 5 we are told to answer a fool. It all depends upon the situation. Not situation ethics mind you. The Bible gives us unchanging ethics. But these ethics and principles are applied differently to the situational facts in God's ever-improving world. Is the glass half empty or half full? What's really important is the trend. Is the glass being emptied or filled?

In the much quoted John 3:16 we find, "For God so loved the world..." Then over in John 17:9 Jesus says, "...I do not pray for the world..." Whoa! It takes some "discernment" to discover which world is being talked about here by John.

In Psalm 139:21-22 David declares, "Do I not hate them, O Lord, who hate You? And do I not loathe those who rise up against You? I hate them with perfect hatred..." Then over in Matthew 5:44, Jesus says, "But I say to you, love your enemies, bless those who curse you, do good to those who hate you, and pray for those who spitefully use you and persecute you, that you may be sons of your Father in heaven..." Uh oh, just who is correct here? David, or the son of David? Obviously, both are true. Both must be taken in context. Both truths must be applied from time to time depending on the situation at hand. This requires discernment.

These paradoxes, these truths in tension, these "simultaneous co-existence of apparent opposites," found in Scripture are nothing more than a reflection of the very essence of God Himself. God is

Three in One in the Trinity, separate, yet united. God is both many and One. Jesus Christ is both God and perfect man. Why should we expect God's model to be any different in His creation?

Let's face it. Life is not all that simple. Only the religious try to make it so. Those who rise to positions of occupation dominion, and stewardship - to positions of leadership - have reached such elevated levels in large measure because they have developed the skill of discernment. Those who pay the price and acquire wisdom, knowledge, understanding, discretion and discernment cannot help but grow in favor with both God and man. God is perfect unity. He reconciles and harmonizes all things unto Himself. There can be no conflict with God. The better our discernment, the more peacefully we will live with all sane men unto God. And the more wealthy we will become as well. A well-ordered mind put to work leads to the blessing of prosperity. "The rich rules over the poor..." - Proverbs 22:7.

Albert Einstein once commented, "Science without religion is lame, religion without science is blind." In other words, Einstein was recognizing the truth that we must take the ever-changing facts of God's creation back to the unchanging principles of His Word, just as we are required to take the unchanging ethics of God's Law-Word and apply them to the situational facts of His creation. This is indeed no simple task. In fact, it will never be perfectly achieved. All men have imperfect knowledge of the mind and Word of God and also have limited knowledge with regard to the facts of God's creation. In this sense, all men are liars (Romans 3:4). All men have imperfect, limited truth and facts.

At minimum, the recognition of our imperfect state should keep us humble. Further, it should make us sensitive to the reality that we require the Holy Spirit to lead us and teach us all truth. We are dependent upon Him. Only with the Holy Spirit can we perfectly take the principles of God's Law-Word and the facts of His creation and apply them in His world to His glory. In this regard, Jeremiah 16:11-12 stops us dead in our tracks. In these two verses, the prophet Jeremiah tells us in no uncertain terms that there is a worse sin than walking, serving and worshipping after other gods, and that there is also a worse sin than forsaking God and not keeping His law. What heinous sin could be worse than these? Jeremiah 16:12 tells us: "And you have done worse than your fathers, for behold, each one walks according to the imagination of his own evil heart, so that no one listens to Me."

That says it all. Worse than walking after, serving and worshipping other gods, worse than forsaking God and not keeping His law, is the abominable sin of a man thinking his own thoughts, imagining things in his own evil heart, and not listening to God. Such a man effectively blasphemes the Holy Spirit. He resists, grieves and quenches the Holy Spirit. Thus, we flounder and sin egregiously in the discipleship and stewardship responsibilities God has given us. We must be led day by day, moment by moment, by the Holy Spirit.

Without the ever-present work of the Holy Spirit in our lives, working off God's Law-Word which we have established in our hearts and minds, we have no true discernment. We become despicable New Age humanists in God's sight. Therefore, just as God's eternal salvation for mankind required a supernatural solution through the person and work of the Lord Jesus Christ, the temporal salvation necessary for the redemption of His creation also demands a supernatural solution. ("Thy kingdom come, Thy will be done, on earth, as it is in heaven.")

Regardless of how much Bible we know and apply, regardless of how many facts we can recite and apply, unless we pray and submit to the guidance of the Holy Spirit in all matters, we have no comprehensive biblical discernment. The Christian way of thought and life is thoroughly supernatural!

The Holy Spirit is what the New Agers are attempting to counterfeit with their "spirit guides" - demons, much like witchcraft is a counterfeit for prayer. How dare we as Christians leave our discernment to our fallen natural minds? The unseen battleground of Ephesians 6 is manifested in our visible world. Spirit is living energy possessed of personality and purpose for influencing the creation. The purpose of the Holy Spirit is to tie things together for us so that we might reign victorious and Jesus Christ be glorified in us. We cannot defeat the supernatural with only the natural. We need supernatural discernment for victory.

PRAYER

I now conclude my prayers with, "In the name of the Lord-God Jesus Christ, Through the power of His precious, holy and redeeming blood and Word, Through the enabling work of the Holy Spirit," prior to "Amen." Why? "In the name of the Lord-God Jesus Christ" establishes Jesus Christ as the highest authority in heaven and earth, the Creator and Ruler of all His creation. "Through the power of His precious, holy and redeeming blood and Word" takes us from His throne room in the heavens back down to the earth where His perfect keeping of His Law-Word and His blood sacrifice provided the eternal and temporal salvation for mankind, also redeeming His creation. Finally, we have, "Through the enabling work of the Holy Spirit," the most powerful force in the spiritual universe to activate our prayers as sanctioned by God.

Given the power of the above, it is no surprise that when Christians truly have the faith to take prayer from their heads (knosis) down into their hearts (epiknosis), that one Christian prayer warrior can put a thousand of the enemy to flight, and two can put ten thousand to flight.

Of course, Lucifer has his counterfeits, astrology and witchcraft. Astrology is using the heavens, specifically planetary angles which affect the human organ systems as well as the phosphorus/nitrogen ratio in the human body, at precise times in order to attempt to influence or determine the behavior of the natural man. The natural man is influenced by such astrological activities because he is subject, in fact enslaved, to the natural fallen, imperfect order. Thus, his/her pineal gland, which is geometrically programmed at his/her first breath at birth, the programming determined by where he/she was born, the time of birth, and longitude and latitude, can be accessed by astrologers for the purpose of working their nefarious will individually. Collectively, astrology is used to time events in the collective consciousness. Astrology is thus the Luciferian occult attempt to usurp the rightful predestinating will of the Lord-God Jesus Christ, as He sits at the right hand of God the Father, ruling over the heavens and earth.

The blood sacrifices of the likes of chickens, goats and even humans by witches is a counterfeit occult attempt to steal the living magnetic grounding reality of blood and use it for incantations and spells to influence human behavior and other forms of matter. Like astrology, witchcraft - particularly when it involves blood sacrifices - also uses living energy for the purpose of significantly influencing matter, specific humans, events or whatever. But when we compare the historic personal blood sacrifice of the Lord-God Jesus Christ to the blood sacrifices of witches, and Jesus Christ's rulership of the heavens versus the astrological use of planets by astrologers, we can readily see how much more powerful Christian prayer can and should be when it correctly accesses the heavens, "In the name of the Lord-God Jesus Christ," and then accesses His blood and Law-Word on the earth, and then calls on the activation of the Holy Spirit for implementation of prayer.

It has been purported it would only take 27 pure-hearted Christians, united in focused intent and prayful purpose, to put the entire army of Satan to rout on any particular matter. Ideally, this would occur in church. For an excellent discussion of "What Is The Church?" order the September 1995 Chalcedon Report, No. 362, P. O. Box 158, Vallecito, California 95251. Because of the power of prayer, Satan, the master of deception, uses so many distractions to keep Christians from praying, from having faith in their prayers, and from praying with focused intent together, particularly in church.

When we confess our sins to God and forgive others, it effectively puts us in the same position with respect to God as the High Priest of Israel enjoyed in the holy of holies, when he wore the 12 gemstones on the breastplate and communicated with God. It also establishes us in Christ, for these 12 living gemstones perfectly networked in the 12 organ systems of Jesus Christ, who was in constant contact with both heaven and earth. We become living laser beams, living plumb lines, when we truly forgive others, ask for forgiveness personally, and have the faith that Jesus Christ as our advocate and propitiation has covered our sins and will handle our prayer request.

It is also important that as we petition God the Father, we then offer up heartfelt words of praise, worship and gratitude. Next comes our prayerful petitions for the needs of others and then ourselves. We bind on earth so it is bound in heaven. We loose on earth so it is loosed in heaven.

Then, when we hold our prayers in faith in the parasympathetic side of the autonomic nervous system as connected to our hearts, after we have first activated our prayer through the sympathetic side of the autonomic nervous system as connected to our hearts, we have initiated the most powerful activating and holding forces in creation. Prayer is a head/heart (masculine/feminine) integration. Thus, when husbands pray with their wives, it is like a microphone integrated with an amplifier. We may then end our prayers appropriately, "In the name of the Lord-God Jesus Christ, Through the power of His precious, holy and redeeming blood and Word, Through the enabling work of the Holy Spirit. Amen."

SECTION C

LOVE

LOVE: THE SECOND GREAT COMMANDMENT

The practical application of the Second Great Commandment in our day-to-day lives is one of the true blessings that demonstrates God's love, blessings that extend not only to His chosen but to all men through the principle of common grace. When applied in the marketplace of life, particularly where liberty exists, it means all men have the opportunity to live together peacefully.

Where the Spirit of the Lord is, there is liberty. Why is that true? It is true because the sword of the Spirit is the word of God and comes from God's supernatural realm - His open system. God's law enters time here on earth where the law of sin and death applies (law of entropy). When His law is applied here, then the individual or the masculine principle (yang) can be emphasized, and that's the principle of liberty. Basic to our heritage is the idea that an individual has importance because he is created by God for a purpose. The purpose has to do with fulfilling his calling. So, if he is created for a purpose and he is fulfilling his calling, this means he has to have freedom for that to occur. Freedom is very precious because it is absolutely tied into God's will for mankind, man's individual destiny, on the earth. This in turn led to the free marketplace, where men exchanged their wares, the output resulting from the development of their God-given calling.

Let's begin with the basics, the Scriptures. In the First Great Commandment Jesus said, "'You shall love the Lord your God with all your heart, with all your soul, and with all your mind.' This is the first great commandment. And the second is like the first, 'You shall love your neighbor as yourself.'" Here's where the rubber meets the road.

"If someone says, 'I love God,' and hates his brother, he is a liar; for he who does not love his brother whom he has seen, how can he love God whom he has not seen?" - I John 4:20. "Let each of you look out not only for his own interests, but also for the interests of others." - Philippians 2:4. In other words, if we're going to fulfill the First Great Commandment, we first have to fulfill the Second Great Commandment. Unless we love our neighbors as ourselves, how can we love God? This is a real line in the dirt that distinguishes Christianity from religion. This is a very important difference because those who practice "religion" always make a pretense of serving God, while riding roughshod over their fellow man and/or doing their own thing. In Christianity, faith is demonstrated by service to one's fellow man and loving one's fellow man whom one has seen, a demonstration of the fact that one does love God.

This creates a problem, because not only are we made in the image of God, but we are also formed from the dust of the earth, so we have a spiritual nature and we have a physical or an economic nature. If we're always serving our fellow man without something coming back to us as so many well-meaning ministers and other caretakers have done over the past two or three decades, we get burned out, used up, drained dry - there's nothing left. Then what do we do? How do we find a balance?

If we can understand the principle of how the Second Great Commandment applies in life to our fellow man, it will free us from all the anxiety, all the tension, and all the guilt that so many Christians have wrestled with and felt. It will also resolve the internal dialectic tension between how to meet our own needs and how to serve God by serving our fellow man. More specifically, in serving our fellow man, how do we demonstrate that we are fulfilling not only the Second Great Commandment, but also the First Great Commandment, and simultaneously that each of us not only looks out for our own interests, but also for the interests of others?

Beginning with Philippians 2:3, "Let nothing be done through selfish ambition or conceit, but in lowliness of mind (humility) let each esteem others better than himself." It can be seen again that we are not to look to our interests only, but also the interests of others. I John 2:15 states, "Do not love the world or the things in the world. If anyone loves the world, the love of the Father is not in him." Then if we move over to I Timothy 6:10 we read, "For the love of money is the root of all evil." The love of money - greed, is the root of all evil. But if we look up that word in the Greek and really dig into the base meanings of love of money or greed, what it comes down to is selfishness. So, it is really selfishness that is the root of all evil. This is just the opposite of what love is, because love serves and love gives. Selfishness takes.

Now, a basic principle in the Bible is what I call the T-N-T principle, the principle of the paradox, the simultaneous co-existence of apparent opposites, or the Truth-In-Tension. We find apparent conflict in a situation. For example, in a scientific sense, just as there is a left brain and a right brain and a corpus collosum that creates balance between them in the male and female, in truth in tension in the Trinity there is a Father, Son and Holy Spirit, separate but united.

This same principle exists all through Scripture. What we are going to address here is how we as individuals can deal with our fellow man in every endeavor in life, the human action marketplace, and meet our own needs while serving God and our fellow man (the definition of economics is human action, according to the great Austrian economist Ludwig Von Mises).

We all need love and money; love, representing our spiritual needs (made in the image of God) and money, our physical or economic needs (formed from the dust of the earth). There is only one way to have both love and money, and that's God's way - living according to the Second Great Commandment. This commandment, "You shall love your neighbor as yourself," in Matthew 22:39 is quoted from Leviticus 19:18 - the New Testament again building on the Old Testament. A master biblical principle that comes out of this is the principle of reciprocity. In other words, "Do unto others as you would have them do unto you" - the Golden Rule. This principle resolves the ultimate religious, political and economic question of how to reconcile the rights of the individual with those of the collective. Every society wrestles with whether to emphasize the rights of the individual or the rights of the collective, a dilemma first resolved in the Christian Godhead (Trinity).

Now, the natural man - what the Bible also refers to as the old man - will naturally be conflict-oriented and take a short-term view. The interpersonal transaction between people (you vs. others) will lead to a win/lose situation. However, the long-term outcome is lose/lose.

On the old TV series, Dallas, the character of J.R. Ewing was a rascal if there ever was one. Certainly, he believed in the win/lose philosophy, and the conflict-oriented, survival-of-the-fittest, evolutionary standard that undergirds Western civilization today. Remember, it is not conflict that brings about prosperity, it's cooperation contracting in the marketplace that brings about prosperity. If conflict brought about prosperity, all of us would be rushing to invest in Iraq and Lebanon, or maybe North Korea or Bosnia. But money flows to where there's peace and harmony so there can be a cooperative exchange of goods and services, and people can network. In the concept of the heavenly city, where we have saints in God's presence, the environment is one of cooperation and joy. J.R. Ewing certainly became rich and met his money needs, but he was always frustrated in terms of being loved. This is certainly often true among the rich and, particularly, the super rich in this nation.

There is no real joy in being a hermit, in being a loner. Real meaning in life comes from relationships with people. So, how do we serve God, serve our fellow man, and also serve ourselves in a balance? We don't do it with a short-term view. Again, what God requires if we as individuals, and our society (the collective), are to win, is to take the long-term view. This is the closest we can come to being God-like, because God is eternal. The Christian perspective is one of work and of service to others. This way we serve God. As a result of serving others or esteeming others better than ourselves and looking out for their interests, we are paid and then we win. We serve God by serving our fellow man and as a by-product we serve ourselves, which leads to cooperation long-term, truly a win-win transaction. Thus, this scenario achieves the reconciliation of the rights of the one with those of the many and resolves the conflict between the collective and individual.

The caveat with achieving this desirable situation is that living the Second Great Commandment requires risk-taking. Nevertheless, risk is basic to reward in life - the greater the risk, the greater the reward. Why do bankers often lose so much money making real estate loans? Because they really don't want to take any risks. They tend to wait until all the information is available and then they are willing to loan money. Well, when everything is known about something, then the risk is not there. If the risk is not there, the reward is not there. So, any time we know everything about an investment - it's on the front page of The Wall Street Journal or the cover of Time magazine or U.S. News and World Report - it's time to be careful.

Being willing to take a risk applies to people as well as any area of life. This means that we have to have some faith in the unknown, in the unseen, in the future. A way to handle this, in choosing to be involved with people, relationships and business opportunities in all areas of life, is to always run the risk of getting hurt or losing money short-term. In other words, we give an individual enough rope to either build a bridge or hang themself, and we pay for the rope. Then we will find out the nature of their character. By contrast, when we find ourselves turning inward and being defensive, then we've buried our talents, whether it's in an economic sense or a political sense, a personal sense, or an action with our family, friends, or church, etc. God expects us to multiply our talents; that means there is a risk involved. So, we extend enough rope to an individual to either build a bridge for our relationship long-term, or to hang himself short-term. We may get hurt short-term. On the other hand, if a great relationship comes out of it, the rewards could be many times over what the risk would be. That's the long-term view. It's not a natural security-based view, but it is certainly in keeping with what God intends for us to do in His Second Great Commandment. In a biblical sense then, we are all to be entrepreneurs, to take risks.

Look at the difference between the Hebron slaves that came out of Egypt and the Israelites after 40 years of hardened risk taking in the wilderness. There was a real difference in perspective, in courage, in risk-taking, when it came time to take the land.

Inescapably, throughout economic history, people of a culture who are willing to take the long-term view - who save, invest and accumulate capital - are the ones who end up with the wealth. This leads to the second golden rule: whoever has the gold makes the rules. Again, every scriptural principle, applied in the realm of time, requires us to take that long-term view. So, we must think and act long-term. In 1992, I had a meeting with a number of Singaporeans when I visited that country. Their long-term plan extends 250 years. When I was in London back in the early '80s I had dinner with one of my clients. I asked him about his investments. He said one investment was his annual purchase of port from the south of Spain which he stores in temperature-controlled, underground caverns in Scotland for his yet unborn grandchildren. As Americans, are we thinking long-term, multi-generationally, in saving up a heritage or inheritance for our children's children as Scripture commands?

If we are to be successful overall, there are four basic underlying principles of behavior that make it possible: 1) humility; 2) responsibility; 3) empathy and 4) duty. These principles are nothing more than reflections of the individual (the masculine principle) and collective society (the feminine principle) coming into balance.

Humility, a basic Christian virtue, and responsibility are individual and personal. We don't grow from milk to meat personally unless we have humility and responsibility.

What about with respect to other people, collective? We have to exhibit empathy, understand what they are thinking and feeling, what their needs are and then perform our duty toward them. When these four principles are first applied in the basic voluntary institutions of family and the church, they bring us into harmony with what God intends as foundational in terms of serving Him, serving our fellow man and, as a by-product, serving ourselves.

Additionally, where there is economic prosperity, there is a fourth win - the win of the creation. The creation can only win when there is economic prosperity. In poverty-stricken Third World nations, the environment is plundered as inhabitants attempt to scratch a living out of the land. In bureaucratic empires like the former Soviet Union, the environment is plundered and ravaged.

The way we interact in a godly manner with our fellow man is through the covenant or contract. Covenants are personal. The contract is basic to impersonal interpersonal interaction. What is a contract? A contract is a governmental, religious and economic document. A contract has a legal basis; if I don't fulfill my part of the contract and you don't fulfill yours, we have access to the courts for relief at law, for damages. We've been injured. A contract is religious because it is no better than the morality of the two parties to the contract. It is economic because there is consideration given and consideration received. So, we're back to the basic equation that undergirds all of life as it is first implemented or activated in the Second Great Commandment - that is, government everywhere is always religion applied to economics.

There is no such thing in the abstract world as the separation of church and state. Sure, we can separate the church as an institution from the state. Different men run the church than those who run the government. But because all governments through their legislation enact religious ideas about right and wrong, good and evil - ethics and morality frame the arena that we call human action or economics. Therefore, what kind of religion we have determines what kind of government we have and what kind of economic system we have.

Personally, we have the contract, such as the marriage contract. The best way to establish this comes from our having a personal sense of humility and responsibility, and having a sense of empathy and duty toward our mate. This means government, in a Christian sense, is first self-government, then the government of the home, the local church, the local business, the local community.

This winning perspective doesn't come naturally. Children have to be taught it. Children are like slaves; they live what is called a vertical lifestyle - they are dependent. If we grow older and still remain dependent upon the government, we're just older children, or larger, older and heavier slaves. A contract, on the other hand, is horizontal, establishing a balance of power between the many and the one, between individuals and their government. The U. S. Constitution is a contract between "we the people" and the government. Put differently, when the masculine or individualistic principle is emphasized in society there will be a balance of power, greater prosperity and more peace because it's horizontal, not vertical, plus, it is "bottom up." "As iron sharpens iron, So a man sharpens the countenance of his friend." - Proverbs 27:17.

What happens when things go wrong in our lives? First of all, it's critical that we forgive, so we are forgiven. Moreover, from all the verses on forgiveness, it's clear that God doesn't have us forgive for the benefit of the person who has wronged us. He has us forgive that we might release the burden of anger and resentment. For example, let's say a car salesman rips us off and sells us a "lemon." Do we think he's going to care that we're carrying a grudge against him for the next two years? Is that going to hurt him in any way? Probably not, but it's certainly going to do damage to us. It's going to create all this negative E-motion, this hostile, harmful energy-in-motion inside our systems. We're going to have negative thoughts and negative emotions that will be hard on our countenances, our physical systems, our spirits, and our fellowship with God. We have to confess our sins, and we have to forgive others, if we're to be forgiven. That does not preclude the fact that this car salesman who sold us a "lemon" owes us restitution. Restitution is the flip side of forgiveness.

There are unforeseen circumstances in life where charity is required. But Christian charity is for the purpose of restoration. It is not for the purpose of putting someone on the dole who then stays dependent, like a slave or a child, forever. The purpose of Christian charity is a short-term remedy, thereby helping our fellow man get back on his feet so that he can again become productive.

The underlying principles of humility, personal responsibility, empathy and duty are basic all over the world, a sign of God's common grace. Let's take the automobile traffic system - whether it's in Japan, the United States, Mexico (horror of horrors), Panama (even worse), or England (where they drive on the wrong side of the road). These four principles must be utilized in the traffic systems all over the world or the system won't work. For example, what if everyone got into an automobile and decided, "Hey, I'm going to do my own thing. I'm going to drive on the side of the road that I want to drive on, whatever is convenient. I'm going to do my own thing behind the wheel. I may drive down the center stripe backwards, going 60 mph, and ignore stop signs, red lights, and yield signs. I'm going to even go off the on ramp on the freeway." If everyone did this or something similar, it would be chaos, anarchy, and collective confusion/misery. Whether it's the marketplace of international currencies that trade a trillion dollars a day, or the automobile traffic system - the system works because of the Second Great Commandment. It functions according to the underlying principles of humility, responsibility, empathy and duty. When we get behind the wheel of a car, we do unto others as we would have them do unto us, we love our neighbor as ourself. With humility, we obey the rules of the road. We take responsibility for our vehicle. If our brake pads need changing, we change them. We make sure that our turn signals are operative and that our headlights are working. At the same time we are empathetic, watching what the other driver is doing, seeing what his needs are. If there is a yield sign on our side, then we yield to him. We have a duty to perform for our fellow man so he can also drive safely.

Think of it. All these individuals of all ages, of all languages, races, cultures and religions, with their own personal needs, are driving these potentially dangerous machines while serving the greater common or collective good. Everyone (individual/masculine/yang) meets his highest and best needs in terms of God's law of liberty and the law of love, maximizing his freedom and personal satisfaction, by living according to the Second Great Commandment and its basic principles. God has given mankind common grace. The world is at war with God's law, deceived, and yet the basic way our systems function best depends upon resting in the hands of God's law and obeying same.

A question which troubles us is, "Why do men and women return evil for good?" There is an old Scottish proverb that says, "You put a beggar on horseback, and he'll ride you down." A similar modern idiom is, "No good deed goes unpunished." Why do men and women return evil for good? They do so when they feel guilty, when they lack the character and/or ability to return good for good. Such men/women are lawless. They don't repay what they owe or they cannot repay what they owe, so they violate the principle of reciprocity, whereby we achieve relative equality. Men need to have a sense of equality with each other. Relative equality, comes through the uniqueness in each of us. If we all had the same talent for playing the violin, who would there be among us to appreciate another? It is our uniqueness, our individuality, our God-given talents that make us important to God, that make us important to our fellow man, and therefore decree our significance in terms of how good we feel about ourselves. Each of us has different skills, talents and callings.

When we develop our talents, we grow in terms of living according to the Second Great Commandment and we can then be in a position to trade with one another our talents, callings and gifts. We swap. There can be sharing and a mutual support system. We need and appreciate each other. As I serve you and you are satisfied, I have served God as He has commanded me to do. The by-product is getting paid with goods and services. If I have done a fine job, I receive your approval. Also, those psychological needs for approval and affection are often times as strong, if not stronger, than the financial needs because spirit rules over flesh. Living energy with purpose and personality (spirit) creates matter.

Sadly, those who return evil for good have to justify their wrongful behavior so that they can attempt to feel good about themselves. Even in prisons, studies by psychiatrists and psychologists indicate that hardened criminals have found a way to justify what they've done in order to feel good about themselves. People cannot live long feeling guilty. So, if someone has wronged us and they feel guilty and don't or can't repay what they owe, they violate the principle of reciprocity, of the Second Great Commandment. They break covenant or contract in order to feel good about themselves, then to justify their wrongful behavior, they manufacture lies or perform other evil that attempts to transform their benefactor into a devil.

How many people have we helped that have ended up shooting arrows in our backs with absolutely no justification whatsoever in terms of logic, reason or fair play? They have to turn us into devils to justify the wrong that they've done us. This justifies the evil that they do in their eyes and egos. This is why, in a real sense, the world hates Jesus Christ. The world is guilty before His perfection. It is guilty because we can't duplicate His sacrifice, the price He paid for our sins, our errors. There's no way we can repay Him for what He did. Moreover, the natural world will not pass onto others the fruit of His character and good works. Also, if we don't do as He has done and commanded, and forgive 70 times 7, then ultimately what we end up doing is warring with the King. The unredeemed world is at war with Jesus Christ because it's guilty before His law and can't repay and won't obey (rebellion) - so it has to repay evil for good.

We are all feminine (yin/collective) in a sense with respect to Jesus Christ, the bridegroom, because we are His bride. We are under His authority and thus, are obedient and accountable. If there is anything a response un-able (irresponsible) world doesn't want to be, it is obedient and accountable.

Three major subcategories of sin stemming from guilt are: 1) lust of the eye (gold); 2) lust of the flesh (gals); and 3) pride (glory). It is the same thing with reference to money, sex and power, which goes back to the natural, feminine, collective, childlike, basic needs for security, approval and control. Then the subclusters of sins arising from these three come forth like a stampeding herd of horses - sins such as being unappreciative, inhospitable, ambitious, jealous, envious, greedy, stubborn, inconsiderate, selfish, legalistic, judgmental, critical, quarrelsome, opinionated, attention-seeking, self-righteous, religious, full of delusion, fearful and ungrateful. How many pastors have seen this in their churches? Until the church cleans up its own act, the world is not going to take a good, hard, serious look at Christianity.

Hardened hearts crucify their benefactor, but by the mouth of two or more witnesses guilt is established. Repentance, restitution, forgiveness, compassion and mercy are all better than judgment. After all, those who are angry and those who hurt others are only hurting themselves long-term, as well as sinning against God. We strive to live according to the maturity of the Scriptures. The Second Great Commandment will not only resolve our personal problems, but will also be a light on a hill that cannot be hidden from the world. We will be less likely to return evil for good, and when such is coming toward us, we will be able to recognize it.

Christians, when dealing with God's Word day in and day out in its applications to all areas of life, come up against and have to go through, what I call the truth barrier. It's like a plane going through the sound barrier; it shakes a little, then it passes through or peels off and fails. When Christians come up against God's truth barrier, it will either quicken their spirits, change their hearts, their emotions, their minds, their behavior and they will pass through it and grow, or they will get locked into their own dark habits. It draws them down and they peel off. It's life or death.

Herein lies the real challenge. As mature Christians, we want to be marathon runners. At the same time, we don't know what other potential marathon runners are out there. Therefore, we always want to be able to give the Gospel to anyone who may be a potential member of God's elect by word or example, so they too can be awakened to the reality of their salvation and join us in the mission that God has given us here on earth to occupy until He comes.

Returning to the concept of T-N-T, Truth-In-Tension, there exists this dialectic - a simultaneous co-existence of variables that appear to be in opposition but really are complimentary. That's the way God operates, and the way He commands us to function. For example, to be a good leader we must serve. This is what Jesus Christ did. We have to take risks if we really want to be secure. We don't become secure by wanting to become secure - we become secure by taking risks. (Risk assumption is primarily a masculine/yang trait. Security, by contrast, is womb-based, feminine.) How many risk-averse investors have we seen lose fortunes by playing it safe and secure? There is only profit where risk exists.

How about approval? We all want approval, which is a feminine, womb-based need, just like security. But to gain approval, we have to give to others what they want first, both in the tangible and the intangible realms. The best listeners have the approval of others because they are empathetic and dutiful toward their fellow man. They're feeling, understanding and hearing others' problems just as a good salesman does. In a sense all of us are always selling ourselves and whatever we're doing. So, if we want approval, we have to give to others first what they want. This means that our own emotional and physical needs have to be subordinated first for us to be empathetic with the needs of others. We have to possess humility to recognize and align with the highest and best in others, and be responseable to meet their needs empathetically and with a sense of duty.

Finally, the third of the basic womb-based needs is for control. If we seek control in life it inevitably eludes us. We all have limited time, resources, knowledge, ability, power, mobility and energy. Total control is thus beyond us. We can't even totally control ourselves, much less others. Besides, we are only invulnerable when we are without defenses. Where we are defensive, we're vulnerable. When we leave everything in God's hands, have Christian love and faith, are anxious about nothing, and give thanks for all things, there is no fear because perfect love casts out fear. God is in control - omniscient, omnipresent, and all-powerful.

As we get older in life, energy-in-motion - E-motion - takes its toll on our bodies if we don't handle our E-motion correctly. As we approach 40, we either get bitter or we get better. Stated differently, as we grow older, we either live more by faith or by fear. Faith, again, is risk-based, and masculine (yang) because it involves hope for the future, hope in something which does not yet exist in the tangible world, but instead exists in the minds and hearts of men in the intangible and abstract world of spirit. (There is a piece of vacant land out there. I'm an architect, I see a golf course. It takes faith and work to create it. How about faith and work to restore a nation to its godly heritage?) Faith is followed by works because faith without works is dead. Faith is sightless and also futuristic.

Faith is thus the essence of growth and progress. The antithesis, the opposite, is uniform control, retrenching fear, security craving and the need for group approval which leads to stagnation, decay and death. "All who war against God wrong their own souls; all those who hate God love death." How many football teams have we seen attempt to sit on and control a lead only to have it erode away? Fear, security, control and being comfortable in the approval of the status quo will all inevitably lead to failure.

Life, which is energy in motion, E-motion if you will, is dynamic; it is never stagnant. Any time we are coasting, we're going downhill, and we do that naturally according to the laws of sin and death, which is the same thing as Newtonian physics' Second Law of Thermodynamics: entropy. We have established the importance of grounding ourselves in values arising from God's supernatural law to escape this earthly curse. This is law from outside of a fallen nature, coming from a Source who exists in His open system, the supernatural system. Scientists may call it the zero crossover point of the sine wave, integrating linear and cyclical time, so that our own natural emotion, E-motion, and chaotically flawed values stemming from our ancestry and culture don't lead us into error. In other words, we have to establish God's rule and law in our own beings and activate them, just as this basic principle of the Second Great Commandment demonstrates, if we're to have a chance of being successful in life and not fall victim to the womb-based needs of the natural, fallen man - the needs for security, control and approval. When we fall victim to them, we slip into error, which is one of the definitions of sin: "to miss the mark."

Scripture tells us to be anxious about nothing; to bring every thought into captivity to the obedience of Christ; to give thanks in all things; to renew our minds; that all things work together for good for them that love the Lord, to them who are called according to His purpose; that we are to overcome evil with good - not that we are to return evil for evil. We are to bless our enemies; to think on whatsoever is true, noble and just (masculine principle); and whatsoever is pure, lovely and of good report (the feminine matrix); and to meditate on whatever is praiseworthy and virtuous. As we do this we grow in grace. Growing in grace is growing in power. Total power is complete love.

A distinction I find helpful is the difference between grace and mercy. If I'm driving down the road at 70 mph on the way to the hospital with a man who has a broken arm and a highway patrolman pulls me over, sees that I'm in an emergency situation and doesn't give me a ticket - that's mercy. Same situation, and a highway patrolman pulls me over and now he's going to give me an escort at 90 mph to get to the hospital - that's grace, that's power.

As we grow in grace/power and love, our E-motions become increasingly still, quiet and at peace. "Be still, and know that I am God." - Psalms 46:10. Joy takes over. There is only joy in the present. The more grace and love we have, the more still we become, the more quiet and joy we experience. The past doesn't exist. We can learn from the past and it helps us make decisions in the present and for the future, but the past is gone. We always only live right here, right now. The future doesn't yet exist. When we are better able to live in the present moment, to be fully conscious in the now, then we can truly be. Then we are able to respond, to be responsible or response-able. The intangible things - the best things in life that are free - such as love, freedom, joy and health, become more manifest in our being. We become more relaxed, more at ease. We become more full of thought, or thoughtful. As we become more faithful, or full of faith, we are less full of fear, less fearful. The more we become this way, then the higher traits of God's spirit, the feminine/yin matrix so to speak, traits of compassion, kindness, gentleness and mercy, become manifest. We become overall more loving. Love is the primary characteristic of the supernatural Lawgiver covering both ends of the spectrum, yang and yin. This establishes the foundation (grounding) that makes life-giving E-motion possible. The Most High God is The Great Eternal E-motion, The Great Eternal Energy In Motion, who paradoxically, in T-N-T fashion, simultaneously stands still.

LOVE: MEN AND WOMEN

Part I

What we're going to explore in this chapter is how the principle of the masculine vector/impulse is linked to the feminine matrix. The masculine principle (yang) is individualistic, the many, linear like a laser, light-based, cause-and-effect-like law, and progressive with logical reasoning. The feminine matrix (yin) is holistic, dark, delicate, collective and more gentle and feeling. We want to examine these two perspectives in opposition to each other (which is a humanistic principle), and how they should be working together in integration - man at one end of the spectrum and wo-man at the other - coming together in the way that God intended, complementing and fulfilling each other.

Turning to Scripture, we obtain an understanding of why this perspective of the integration of man with wo-man is important. The theme is love - that God is love, and that God so loved the world He gave His only son, Jesus Christ. He didn't give a wo-man, He gave a Son, because it took a Son, who in His humanity, had a left brain tied to the positive masculine ground of the right foot, to ground with a feminine, dialectic, negatively-charged "Mother Earth." It had to be a Son because wo-men are ungrounded. This is why they are commanded to be covered. Moreover, Jesus had to be a Son (yang) to make progress in linear time, to restore the creation to its Creator, and to bring light to a dark and dying world.

Hopefully, we move to perfect love as we mature as Christians because we know that love covers all sins. In Psalms 119:97, David said, "I love thy law." It is called in the New Testament, "the law of love." Law is basic to love. Law is masculine (yang) - a linear principle. It is a sword, a vector; it is cause and effect that moves in a progression and is logical. "Thou shalt not..." Love, the feminine (yin), rests on law, just as the New Testament rests on the Old Testament. Here "love is patient, kind, does not envy..."

Both men and women have a masculine side and a feminine side. Men have a feminine core and women have a masculine core. When either sex operates out of feelings alone, without the law base, it is exhibiting the ungrounded feminine characteristic of lawlessness. When our modern culture operates on feelings, it means we have become overall a feminine and lawless society, like a mob.

In the United States today, not much is known about God's love or His law because we're living in an era of secular humanism where man - unlike what the Scripture admonishes us - trusts his own heart and his own feelings as to what is foremost in his life. This is dangerous. All values are religious because values are ideas about right and wrong, ethics, good and evil, morality, etc. When we have emotional responses, positive or negative, it's because we are experiencing the positive reinforcement of a value or the negative reinforcement of a value (or the reinforcement or support of a religious principle which we believe, or the violation of a religious principle or value which we hold). So, all emotional reactions ultimately come from values which are, at base, religious. The question is: What are our values? What is our law source which underlies those values, that gives rise to our thinking and emotional responses? Are they Scripture-based in a supernatural law? Or, are they coming from the human heart which is subject to the law of sin and death? Or, as the scientist would say, are we subject to the Second Law of Thermodynamics, entropy, winding down into death.

Dr. Peter Rothschild has written that the Sabbath is so very important because the created 6-1 quantum impulse leads to God's wonderful open system. (When the Scripture refers to the supernatural it means the quantum open system, not the closed system of Newtonian physics.) The open system's quantum (n) pulse is 6-1,6-1,6-1, which leads to growth and progress. So, we work six days and take a day off. If we are going to have progress, if there is going to be "occupying until I come" and dominion and stewardship of the earth, there has to be that 6-1 impulse. If we work seven days, then we are doing the same thing continually; it will lead to death and decay. So, keeping God's law is very critical. God's law is love. It's also life! Fear of the Lord and obedience to His Law-Word are masculine.

In Proverbs 8:36 we read, "But he who sins against me wrongs his own soul; all those who hate me love death." What is sin? Sin, by definition, is transgression of the law. So, there is a difference in obedience to law bringing life from God's perspective, and bringing death when we transgress, and are in opposition to God's law. Today, the United States is broadcasting death as a country. One of the root meanings of the word "debt" is death. Abortion is death. Arms sales promote death. Hollywood's production of violence is death-based, as are drugs. Ninety-five percent of the civil lawsuits in the world occur in the United States, which comprises 5 percent of the global population. Our Standard American Diet (SAD) is comprised of mainly fats and sugars. This is not life-bringing.

So, where are God's love and law in harmony? We read from the Master, Jesus, in John 14:15, "If you love Me, keep My commandments." In this scripture, love is linked inescapably to law. In I Samuel 15:23, we find that rebellion against God's law is as the sin of witchcraft. Witchcraft is feminine, tied to Mother Earth. Lawlessness is a feminine trait of all mankind. Witchcraft, by definition, is a humanistic, self-willed manipulation of energy for personal power or gain. Witchcraft is basic to Luciferianism. Witchcraft worships the creation, the "Mother Earth," Gaia, the feminine, rather than the Creator, the masculine - God the Father. Satan's (Lucifer's) first sin was the sin of rebellion. Eve's first sin was one of rebellion. Rebellion is lawlessness or, in the modern idiom, "doing your own thing," or "if it feels good, do it." By contrast, God's love is based on His law and again, is masculine.

But that's not the end of it. Our purpose is to build the New Testament on top of the Old; it is a progression. God's plan is for the progressive redemption of His people and His creation. It's not only, "If you love me keep my commandments," which is the masculine end, the grounding end, on which justice is based; there is also the merciful side of it. For that we go to I Corinthians 13:1-8. "Love is patient, love is kind; it does not envy; it does not boast, it is not proud; it is not rude, it is not self-seeking, it is not easily angered, it does not keep a record of wrongs.... Love bears all things, believes all things, hopes all things, endures all things. Love never fails."

So, we see that there is a principle here that used to exist in our legal system. We are to love mercy and do justly, as in Micah 6:8 and Matthew 9:13, and to love our enemies, Matthew 5:44. Mercy is better than judgment. I Corinthians 8:1 tells us that "Love edifies." The fruit of the Spirit is love: love, joy, peace, goodness, kindness, gentleness, faithfulness, patience, long-suffering, humility, self-control. The legal principle of justice tempered with mercy built the United States. The masculine is primary and the feminine is secondary. But mercy is better than judgment. In other words, it is better to live in the feminine. As in Scripture, "Wives, obey your husbands." Then it is, "husbands love your wives as Christ loved the church." The truth is that God's love is based in His law. We are to speak the truth, God's law, in love. It's not an either/or situation, it's both ends of the same spectrum simultaneously, masculine (yang) and feminine (yin), man and wo-man. These are co-existent equitable principles with the yin under the covering of the yang.

God is the One and the Many, separate, yet united. The Many is the individualistic or the masculine vector principle; the One is the collective or the feminine principle - the feminine matrix. Another way of looking at it is the forest and the trees. The trees are the masculine impulse/vector - individuals. The forest is the feminine matrix. God's creation is an expression of who and what God is, Father, Son and Holy Spirit - separate, individual, masculine, yet united as one - the individual and the collective, the masculine and the feminine together. We see the trees individually; we see the forest collectively.

When it comes to Christ's church, the non-bloodline family of God, we are all feminine. That's where we're headed, but we only get there on a masculine vector, voluntarily, individually, from the bottom up, horizontally. So, when the state tries to force collectivism or the feminine matrix principle from the top down, it gets into coercion. The Scripture says we have to die to live; we have to give if we want to receive. We have to go with the masculine individual principle before we are able to achieve the feminine matrix - and it's voluntary! God is a gentleman. He views our freedom of choice as more important than coercion. So, the government is really usurping the role of God as the ultimate lawmaker in society, filling the vacuum of unbelief. Remember, the source of law in any society is the god of that society. The state today fills the vacuum of what husbands should be in families and what elders - male elders - should be in churches voluntarily. When our homes and churches are in order, our nation will come into order.

In the 1930s, 60 percent of the black children in this nation were not born illegitimately. There was some black pride. As Dr. Walter Williams and Dr. Thomas Sowell, two black economists, have carefully researched and documented, in the 1930s, the black family was an integrated unit. It was a Christian unit. Black men as head of their families (light-filled masculine vectors) took pride in their wives and their children. Then the state came along as a substitute father and god and usurped their role. In doing so, it stripped the black man of his sense of manhood and his ability to be responseable. He really became response-unable. He lost his sense of response-ability, so to speak, and he had to do other things. As a result we've seen the fragmenting of the black family. Essentially, what we have now is a very chaotic situation - an uncovered, ungrounded feminine matrix, the root of chaos - in the black ghettos of our cities. That's what happens when a feminine, lawless principle exists in any society, in any particular group without the male, law base anchored in God's Law-Word. With its anchor, the feminine matrix brings beauty and meaning.

The many - individuals (masculine/yang) - leads to diversity. Only when there's diversity, as in the free moral market, is there progress and prosperity. By contrast, the collective (the feminine matrix/yin), the community, can be constructive if it's voluntary, or it can result in a mob, or disintegration of society as did the collectivism of socialism and communism in the former Soviet Union.

Vectors are initiators. That's the male principle - the many principle. The collective is a responder - the feminine principle. The activating force is electrical in the masculine vector, what the Chinese call "yang" or light, while the feminine matrix is magnetic, or what the Chinese call "yin" or dark.

This light/dark, masculine/feminine, yang/yin perspective is not just a Christian principle. This is a principle that falls under the umbrella of common grace that exists worldwide. The Bible makes it very clear that a woman is to be covered by a father, a pastor, and/or a husband, all three at the same time. In the Chinese culture "yin," feminine, means dark; "yang," masculine, means light. In the Hindu culture it's held that if a woman isn't covered, she's giving off destructive, chaotic, negative energy (Pordushukte). In the Islamic culture there is tremendous emphasis on the woman being covered, even in terms of the clothing she wears (purdah). So, in two clearly non-Christian, Far Eastern cultures - the Hindu and the Chinese - as well as in the religion of Islam, and also in Christianity, we see the principle of the importance of a woman being covered, or anchored to a male vector. The natural nature of a woman (the dark magnetic matrix) is that she is always out there in the spirit world, and unless there is a law-based anchor, preferably a godly anchor (covering) to keep her on track, Satan and the demonic realm have direct access to her all the time. The essence of the New Age Movement is feminine, lawless, and self-willed. It attempts to ground in witchcraft and Mother Earth. It is a lawless perspective with no male vector, no anchor, no ground, no law, no light.

The human brain is divided into two hemispheres, a left brain and a right brain. The law-based masculine yang left brain (which is also heavily involved with science, mathematics and engineering), controls the right side of the body. This energy runs down through the gall bladder, which has to do with judgment and law, and grounds out in the right foot which has a positive charge, while the earth has a negative dialectic charge. When there is a positive and negative together, there is a connection. This is not the case with women. Women are primarily right-brain oriented, with the right brain controlling the left side of the body. The bottom of the left foot has a negative charge. A negative charge on the sole of the foot repels the negative dialectical charge of the earth. Therefore, even electromagnetically, there has to be a man's covering for a woman to stay grounded.

The idea of the many, i.e. individualism (masculine/yang), as embraced by Western civilization, is law based. The Eastern perspective is feminine, the collective (yin). Where has progress come from? Why is the per capita income among Western Protestant cultures at least six times that of Catholic cultures and up to 20-22 times per capita greater than that of Eastern cultures unless/until they adopt Western perspectives? Because law, or the masculine vector, the many, is progressive and oriented towards cause and effect. In the Eastern culture, the collective, or the one, is basically like a squirrel in a cage - it's the same thing over and over again in eternal cycles. There is no real progress. Therefore, there is no real hope, and when there is no hope there is no basis for faith! A progressive culture is one in which individuals are risk-takers because where there is no risk, there are no benefits. And risk is based upon a faith in the future, in something that is not yet seen. Having a future-oriented faith means a society can move in a linear direction and make progress. A collective holistic, holographic perspective is the end result of voluntary vector activity. So, logically gentle-men are the Christian spiritual leaders because men inherently are the faith base for the feminine collective to be achieved in society, beginning within the family and the local church. If men don't rule in their individual families, in their churches and society grows from the bottom up, from individuals, how are they going to rule the nation? Men have to be response-able - able to respond, not irresponsible - not unable to respond. They have to be able to lead in a lawful gentle way, to be gentle-men.

The flip side of this coin is that women have to respect the authority of their male covering. If men aren't obedient to God's law, they are in rebellion against God. If women aren't obedient to the elders in the church, wives to their husbands, sons and daughters to their parents, as God directs - Christ, man, woman, children - then they are out in the dark matrix, the matrix of lawlessness, which is also rebellion. Rebellion is as the sin of witchcraft.

The way the male is grounded is what scientists call a Hertzian carrier wave, versus the ungrounded or the non-Hertzian, scalar, feminine wave. Dr. Glen Rein, speaking at the University of Wisconsin at Milwaukee in July of 1993, stated the Hertzian or the masculine carrier wave is absolutely vital for the non-Hertzian or feminine to ride upon. So, what we're finding is that God's truth applies to every aspect of creation or reality that we would like to investigate. The many (masculine) is a plus, the one (feminine) is a minus. Acidic is masculine, alkaline is feminine. Clockwise or compressing is masculine, counterclockwise or decompressing is feminine. In terms of colors and frequency; it is red vs. violet, do vs. ti in the notes on the piano which correspond in frequency to the colors. We can either use the seven basic tones or the seven basic colors, or we can go to the 12-tone scale which includes sharps and flats, or the 12 expanded colors which correspond with the 12 tribes, 12 gemstones on the high priest's breastplate, 12 acupuncture meridians, 12 quarks, 12 disciples and 12 tribes - God knew what He was doing. His Law-Word balances out and brings into harmony the yang and yin, masculine and feminine, individual and collective, the many and the one.

We as Christians are commanded to walk by faith, not by sight - a masculine principle. This is progress on the plumb line. There's the directional line again, the vector. Amos 7:8 says, "Behold, I am setting a plumb line in the midst of My people Israel." And, John 1:23 states, "Make straight the path of the Lord." There's the vector again. The masculine leads, grounds, covers, protects, and provides direction for and cherishes the feminine, which then can provide meaning and beauty.

In a paradoxical flip, as this works out, behind every successful man stands a supportive woman. Women need to know that they can be the greatest uplift to their man, or the greatest anchor weighing him down; women have incredible power. Remember, the hand that rocks the cradle rules the world, too.

All of us come into the world naturally flawed or sinful. There are three womb-based, psychological needs that all of us, men and women, have coming out of the womb: the need for security, the need for approval and the need for control. This is the equivalent of the lust of the eye (gold); lust of flesh (gals); pride of life (glory), or money, sex and power. We also have four fears which impact us during our formative first three years - the fears of chaos, loud noises, rejection and abandonment. If we don't have a supernatural law - a masculine base and the Holy Spirit - those natural womb-based needs and fears will overwhelm us since we naturally gravitate in that direction.

So, why did God appoint man as head of the household and put male elders in charge of the church? For 300 years, from the time the Pilgrims came here until the 1920s, men exclusively were involved with the law in this country in terms of voting, law enforcement, the military, judges - everything having to do with law. Why? Because it provided the balance! Unless men control the law, the feminine collective overwhelms and chaos results. The feminine womb-based needs, early fears, and the hand that rocks the cradle are too powerful and destructive unless held in balance by male-based law. Men and women alike are drawn to these womb-based needs.

Ideally, what we want to come to - and some of this comes from Dr. Henry Monteiff, a leading scientist, physicist, and mathematician - is the vortex. As the male light vector moves through the dark feminine matrix, the matrix oscillates around it and together they move into a vortex. The vortex can be either very, very healthy when based in God's law (and as has been shown in terms of the type of water that produces the healthiest vortex and is the healthiest water to drink) or it can be very unhealthy, as in a tornado. It depends on the spin; it depends on if it's in control (law) or if it's out of control (lawless). The vector and the matrix ideally unify as a lawful vortex. (See the cover of this book).

Differences between men and women are being discarded today, with the feminine principle primarily being emphasized in our educational systems, in our movies and society. But the differences are absolutely vital. An important book along this line was published in 1991 entitled, "Brain Sex: The Real Difference Between Men And Women." Also, in the moral free market, when there is diversity (masculine), then there is real freedom and real prosperity. Individuals (masculine) working together in the moral free market need each other and they voluntarily come together forming a holistic, peaceful collective (feminine). And when men are men and women are women, there is progress. It is differentiation in nature that results in progress. We're taught in our society that women are the source of light. Actually, the womb - the yin - is dark. It's a matrix; it's potential and magnetic. It is the masculine vector, the electrical charge, which provides the spark in the womb that produces children. Men are the initiators, the source of light. We're also taught in our society that men are the source of war. However, when there's individual power, which is a masculine principle, in the political, economic and religious realms, then there is a balance of power. And when there's a balance of power, peace results, not war. It's only when there is an imbalance between a huge collective in the government with immense power, and the many individuals not having power, that we have war.

This is not to minimize the importance of the feminine. Without the feminine, life would be unfulfilling. The feminine controls the visual, the spiritual, the emotional, the overall picture. The right brain, the feminine brain, provides embellishment. It is like art. Art is possible in a society that has excess capital and economic prosperity, just like environmental integrity is possible when a society has enough wealth or excess above that which is necessary to provide for its subsistence. Is there environmental integrity, a very feminine collective "Mother Earth" issue, in Somalia? No, there's not. There is no economic prosperity - no basic subsistence level of economic livelihood is available there - so there cannot be integrity of the environment. How about in the former Soviet Union where the state was the epitome of the feminine collective? Was there environmental integrity there? No, Chernobyl is a good example. The old USSR is very polluted. But where the feminine matrix is able to ride on the masculine vector, preferably of God's law, then we have excess capital, by which the beauty of the feminine matrix can come forth and allow for the things in life that make it so much more enriching, creative and beautiful. But taken by itself, such cannot exist because the matrix is just potential. It is dark and empty, and implodes on itself in lawlessness and chaos when on its own. Think of a woman with a barren womb who blossoms into a mother with a loving husband providing covering.

The left brain is verbal, linguistic, detail-oriented, practical, concrete and orderly - that's a law of perspective. It is masculine. Men have to be response-able, responsible. So, ultimately, if we look at the problems of society, it comes down to men not running their households (as it did with Adam); or leading their local churches; or exercising merciful, lawful authority generally. If those two basic institutions are handled correctly, with mercy preferred over judgment, from that the nation-state will arise in a godly, limited fashion. Do we have anything close to this today? Not by a long shot.

The natural godless tendency of men is to be irresponsible, giving up their lawful authority. Men, as initiators, should be responsible. With responsibility flows authority. The natural godless tendency for women is to become dominant, just exactly what they shouldn't be, the law-head. Women are receivers by design. When each assumes the other's role, both self-destruct. In society-at-large - the collective - risk is faith in the unseen and it is male, whereas security, approval and control operate in the realm of the seen. This is feminine. Who makes money in society? Those who take risks, the entrepreneurs. It's only with risk, stemming from faith, looking forward in a linear fashion to the future, that prosperity and progress come. If we instead reemphasize approval, control and especially, security, in the seen world, what happens? We fall behind. We stagnate and decay. Life is progressive.

Given this perspective, a paradox arises: The right brain of the woman is naturally always out there in the spiritual, but she naturally gravitates to the seen. Yet it was the man who was given dominion of the earth and put in charge of the church (the spiritual). Adam was created and the first thing he was given was a job to tend the creation. But God saw it was a lonely job, and so Eve was created as a helpmate. However, Eve was not created like Adam from the dust of the earth - she was created from man. In Scripture, the emphasis is on the calling that the man is given. A woman is fulfilled in her calling to be a helpmate to him in his vocation. The children fall in under that united umbrella. We can look at such recent examples as Jimmy and Rosalyn Carter, Ronald and Nancy Reagan, Bill and Hillary Clinton - where the woman is supportive and joins in the man's calling. In these examples, the woman actually made the man. For a man, there is no greater fulfillment, no greater happiness, no greater godly response than being fulfilled in his calling, because the nature of men is to emphasize what God has given them to do in their work, since they are left-brain oriented. Women desire to feel cherished and important, but that's going to happen best for them when they are involved in their man's work.

Seeing it in other ways, it's like a general who is chief of staff and has another general working for him. They're both generals, but there is a superior/subordinate relationship, too. Or, it is like a king and his queen. The king wants to be respected, the queen wants to be cherished. Or, it is like a two-person volleyball team, with the man as the captain. The man in the home has dominion. As a result of having dominion and being the lawful head of the family, the woman gets rest. Rebellion is not just against civil law. Men rebel against God's law, women rebel against their husbands. Children rebel against their parents. Church members rebel against the elders in the church. It is not first overt, political rebellion, it is first rebellion of the mind and of the heart. Remember, God virtually equates the two. "As a man thinketh in his heart, so he is." The New Age tells us to trust the heart, which God says is desperately wicked when not bounded by His Law-Word. Moreover, since rebellion is as the sin of witchcraft, it is no accident the lawless New Age has as its religious base, witchcraft, and as its economic base, a dying Mother Earth.

The correct perspective is that there is to be a contrite spirit and a contrite heart. The masculine moves down in a contrite spirit as the covering and lawful authority over the feminine with her broken spirit. As a result, the feminine spirit responds in obedience. The feminine, in a contrite heart, moves down to rest on the grounding of the masculine broken heart and the masculine response to the feminine is mercy. The masculine moves toward the feminine, the feminine moves toward the masculine and in that comes the unity of equity in the marriage. Do we have this in our society today? Anything but, in far too many cases.

Time magazine, February 1994, headlined, "Are Men Really That Bad?", with a man being portrayed as a pig in a pinstripe suit.

Basically, we are seeing a split, a dichotomy, between men and women rather than the unity God intended. How's this one? "Do white men have a future?" If white men don't have a future, then we're going to end up with the white culture repeating the chaotic history of the black community over the past 60 years. Another headline was "The Demonizing of White Men." This is not a coincidence. We're moving toward chaos, anarchy and revolution. Its foundation is rebellion and lawlessness which is the sin of witchcraft, basically Luciferianism. All these perspectives fit together:

From The New York Times:
"Women might not find this surprising, but one of the most persistent and frustrating problems in evolutionary (not creationary) biology is the male.

"Specifically, where did he come from and why doesn't he just go away?

"After many years of rubbing their chins so hard they are practically scraping bone, scientists say they cannot explain to their satisfaction why the great majority of species on earth reproduce sexually.

"It would be so much neater and more sensible if females were to do the whole reproductive business solo, either by making simple clonal copies of their eggs - as do some lizards and fish or by manufacturing in-house the sperm needed to fertilize the eggs, as do some worms and snails."

Men, Christian gentleman, are an endangered species in the U.S. today. But women do not benefit from their demise. The U.S. News And World Report cover story, March 28, 1994, was "The War Against Women: Violence, Poverty, Abuse." Another example is, "Human-rights Reports Decry Widespread Brutalization of Women," from the Associated Press. When we destroy the male vector, women inevitably implode into a chaotic matrix of darkness, anarchy, chaos and lawlessness. Women are falling further behind in country after country, and - here's the sad thing - in a non-Christian culture, their men like it that way. It happened in the so-called egalitarian Soviet Union. But this isn't a win-lose situation going on today in society, globally. If women lose, men lose. If men lose, women lose. Today the move is toward global anarchy and revolution - this ungrounded feminine perspective of the great collective, the New World Order, the feminine occultism of the New Age. In a pyramid-type New World Order, only the elitists at the top win.

Let's look now at the wise woman in Proverbs 31: "Who can find a virtuous wife? For her worth is far above rubies. The heart of her husband safely trusts in her so he will have no lack of gain." Isn't it interesting? This Proverbs 31 woman is a businesswoman. She wasn't involved in politics, she wasn't involved in animal rights, or in all these other activities that women are so involved with in our society today - the feminist movement, environmentalism, etc. She was involved in business. Her feminine right-brain was anchored in a left-brain activity that brought her balance. And her husband's heart responded to her emotionally and he had no lack of gain.

"She does him good and not evil all the days of her life." What is she doing? She's in business. "She seeks wool and flax, And willingly works with her hands. She is like the merchant ships, she brings her food from afar." Look at all the things she's doing! She's managerial, she's moving in terms of organization. She's operating left-brained, functioning just like an executive or a businessperson functions. Women need to be involved in a family business. Of course, mothers need to take care of their children, particularly during the first 12 years when the basic imprinting is taking place, via the theta, delta and alpha rhythms. Recall this biblical guideline: "Train up a child when he is young, and when he is old he will not depart from it." Why? Because those basic brain patterns in the subconscious of a child have to do with the spiritual knowledge and values that are established in those first six years, and even up to age 10 or 12. So, the husband-and-wife balance for the children in those first six years, and up to age 10 or 12, is critical. But at that point in time, it's time for her to move into a family business.

"She is like the merchant ships. She brings her food from afar. She also rises while it is yet night." Women have incredible energy. Have you men noticed how much more energy women have than we do? It needs to be put to productive use. Women working in business have excess money that their natural nurturing instinct can use to finance charities, and all these things that the civil government is doing that it should not be doing. These things should be financed from the private sector.

"And provides food for her household, and a portion for her maidservants. She considers a field and buys it:" She is managing her home; she is managing her family business. "From her profits she plants a vineyard." Do we hear in the feminine-dominated Hollywood about exalting profits, gains on buying and selling? No, we don't, but we sure hear it in the Bible. She girds herself with strength and strengthens her arms. "She perceives that her merchandise is good." In other words, she is a good analyst. She has a sharp eye for what something is worth. She has solid business judgment.

"And her lamp does not go out by night. She stretches out her hands to the distaff and her hand holds the spindle. She extends her hand to the poor..." Notice she has money and she feels good about how she uses it, in a compassionate way. She's serving her husband and her husband is profiting from her. She's financing all these businesses, and now what does she have to do? Instead of going to the state and saying, "Let's have all these welfare programs," she says, "I've got the money." "She extends her hand to the poor, Yes, she reaches out her hands to the needy. She is not afraid of snow for her household, For all her household is clothed with scarlet." She has taken a long-term view; she has planned and helped those all around her.

"She makes tapestry for herself; Her clothing is fine linen and purple. Her husband is known in the gates." The wife is the reflection of the husband. She has class and dignity. Because the wife is doing all these things, the husband is elevated in terms of his status in the community. So, a good evaluation of a man is to look at his wife. Such establishes the biblical perspective of his standing in society. "She makes linen garments and sells them, and supplies sashes for the merchants. Strength and honor are her clothing; She shall rejoice in time to come." There is that long-term view of future orientation, character and wise service. "She opens her mouth with wisdom, and on her tongue is the law of kindness." There is the balance: wisdom is the left-brain, the law, moving out; yet she has the natural, feminine, nurturing instincts, being right-brained by nature. So, she's in balance.

"She watches over the ways of her household, and does not eat the bread of idleness." She is not watching soap operas. She manages her home and stays productively busy. "Her children (as a result of all this), rise up and call her blessed; Her husband also, and he praises her: 'Many daughters have done well, But you excel them all.'"

In our society, by contrast, glamour is emphasized. What does the Bible say about this in Proverbs 31:30: "Charm is deceitful and beauty is passing, but a woman who fears the Lord, she shall be praised."

"The fear of the Lord is the beginning of wisdom..." - Proverbs 9:10. What is the first requirement that has to do with the fear of the Lord? It has to do with keeping His commandments, with keeping His law.

"Give her of the fruit of her hands, and let her own works praise her in the gates." This is like faith coming down to works. We look at someone's works and we can see where their faith is.

Today we have the opposite perspective as discussed in Isaiah 3: "As for My people, children are their oppressors." Children react emotionally naturally, and are not law-based, logical and linear. "And women rule over them." What is the result of women ruling? "O My people! Those who lead you cause you to err, and destroy the way of your paths."

Let's look at some history, from a book published in 1956 entitled "The Coming Caesars" written by a French historian, Amaury de Reincourt. This French historian observed, going back to ancient Rome toward the end of the Hellenistic age, that there was no greater revolution in Rome than that of women's rights. In the second century B.C., women became emancipated in every way, including economically. The United States' declaration that all men are created equal excluded women. Apparently the difference in essence was enough. "The growing role of women in the United States has led to many changes in public opinion, including the following: the desire for freedom to be replaced by security...."

In the feminine matrix we find the basics of security, control, approval, - needs that don't lead to progress. Security is feminine, freedom is masculine.

Quoting de Reincourt again: "In Rome, the increasing voice of women in formulating public opinion resulted in the establishment ultimately of a virile Caesar." Or, in our case, a result of feminine chaos and anarchy leads to a masculine-ruled bureaucracy, a fascist state that rules with an iron hand. The feminization of society is setting the U.S. up for a hard-core, Nazi-like, masculine rule. It's a trap. Masses of people, such as are found in the cities in the United States today, collectively display the emotionalism that's common to women. They must instinctively look for masculine leadership, which cannot be found in a congress, but in a Caesar, according to de Reincourt.

All this being said, men are ultimately accountable for not being response-able, for not providing justice tempered with mercy. This is the problem that de Tocqueville, the French historian, saw when he was in the U.S. in the 1850s. That is where America missed it. We stayed in legalism and/or materialism and we never really got into the law of God sufficiently. Therefore, it developed with what we might call the feminine matrix of the New Testament, so that the New Testament rode upon the legal masculine base that God gave us.

One of the reasons men were put in charge of the law is because men naturally understand mercy better than women. Men tend to be naturally irresponsible, so they tend to be more forgiving since in their irresponsibility they need mercy. Even in publications such as Lawyers Alert, we learn that if we are a defendant, we do not want women jurors because women do not understand mercy. A study was done of women gangs in Denver. It showed that the women gang members were unmerciful. Ask divorce lawyers. They say that far more often than not, men are more fair and just, and women are cruel and unforgiving. So, God in His wisdom knew what He was doing when He set up His order and put men in charge of the law.

Let's finally look at some comments made by the late Taylor Caldwell, a prolific author. One of her books, "The Pillar Of Iron," is about the time when Rome was sinking from a republic into a dictatorship. She wrote, in "The Devil's Advocate," about America 20 years after a socialistic dictatorship had taken over; she also penned "Captains And The Kings," which was about the power structure and the families that rule America.

Over a decade ago, Caldwell made a speech entitled, "Restore Your Dead Republic," about how American men have abdicated their courage, leadership, and fighting spirit, and how, because of that abdication, wickedness and tyranny are coming to rule America. "I hate to throw a somber bombshell into this festive gathering of patriotic people of good will, but life is too short to be sweet. With the matter of a catastrophe facing this country, we have a terrible alternative now. We actually have two alternatives. We can say, 'Hail, Caesar! We who are about to die salute you.' Or we can say what John Quincy Adams said in the first Congress, 'One day we freemen will have to exit. It is inevitable, but whosoever, whenever or however we go down we will exit as freemen.' I'm going to castigate all of you men here for what you have done to America, every mother's son of you. How did we arrive at this disastrous hour in time? I will tell you. You men, not your women, abdicated your manhood. You deserted your republic. Aristotle said 2,500 years ago, 'Masculine republics (individualism/yang) decline into feminine (collectives/yin) democracies and democracies into despotism.' This is what has happened to America now. We call ourselves a free country. We are not free. Tomorrow the tyranny will be overt instead of covert, as it is now.

"Now, above all, all you men have - what is that phrase - you have chickened out on your women and thrown them into confusion and terror. I've listened to some of you men who have defended yourselves to me. 'We want peace and tranquility,' men say. This will never be a peaceful and tranquil world until the last human being is dead (or Jesus Christ returns). Humanity by nature is violent and predatory. We are made that way. That's our natural instinct. And all the Sunday School teachers and the nice Nellies and psychiatrists will never change that. They are trying to make us all sweet and docile so we will offer no resistance to despotism. Is there any hope? Well, only a little, and I'm afraid that few men will take advantage of it. 1) Challenge your government, and if you suffer for it, to hell with sweet peace. 2) Fight gun control. It is your right to bear arms under the Constitution, but the tyrants want to take away your arms so you won't be able to offer any resistance to bayonets. Last but not least, remember what Paul said: 'Man is for the glory of God and woman is for the glory of man.'

"Gentlemen, you can restore your dead republic, but be again the masters of your government, and be again the masters of your women. Or will you meekly say, 'Hail, Caesar, we who are about to die salute you.'"

LOVE: MEN AND WOMEN

Part II

Both men and women alike naturally gravitate toward the feminine womb-based needs of control, approval and security. When those needs take priority and dominate a society, it means the collective will rule and the civil government will be omnipotent. These instincts are such a powerful influence because every man, woman and child picks them up from the feminine womb. So, in a very real sense, women are far more psychologically powerful than men. God's plan to offset this natural tendency and to maintain a male/female balance is to put men in charge of the home, the church and the law.

The New Age is the lawless, witchcraft-based, Mother Earth-worshiping, Luciferian attempt to establish a counterfeit New Testament "Christian New Age" without Jesus Christ and without His laws of love and liberty. The New Age tells us to trust our hearts, contrary to Jeremiah 17:9 which tells us, "The heart is deceitful above all things and desperately wicked: who can know it?" The New Age philosophy tells us we are reincarnated, yet the Bible tells us that it is appointed to man once to die, and then face the judgment. Biblically, we make progress through dominion over a lawless and dying Mother Earth, and then we exercise stewardship. In the New Age, by contrast, we evolve. There are some very subtle dividing lines between what the New Age is teaching, with the counterfeit millennium that it is attempting to create, and the Christian perspective.

The feminine magnetic matrix, which is like an empty womb or a black hole, without masculine covering, grounding and vectors, will implode and crash in on itself, resulting in chaos and anarchy. Democracies historically result in chaos and anarchy anyway, because they are in essence mob rule, which is emotional and collective. Order then will be attempted out of chaos which is the pagan idea of the phoenix arising from the ashes. There is a Luciferian plan in existence now for the year 2000, and by no later than 2008-2012, for the New World Order to arise from the chaotic ashes of present civilization. Out of that comes a very harsh, masculine rulership executed by a harsh inhumane bureaucracy, in which neither men nor women win. It's a most dangerous time for a woman, because in a violent, chaotic time of anarchy, the harsh male vector rules without compassion. The most dangerous position for a woman to be in today is to be ungrounded, uncovered, practicing New Age witchcraft lawlessly out in the dark spiritual matrix, particularly with the increase in occultic and demonic activity.

In 1850, the historian Alexis de Tocqueville, in his classic work, "Democracy in America," noted that the United States emphasized either legalism or materialism. That's still true in this century. The Reagan era epitomized materialism; the Clintons are legalistic, advocating more government laws. The U.S. is governed by more laws than any other people on the face of the earth. We squandered our potential because we became response-unable. Responsible Christian men should have established a gentle, kind basis for the implementation of God's Law-Word and His commandments so that the feminine matrix could blossom in this country. This did not occur, so we stayed with legalism or materialism. We never understood how to develop our culture in a gentle, kind way. There was too much, to put it in Hollywood's terminology, of a John Wayne mentality that doesn't reveal that love is patient, love is kind, it does not envy, it does not boast, it is not proud, it is not rude - all those things that are part of the feminine matrix aspect of Christianity. One of the most difficult things we must learn is to have God's Law-Word work in our hearts, minds and souls, and then eliminate any contrary influences from our culture, parental upbringing and genetic heritage.

Some scriptural passages that reveal how this spiritual feminine matrix operates in terms of the masculine vector are: "Whatever things are true, whatever things are noble, whatever things are just (masculine/yang), whatever things are pure, whatever things are lovely, whatever things are of good report (feminine/yin), if there be any virtue, if there be anything worthy of praise, think, meditate on these things." It's not either/or - it's both, man and wo-man. Woman came out of man. They're different ends of the same spectrum. They go together, but men as initiators lead and wo-men as receivers are team members. Another very good verse is, "The sword of the spirit is the word of God." There is the feminine (yin) resting on the masculine (yang). The woman is the amplifier because she's out there in the spirit and has the holographic right brain. If men want power in their prayers, in their homes they need to have their wives and their daughters submissive to them in prayer life, because they are the amplifiers. The man is a speaker, but unless he has an amplifier out there to broadcast his words, he will not have the power that he could have.

As men and women both approach 40, they either get bitter or they get better, depending on how well the word of God has circumcised their hearts, minds and spirits, and how well they become conformed to Jesus Christ. Men, if they become bitter, tend to become withdrawn. Women tend to move toward rage ("I am woman, hear me roar," as Helen Reddy sang). The key is to clear out the sin, or it starts to eat people up by the time they hit 40.

In early America, 90-95 percent of all American families were basically entrepreneurial families. They were farmers, ranchers or had small businesses, so it was a very natural thing for the wife to be working with her husband in the calling. That's what it took for them to make it economically. Today, for family continuity, a woman's business needs to be tied to her home, like a cottage industry, or if it's outside the home, it needs to be entrepreneurial, with the financial or managerial support of her husband, so that the godly covering is still maintained.

Historically, biblically, the husband's purpose has been to provide for, cherish, defend and instruct his family - his wife and then the children. Provision has an economic basis, because we know if a man does not provide for his family, he's worse than an infidel, or an unbeliever. This means that Christians who go off and serve the Lord and leave their families destitute are not doing God's will. Secondly, women need to feel cherished, usually with non-sexual touch, supportive and encouraging words and acts of kindness. Next, to defend comes from the concept that men are to love their families as Christ loved the church and gave Himself for it. Christ died for the church, so a man is to give his life to defend his family. The final point has to do with instruction. The best way to communicate is in a kind and gentle way according to I Corinthians 13. Being able to forgive and be merciful goes a long way; we catch more flies with honey than we do with vinegar.

A man tends to value only what he has a stake in. Therefore, the wife's family should not be paying for the wedding. The groom should pay for the wedding. He should pay a ransom or a dowry to the parents of the bride for the asset he is receiving. After all, the bride's parents raised their daughter and trained her in a godly way, and he's acquiring that asset. He'll appreciate her more, and her parents will be compensated for their efforts. This is a scriptural perspective, although it's certainly not our western culture's perspective. (If the feminists want to get behind an issue that's biblical, they ought to hop on board this one.) As a check against the immaturity, indiscretions and poor choices of youth, both sets of parents should approve of their children's marriages.

Men like to be honored, respected and to feel like they are most important in their home, that they are king of their family's castle, and that they have first place and final word there. If a woman helps a man feel this way, even if she's a little surreptitious, he's going to feel good about his wife and his home. Home is one of the few places, particularly today, where a man can have dominion. That's important to men. A woman, if she expects to feel cherished, will align with what's important to him. Her husband will come first - not the children, not her job. God created the woman out of the man; godly men therefore see their women as extensions of themselves. So, when a woman sees herself as an extension of who and what he is and who and what he thinks is important, she will feel cherished and fulfilled. This means it is very important that a woman's interests align with those of her man. Moreover, this is a practical consideration as men do not like to compete with women. There is no honor for a man in defeating a woman and there is only humiliation when he loses. So if a man competes with a woman, it's a lose-lose situation. Such will drive him away. Also, criticism, instructing and nagging do not change men. The overwhelming psychological, even contemporary, humanistic evidence supports this biblical perspective. It is a faithful, loving wife who, by her godly example, turns a man's heart. Even when the husband is incorrect, as long as he is moral, ethical and civil, he deserves the faithful obedience of his wife. Following her leader in that circumstance will cause God and most men who are devoted to their wives to see what a cherished vessel she is. At the same time, men must not put their wives down. Women have unique, God-given talents that are to be developed in the best interests of the family and themselves. (Again, Proverbs 31.) Women bring beauty and meaning to life.

Husbands and wives should ideally be in alignment on all four levels: spiritually, mentally, emotionally and physically. Religion is the basis of everything, because our religious ideas give rise to our values, and our values give rise to our emotional responses, both positive and negative. If husbands and wives aren't getting along emotionally, it is because there is a conflict of values, which means that at the base there is a religious conflict. If there is going to be a good marriage, it has to be spiritually grounded in the same basic beliefs; then there can be emotional harmony. In other words, as a man believes and thinks, so he is. If we have the same values, and if the Bible and its principles are shared in terms of commonly held beliefs, then not only will there be potential emotional compatibility, but mental perceptions will tend to be in harmony as well, as we subjectively interpret the reality that we see in the day-to-day world. From this comes physical compatibility.

Divorce obviously is not desirable. That is very clear in both the Old and New Testaments. Divorce brings violence upon the children. If not handled exactly right, which it seldom is, it is devastating to children. God hates divorce. However, there are cases of divorce in the Old Testament, as in the book of Esther, where the queen was put away (divorced) for her rebellion against the king. Additionally, Deuteronomy 24:1-4 gives the basis for a certificate of divorce. The New Testament, I Corinthians 7:15 says that a believer married to an unbeliever should not try to prevent divorce. (As an aside, a requirement for eldership [church leadership] in Titus 1:6 is for a man to be the husband of one wife. In other words, if a man had two or more wives, he's too busy to handle the responsibilities of eldership in the church.)

The male vector is basic, because the source of law is the god of any society. Law is masculine. Law rules. Are we going to be lawless or not? Will we be obedient or rebellious? That is the issue on which everything pivots. Matthew 7:21-23 states, "Not everyone who says to me 'Lord, Lord,' shall enter the kingdom of heaven, but he who does the will of My Father in heaven.

"Many will say to Me in that day, 'Lord, Lord, have we not prophesied in Your name, cast out demons in Your name, and done many wonders in Your name?'

"And then I will declare to them, 'I never knew you; depart from Me, you who practice lawlessness!'"

In the April, 1994 Chalcedon Report, Harold and Donna Kupp point out additional Bible verses which confirm the above: "'If you keep My commandments, you shall abide in My love' - John 15:10; 'If a man loves Me, he will keep My words and My Father will love him' - John 14:23; 'He that hath My commandments and keepeth them, he it is that loveth Me: And he that loveth Me shall be loved of My Father...' - John 14:21.

"Those verses clearly say that God will love someone IF they keep His commandments. Therefore, the doctrine of God's unconditional love of mankind is false. We must stop listening to the ear-tickling sermons of modern Christianity and let the scriptures speak for themselves about whom God loves...

"'The Lord loveth the righteous' - Psalms 146:8; 'He loveth him that followeth after righteousness' - Proverbs 15:9; 'I love them that love Me' - Proverbs 8:17; 'For I the Lord your God am a jealous God...showing steadfast love to thousands of those who love Me and keep My commandments.' - Exodus 20:5-6.

"According to those verses, whatever they may call themselves, all who are not keeping the Ten Commandments of God can be certain that God does not love them...The sinning Christian has been repeatedly told that: 'God loves you and has a wonderful plan for your life!'...Sadly, nothing could be farther from the truth, for their end shall be eternal destruction. Can we despise God's grace by flouting His law and be loved?" "All that war against Me wrong their own soul; all those who hate Me love death." - Proverbs 8:36.

Here is some scientific and other evidence that supports this legal/male perspective, with insights into the mother's/female's role. From Dr. Charles W. Littlefield's book, "Man, Minerals And Masters": "The differences we observe among individuals are not accidental. Nor are they mere arbitrary marks without meaning. There is a cause in the innermost nature of man which each individual should possess, a precise personality, and this cause may be found in the mental state which dominated the mother during the time of gestation." We are talking about the mother establishing the personality of a child. Dorothy Rushdoony commented in the August 1993 issue of Chalcedon Report: "And now we come to the role of the woman. She, because of her role as mother, represents the future. The old saying is, 'The hand that rocks the cradle rules the world.' This is not an exaggeration nor poetic. It is simply the truth. A child begins life utterly dependent upon the mother, and after birth the dependence usually continues. She teaches him or her to speak the mother tongue." ...It cannot be overemphasized how important a lawful, peaceful, God-fearing mother is to the welfare of a child.

The humanistic theme makes man the measure of all things, without faith. Humanism sees man only as worldly. It opens man up spiritually and what fills the vacuum of unbelief in humanism is very dangerous and demonic. At least, the elect has a personal experience with God. But all men are held accountable because all men have knowledge of God. Even the heavens speak of His handiwork. The law is written on the hearts of God's people. However, the unbeliever holds the truth in unrighteousness. Knowledge of God is omnipresent. All men know and are thus guilty and accountable. Humanistic man-centered psychology is accordingly antagonistic to God-centered Christianity. Humanistic psychology has at its base a displaced bonding to God, in other words a warp, and has never gone down to the core level of where the reality of God exists in the human heart and subconscious. It only gets down to betrayal where people are like wounded animals. That's why there's so much anger in society. We never get to the point of complete trust or complete faith or to where betrayal is by the mother, not the father.

One of the greatest European psychologists of this century was Dr. Carl Jung, the father of analytical psychology. He was a contemporary of Freud. Perhaps his most famous book is "Man And His Symbols." In it, he integrated all parts of the person, including instincts, personality, rejections, stress analysis, history, synchronicity, archetypes and mythology. Human growth he called individualism. That's the masculine principle. But Jung also spoke of being "born of the unconscious" (which is the feminine principle). He attributes a mother archetype to it, saying that one can ignore other relationships, but one cannot ignore one's mother. In other words, until one grows through the womb-based needs for control, approval and security, one never reaches maturity.

Dr. Henry Monteith is professor of physics and mathematics at Eastern New Mexico University. Though he is not a Christian, he stated that at the University of Wisconsin in 1993, female bodies, particularly today, are being indwelt by animal spirits, which is what the Bible calls demons. ("Hu" means animal, thus human is "animal-man.") Women are vulnerable; they are out there alone in the dark spiritual magnetic matrix unless they are covered. Plus, with the weakening of the earth's magnetic field, and with the Chandler Wobble increasing, what we're seeing more and more is a blurring of what once was a distinct line between the natural and supernatural. New Age-type women particularly are out there like sitting ducks primed for incredible invasion, unless they're covered. A number of them are actually inviting demons in. Many are calling upon their own spirit guides, such as wolves or cougars. In this manner the hosts of hell increasingly have access to the human race.

So, it is vital that the masculine vector anchors civilization. Virtually all thinking is linear, a masculine principle dealing with logic and law. That means progress is linear - past, present, future. Society must be guided by a true law to be progressive. And that law must be supernatural, coming from outside the fallen state of Newtonian nature. Even heredity, the software programming that comes down through the DNA and the RNA, is passed down linearly in biological systems from bloodline to bloodline, from generation to generation. That is masculine. We cannot even think without division (categorization). When we think with division, diversity is created. Diversity is a masculine principle. When everyone thinks alike, no one is thinking. That is the feminine principle of the one. Therefore, there is no change and no diversity because there's no new information coming in, consequently there is no growth. The subconscious is non-Hertzian and feminine/yin, with most people operating automatically out of the subconscious programming that comes to them from the womb, when their brain waves in the delta, theta and alpha regions were programmed up to the age of 10-12 years. Obviously, if one receives good programming from a Christian mother and father with correct principles established, it will carry one through life. If one is programmed to behave emotionally and trust one's own heart and feelings to the exclusion of God's boundaries, then one has a lot of work to do after age 12 to get back on track.

The initial impulses of all life are male, as in the linear vector. The female is nonlinear, so the female womb is a magnetic, dark, scalar, chaotic, holographic chalice, a latticework, a matrix. This reality manifests biologically through sexual reproduction; babies are conceived via the male thrust or linear vector that brings light/life into the dark magnetic matrix. The male, being the initiator, assumes responsibility and authority - the basis of law.

Again, these typically unexplored differences between the masculine and the feminine echo throughout the world, with the truth being evident in many different cultures. From the book, "Feng Shui, The Chinese Art Of Placement," we learn that, "Yin and yang, the two primordial forces that govern the universe, symbolize harmony. They are opposites. Yin is dark; yang is light. Yin is passive; yang is active. Yin is female; yang is male." In the Islamic and Hindu cultures, the covering of a woman is critical, or else she puts out destructive dark energy. In the Christian culture, this concept is illustrated by the traditional marriage ceremony which begins with the father giving the bride away, transferring her in effect from his protective covering to her new husband's. Even adherents to the New Age Movement have, in their own way, come to deal with this basic truth: a carrier frequency or Hertzian wave, a male vector, is necessary for a psychic to be able to tune in. It is that a feminine spirit requires a carrier or male Hertzian wave.

Despite the evidence, we in the West have denied this basic understanding of the nature of things, much to our detriment. The following quote from Lance Morrow's writing in Time magazine, February 14, 1994, demonstrates how out of touch we are and how close we are to chaotic anarchy: "After God cast Lucifer and his followers into darkness, all the fallen angels came straggling together on the plains of hell to recriminate, to console themselves, and to discuss their new identities as devils. It may be time for men to hold a convention for the same purpose. The manly virtues, bravery, strength, discipline, and, egad, machoism itself, remain admirable only by being quietly reassigned to women, to Janet Reno and Hillary Clinton, say. People come in two models: women (good, nice) and men, the heavier, hairier life form. Allen Carlson, president of the Rockford Institute, a conservative think tank in Illinois, offers this analysis: We are at the tail end of the deconstruction of patriarchy, which has been going on since the turn of the century. The last acceptable villain is a prototypical white male. The cold war is over. The war between the sexes has the potential to take its place. The market economy has found that man-bashing sells. An established genre of movies routinely assumes the awfulness of men and portrays them in a way that would be judged bigoted and stereotyped if applied to blacks, Jews, Orientals or, for that matter, women. In this sequence, the good guys are women and children. The bad guys are adult white men, almost inevitably brutal, stupid, violent, seething with rage against women. The assumption is that men are fair game. Any man-insulting is retributive, a payback for the years, the centuries, of male dominance and oppression, and for the continuing awfulness of men."

Christian men need to understand that beyond the bravado of machoism is a true strength, which is found in gentleness and kindness. That is a struggle in an evolutionary-based culture that, of essence, is warlike. In Colossians 3:19, we read, "Husbands, love your wives and do not be bitter toward them." Of course, verse 18 says, "Wives, submit to your own husbands..." Ephesians 5:25 reads, "Husbands, love your wives, just as Christ also loved the church and gave Himself for her..." There has been a significant amount of preaching of late which discusses how husbands are commanded to love their wives, but wives are not commanded to love their husbands. However, Titus 2:4 says women are to love their husbands and their children. The younger women are supposed to be taught this by the older women, because apparently the younger women don't understand it naturally.

The reason Jesus taught in parables was because His creation is really different levels of harmonics of the same reality. The information presented here has come from many different perspectives, but they all come together to support the same point because God speaks consistently in many different ways to demonstrate that He is the great All-in-All.

For example, scientifically speaking, at the sub-atomic level, there is a male and female neutrino. This fact is illustrative of what a husband and wife are to be in terms of perfect harmony. The male spins clockwise, the female counterclockwise. Each has three electrical bands and seven magnetic bands for a total of 10 vibrating strings, equal to the 10 super strings. The 10 super strings are the basis of creation in terms of the way scientists today look at it. This is very important, because in terms of male/female companionship, humans reflect this on a higher level. The human body is composed of space and time, according to Lee Richard Donahue, a research anthropologist and physicist. We know a great deal about the physical half of the equation, where the body exists in time. But it is important to note that we possess an analog as well as a digital computer in terms of the way we are created. The super strings we have provide a network, or a spider web of communication that can access information all across the planet and the galaxy. I expect to see more and more of this coming up, particularly in the New Age, because we're entering the age of magicians, where we will see a significant amount of supernatural power manifest by the occult.

In the natural world, both men and women face an age-old dilemma, the solution to which continues to elude our society. Man's dilemma is that life is lonely, incomplete and unfulfilling without a female helpmate or companion to share his beliefs and work. Going back to Genesis, God recognized that man (Adam) was lonely, and He created woman out of the side of man - "Flesh of my flesh, bone of my bone." So, woman is an extension of man. When a man sees a woman as an extension of himself, she is of true value to him. A female helpmate or companion will share his beliefs, values, calling, occupation, interests, thoughts and feelings. She will support him when he's down, nurture and love him, do the things with him he likes to do, help him feel important and produce his offspring. When these supportive activities are provided by a woman to her man, it will tend to offset his natural unbiblical tendency to be irresponsible - response-unable. In his biblical responsibility, a man will economically provide for, cherish, defend and instruct his wife. But for her to respond and not rebel or seek dominance, he must do so kindly, gently, patiently. He must see their relationship as a team effort, be sensitive to her unique needs and interests, be considerate, serving, calm, forgiving, enduring, joyful, faithful, long-suffering and self-controlled. How many men have fulfilled these requirements? The male vector standing alone is cold, harsh, lacks beauty. It is sterile, conflict-prone, rigid, limited, inflexible, legalistic and is void of spontaneous, warm, beautiful, nurturing creativity and love. If a man has a covenantal list of what he is looking for in a woman, as discussed above, he has an opportunity for a fulfilling and an enriched life. Few men like an angry woman or an expensive, haughty woman, or a self-centered, loud, autonomous, unfaithful woman who has her own agenda. In a marriage a man's ultimate test is: Will he be willing to give up his life for her?

Here's the woman's dilemma: She desires to be dominant, which is naturally unbiblical. A dominant woman destroys herself, because the feminine, non-Hertzian matrix must be anchored to a masculine, Hertzian vector to avoid chaos, destruction, anarchy, lawlessness and death. A woman needs to receive before she can give. Feminine dominance in turn destroys the feminine need for approval and security provided by a man. It is a catch-22. Feminine dominance turns a man into a dependent, irresponsible, unfaithful, wimp or a raging, oppressive, cruel, abusive bully, or he simply leaves. All are irresponsible acts, which are his natural, unbiblical tendencies. Either way a woman's needs are left unmet. All the while, a dominant female is betrayed by her very nature in that 1) she can't control her own body like a man, i.e., menstrual cycle, pregnancy. 2) She is primarily E-motional, and right-brained. Men are left-brain oriented, logical and linear. Logic rules over emotion; the male vector anchors. 3) She's physically weaker. We don't see women competing against men in the Olympics or on professional football or basketball teams. Nor do they fight shoulder to shoulder, bayonet to bayonet, with men in war. 4) Women are not naturally merciful. Men better understand justice tempered with mercy because men are left-brained, law-based and naturally tend to be irresponsible, which means they understand mercy because in their irresponsibility they need it.

Question: How does the weaker vessel (women) avoid the anger and resentment that comes from the past, the hurt and sadness in the present, and the anxiety and fear that has to do with the future, that arises from the spiritual, mental and physical dominance of man, when her natural instincts are to be dominant? The answer is rooted in the biblical perspective that she be submissive, obedient and a helpmate. In addition, a woman must find a man she respects and loves, who is aligned with her beliefs, values, work and family ethics, her calling and occupation, interests and recreational likes, so that her subordinate role's negative emotional response of dominance is naturally minimized. In other words, she must join a man's team with whom she identifies. Otherwise, she is likely to be forever frustrated and unfulfilled. Her test is whether or not she can say, "Yes, Lord" in submission and obedience to her man and really mean it. It helps if he is leading in the direction she is motivated to go.

AT THE CORE

At the core of every created human being is a primal need for true, righteous unconditional love, a love that never fails. Spiritually, this need is first met by the love of God which passes all understanding and is grounded by His laws. It is next met by a righteous natural father and an unconditionally loving mother, and finally by true, righteous, unconditional love in a man/woman relationship (marriage). When this type of love is present, the natural fear-based, womb-based needs for approval, security and control are offset. The male vector (the light and direction of God the Father, an earthly father, and for a woman, the right man) at the conscious (masculine/left brain) level, fills and merges with the female matrix at the unconscious (feminine/right brain) level to form a beautiful crystalline, rainbow-colored vortex of love, light, life, liberty, law, laughter and long-term prosperity and fulfillment. Men and women who would be right for each other are attracted to each other if they are of the same frequencies and wave length in phase, and have grown harmonically.

When we enter into the world at birth, we immediately are tuned to our own personal matrix of frequencies which defines the wave lengths at which we broadcast, receive and operate. This matrix is determined by the 45 aspects of planetary alignment at the time of birth. This information is then encoded in geometric angles formed in the pineal gland. Therefore, the right man and right woman are literally on each other's frequencies, with similar genetic background and early upbringing helpful. If they can cut through their fear and defenses and relate to each other's cores, they can come as close as it gets to heaven on earth. It is imperative that we are freed from much of our personal emotional "baggage" in order to operate clearly and consciously so we might be tuned into ourselves and others. When we are in this state, we are in a position to attract another based on our true selves, thus making possible a good match.

When a man and a woman have even 10 out of the 45 planetary aspects in common, they get along well in terms of touch, smell, taste, bio-chemistry, shared thoughts, feelings, interests and the shared capacity for incredible love. When understood this way, it makes sense for couples who have been together for years to begin to resemble each other. Even people simply attracted to another often resemble the focus of their desire. However, their values, hopefully Godly values, the highest band of frequencies at 9C (C = speed of light), need to first be aligned, so that everything else tumbles into place (mental - 3C, emotional - 2.5C, and physical - 1C). Ironically, the normal romantic attraction is the physical first. Putting the physical first makes the relationship "iffy."

As mirrors of each other, a man and a woman with more than 10 aspects in common, as close equal opposites, also have similar faults, similar negative emotions, similar weak body organs, naturally. The beauty of this is that as each mirrors the other, it provides the opportunity for each to clear his/her sin (error) in his/her genetic programming, faulty womb and early training, bad habits, and their brain's delta, theta and alpha subconscious programs. Therefore, they can become more clear, more super-conductive, more integrated, more Christ-like. As this clearing process occurs, eliminating blockages in the body (dark crystals), there is more light integrated into their bodies which is evident in their eyes. The eyes are the light of the body. The "look of love" then fills their eyes as light increases.

God so loves mankind that He wants mankind to be perfect like Jesus Christ is perfect. He keeps bringing emotionally trying situations into human life, over and over again, giving the man and the woman the opportunity to "clear" the negative spiritual, mental and emotional programming, and rid themselves of the "death" (sin) which abides in their systems. Challenges not handled calmly and correctly with loving care are recycled painfully over and over again until they are cleared or the human self-destructs. It's either change, grow or die on this earth.

God's true love is both righteous and unconditional. It is righteous because it is in love that God establishes correct standards of conduct. God's rules of behavior define the playing field and the rules of engagement between individuals and everyone else, so as to maximize everyone's love, light, life, liberty, laughter, and long-term prosperity and fulfillment. Thus God's values, boundaries if you will, are rooted first in the spirit and mentality, and then are reflected in the emotional response of an individual to life's situations (a changed heart), and then become fully integrated physically in the human body. This way a person is spiritually, mentally, emotionally and physically "at ease" rather than at "dis-ease." In other words, God's rules (boundaries) are for our own good, to maximize the opportunities and benefits to each of us here during our brief time on earth. When we truly learn who God is and the nature of His righteous and unconditional love, we can truly learn who we are. We can establish a grounded sense of self-worth and find the true, righteous, unconditional love we all seek on earth.

God's unconditional love means He still loves us even when we fail, thanks to the redeeming work of Jesus Christ. To put that in human context, if a man loves a woman unconditionally, he wants the best for her in every way - spiritually, mentally, emotionally and physically. He cherishes her. He loves her as Christ loves the church. At the same time, the man, as the righteous keeper and implementer of God's law-rules (His righteousness), is commanded not only to provide for and protect, but also to instruct his woman in a gentle and kind way regarding God's laws of love and liberty. For example, a man may love a woman unconditionally and still withdraw support from her when she becomes rebellious of his beneficial instruction (Eve's first sin, following Satan, was the sin of rebellion, which God classifies as akin to witchcraft). For a man not to execute his responsibility in this fashion would be to do the woman a disservice and at the same time manifest his basic weakness, that is to become response-unable, or irresponsible (like Adam). Such destroys a man, who is by design spiritually, mentally, emotionally and physically, an initiator. For a woman to become rebellious and seek to dominate her man likewise destroys her for she is by design spiritually, mentally, emotionally and physically a receiving unit. Men need to do good to feel good. Women need to feel good to do good. Men need respect. Women need to be cherished. Respect and responsibility mean leadership/team captain (men). Being cherished means being a team player (women).

God's purpose is for the two of them to be a team, to become "one," an electrical, light-based, male, linear, conscious vector which provides direction, matched by the dark, rich, magnetic, feminine, unconscious matrix which provides meaning. Together they become a beautiful, life-filled, rainbow-colored, crystalline vortex. As such, they are an equitable team, but as in any team, there is a team captain to prevent chaos, confusion and anarchy. The man provides direction and leadership as the initiator, which he is designed to do. He leads gently and primarily, by example. The woman responds and provides meaning. Otherwise, misery results for both. The relationship is not equal, but equitable, complimenting the spiritual, mental, emotional and physical natures and uniqueness of man and wo-man. In becoming "one" in this fashion, they each find their true individuality.

What frustrates this process? In opposition to faith, hope and love stands fear of betrayal, abandonment and rejection. Fear frustrates true, righteous, unconditional love. Fear is often masked by anger and pain. Sadly, too many people today would rather stay unconscious by going and "doing" all the time, feeding their addictions (drugs, alcohol, sex, sports, work, business) in a frantic dissatisfying pursuit of happiness, rather than "being still." They avoid dealing with the unconscious anger, pain, and fear of their own emotional inadequacies. But dealing with such is necessary to clear the emotional subconscious (feminine/right brain) and integrate it with the conscious (masculine/left brain) so that true, righteous and unconditional love can be experienced and accepted. It is a head/heart link up for both men and women.

God's rules require short-term pain for long-term gain. He requires us to serve before we receive. We have to be disciplined in thought, emotion, word and deed to His values (First Great Commandment). If we want true, righteous and unconditional love, we must first give true, righteous and unconditional love, particularly men (Second Great Commandment). After all, man is the initiator. For a woman to be able to receive and reflect back to her man true, righteous, unconditional love, she must follow his constructive lead, be a team player with her man, and be clear of her own "stuff" (emotional baggage) as well. True love serves both ways, and looks to the other's interest first. We really cross the bridge from death to life, from sickness to health, from darkness to light when it feels better to give than receive, both personally and professionally. This is the only way true self-worth is established.

The safer and more trusting the environment, the easier it is for detrimental emotional blockages to clear. So, the greatest of blessings is to have someone who is our equal opposite, with similar genetic background and early training, having more than 10 planetary aspects in common with ours, who loves us truly, both righteously and unconditionally, providing a safe, accepting environment for us to clear. This is why open, honest, intimate communication deepens love. This way we can become everything God wants us to be, more fully complete and "unique" in ourselves, while at the same time becoming more fully and completely integrated together as "one," in each other, and with God. Then, true righteous and unconditional love can replace, at the core, alienation and fear. For a woman this means, wrapped in the reins of her Heavenly Father, her earthly father and her husband, she is free. For a man, this means to risk all to love and obey God, and to risk all as he loves and "does good" for his woman. The man and woman then are mirrors of each other - totally "unique," totally "one." Both are true. This is total fulfillment. This may be the ultimate earthly blessing for God's humble and tenderhearted. Thus, the most important decision a man and woman can make is to drop their defenses, let go of their fear, and yield to the true, righteous, unconditional love of God, and of each other. We, after all, are only vulnerable where we are defensive, when we fear. To reject true, righteous, unconditional love is for a man or a woman to ultimately reject themselves. We compound our error (sin) and increase our misery when we run from our emotional pain and reject God, and reject those who God has given to love us and to love.

At the core, going back to Genesis and the creation of Adam of Eve, man was created to work and wo-man was created to be a helpmate to man's work and a companion to preclude his loneliness. This basis, grounded in shared Christian values, thoughts, feelings and physical intimacy, covered by prayer, is the essence of true intimacy.

CREATING LOVE

In our lawless romantic age, marked by fractured relationships, alienation and loneliness, one of the overwhelming driving needs is the need for love. This hunger for love is everywhere. It is inflamed by the mass media, particularly in the love stories which saturate television and the movies. It is evidenced by the plethora of best-selling romantic novels. Love is lost in our society due to such things as the breakup of the family, the destruction of both men and women who are removed from the harmonious roles for which they were inescapably biologically created, lawlessness, selfishness, a lack of grounding, a low sense of self-worth, a lack of integration of con-sciousness into the subconsciousness, failure to link up the anima with the animus, the yang not illuminating and integrating itself with the yin, knosis not translating into epiknosis, etc. Most importantly, in a society where God is reputed to be dead, there is no love. After all, basic to everything is the reality that God is love.

In terms of men and women seeking that most excellent lifetime partner, everyone consciously or subconsciously looks for that per-fect balance of yang and yin, a male and female neutrino that move together while separate in perfect harmony intuitively, the equivalent of the perfectly matched 64 fields equal and opposite each other in the North and South poles of a magnet. When all these line up, values, intellectual, emotional, and physical harmony exist. The spiritual, mental, emotional and physical aspects of male and female are totally complimentary. They work together for the greater good, and in their unity, find paradoxically greater individual identity. True love, which is based on giving/sacrificial service, simultane-ously framed by God's lawful boundaries, fully blossoms the light male vector in the female magnetic matrix into a holistic one, which synergistically is much greater than either of them individually. Life literally becomes a beautiful upward spiral in every way.

Given the way American society operates - lawlessly, romanti-cally, without boundaries in its random attempt to create love - it is a miracle any man and woman link up successfully and are able to make it work. And those who do make it work usually have to work hard at it.

This mass randomly produced matched drudgery is unnecessary. All the time, money, effort, energy, fear, doubt, and wasted torn emotion put forth in the typical Western dating/courting process is ludicrous. If a person doesn't know who he/she is, a relationship won't work long term. If the man or woman has not developed the ability to give/serve/love as primary, where he/she literally feels better by bringing joy to the other than in receiving personally, the relationship won't work. Unless an individual can stand on his/her own alone, is winning in life, is able to give what he/she wants back, and wants a relationship, it won't work. Moreover, because values oscillate at a higher frequency than mentality, emotion and the physical being, unless values are in harmony to begin with, the long-term relationship won't work either. Finally, if a person is unwilling to grow spiritually, mentally and emotionally, they have no business in a relationship. Life is change. We either grow or die. It is more true within a relationship.

Just like we build a shopping center - first doing the ground work, planning, carefully choosing the land, drawing up the appropriate architectural plans, arranging financing, procuring tenants, etc., in like manner, we can systematically approach building a relationship that works and is successful long-term. We don't go out and build shopping centers on emotional/romantic whims. And more importantly, given the complex nature of this spiritual/biological/emotional computer we call man, we can best build relationships on a systematic foundation. Some of the key operating principles in life are: "Never guess when the information is available." "It's lazy and unprofessional to guess when the information in available." "Trust, but verify." "When in doubt, check it out."

Most relationships are built electromagnetically, through trial and error, over much time, in much space, with much stumbling. However, when the proper tools are utilized initially, a relationship can be built magnetoelectrically, beyond time and space, with a quantum leap, if you will. Put differently, why suffer unnecessarily in a primitive trial and error way?

While at first, this may seem to be cold and calculating, the paradox - the truth - is that this approach results in much greater emotional fulfillment and romance long-term than the present woefully lacking process. A good relationship between a man and a woman is for the purpose of building something together - a calling under God, a home, a family, a comprehensive purpose in life with mutually edifying individual growth and pleasure. When people are willing to go through the pain of continual growth, deal with the likes of their emotional baggage, and they are with the right person in a harmonic match up, the growth, the joy, the fulfillment, the exhilaration of life is absolutely incredible. There's nothing like it. It is worth pursuing and defending at all costs. Dr. Gary Smalley's book and video series, "Hidden Keys Of A Loving Lasting Marriage," is helpful in achieving this, as is Dr. Patricia Allen's book, "Getting to 'I DO.'"

Now, I know this is challenging. It has to do with having heart. Think of the movies, such as the Robert Redford classic, "Jeremiah Johnson," the Clint Eastwood classic, "The Outlaw Josey Wales," and Mel Gibson's latest hit, "Braveheart." All three of these movies speak of the balance that men struggle for in life, as their character develops, to become courageous gentle-men, fully male and yet with the tenderness to operate out of their female side. It takes such men to establish an equitable relationship with a woman, and simultaneously be a compassionate leader of their two-person team.

For effectiveness and efficiency, I have narrowed down to five tests, whether two people will be compatible for a lifetime. Three of these tests can be found in two books. Another test takes a couple of hours for each person to complete and then a comparative analysis is done between them. The final test involves an extensive computer run on each individual, followed by an interpretive analysis. All of this can be accomplished for under $500. That's an inexpensive investment for a wonderful, high probability opportunity for a fulfilling lifetime relationship.

One test is Middle Eastern, one test is European and color-based. The third test is Western analytical, the fourth test is computerized motivational and apptitudinal, and the fifth test is astrophysical. Four of these five sources I can give you readily so you can purchase them and pursue them on your own. The fifth source, however, the astrosonic/astrophysical source, has to remain confidential. For nearly all of you, the four sources will be sufficient. Please remember, however, that you will have to purchase these four items/services on your own. These sources are: "The Luscher Color Test" by Ian Scott, ISBN 0-671-63882-3, Washington Square Press Books, NY; "The Enneagram Made Easy" by Renee Baron & Elizabeth Wagele, ISBN 0-06-251026-6, Harper, San Francisco, CA (2 Tests); Potentials Development, P. O. Box 55339, Seattle, WA 98155 (206)364-0737, Fax (206)364-3303.

Let me provide you with a little more insight. I presently hold that there are three primary determinants of an individual's personality: heredity, spirit, and environment. The first is the genetic family lineage, going back at least four generations. This means there are 30 possible genetic personality considerations involved in the make-up of an individual. Second is the geometric angular programming of the pineal gland, the master spiritual gland, which takes place at birth. The pineal gland is a crystal. The time an individual is born, as well as the location of his/her birth (longitude and latitude) when he/she takes that first breath programs the geometric angles of the pineal gland which help determine his/her unique personality. The 45 aspects of planetary alignments at that particular moment at time of birth, in their angular relationships, emit frequencies in the infra-red range which establish not only personality traits but also bio-chemical aspects of an individual. This is why competent Indian M.D.s (in India) evaluate both an individual's urine (biochemical) and his/her birth chart (electromagnetic) to determine comprehensively who they are dealing with, when a person is not at ease, or is dis-eased. Thirdly, the environmental programming of an individual in his/her mother's womb, during the first six years, and even up to ages 10-12, when the subconscious mind is programmed in an individual, establishes the framework upon which 98 percent of people operate throughout life.

Am I saying that most people go through life literally uncon-scious, on automatic pilot? Yes. The Roman Catholic Church and the Communist Party have long known that if they captured a child in his/her first six years and educated/indoctrinated him/her then, the party would probably hold that person for life. Why? Because the spiritual subconscious regions of the mind - the delicate delta, theta, and even some alpha rhythms - are primarily programmed in the for-mative six years, with the rest of the alpha region being filled out from ages 6-10 or 12. This is the programming, the mind set, with which most people operate throughout their lives without even giving it a second thought. Most people think they are thinking, when what they are really doing is reacting subjectively to perceived realities, filtered through the values, opinions and beliefs which are pro-grammed in the subconscious genetically, at birth, and in the first six to 12 years of life. This explanation helps us understand mankind's sad plight, and why change usually takes place slowly and painfully. Most folks do not change until the pain of change is less than con-tinuing on their present paths.

These five tests do a comprehensive job of going to the core of an individual's personality and discovering with high probability the essence of what makes him/her tick. When these matchups are made, life between a man and a woman can more readily operate on a faith and trust basis, rather than a fearful and trustless one. Life is a struggle when two people have to work to exhaustion to make things happen together. They instead can flow harmoniously with each other with much less effort, and that effort can become literally recreational. It's fun.

Two people can be on the same frequency, on the same wave length, actually many of the same frequencies (at least 10). But I've discovered, too, that if one individual is more progressed, living at a higher harmonic of the frequencies than the other, it takes some time and work for the lower harmonic individual to catch up. But my experience also is that it is worth the effort. It does ultimately, however, come down to individual choice, and the willingness to do the hard painful work to look at one's value system, mental processes and emotional baggage to clear and become all that one was created to be, individually and together.

In the emotional clearing area, I still very much like Dr. Michael Ryce's work, "Why is This Happening To Me...Again?" Dr. Michael Ryce's tapes are available from New Horizon Trust (800) 755-6360 or directly from Dr. Michael Ryce, Rt. 3, Box 3280, Theodosia, MO   65761, Phone (417) 273-4838.   Also, The Sedona Method is easy and effective for emotional clearing. Phone (602) 553-3770 or (800) 875-2256. A third course men and women might consider going through together if possible, but in any case, is beneficial in helping an individual to deal with and clear his/her "stuff" is the Context Associated Program entitled, "The Excellence Series." Contact Context Associated, 2101 Fourth Avenue, Suite 260, Seattle WA 98121. Phone: (206) 727-4360 or fax (206) 727-4379. An excellent book on helping one deal with one's issues is Judith Sills' "Excess Baggage." These are the four best ways I know, following prayer and faith, for individuals to clear their emotional baggage so they can truly create love.

I thoroughly investigated the components which made up relationships between men and women that have proven to be comprehensively successful long term. After identifying the common factors, I then backed into the "test" which allowed these factors to be identified front end rather than be discovered painfully through trial and error over a period of time. After all, the two most important decisions any of us make in life encompass our choice of an occupation and our choice of a lifetime mate.

* * *

Men tend to intimidate. Women tend to seduce. Long-term, the only thing that works is negotiation.

* * *

Men need to do good to feel good. Women need to feel good to do good. When men are respected, they feel cherished. When women are cherished, they feel respected.

* * *

It is important to discover if kind and supportive words, deeds or nonsexual touch is most important to your mate.

* * *

Long-term, relationships improve in an environment of acceptance, trust, honesty, security, openness and growth. Relationships bring up intense personal issues and it is only in such an environment that these issues can be successfully resolved, allowing both individual and collective growth.

* * *

Needs and hurts must be communicated verbally.

GOD'S WAY FOR THE WORLD TO WORK: A RECONCILIATION OF EAST AND WEST

Part I

It is no accident in God's plan for history, Christianity is a Middle Eastern religion. As such, geographically, Christianity is placed to reconcile the holistic feminine/yin cultures of the East with the individualistic masculine/yang cultures of the West. Moreover, as George M. Lamsa pointed out, the Gospels were written in Aramaic, a language which captured five major religions of the world. This is the geographic and communicative basis for God's reconciliation of mankind unto Himself, the Great All in All.

One reason the occult New World Order is in such a rush to become established is because it knows that God's plan for "His kingdom come, His will be done, on earth as it is in heaven," is moving toward completion. Ever since Jesus Christ ascended into Heaven and sat down at the right hand of the Father, progressively throughout history, Jesus' authority has slowly, but surely, extended toward His total dominion, His rulership over all the earth, His creation. We are not there yet, but we're getting closer. The wheat is being separated from chaff, the sheep from the goats, good from evil, as men wax either worse or better, as we move toward final judgment. Eventually, "every knee will bow and every tongue will confess that Jesus is Lord." Therefore, the sooner the truth of the operational plan for the King's kingdom becomes apparent to man, the sooner will be the open evidence of the tenderhearted, humble, sane, loving obedience of His children bringing in the kingdom, and conversely, the rebellious, hardhearted, insane, death-loving spoiled fruit of those who war against God.

Modern technological man is bringing us closer and closer to this great spiritual division. Whether one looks at Silva Mind Control, parapsychological studies done at Duke University, or even Hollywood movies having to do with dreams, the occult, or science fiction, the frequencies which govern the human mind (the brain's delta frequencies, 1 through 3-4 Hz [cycles per second], theta, 3-4 through 6-7 Hz [cycles per second], and alpha, 6-7 through 12-14 Hz [cycles per second]), it has been demonstrated conclusively these are the windows where the spirit world interfaces with the human mind.

Thus, it cannot be minimized how important it is for a Christian to "bring every thought into captivity to the obedience of the Lord Jesus Christ."

Today, there are even high-tech "mind machines" where one can dial in a frequency and entrain the brain to a specific frequency, and move out to a specific segment of the spirit world for the purpose of achieving pleasure, power, or some other sensation. This is what the "spiritual gurus" of the East have long done, minus technology, minus the grounding of Living Truth (vector) of the Lord Jesus Christ. It is what Eastern meditation at ground level is all about - the integration of the masculine conscious level (beta brain frequency) 12-14 Hz (cycles per second) and higher with the feminine subconscious of alpha, theta and delta, punctuated and integrated with the spirit world. Obviously, the difference between the Christian and the non-Christian is there is only one spirit for the Christian: a righteous, Law-abiding Holy Spirit, who interfaces ideally comprehensively with the human mind (and heart) at all its frequency levels. Such righteousness is the result of complete discipled obedience to God's living Law-Word - Jesus Christ.

Modern psychology, often a secular humanistic replacement for God's theology, has recognized the truth of the above and is well on the road to implementing spiritual ungodliness into Western civilization. In Christianity, it has only been Mid-Eastern Christianity, such as the Egyptian Coptic Church, the Greek Orthodox Church, the Russian Orthodox Church, and some segments of the Roman Catholic Church, that have even had a clue as to the nature of this battle. By and large, law-based Western Christianity has only a superficial understanding of the supernatural battle, with the exception of a few charismatics. Yet, if Christianity is anything, it is at its base, supernatural. Spirit is living energy with personality and purpose. God's Holy Spirit is personal and righteous living energy with personality and purpose. Satan's demonic world is fallen, evil, unrighteous living energy with personality and purpose.

Quantum physics has taught us that energy precedes and forms matter. The supernatural - the quantum - thus determines the natural - the Newtonian - in a scientific, physical sense. It is this reality which is permeating the exploding interest in holistic medicine and also humanistic psychology. The influence of the secular humanistic public schools and the entertainment industry is obviously not Holy Spirit-based, not righteous, and thus, ungodly. If C.S. Lewis were alive, he would call it the infection of "That Hideous Strength."

Let's look more closely at the psychology of the matter. One of the greatest psychologists of the 20th century, who has influenced nearly every field of psychological thought, was the great Austrian, C.G. Jung. Jung did more to integrate Eastern and Western thought than any other psychologist up to his time. He is to such psychological integration what the Beatles were to rock music. Unknown for the most part in the West, is that Carl (C.G.) Jung understood the key elements of Christianity as basic to any expansive adoption or integration of Eastern thought into Western thinking. This fact has been ignored by the rebellious, God-hating, Western, Freudian, and other psychological humanists. Moreover, Jung understood and explained the masculine (yang) and feminine (yin) parts of every human, male or female both. He also discussed the relationship between consciousness (yang/masculine) and subconsciousness (yin/feminine).

In an important book by Richard Wilhelm first published in the United States in 1931, "The Secret Of The Golden Flower: A Chinese Book Of Life," (A Harvest/HBJ Book, Harcourt Brace Jovanovich, Publishers, 1250 Sixth Avenue, San Diego, CA 92101 - ISBN 0-15-679980-4) C. G. Jung follows with a comprehensive commentary on the presentation of the ancient 1,000-year old Chinese text. What did C. G. Jung have to say? "Is it that our eyes are open to the spirit only when the laws of earth are obeyed?" We have physical eyes and we have spiritual eyes. The Bible makes it clear that when we become alive to God (born again), our eyes and ears are opened. What Jung is saying, is that when God's laws intended for earth are obeyed, when we have that ground, that foundation, that masculine vector, we can then be open to His Spirit.

Jung knew well the importance of the spiritual base of man as primary, preceding every other aspect of his nature: "In our Christian culture, spirit, and the passion of the spirit, were for a long time the greatest values and the things most worth striving for. Only after the decline of the Middle Ages, that is, in the course of the 19th century, when spirit began to degenerate into intellect, did a reaction set in against the unbearable dominance of intellectualism. This movement, it is true, first committed the pardonable mistake of confusing intellect with spirit, and blaming the latter for the misdeeds of the former. Intellect does, in fact, harm the soul when it dares to possess itself of the heritage of the spirit. It is no way fitted to do this, because spirit is something higher than intellect in that it includes not only the latter, but the feelings as well. It is a direction, a principle of life that strives toward shining, super-human heights. In opposition to it stands the dark, feminine earth-bound principle (yin) with its emotionality and instinctiveness that reach far back into the depths of time and into the roots of physiological continuity."

Carl Jung, recognizing truth, realized that the law-based West, with its heavy intellectualism, missed the integration with God's supernatural reality, His Spirit. Of course, it was during the last half of the 19th century, when evolution became prominent, when the fall of the Christian South occurred, and with it the demise of masculine Calvinistic culture, that the United States lost its grounding. Since that time, the United States has increasingly exported death to the rest of the world, whether in the form of debt (death), pornography (Hollywood), dead food, abortion, drugs, or arms. Reaping what we sow, the judgment of the West will be accordingly fearful.

We must seek the counsel of God's Holy Spirit in guiding our intellects, our thoughts, our emotions and our behavior. The Holy Spirit is given to us to guide us in all truth. In the late 20th century, we have seen the folly of relying on the Western-based legalistic intellectualism. Its inadequate hollowness has yielded to as Jung put it, "emotionality and instinctiveness," which he called, "the dark, feminine earth-bound principle (yin)," which reaches deep into the depths of time and the "roots of physiological continuity." We have fallen back into the status of the "natural man" in the West. Natural man, being alien to God, always seeks his greatest strength in earthly things, and in the "collective." The "collective" is the feminine principle, as is usually manifest in primitives in the "tribe" and in advanced cultures in the "state" (federal government). So, here we are again back to a basic biblical truth, that the nations which war against God are those linked up to the "whore of Babylon," the ungodly feminine collective, where civil government as the collective is the final source of authority, the ultimate lawmaker and god of a society. Law needs to come from outside of man and from above nature. It needs to be supernatural.

C.G. Jung was clear in his perspective on this issue. "...anyone with a more than superficial desire to understand cannot fail to discover that without the most serious application of Christian values we have acquired, the new integration can never take place." Carl Jung understood that the personal living truth of the Lord God Lawgiver and Creator, Jesus Christ, and the living principles and values He gave us to operate with on earth, taught by the Holy Spirit, were basic to any integration on an individual level of the conscious with the subconscious, and on a social level of the individual/masculine based West with the holistic/feminine East and the collective. We might visualize the linear, directional, purposeful, cause-and-effect of

God's law as a masculine vector, around which the feminine collective matrix can wind or wrap itself. Or, put another way, we might see it as the masculine Hertzian wave being the carrier wave for the feminine non-Hertzian scalar wave.

Historians such as Frenchman Amaury de Reincourt, would see it as a primary reason for the fall of a civilization - when the collective feminine matrix, dark, yin and chaotic in nature, rules supreme, having emasculated the directional, law-based male vector in society, leaving nothing left for it to ground to and thus, leaving the feminine collective matrix to implode and self-destruct. Accordingly, great civilizations (collectives) die from within, and are marked by the emasculation of their men and the predominance of their women. The antedote to this is for men to be response-able Christian gentle-men - gentleness being a character trait that only exists in Christianity, and for women to be team members. In the East, there has never been a supernatural basis for the masculine vector of individualism, and so the collective feminine matrix has manifest itself in a top-down, centralized, governing authority, such as in dynasties and bureaucratic governments.

How clearly Carl Jung saw this is evidenced by another quote: "My admiration for the great Eastern philosophers is as genuine as my attitude toward their metaphysics is irreverent.

"...It is a change also known to us through the testimony of the Apostle Paul: 'not I (live), but Christ liveth in me.' The symbol 'Christ' as a 'son of man' is an analogous psychic experience: a higher, spiritual being of human form is invisibly born in the individual, a spiritual body, which is to serve as a future dwelling, a body, which, as Paul expresses himself, is 'put on like a garment,' ('for as many of you who have been baptized into Christ have put on Christ'). Obviously it is always a difficult thing to express, in intellectual terms, subtle feelings which are, none the less, infinitely important for the life and well-being of the individual. In a certain sense, the thing we are trying to express, is the feeling of having been 'replaced' but without the connotation of having been 'deposed.' It is as if the directions of the affairs of life have gone over to an invisible center. Nietzsche's metaphor, 'in the most loving bondage, free' would be appropriate here. This is the essence of 2 Corinthians 4:7-12." Jung saw the same thing as Paul, but framed it in different language. It is also confirmed by the scientist, Sheldrake, who identified metaphysical information fields, morphogenic fields, which always attach themselves to living energy systems - humans. In other words, the choice is God's Holy Spirit and angels, or Satan and his fallen angels.

The Eastern philosophers had no great supernatural philosophy that could be applied successfully to the world from the bottom up. The paradox is that when law comes supernaturally from God, from above and outside of nature, then man individually is free to develop and build the collective from the bottom up. That's why the East never progressed in an individualistic sense, until it included at least the common grace application economically, socially and politically of Western Christian law. The holistic Eastern philosophy (feminine), minus God's Law-Word (masculine) operated in terms of the top-down collective, with the rulership from above. Therefore, it never progressed in terms of individual achievement. This is what C.G. Jung addressed when he referred to the spiritual being of the Lord Jesus Christ, the Son of Man, being born into the individual in a spiritual body which transformed that spiritual body and reconciled the paradoxes, the oxymorons, the TNTs (Truths-In-Tension) of life. We are replaced without being deposed. We are born again. We lose ourselves to find ourselves as the Bible puts it. The Law of God is written on our hearts to transform that emotional center so that the heart of man is no longer unbounded, tossed to and fro by every circumstance of life, by every whim of doctrine. Instead it has a ground, a vector, an anchor, to carry it through the storms of life. A born-again Christian man can thus be stable in all his ways, if he matures. It is also why women need men, for a covering. Writes Jung, "What, on a lower level, had led to the wildest conflicts and to panicky outbursts of emotion, viewed from the higher level of the personality, now seemed like a storm in the valley seen from a high mountain-top. This does not mean that the thunderstorm is robbed of its reality, but instead of being in it, one is now above it." Jung is expressing what biblically is referred to as overcoming. Jung went on to write, "The greatest and most important problems in life are all in a certain sense insoluble. They must be so because they express the necessary polarity inherent in every self-governing system. They can never be solved, but only outgrown."

Self-government is an individual/masculine/yang concept. These polarities/paradoxes/oxymorons/TNTs are first resolved in the Christian Godhead, in the Trinity. We must grow and overcome, as individuals, toward this end.

This Christian perspective of internal spiritual growth, outwardly manifest, is also "faith" leading to "works" as discussed in the New Testament book of James. Christians who mature are also to reach the point where they give thanks for all things and are anxious about nothing. This is why the basic form of Christian government is self-government. When God's Law-Word, Christian values/principles, are established in men's hearts at 9 times the speed of light, then the lower vibrations of the human mind (3 times the speed of light), emotion (2.5 times the speed of light), and even the physical body (1 times the speed of light), are so integrated, that men can remain at ease, without "dis-ease." In such a state, men/individuals can stand unwavering throughout the up and down circumstances of life, the conflicts between the yang and yin, the masculine and feminine, the polarities of life. Such are solved by being outgrown in the character of the individual who becomes increasingly Christ-like as he walks his life's path.

Through prayer (talking to God) and meditation (listening to God), the consciousness of man (masculine/yang) for the Christian must penetrate the spiritual sub/unconscious (feminine/yin), to re-place the monkeys (fallen spirits) that pull our strings in the dark so that God's light (yang) is brought to full illumination in the dark subconscious (yin); so that both consciousness and sub/un-consciousness coexist in balance, bathed in the righteous illumina-tion of God's Holy Light bringing Truth by the Holy Spirit. As C.G. Jung wrote, "An external law, in the course of time, becomes an inner conviction. Thus it might easily happen to contemporary man, especially the Protestant, that the person Jesus, now existing outside in the realm of history, might become the superior man within himself. Then we would have attained, in a European way, the psychological state corresponding to 'enlightenment' in the Eastern sense."

It is noteworthy that Jung would see this as unique to the Protes-tant. Why would this be? Because Protestants historically focus on the development of the individual (the "many"/masculine), as op-posed to the Catholic focus on the collective (the "one"/feminine). This is the essential difference between North and South America. Even though those Europeans who settled South America had better education, greater status, and greater natural resources, North Amer-ica developed while South America did not. As Irving Kristol, the great scholar who long wrote for The Wall Street Journal, declared, the reason North America developed and South America did not was because North America had a Protestant Reformation. This posited power in the individual and led to the (masculine/yang/many) bot-tom-up development in the Christian free market rather than the top-down (feminine/yin/collective) approach, the Catholic one, which dominated South America. It is no accident that throughout the world in Protestant versus Catholic economic cultures, the per capita income in Protestant cultures exceeds that of Catholic cultures by as much as 6:1, as the late Dr. Iben Browning documented.

On a perverted individual basis, Western men seized this posited power in the individual as Nietzsche's anti-Christ effort to humanistically become superman, while the real Superman is the person of the Lord Jesus Christ dwelling within, manifesting outwardly in the individual.

We cannot discount how important spirit is as it filters down to the levels of man's existence mentally, emotionally and physically. How important Christian values are God makes clear over and over again in His Law-Word. When such values are not installed internally, men are in essence in rebellion against God - lawless. Man will always be drawn to a supernatural information field, a godly or an ungodly one. Jung wrote, "If the values are not retained, the individual goes over to the other side, and passes from fitness to unfitness, from adaptation to the lack of it, from sense to nonsense, and even from rationality to mental disturbance."

Societies at war with God go insane and self-destruct. Before Rome self destructed, it first went mad. It is a common observation in Western civilization today that lack of rationality, in Jung's words, "mental disturbance," rules. It is the clear evidence of lawless rebellion against God and His "values."

Being disciplined, being a law-abiding disciple of Christ, is not an easy path to follow. Narrow is the gate, and not many pass through. Jung saw this: "The way is not without danger. Everything good is costly, and the development of the personality is one of the most costly of all things. It is a question of yea-saying to oneself, of taking one's self as the most serious of tasks, of being conscious of everything one does, and keeping it constantly before one's eyes and all its dubious aspects - truly a task that taxes us to the utmost.

"...The step to high consciousness leads us out and away from all rear-guard cover and away from all safety measures. The individual must give himself to the new way, for it is only by means of his integrity that he can go further, and only his integrity can guarantee that his way does not turn out to be an absurd adventure."

How clear, how precise. It costs man everything in an earthly sense to follow the Lord Jesus Christ. He must pick up his cross, and follow Him, forsaking everything that is important to him in an earthly sense. The irony, the paradox, the beauty of this, however, is that by doing so, when a man/woman dies to his/herself, he/she becomes a new creature in Christ - just the way when a seed dies as it is planted in the ground, it brings forth a new plant and fruit. The joyful result is that the yoke of Christ is not heavy, unlike the death-based natural yoke, embedded in his subconscious (alpha/theta/delta rhythms of the mind) which kept him/her trapped in the natural chains of death. As Jung pointed out, the importance of being conscious is the importance of the conscious ruling over, but in consonance with, the un/subconscious - of the masculine ruling over, but in harmony with the feminine. (Conscious is masculine, unconscious is feminine). This moves us away, as Jung stated, "from all safety measures," from all our security blankets. We must take risks. But we find a new security, looking down on the thunderstorms of life. Recall that safety is one of the basic womb-based needs of the feminine matrix which entrap man in the natural system, the need for security, safety, control and approval. When we are fully conscious, we are anxious about nothing. We live in the joy and pain of the present, not in the guilt, anger, bitterness, resentment and regret of the past, nor the fear and anxiety of the future.

Jung's "the new way" is Jesus Christ, for He is "the way, the truth and the life." This way only comes by means of "integrity," of establishing the rulership of Jesus Christ's Law-Word in the warring human heart which naturally is desperately wicked, and wants to emotionally do its own thing. Such a transformation has to begin at the individual (many/masculine) level, because the whole can only be greater synergistically than the sum of its parts when the whole is a voluntary collective of individuals of integrity. The kingdom of God must first be within individuals before it can be externalized. Ann Douglas, in her book, "The Feminization of American Culture," documented the death of this perspective.

In Jesus Christ, we lose all to gain all, as He did. Jung wrote: "Wherever we are still attached, we are possessed: when one is possessed, it means the existence of something stronger than one's self. ...Where the god is not acknowledged, ego-mania develops, and out of this mania comes illness." When Christianity really has it right, when Christianity truly becomes biblical in every sense of the word, the values of the Living Word, Jesus Christ, will rule in the human mind and heart, in the conscious and un/subconscious, head over heart, yet in harmony. Then peace in the mentality will result in peace in the emotion, which will result in being "at ease" in the physical body, rather than at "dis-ease." And isn't it interesting that illness comes from ego, from the mental and emotional state (according to Jung). The basis of ego is pride. Pride, as Proverbs teach us, is the foremost mental attitude sin against God. Mature Christians are not attached. They don't own anything, but are the steward of everything. They are humble, and never take credit, but give credit to others and glory to God. Mature Christians take full personal responsibility for sin, never pass on anything bad about anyone else, never defend themselves, and are full of compassion and forgiveness.

C.G. Jung wrote in "The Secret Of The Golden Flower," "In accordance with this conception, the Christian subordinates himself to the superior, divine person in expectation that He has grace; but the Eastern man knows that redemption depends on the 'work' the individual does upon himself." The Christian, rightly dividing the Word of Truth, recognizes there is no contradiction here between what the Bible declares and the partial truths of both Western and Eastern thought. As the Spirit of Christ is instilled in the character of the individual, the "work" is done in the individual at the mental, emotional and physical levels. This is an "Eastern" perspective. But the Western truth then kicks in, as is written in the book of James, that "faith without works is dead." Faith is manifested outwardly in works. Thus, the inner Eastern truth of Christianity and the outer Western truth of Christianity are harmonized in the whole individual man, the complete Christian disciple, who then goes forth to form the "one" in voluntary organizations in the world, establishing dominion (masculine) along with stewardship (feminine). When this occurs, the mid-Eastern reality of Christianity - the link between East and West - is realized.

GOD'S WAY FOR THE WORLD TO WORK: A RECONCILIATION OF EAST AND WEST

Part II

Examining in more depth the spiritual battle within the individual, the Christian perspective of theology, expanded by an understanding of the humanistic perspective of psychology, we find the work of C.G. Jung integrative. Men and women are sexually masculine and feminine, respectively. However, in terms of the way their brains work, and their organ systems and bodies are constructed, men and women both have a masculine and a feminine side. Men are more left-brain oriented, law-based, masculine. Women are more right-brain oriented, feminine (holistic). Men have an inner feminine core and women have a masculine inner core. The left side of a male body spins clockwise, the left side of a female body spins counterclockwise, etc. Together, they become one in balance. Thus, in the true development of the individual over time, men become more feminine - gentlemen, and women move toward ground, and become more masculine. God's intention is for a balance, an integration. Jung saw the conscious as masculine, the unconscious as feminine. Jung's associate, Salome Wilhelm, wrote "Consciousness is the element marking what is separated off, individualized (masculine) in a person and the unconscious (feminine) is the element that unites him with the cosmos. ...The unconscious (feminine) must be inseminated by consciousness (masculine) being immersed in it. In this way the unconscious (feminine) is activated and thus, together with an enriched consciousness (masculine), enters upon a super-personal mental level in the form of a spiritual rebirth." The unconscious, the feminine, is always in the spirit, linked to the delta, theta and alpha rhythms of the mind and further linked to the autonomic nervous system. There is no light without consciousness.

In "The Secret Of The Golden Flower," another Jungian associate, Richard Wilhelm confirmed this perspective, "Where yang (masculine) appears as the active principle and conditions, and yin (feminine) as a passive principle is derived and conditioned..." The masculine/yang consciousness is further equated to the animus while the feminine/yin unconsciousness is equated to the anima. Richard Wilhelm penned, "The anima (feminine) was thought of as especially linked with the bodily processes; at death it sinks to the earth and decays. The animus (masculine) on the other hand, is the higher soul; after death it rises in the air, where at first it is still active for a time and then evaporates in ethereal space, or flows back into the common reservoir of life. In living men, the two correspond in a certain degree to the cerebral system (masculine) and the system of the solar plexus (feminine) respectively. The animus (masculine) dwells in the eyes, the anima (feminine) in the abdomen. The animus (masculine) is bright and active, the anima (feminine) is dark and earth-bound."

"As a rule, it will be the anima (feminine), the undiscriminating will, which, goaded by passions, forces the animus (masculine) or intellect into its service (as Eve did Adam). At least the anima will do this to the extent that the intellect directs itself outward, whereby the energies of both animus (masculine) and anima (feminine) leak away and life consumes itself."

A natural male can be captured by the earth-bound sexual energy of a female. She can control him by rewarding him with sex and punish him by withholding sex. Throughout the Old Testament, this was unfortunately true for many of God's saints, from Adam to Sampson to David, their animus was compromised by an anima. This is in contrast to what God intends. God intends for the anima (feminine/yin) to be a helpmate to the animus (masculine/yang), for God's work to be done on earth.

Richard Wilhelm, Salome Wilhelm, and C.G. Jung address this point. C.G. Jung wrote, "Instincts suffice only for the individual embedded in nature, which, on the whole, remains always the same. An individual who is more guided by unconscious (feminine) than by conscious (masculine) choice tends therefore toward marked psychic conservatism. This is a reason the primitive does not change in the course of thousands of years, and it is also the reason why he fears everything strange and unusual. It might lead him to maladaptation, and thus to the greatest of psychic dangers, to a kind of neurosis in fact." In other words, unless the God of the Bible rules in the hearts and minds of men, in their consciousness (masculine), they will be guided by their unconsciousness (feminine), which leaves them in darkness, the depraved status of the primitive, natural man who cannot progress or change, who fears everything, and who becomes neurotic, mad. It is much easier for man to naturally fall under the influence of the unconscious because this is what he first knew, the feminine womb. It takes disciplined discipleship to do otherwise. C.G. Jung wrote, "Whenever the narrowly delimited, but intensely clear, individual consciousness (masculine) meets the immense expansion of a collective unconscious (feminine), there is danger because the latter (feminine) has a definitely disintegrating effect on consciousness (masculine)."

When women follow their death-based natural tendency to be dominant, they destroy themselves and men. Women are by design receiving units. When men follow their death-based natural tendency to be response-unable (irresponsible), they destroy themselves and women. Men are by design initiating units. But, not only does the feminine unconscious have a "disintegrating effect," but C.G. Jung also warned of the animus of a woman, the masculine side of her brain, when it is unregenerated. It is of a subjective, collective nature. "...the animus of woman consists in a plurality of preconceived opinions, and is therefore not so susceptible of personification by one figure, but appears more often as a group or crowd. ...So the animus of a woman consists of inferior judgments or better said, opinions."

Preconceived opinions are by their very nature subjective opinions, and are emotionally unstable. Crowds or groups are collectives; they are ruled by emotion. They are accordingly lawless. If individuals and following collective mankind are ruled by their emotions, yielding inferior judgments or opinions, then where is the standard of law? There is none. Then every man/woman thus becomes his own law, his own New Age god or goddess, which duplicates Satan's desire "to be like the Most High." This results in massive lawlessness, anarchy, which gives rise to a Caesar, a dictator, a compensating masculine anti-Christ, a top-down authoritarian male vector-ruled bureaucracy, a New World Order, to offset the disintegrating darkness of the feminine collective matrix.

GOD'S WAY FOR THE WORLD TO WORK: A RECONCILIATION OF EAST AND WEST

Part III

Let's tie some more things together. The Lord God established in His Living Law-Word the balance between yang and yin to promote peace, prosperity and progress, both individually (masculine) and collectively (feminine). The Christian God, the Trinity, is the only God that unites both the one and the many, the collective and the individual, the feminine yin and the masculine yang. Moreover, because government is always religion applied to economics, and because the God of the Bible reconciles the ultimate religious, political and economic question, His harmony and reality can therefore be manifest on earth as, "Thy kingdom come, thy will be done, on earth as it is in heaven." The key problem, however, is that by nature, fallen man always wants to be as God, to be like the Most High, by being his own law and determining for himself good and evil. This begins with the mental attitude sin of pride and results in the first overt sin of rebellion against God's lawful authority. This is the exact pattern of Satan's first sin, as well as Adam's and Eve's. A result of man's fallen state is his lack of balance between the one and the many, between yin and yang, between feminine and masculine, between the collective and individuals. Therefore, mankind oscillates between the one and the many in his lawless state, swinging from one extreme to the other. This lack of God's lawful boundaries is the source of cycles in human affairs. There is no equitable balance. The fallen male's natural pre-disposition is to become response-unable (irresponsible) and the female predisposition is to be dominant. As such, man/yang/light/the initiator/an individual, who has responsibility, and the authority commensurate with the responsibility, gives up his lawful leadership as head of the family, church, government, etc., thus sacrificing his feminine inner core where mercy exists (justice tempered with mercy). Man thus ceases to feel good about himself and has low self-worth, and insecurity because he hasn't first done good. Man must do good to feel good. On the other hand, a dominant woman, in a state of low self-worth, insecurity, separated from God, also self-destructs, because she is sexually, emotionally and mentally designed to be a receiving unit, biblically an "empty vessel," who has to receive first before she can give. In other words, she has to feel good to do good. Thus, God's pattern is of gentle-men ruling mercifully with service, covering, with lawful authority over their wives, cherishing them as Christ loved the church and grounding/anchoring them, while women, biblically speaking, re-spond in submission and obedience as helpmates/team members to their "gentle-men" husbands, providing meaning, embellishment, beauty, warmth, nourishment and love holistically to their husband's linear/lawful direction. The male vector and the female matrix thus became together a beautiful light-filled upward spiral under God.

Men were put in charge of the civil law by God as an offset to the natural state in which mankind, both male and female, find them-selves, always seeking to fulfill the womb-based desires for control, security and approval (power/money/sex). Unless men are in charge of the civil law, there is no check against the natural draw that man-kind has to return to the desires normally fulfilled in the womb of the mother. The feminine unconscious/anima is not equipped physi-ologically, psychologically or mentally to handle the law. Precon-ceived opinions are of their very nature antithetical to the objectivity of law. Moreover, because the feminine core is masculine, it lacks mercy, as has been demonstrated consistently in the United States in women gangs which are far less merciful than male gangs, by women jurors, and by divorce and defense attorneys who testify that women are far less merciful and more vindictive and less fair than are men. If the hand that rocks the cradle rules the world, it is a fearful place to live.

In terms of the collective "organizations," God's way is from the bottom up (masculine/individuals), while the natural fallen rebellious man's way is from the top down (feminine/collective). God's way is what Thomas Jefferson called the "natural aristocracy," where the very best individuals through character and performance, rise to top leadership from below. They earn their exalted positions. By con-trast, top-down organizations are the collective "one" over the indi-vidual "many," feminine over masculine, and use force or the threat of force for compliance in an attempt to bring about harmony among the many/the individuals/the masculine. In bottom-up organizations, the many/individuals/masculine rely upon freedom of voluntary asso-ciation. Individuals are held accountable. They have freedom of choice. But this way, God's way, requires more discipline and the application on earth of His supernatural law. It is more painful short-term; it does not cater to the security, control or approval needs of the womb. It is risky, insecure, controversial, uncomfortable, un-fashionable. Thus, man naturally does not tend toward it. However, when these bottom-up organizations are framed by God's law, and man follows His pattern, a balance is provided between the masculine and feminine, between the many and the one, between yang and yin, that promotes peace, prosperity and progress.

The Creator (the Lord God Jesus Christ) is separated from His creation, and so He can provide a law that is ultimate in authority to rule over mankind. The living Law-Word of the Lord Jesus Christ thus resolves man's ultimate religious, political and economic question, which is, "how does man reconcile or balance the rights of the many (individuals/masculine/yang) with the rights of the one (the collective/feminine/yin)?" The top-down (removed from nature), supernatural, personal and caring Law-Word of love and liberty of the Creator Lord Jesus Christ is given, implemented and enabled in His creation by the Holy Spirit, applied first bottom up by born-again discipled individuals, who then are growing both internally spiritually in character and externally by their works, who voluntarily join groups to become the collective, first in the family, then in the local church, then in the community, the job and the state. Because the whole (collective) is no better than the sum of its parts (individuals), the focus first is on the development of the individual who learns responsibly and peacefully to take a long-term view and establish covenants and contracts. Godly covenants and contracts thus fulfill the Second Great Commandment (to love thy neighbor as thyself), which is necessary for the First Great Commandment (to love God) to be fulfilled. Covenants and contracts are basic because they are the evidence of how government is always religion applied to economics.

Government always sits in the middle between religion and economics. Civil government is the religious enactment of ideas about right or wrong, good and evil, ethics and morality, which in turn is applied to the arena of human action which the great Austrian economist, Ludwig Von Mises, called economics. A contract is a legal document, with sanctions and rewards; it is religious, too, because it is no better than the moral/ethical (religious) aspects of its makers, who also have economic duties to perform to fulfill the contract. This contractual bonding between free men (where the Spirit of the Lord is, there is liberty) is a reflection of the Lord Jesus Christ who Himself is the King of Kings (government), Lord of Lords (religion) and Creator of the universe (economics). No wonder the free market framed by God's law works, and forms beautiful collectives.

The many (masculine/individuals/yang) "naturally" become voluntarily the one (feminine/collective/yin) when they form natural bloodline biological families. The "many" also become the "one" spiritually when they voluntarily join the first non-bloodline family, the local church. Thus, God's two basic and most sacredly protected institutions are the family and the church. They are how the "many" first harmonize and then become the "one" - peacefully, voluntarily, spiritually and physically. In such a collective form, the male vector and the feminine matrix join together to become a spiral up, a progression of becoming Christ-like, both individually and collectively, through the making and keeping of covenants and contracts, through voluntary associations, and by taking a long-term view - all framed by the teaching and the keeping of God's Law-Word.

The family correctly programs this righteous, masculine, biblical Christian perspective of reality into their children's un/subconscious up to ages 10-12. The feminine, spiritual un/subconscious delta, theta and alpha rhythms are programmed, hopefully preceded by a godly genetic code coming down at least four generations, so that throughout life, these children will have a blessing from which they will not depart. The church reinforces this godly perspective, the church being at base God's law school, filling in the gaps and providing the linkage between these bloodline and non-bloodline voluntary associations.

Thus, as solid nuclear families are biblical and extant throughout the world, and as the church is biblical and grows throughout the world, inescapably the kingdom of God expands and permeates the world. After all, this is God's world, Satan is a trespasser here. God's Word moves man from the masculine/yang/individuals voluntarily into the feminine/yin/collective peacefully, where like God who is the Great All-in-All, man becomes the unified one, without individuals losing their distinctiveness. This is unity amid diversity. Again, this is reflected in the Godhead - Father, Son and Holy Spirit, individual, yet united, individuals in the collective, the yang in the yin.

The Father, Son and Holy Spirit had to be inescapably labeled as masculine biblically because they are individuals and thus retain their unique personalities and distinctiveness within the "feminine" collective. In other words, it takes the masculine to create the feminine collective. (It might be helpful to visualize vectors shooting out all 360 degrees from a point, thus forming a ball, a collective whole, like a dandelion seed puff.)

A man and a wo-man, two individuals, join together voluntarily and covenantally to become one in a family, a collective. It takes the male initiative sexually, the vector (penis), penetrating into the feminine dark matrix, the vagina, to complete the collective in a family with children. The church, made up of individuals (masculine/yang), becomes the collective (feminine/yin) as the bride of Christ. Here the Word of God is intended to be alive and powerful, sharper than any two-edged sword.

The New Testament, in a sense, because the fruit of the Spirit seems feminine and collective, rides on the masculine vector of the Old Testament law in order to become one - just as a non-Hertzian feminine scalar wave rides on a Hertzian masculine carrier wave, or like a wife depends on her husband for grounding and leadership.

Entering into the realm of time, all of God's lawful principles require a long-term view, which is the closest man can come to being as God, who is eternal. The long-term view has always marked the upper class of any society - those who plan, save, and execute. These are the individuals and societies that prosper long-term. The execution of law is a left-brain, masculine activity. Thus, patriarchs (men) were put in charge of families by God. The patriarch had the greatest power of anyone in the Old Testament. Men (elders) are put in charge of churches, too. God also puts men primarily in charge of law for society, as attorneys, judges, statesmen, police officers, military soldiers, etc. In this way, unity (feminine/yin) can arise out of diversity (masculine/yang). Men in charge of the law offset wo-men's womb-based draw of control, security and approval. Together there is balance.

With Christian gentle-men leading, they speak the truth in love and are sensitive to the feelings which are basic to women. They do not cause pain in their leadership, as is evidenced by their indwelling fruit of the Spirit (love, joy, peace, goodness, kindness, gentleness, faithfulness, patience, long suffering, humility, self control). When men speak the truth in love, they are response-able. In this way they checkmate women's naturally sinful tendency to become rebellious and dominant. These born-again men and women move from their natural fallen states, no longer co-opted by the lust of the eye, the lust of the flesh, the pride of life, by money, sex, or power, and remain godly long-term response-able - responsible. Born-again women yield their feeling sub/unconscious (matrix) to the word of God under the male leadership (vector) of a father/pastor/husband to become fully conscious and frame/ground their feelings. Men are nourished in return. In such a state, the born-again Christian becomes complete, in balance with male and female, yang and yin, conscious and sub/unconscious, animus and anima, individual and collective.

GOD'S WAY FOR THE WORLD TO WORK: A RECONCILIATION OF EAST AND WEST

Part IV

God is life. Any time we're not a-"live," we're 180 degree out of phase and instead, are "evil." ("Live" spelled backwards is "evil".) To be a-live and not evil we need to be conscious. We can only be conscious in the present - now, today, at this very moment. Thus, when we are feeling the E-motions of regret, bitterness, anger, resentment, guilt and the like, we are living in the past. When we are experiencing the E-motions of fear, anxiety, worry and the like, we are living in the future. When we are living in the past or the future we are not truly a-live. We are unconscious. We are evil.

The past is over. It's history. The future is unknown and uncertain. We are only a-live, conscious, in the present moment. Further, in the present, the now, there is only pain and joy. In Christ Jesus our joy is to be full. This means we are to be conscious and live in the present tense, the moment, now, at all times. And when there is pain, we are to feel it in the present and release it; we don't stuff it or ignore it. We process it.

We know our sins of the past are forgiven. We are commanded to be anxious about nothing regarding the future. We know in this world we either grow or we die. Any time we are coasting, we are going downhill. Such is the nature of nature, the Second Law of Thermodynamics in operation.

Growth is painful. It means change and change is uncomfortable. This means to be truly a-live we must embrace growth, change, and pain. We must welcome it. Anything else is death, and God is life. We want to be a-live.

It is different to think of welcoming pain as good for us, but in this sense, it is. Short-term pain keeps us a-live long term. Moreover, when we let go of our fear of being hurt, and instead have faith that God's plan is being worked out in our lives, and thus let go of expectations for the future and release ourselves from attempting to control outcomes, we are free to flow with God's perfect plan for our lives. Then we can continually be surprised by joy. In this state, we are not hurt by what occurs in our lives. We know that all things work together for good. Moreover, we are only vulnerable where we are protective, defensive.

We know far too many people avoid pain at all cost, and would rather die than change. And in truth, when they don't change, they do die. That's real pain! Change equals growth equals life equals pain. No change equals deterioration equals death in the entropic spiral down in the natural Second Law of Thermodynamics. When we look at the magnificent complexity of life and how limited we are in every aspect of our being, we get a glimpse of the folly of our thinking we can control much of anything and/or keep things the same. We might as well just let go and let God take over, rule our lives and progress. This is the point of total brokenness and submission of the mind, heart and will to Him, the yielding of the conscious and subconscious, so He can then use us for the purpose for which we were created, and in the miracle of His love, we can experience all we could ever hope for in the fulfillment of our own dreams. It is in this space, His place, that we can become truly self-actualized and self-realized, manifest what is truly good for us all, as we become Christ-like.

We know there are three primary determinants of personality; heredity, environment, and the programming of the pineal gland astrophysically at birth. Heredity we can seemingly do nothing about. It can be either a blessing or a curse. We know the sins of our ancestors, the mistakes of our mothers and fathers and grandmothers and grandfathers, etc., impact us for at least four generations back (30 possible genetic inputs). Certainly our ancestors weren't perfect, and what we pick up in our RNA/DNA genetic code programs us (partly) mentally, psychologically, emotionally and physically. This natural program can be altered, however, through the supernatural intervention of God the Holy Spirit in our lives. Yes, there are documented examples of genes being supernaturally altered. Ancestral curses can be and are reversible. When the supernatural mind field of the Lord God Jesus Christ replaces our mind field with His values and His thoughts, as our spiritual mind field alters, so does our physically connected mental, emotional and physical being. We cannot change ourselves without being at war with ourselves. Besides, naturally we are a death-based system. Therefore, our salvation must come from outside of us, from God's open supernatural system, from Jesus Christ and the Holy Spirit.

Next, if a child is trained up properly, when he is old, he will not depart from it. This is the most important of the three determinants of personality. The programming parents instill in their children's delta, theta and alpha rhythms of their brains in the first six years of their lives particularly, and even up to ages 10-12, is foundational. This subconscious programming will determine most people's actions throughout their lives. However, if we are to be truly conscious and Christ-like, we will test and prove all things, holding fast to that which is good. We will replace any of the ungodly beliefs, values, thoughts, attitudes, opinions and habits that were programmed in us in our early formative years with those of the Lord God Jesus Christ and consciously make the change. All things positive begin with being conscious. Again, if we are not conscious, we are not a-live, and instead are evil. As God brings us the opportunities through the circumstances of living to endure pain, change and grow, we can walk out our new godly beliefs, values, thoughts, attitudes, opinions and habits in a Christ-like manner, thus placing this new live Christ-centered software programming in place of the old errant ones. We start to think, feel and act differently as we are transformed into being Christ-like. This is truly Christ consciousness. Christ's consciousness (masculine) literally illuminates our subconscious (feminine) where we were previously unconscious, as everything is increasingly brought to light. We become more conscious, live in the present, become like a light on a hill which cannot be hid, and experience joy in Him. Sadly, men love darkness (subconscious/feminine/yin) more than light (conscious/masculine/yang).

The last area of our dark subconscious programming to be changed and overcome is what is uniquely us - that part of us that was programmed at birth, determined by where we were born (longitude and latitude), the time we were born, and the unique vibratory qualities (frequency) of our name at birth. This is our unique frequency signature in all the universe. It is established at birth in the geometric angular programming of the pineal gland, the master spiritual gland of the body. Here is where we get to the core of our unique E-motional challenges in life to become conscious, Christ-like, and truly overcome. Here we deal with the unique issues of our hearts, the darkness inherent in our inner subconscious cores, which need to be challenged and reprogrammed. This is our spiritual core. It is here that religion blocks the E-motional heart clearing which allows true Christianity to be established in believers. It is here where witchcraft attacks. But, when this region of the subconscious is cleared and becomes integrated with Christ's consciousness, brought to His light, then the tender, kind, gentle, loving heart of God is truly established in us, and we can begin to manifest the fruit of the Spirit and the gifts of the Spirit. Life flows and we live in what I call parallel universes, God's created realm and his supernatural spiritual realm simultaneously, being conscious of both. It is at this point God can use us more fully in line with His purpose, to the best service of our fellow man and to our own best interest long-term. We can execute our plans for our lives, as God leads, day by day, and simultaneously experience His supernatural intervention in our lives, providing us opportunities to be Good Samaritans. It is at this point, too, that the ungodly, ancestral, genetic programming begins to alter.

Yes, we do need nutritional support (including eating red meat), rest and exercise to back up this process. Life after all is comprehensive. We have a physical base. Everything we do must be life bringing and possessed of a long-term view. At this point we can truly give thanks for all things. Victory is ours, for we have overcome the world, the natural fallen world of sin and death. The kingdom of God is within us. We are the temple of the Holy Spirit. We love comprehensively. We are living stones, literally crystal christs.

SECTION D
GOD'S LAW

THE DANGER OF THE EXTREMES
OF LAW OR GRACE

Any truth, taken to an extreme, is no longer true. It becomes out-of-balance. Nothing hurts the witness of the basic, fundamental, Bible-believing Christian community more than the friction caused by the divisive extremes of the "grace"-only and "law"-only camps. This immaturity gives the unbelieving secular world another excuse to reject a serious investigation of the truths of Christianity.

The natural man, who the Bible calls the "old man," is identified with a conflict-based modus operandi. In other words, our sin/error nature is to favor "either/or," rather than "both." We naturally like to take sides. We naturally gravitate toward the win-lose philosophy. The desire for conflict is inherent within us. Since there is very little difference overtly between an unbeliever who operates as a "natural man" and the new born-again believer who is a babe in Christ, we should rightfully expect their behavior patterns to be similar. This is what Peter refers to in I Peter 2:1 when he calls new believers new-born babes. Peter requires these new believers to lay aside "all malice, all guile, hypocrisy, envy, and all evil speaking...." In other words, new believers have to quit behaving like their old selves, like natural men. New believers have to cease from their strife and conflict.

As a new believer, the tendency is to gravitate in the same old sinful "either/or" fashion toward the sect of Christianity that most readily matches and harmonizes with one's natural bent. For this reason, new believers who are primarily spiritual, feminine, emotional and subjective will gravitate toward grace. New believers who are more intellectual, thoughtful, masculine, reserved and objective will tend toward law. The result of taking the extreme position of grace without law, or the extreme position of law without grace results in the either/or conflict that is so apparent in the fundamental, Bible-believing, collective church today. It is a hallmark of our national Christian immaturity. It is why divided, we fall. After all, we have eight times the number of "born-again" believers we need to turn this country around toward revival and reconstruction.

A biblical truth that becomes autonomous is no longer true. This is the case with the extreme positions of either grace or law. The answer biblically is not either/or, but both grace and law. We must "rightfully divide the Word of Truth."

Where Christians become exclusively grace-orientated, the over-whelming tendency is to become lawless, which Scripture clearly prohibits. "Grace-only" believers in their spiritual subjectivity and emotionalism can and do justify almost anything they want to do as "right in their own eyes" since they have no firm, clear-cut stand-ards. They have no law to guide them. Feelings, on these opinions, are all that count. They are generally very poor at following through with their covenants and contracts. Thus, grace turns into ruthless lawlessness whereby these believers can and effectively do adopt the humanistic cultural heresy of "do your own thing." Grace becomes a license to run roughshod over fellow believers, as well as unbeliev-ers, all in the name of the Lord. Such believers miss the law of the covenant and the contract, as summarized in the Golden Rule and Christ's Second Great Commandment. They forget and/or ignore what Paul told Timothy in I Timothy 1:8, "that the law is good if one uses it lawfully..." They seldom if ever make restitution for the wrong they have done (Matthew 5:23-24). Such grace believers fail to link the potentiality of the law that is "written on their hearts," (in their subconscious minds - feminine) with the necessary mental un-derstanding of the law that comes to the conscious mind (masculine) only by "studying to show themselves approved." The end result is that the grace believer becomes autonomous, a law unto himself. He may become self-righteous. He is no longer under authority. He adheres to no unchanging standard on earth or from heaven. He has manifested Satan's first sin as recorded in Isaiah 14:12-14, the sins of pride and lawless rebellion leading to autonomy. This is secular hu-manism. An autonomous superman is a counterfeit Jesus Christ.

On the other hand, the law-orientated believer paradoxically ends up in the same final place on earth as the grace-only believer. He, too, becomes autonomous, subject only to his personal interpretation of God's law. He arrives there, however, by traveling a different path. The "law-only" believer rightfully condemns the grace-only perspective as akin to magic. He sees that God is something more than a genie who pops out of a lamp when rubbed, or who appears when He is sung to, His name is mentioned or He is called forth by some indiscernible chant. He rightfully sees that the Bible also re-quires both ethics (discipleship) and work (stewardship) for promo-tion in the Christian life (Luke 16:10-11). But more times than not, the law-only believer accomplishes all his works "in the flesh." This results in internal tension and anger, and often cynicism, followed by burnout. Knowledge and works "in the flesh" produce anger, in-dicative of conflict within, unless there is a changed heart.

The law-only believer also misses the major, primary unseen battle of the spiritual and supernatural world. For this believer, the vital supernatural function of the Holy Spirit is "grieved" and "quenched" from teaching him all truth and guiding him day-by-day. The result is that this believer attempts to become righteous by his own efforts. Therefore, his "good works" biblically, become "wood, hay and stubble," rather than "gold, silver and precious stones." Furthermore, because he sees that God's laws do work for the natural man in the seen, visible world, as common grace, he tends to become self-righteous and proud of his efforts. He glories in his "fruit." Pride, biblically, is the first mental attitude sin.

The law-only believer often becomes a member of the "frozen chosen," who know all the answers but rarely apply them, particularly in a grace-orientated or compassionate way. He is often quick to condemn and slow to help, while the grace-only believer may be emotionally quick to serve and help others, even to the point of throwing himself figuratively in front of an oncoming truck.

The law-only believer also tends to be slow to forgive, although he may make restitution for his personal wrongs. He is often out of touch with his feelings, although he tends to keep his covenants. In such realms, the "letter of the law," rather than the "spirit of the law" is upheld. But, by keeping the law by his own efforts, a believer slips into autonomy. He becomes his own law (since he keeps the law), and thus is not under the authority of anyone. Being proud and autonomous, he also manifests Satan's first (and worst) sin, matching his brother believer on the other extreme, the grace-only believer. Both are insidiously in rebellion against authority. Such secular humanism, man as his own god, is the basic conflict between man and God.

The God of the Bible will have nothing to do with the pride, autonomy, rebellion, subjectivity or self-righteousness of either the grace-only or law-only believer. The God of the Bible is not an either/or God. He is not pleased when we follow our natural bent toward either grace or law. The God of the Bible is not a God of conflict; He is a God of harmony and of peace. He is not a God of division, but of reconciliation. This is manifested in His very nature - the Trinity.

The Trinity is comprised of three persons - Father, Son, Holy Spirit - separate, yet united. Put differently, in the Trinity, the answer is not either/or, the answer is both, simultaneously. This is also evident in the person of Jesus Christ. He is both God and perfect man, separate, yet united. It follows that God's truth is also a dialectic tension when it comes to both grace and law. God is neither judgment or mercy. He is both judgment and mercy.

It is quite difficult for the Western mind to hold these two seemingly opposing concepts simultaneously in dialectic tension. It is hard to see that God's law is His grace gift to mankind, given to us for our own good (Deuteronomy 6:23 and 10:13). God even tells us He perfects us through His law, through the "grace"-ful teaching, intervention, and help of the Holy Spirit. We are to speak God's law - His truth, in love, with grace. Christ commands that if we love Him, we will keep His law, His commandments. Scripture teaches us that until heaven and earth pass away, God's law is valid. Yet Scripture also teaches us that God's law kills, particularly the letter rather than the spirit of the law. If we attempt to keep the law by our own efforts, we will fail. We need the grace of God's Holy Spirit to keep His law. The answer is again both - grace and law.

Too often Christians miss the reality that God's law has both an eternal purpose and a purpose on earth in His creation, just as Christians often miss that the New Testament is a commentary on, and a continuation of, the Old Testament rather than a refutation of it. Scripture cannot be broken. It is the lack of such distinctions that causes much confusion among believers.

True enough, with regard to our eternal salvation, God's "law" condemned us. None of us could keep it perfectly. Therefore, we were doomed. An imperfect, sinful natural man cannot have fellowship with a perfect righteous God. In this eternal salvation sense then, the law of God brought death. This is why Jesus Christ had to come, be born of a virgin, live a perfect life, perfectly keep the law and take onto Himself all of the law-breaking sins of man's world. Jesus Christ paid for all the sins (errors) of us lawbreakers on the cross. The fact that He did this was pure grace and a merciful, compassionate act. The fact that God, the Father, let His only Son, Jesus Christ, perform such an act is perfect grace, and an act of love. At the same time, the holiness of God's law was so absolutely righteous and unbending, that once man broke the covenant of grace in the Garden of Eden and violated God's law, there was no way God could love man until the price for the lawbreaking was paid through the grace of Jesus Christ's work.

Any time we find ourselves in the extreme of either law or grace, the biblical requirement is that the other be immediately implemented in order for the Christian to function correctly, biblically. When the law abided perfectly in the garden of Eden, perfect grace also existed. When the law was broken there, grace no longer abounded. But then God, in His grace, began the great restoration of fellowship between man and Himself as told through the Old Testament, up until the completion of Jesus Christ's work on earth. Thus, the crowning glory of Jesus Christ's resurrection was the perfect keeping and fulfillment of the restitution-requirement of God's law, as well as the perfect manifestation of His grace and love. In His grace and mercy God loved us so much that He sent His own Son, Jesus Christ. God became flesh through Christ Jesus and perfectly kept the law on our behalf to resolve the problem of the eternal penalty of lawbreaking, of sin. Once the work of Christ was completed, this again turned the curse of the law into a blessing on earth during history. It became the law of love and liberty. Such a blessing is grace.

Since we are no longer faced with the penalty of eternal condemnation demanded by God's Old Testament law, thanks to the work of Jesus Christ, we are now free through the Power of the Holy Spirit to work out our salvation in our time on earth by living according to the standards of God's law of love and liberty. By way of the Holy Spirit linking up with our spirit in our study of God's Law-Word, and tying it together with the law that was written on our hearts (subconscious) at the moment of our eternally realized salvation, we exercise faith through grace in working out our temporal salvation toward our position of eternal salvation. We become in time what we are positionally - eternally saved.

God's law is the standard by which the Christian makes decisions and then acts. This keeps the Christian from being humanistic and "doing whatever is right in his own eyes" - Deuteronomy 12:8. The mature Christian lives the law of God in a grace-orientated way according to the guidelines of I Corinthians 13. It's not either/or, it's both. Grace solved the eternal penalty problem of God's law. God's grace then and now enables us to live victoriously, fulfilling God's law. Love (grace) is the keeping of the law (Romans 13:10). After all, if not God's law, whose law? The laws of the kings of the earth? The laws of the rulers who take counsel against the Lord while the nations rage? (Psalm 2) Hardly! The Christian is to be self-governing just like Jesus. Perfect, grace-orientated, mature, law-abiding Christians require no externally imposed manmade regulations. Given that we aren't perfect, God has instituted civil government to serve as an administrator and enforcer of God's Law for collective mankind.

We need the grace given us by the supernatural function of God's Holy Spirit to work through us in fulfilling God's law in our hearts, thoughts, and works, moment-by-moment, day-by-day. Just as a young son, naturally desiring autonomy, looks upon the law of his human father as a millstone around his neck, a burden to be suffered quietly under threat of punishment for disobedience, so, too, in like manner does the young believer view the law of God. By contrast, a mature son looks at his father's law as a gift of grace, a gift of love, obedience, to which results in blessings for the son. In like manner, the mature Christian in his study of the law also eagerly awaits the teaching of the Holy Spirit regarding God's law, because he both wants to please his heavenly Father, serve his fellow man and reap the blessings for himself both on earth and eternally. God's grace therefore enables us to keep his law, to "speak the truth in love," to exercise justice tempered with mercy, and to do good works. Indeed, the "sword of the Spirit is the Law-Word" of God (Ephesians 6:17).

God's way is not either/or, it's both law and grace simultaneously. If a Christian is to become mature, he must strive to grow in the areas of grace and law. He must emphasize the area that is not his natural bent. For the extremes of either grace or law tend to lead to rebellious autonomy which was Satan's first manifest sin, a sin condemned by God as one, if not the worst, of sins (Jeremiah 16:11-12). A Christian instead is called to individual maturity for the purpose of service in the Christian community.

GOD'S TEETH

Many of us have beloved sons. Imagine that your precious son gave his life to save one of his friends, some kid you don't even know. Then imagine yourself adopting this alien kid in an act of compassion, kindness, love, mercy and goodness. Next, imagine this adopted kid spitting on your son's grave and telling you what a fool your dead son was, and what an idiot you are to adopt him. How would you feel toward this kid? This is roughly the way God feels when we, His adopted sons, sin/rebel willfully against Him.

How many times have we read the New Testament? How many sermons and Bible study classes have we attended? How many Christian articles, publications, tracts and books have we read? Over the past 25 years of serious Christianity - hundreds. How many times have we read the book of Hebrews? Several. So why does Hebrews 10:26-31 cause us to sit up straight in our chairs? Because in all these years, we've never heard any Christian religious leader, writer, teacher or pastor speak or write on these verses. Why? Because "easy-believism" Christianity dominates, nay, even saturates, the American Christian church today.

Sin? Christians are told that sin is no longer an issue, that Jesus Christ died for our sins, and that we are eternally saved as members of his called, elect, chosen, etc. Good enough. But that's not the end of the story. We have seen numerous articles written and heard sermons about I John 1:9, "If we confess our sins, He is faithful and just to forgive us our sins and to cleanse us from all unrighteousness." Okay. We're not perfect, not by a long shot. We have to grow up from milk to meat. Along the way we're going to transgress the law, because sin is transgression of the law. We're going to err, to miss the mark, and if we do, then repent, confess our sins, have a change of heart and a subsequent change of behavior (which is the real meaning of repentance). Then "He is faithful and just to forgive us our sins and to cleanse us from all unrighteousness." Hallelujah!

Now here is the stick, or to put it more bluntly, the hammer. What if we sin willfully, knowingly? What if, as Christians, we know the right thing to do and don't do it, or purposefully do the wrong thing? Reference Hebrews 10:26-31. Even in Thomas Nelson's New King James Version, sinning willfully exacts a terrible price: "For if we sin willingly after we have received the knowledge of the truth, there no longer remains a sacrifice for sins, but a certain fearful expectation of judgment, and fiery indignation which will devour the adversaries. Anyone who has rejected Moses' law dies without mercy on the testimony of two or three witnesses. Of how much worse punishment, do you suppose, will he be thought worthy who has trampled the Son of God underfoot, counted the blood of the covenant by which he was sanctified a common thing, and insulted the Spirit of grace? For we know Him who said, 'Vengeance is Mine, I will repay, says the Lord.' And again, 'The Lord will judge His people.' It is a fearful thing to fall into the hands of the living God."

That's pretty clear. There are not many weasely, soft-sell interpretations that could come out of those straightforward verses. Not many modern commentaries are written on it. Why? Easy-believism Christianity, which is so dominant today, dies a quick death under these verses. God's Word here has teeth and brings to mind thoughts of discipline, discipleship, being a soldier of the cross, judgment and the true fear of the Lord.

Let's be clear on this. If we are born-again Christians, and we know what God's Word requires, and we deliberately, purposely and willfully violate the Word, insulting the Holy Spirit, discounting the blood covenant made perfect by the Lord Jesus Christ on the cross, effectively walking all over Jesus, it subjects us to worse punishment from God than those who violated the law of Moses, and they died without mercy! The Lord God judges His people. This is consistent with the fact that when Jesus Christ returns to earth, He takes no prisoners.

The implications of these verses are obvious. It is a dangerous and fearful thing to be a sinner in the hands of an angry God. Again, Hebrews 10, verses 26 and 27 say it all, "For if we sin willfully after we have received the knowledge of the truth, there no longer remains a sacrifice for sins, but a certain fearful expectation of judgment, and fiery indignation which will devour...."

Do any of us really want this type of exposure to our angry God? Do we want to live an uncovered life and be subject to Satan's demonic realm? No! Then why aren't the churches teaching the fear of the Lord, His Law-Word, and the humility which leads to obedience after they have preached the blood of Christ? Why aren't the churches disciplining their members and holding them accountable for their sins? Whatever happened to accountability, church discipline, forgiveness, restitution and restoration? Why aren't Christian believers rebuking one another day in and day out, and simultaneously supporting and exhorting each other, to avoid willful sinning? If we do not see our errors/sins, if we are unconscious with regard to them, then we will commit them over and over again to our own detriment. We, thus, should be thankful if a fellow Christian points out to us our errors/sins that we cannot see. This way we can repent and change the easy way, from instruction, without learning the hard way. We can become conscious.

Where is the basic fear of the Lord today demanded by these verses in Hebrews 10? Have American Christians' hearts become so hardened that they continuously grieve the Spirit? The Holy Spirit's activity rests on the Word of God as the sword of the Spirit. Is God's Word really hidden in our hearts so that we do not sin against Him?

Today, far and away, the majority who call themselves Christians, treat sin lightly, much like a light beer. Sin, it seems, goes down easy and is eliminated quickly, without exacting much of a price. Members of too many modern churches, if they are biblical at all, when they recognize sin, run quickly to I John 1:9 after they sin, and then go along their merry way, never giving their offense to God a second thought. Then they sin the same sin again. How many Christians, when they sin willfully, truly ponder the fact that they have insulted the Holy Spirit, stomped on the Lord Jesus Christ, and considered His blood sacrifice, His sacred covenant, a common thing?

All too often today, God is pictured as this great gentle genie in the sky, almost exclusively like a mother - compassionate, loving, forgiving, merciful, giving us anything we ask for when we ask for it, patting us on the head when we're hurt, telling us it's okay when we go wrong, and generally helping us feel good about ourselves. (If we're always feeling good about ourselves we have no reason or incentive to grow or change.) Well, certainly God's mercy covers some of this, and we're to cast our cares on Him for He cares for us. But this perspective, standing alone, is an incomplete picture, and is not representative of the God of the Bible. Scripture clearly teaches that these merciful characteristics of God apply only to those who are obedient, who do not sin willfully.

In summary, there is no fear of the Lord today. And "it is a fearful thing to fall into the hands of the living God." The modern American church has bought a feminist lie, a whore of Babylon deception. Can there be any doubt that the willful sinning which occurs by so-called American Christians today will exact a greater judgment by God upon this nation than most Christians can even conceive? Jonathan Edwards, where are your spiritual descendants who are willing to courageously preach God's Word, balancing His justice with His mercy? Where is the true faith today that takes the whole counsel of God seriously? Where is the faith leading to fear of the Lord that puts the brakes on Christians' willingness to sin willfully?

POLARITY AND GOD'S LAW

In what the Bible calls the "fallen" or "natural" world, the realm of the physical and visible that is referred to in science as Newtonian physics, there exists polarity which is in apparent conflict. This conflict accelerates entropy, producing poverty and death, works in cycles and makes life chancy. Examples of the polarity are: positive - negative, male - female, patriarchal - matriarchal, individual - collective, diversity - unity, Western - Eastern, yang - yin, linear - cyclical, risk/faith/unseen - security/approval/control/seen.

One of the purposes of God's law is to resolve the conflict between polarities, eliminate the cycles, and "make straight the way of the Lord." This provides greater certainty in life, promotes prosperity, shifts the orientation from a short-term to a long-term perspective, moves mankind from operating in a death-based closed system to a life-bringing open system - all which effectively bring about "Thy kingdom come, Thy will be done, on earth as it is in heaven."

There are two ways in which progressive change can occur - God's way, or the evolutionary way (order out of chaos). (The latter may not be progressive.) God's law, in scientific terms, acts like a scalar interferometer. That is to say, it holds the yin and yang factors in tension, Truth-In-Tension if you will, establishing the simultaneous coexistence of apparent opposites, which neutralizes and resolves conflict and promotes cooperation. This allows peaceful and harmonious change and steady progress in a life-bringing open system on earth, brought about by God's supernatural (quantum/open system) law. This is literally the kingdom of God come to earth His creation. Jesus Christ, His person, work and life repaired the rift in time, making reconciliation and restoration possible.

The second method of change comes in the natural, fallen and closed Newtonian system of conflict, chance, cycles, poverty and death. Here, conflict between the yin-yang factors disintegrates into chaos out of which supposedly, a new order arises. This is a very painful way for man to learn and change. And rather than an evolution up, there may be a devolution down. In actuality, evolution promotes slavery of the masses, whereby a Luciferian elite rule.

Let's look at these yin and yang factors to better understand how God wants redeemed men - gentlemen - to work with the helpmates - women - to turn the wild wildernesses of the earth and human hearts into peaceful gardens.

We know God is sexless. Yet, God the Father, God the Son and God the Holy Spirit are all clearly defined as masculine when it comes to their dealings with man and the earth (the creation). Why? Because it takes the masculine/individuals to correctly create the feminine/collective. We also know all the way from Eve in Genesis to the whore of Babylon in Revelation, that the feminine matrix personality is often used to depict enmity with God when it is created from the top down. No wonder modern witches and feminists hate the Bible and its patriarchy. They view the Bible as sexist. But witchcraft is sexist. In Wiccan witchcraft, female witches are far more powerful than male "witches."

Yang means light and is masculine, male, electrical and can be depicted as a vector, a spear, an impulse. Yang includes linear progress, is individualistic, progressive, discriminating, law-based and logical. By contrast, yin, which is feminine and means dark, should be seen as a magnetic matrix, like a womb. It is the collective principle, stagnant, chaotic and emotional. From the feminine matrix arise the needs for security, approval and control, which translate in life into gold, gals, glory, or money, sex and power, or the lust of the eye, the lust of the flesh, and the pride of life.

The magnetic feminine matrix is naturally spiritual and ungrounded, and seeks to ground in the tangible physical world, the "seen." By contrast, the electrical linear masculine vector is grounded in the tangible physical world, but is more risk-oriented regarding the future, thus having a greater capacity for faith (the unseen future) rather than sight (the seen present). The feminine matrix is by its very essence lawless, and therefore leads naturally to secular humanism. By contrast, by its very essence, the male vector includes the cause-and-effect rule of law and thus by implication, potentially the rule of God. Progress is yang, masculine, not only because it is linear (as opposed to cyclical), but also due to its faith and its according willingness to take risks for potential reward in the unseen future. The ideal combination is a vortex, a spiral of progress, uniting the male vector and feminine matrix.

Here's how this works out politically. In modern times, we have the feminine matrix as predominant. It is dark and spiritual (yin), as manifest in the New Age movement which undergirds American political structure today. It is chaotic, and clearly humanistic, focusing at the collective level on socialism and at the individual level on the egocentric, autonomous development of self. Its religion centers on goddesses and the worship of "Mother Earth," which is the basis of witchcraft. Biblically, rebellion is as the sin of witchcraft since Satan's first overt sin was rebellion against Almighty God. Satan uses witchcraft to manifest his power supernaturally on earth as an extension of his defiance. Rebellion against lawful authority is also natural for fallen, unredeemed man. Supernaturally, witchcraft is Satan's counterfeit to prayer. Naturally, debt (death) money is in opposition to honest money, like gold.

Since the feminine matrix is by nature lawless and collective, it gravitates in its fallen state toward the likes of socialism, communism and democracy as the forms of civil government - collectivist forms of government, which at their end operate lawlessly and self-destruct. Communism/democracy inevitably fail and the "order that comes out of chaos" is literally an occult masculine vector. Caesar-run bureaucratic dictatorships arise out of the lawlessness of anarchy. It is difficult for Americans to realize that democracy is a feminine collective that moves inevitably toward anarchy and chaos, and thus the bureaucratic dictatorship of a Caesar. Until 1980, the U.S. Army's training manual listed democracy as a threat to the republican American form of government.

The communistic/socialistic/democratic state's attempt to fulfill the feminine matrix's womb-based needs for control, approval and security eventually become so all-encompassing that the state consumes the society it governs and eventually implodes, leading to collapse. What else could it do? Civil government is ultimately a parasite which lives off the livelihood (taxes) of the people (the host) until it consumes them. Witness the historical case of the former USSR, and the contemporary case of the U.S. The U.S. civil government today, through its ubiquitous alphabet agencies and unelected judges, is exercising total control through omnipotent regulation, court rulings, and through forcing social consensus via politically correct thinking. This is an attempt to provide total security in a tangible sense for all of society now. There is no risk, short-term, and thus no faith within a civil government-dominated society. Its bankruptcy is assured as the federal debt (death) compounds in the trillions of dollars.

The overriding goal of such a feminine matrix is to become all-in-all, like God, to have the many/individuals/diversity, the masculine principle, forcibly become the one/the collective/the community/unity. The world collective is to be achieved through force by the state (civil government), from the top down, via bureaucratic edict and arbitrary court rulings, moving now toward New World Order fascism. By contrast, God's system for transforming the many/the individualistic/masculine/diversity principle into the one/the collective/the community/unity is voluntary, peaceful, from the bottom up, via covenants and contracts.

God's law, the masculine vector, achieves the harmony of polarity between the many and the one, the masculine and the feminine, the individual and the collective, etc. in the following five ways.

(1) On an individual level, learning is achieved by having everyone become self-governing. A person possessed naturally in his fallen state of the short-term view and conflict, chance, cycles, poverty and death in the closed system, is transformed by God's law into a born-again state through the redemptive blood of the Lord Jesus Christ. He is brought into the open supernatural system of God's kingdom come on earth as it is in Heaven - a kingdom of life, light, love, liberty, law, laughter and a long-term view. The self-governing individual, by living according to the Golden Rule and the Second Great Commandment, first serves his fellow man before receiving benefits for himself. This, in turn, fulfills the First Great Commandment, since we demonstrate our love of God by serving others, and this results in a win-win-win between God, man and his fellow man. (The creation/environment wins too.) The conflict between the masculine vector and the feminine matrix, between the many and the one, the individual and the collective, is thus reconciled. Self-interest is first served by service, and man's spiritual need for love and his physical need for money - reflecting his dual spiritual and physical natures - are met as the polarity conflict is resolved. His sense of self-worth is also increased, the only way it can be, by having God work through him and by serving (loving) his fellow man.

(2) Next comes the family, where the individual (the many/masculine vector) voluntarily becomes the one (the collective/feminine matrix). When this union produces children, a bloodline connection is created which naturally resolves the conflict between diversity and unity, between yang and yin, between the male vector and the feminine matrix. No wonder treason in the Old Testament was against the family, not the state. The family is the basic godly unit (collective) by which conflict is resolved between individuals.

(3) Next comes the church, God's spiritual non-bloodline family, where we (the collective) are all members of the same body. We are all feminine with respect to the Lord God Jesus Christ because we are under His lawful authority. He is the bridegroom (masculine), and we are the bride (feminine). The church is a voluntary organization. It redeems society from the bottom up, one individual (masculine vector) at a time, thus bringing about a voluntary collective

(feminine matrix). Its influence should rightfully permeate society. Government is always religion applied to economics.

(4) The state (the collective), which is created by free men (individuals - the masculine vector), should be a civil government which exists for the benefit of individuals (masculine). This voluntary collective (feminine), the state, is organized to protect life, liberty, and property; provide for the common defense; keep the peace; and enforce contracts - in other words, ensure the freedom and protection of individuals (masculine vector). It does not exist to promote the feminine collective to serve its own self-interest at the expense of individuals, as it does today. The individual properly assumes the risks of life with the family and the church first providing social safety nets so the state does not exercise control by promoting bureaucratically inspired security and approval.

(5) In economics we find that the free market and Adam Smith's so-called "invisible hand" is God's masculine individualistic diversity principle in action. This principle results in men peacefully and voluntarily exchanging goods and services, thus producing the harmonious feminine collective, the market, through the rule of the law of contract. A contract is a religious, governmental and economic document - because a contract is no better than the morality (religion) of the contracting parties; is subject to the rule of law governmentally should either or both parties not perform their duties according to the terms of the contract; and has economic benefits to both parties.

We know from I Timothy 6:10 that the love of money (greed) is the root of all evil. In the original languages it effectively reads that selfishness is the root of all evil. Therefore, if we are to avoid ground level evil (sin), we have to be selfless rather than selfish. In other words, we have to live according to the Golden Rule and the Second Great Commandment - we have to serve or give before we receive. By, fulfilling the Second Great Commandment, we fulfill the First Great Commandment, and as a by-product of serving our fellow man and God, are personally blessed. This is what happens in free market economic contracting. By doing so, we live in the life-bringing, open system of God's voluntary collective of common grace rather than the closed death-based system of the civil government-imposed, collectively controlled economy. Is it any wonder that the nation-states war against God? Their death-based dark, closed, natural system is at complete odds with God's life-bringing, open system, supernatural plan.

By giving before we receive, being selfless rather than selfish, we participate in resolving the polarity conflict between the one and the many. We then move voluntarily, peacefully and harmoniously from the individualistic man of the masculine vector into the one of the collective feminine matrix. A beautiful vortex or spiral results. God's law (yang = masculine, light), literally brings light into darkness (yin = feminine, dark). God's light today shines in the darkness and mankind does not comprehend it due to pride, lack of discernment, deception, rebellion and a love of death. All those who hate God, love death (Proverbs 8:36).

We also see this principle of give versus take, of voluntary harmony versus conflict, in supply side economics versus consumer-based economics. Supply side economics focuses on production (giving based, in savings), while consumer-based economics focuses on taking (spending/borrowing for self). It is selflessness versus selfishness again. It is good versus evil. It is the godly long-term view versus the godless short-term orientation.

In conclusion, God's law neutralizes and resolves the natural fallen conflict of polarities between male and female; diversity and unity; yang and yin; light and dark; active and passive; initiators and responders; Western and Eastern civilization; logic and emotion; progressive linear, cause-and-effect reality and holographic reality; the risk and faith of the unseen and the security, control and approval of the seen; the grounded and the ungrounded; the clockwise and the counterclockwise; the compressing and the decompressing - all by first implementing the masculine vector of God's law in individuals, and then in forming families, churches, communities, nations and economies, so that these "many" (masculine) will voluntarily, peacefully, harmoniously become the "one" (feminine). When this is totally achieved, then the bride (the feminine matrix collective) will be ready for its bridegroom (the ultimate masculine vector), the Lord Jesus Christ. The peaceable kingdom, the open system, the supernatural kingdom of God will then be installed on earth. "Thy kingdom come, Thy will be done, on earth as it is in heaven."

As an example of how all this works.... Imagine it's the early 1800s in the United States and the land in the West is being settled. One man, a farmer, settles a homestead through which the only creek which waters the valley below flows. As a Christian "gentle-man," he is empathetic with the needs of the other farmers. He sees his duty toward his fellow man. He realizes that he needs to balance off his individual need for water with those of his fellow farmers and thus share the water, rather than selfishly hoard it and run the risk that the other farmers downstream either will physically assault and/or kill him for it, or call in the state (civil government) to force him to share the water. He opts against violent conflict or state imposed, top-down dictates as solutions. Instead, he surveys the land and computes how the water can be stored in holding ponds with a series of dams (dominions and stewardship), so that everyone's water needs may be met year-round. His long-term view and plan, whereby his individual self-interest is served by cooperating with the collective group of farmers, results in a farm cooperative that builds and operates the dams and rations the water. Alternatively, he develops a water supply system himself and turns a profit for his water management services, based upon the infrastructure and utility plant he built.

In this way, the farmer (individual masculine vector), has resolved the potential conflict with the feminine collective (all the other farmers). By having a tender heart that is sensitive to the needs of others, this man and the other men and women in the valley remain free and self-governing. Far better this way than to be hard-hearted and operate according to the closed system of survival of the fittest, where he would hoard the water and subject himself to conflict, chance, and possibly even death.

From this example, we discover the only method that ultimately works long-term is for individuals to be self-governing, effectively born again from their natural, conflict-ridden, fallen state. It is only redeemed men, individually, who are able ultimately to provide the solution that resolves the conflict between the individual and the collective, between diversity and unity, and voluntarily transform the masculine vector into the feminine collective, peacefully so.

THE MYTH SURROUNDING WILD HORSES

Hollywood (the "wood" of witchcraft) portrays herds of wild horses as strong and free, roving the plains and hills, and frolicking with reckless abandon. The romantic fantasy communicated is that if horses (men/women) are left alone to do their own thing in an unbridled fashion, they too, will have the best of all worlds. Sadly, nothing could be further from the truth. This is Satan's lie. Wild horses, just like men and women, fall slave to the closed system; the conflict, chance, cycles, poverty and death of fallen Newtonion nature. This is the overwhelming evidence compiled by both the Department of Interior on the mustangs which roam wild in the West on federal lands, and the State of Montana regarding the wild horse population on Wild Horse Island.

What is the truth regarding how wild horses fare when left alone totally free and lawless to roam in the natural realm? First of all, the conformation which improves the breed, brought about by the dominion and stewardship of man, is missing. The breed literally deteriorates. Bloodlines are a mess. Secondly, the horses fall prey to predators, lack of food and natural disasters. They have no peace and no rest. They are not cherished. They live in continual fear concerning their existence, having no safety or security. They fall victim to disease and if they are injured, crippled or have an infection, they often experience a slow, agonizing death. There is no one there to take care of them. They never realize their full potential or the good life that comes from being harnessed, broken to the bit, trained, cared for, groomed, watered, fed with balanced nutrition and loved. Wild horses, in effect, squander their lives because they have not come under the dominion and stewardship of man.

Is life any different for a lawless, rebellious, selfish, unbridled self-willed man or woman who lives in disobedience to God's law in this, His creation? No, not really. Such men and women are like wild horses, lost in a hostile nature, subject to survival of the fittest. Such people never realize their true potential. Their lives are wasted. They might as well be sent, so to speak, to the cannery for dog food, just as the wild horses are food for their predators.

This is what we effectively have in our society today: wild horses - irresponsible men and lawless, dominant, rebellious women. They are no good to themselves, and certainly not to God. Their

lives are dark, empty, shallow and full of pain. They are unconscious, caught up in the anger, bitterness, resentment and guilt of the
past, and the fear and anxiety of the future. They are self-destructive. They never reach consciousness because they never first reach
the God-consciousness that comes from submitting themselves to Jesus Christ and to obedience to God's Word and will. They cannot
know themselves because they do not know their Creator. Because
they are still subject to Satan's closed, fallen, natural system of conflict, chance, cycles, poverty and death, they are always under the
gun, so to speak, suffering, in unconscious pain. Such men never
receive true honor and respect. Such women never enjoy the thrill of
being cherished or loved, and the peace and security of rest. They
are instead always discontent. They maintain a frantic search for
happiness. They live the miserable life of predators or parasites,
preying on one another in search of some fleeting moment of tempo-
rary, self-indulgent gratification. They remain immature, like
spoiled, selfish children.

There is a key difference, however. Man, unlike wild horses,
lives also in his mind. His thoughts are either God's thoughts or
they are the thoughts of Satan's realm. There is no in between. Man
is either a slave to God or a slave to Satan. Autonomous freedom is
a myth. The men and women of the United States today, who live
according to their own lawless thoughts, which are not their own but
the thoughts of their sinful ancestors, erroneous cultural upbringing,
and/or from Satan's demonic realm, have life's vitality sucked out of
them. They are to be pitied. Man (woman) cannot escape his (her)
thoughts. All reality is subjectively interpreted according to God's
values or values arising from the wicked, unstable emotions of the
heart. So, there is no truth which leads to freedom apart from the
standards established by God and His law. Law defines boundaries -
the fences of freedom - and resolves the natural conflict between
individuals, between men and women, and between man and society.
God's law resolves the conflict, chance, cycles, poverty and death of
the natural fallen closed system and opens mankind up to the blessings and benefits of God's open supernatural system.

Thoughts determine actions. If a man thinks God's thoughts,
stemming from having God's values in his heart, he will be far more
successful than if he operates on his own. Thus, such godly attributes as doing the right thing long-term, being empathetic and dutiful
toward his fellow man, being helpful and selfless, as well as humble
and responsible personally, giving before receiving, forgiving others,
being kind and merciful and having God's new heart rather than the

natural fallen wicked one, gives man the ability to possess love and have joy under all circumstances. They are the cause and effect/result of being bridled to God's will. It keeps men and women down-to-earth, grounded, content and out of the demon-filled dark matrix. The addiction to the ever fleeting and unfulfilling selfish pursuits of pleasure and romance, unsatisfying in the end as they always are, is defeated by the bridled heart. After all, it is only with the submission of one's will, of surrendering, of being bridled to godly obedience, that the delusions and illusions of the dying man or woman can fall from the eyes so that he/she can see and hear, and be fully conscious. Then they can truly feel. Then they can be still and find the peace and joy they so seek in fulfilling relationships. The heart-hardening pursuit of power, control, security and approval, through manipulation and deceit, often masking fear and anger, finally departs. Health, wealth and life's vitality then come forth and are restored. godly people no longer make themselves miserable by aimlessly running to and fro like wild horses ever seeking stimulation, trying to survive.

How much better is it for man to responsibly bridle himself and become subject to the Lord God Jesus Christ? In doing so, he becomes a "gentle-man." How much better is it for a woman to submit herself and her will to the loving leadership of her godly, Christian, gentleman's covering? The irony of God's love is that man and woman both achieve what they were pursuing by giving up the struggle, the pursuit of the myth of autonomous freedom, and by yielding and surrendering. (We have to die to ourselves in order to live.) They not only find the peace, security, certainty, prosperity, life and love they are seeking, but they also maximize their freedom.

Which horse (man) does the rancher (God) allow the most freedom? The wild horse who will not be broken and does not submit his/her will? No, certainly not. Such a rebellious horse is kept under tight restrictions, in confined quarters, closely watched in a small corral or paddock. By contrast, the horse which has been broken to the dominion of the rancher will paradoxically receive the greatest freedom to roam the pastures and do pretty much as he/she pleases, except for the times the rancher calls on him/her to work, which is rewarding! Therefore, it is much better to be a submitted, yielded, bridled, obedient man/woman living on God's ranch, than a wild suffering horse roaming in endless fear on the plains of life.

SIGNS OF IMPENDING JUDGMENT

What remains of the grounded Christian church in the U.S. today fears God's impending judgment on this country. To be sure, that voice is a distinct minority. Fewer in number are the churches which begin with the sovereignty of God. Even fewer are grounded and established in obedience to His Law-Word, and are intent on not conforming to the world. Indeed, the vast majority of so-called Christianity, with its thoroughly modern churches, are rushing headlong into conformation with the world. So, the question of judgment, as always, becomes one of timing - not if, but when.

Actually, the judgment of God and reaping what has been sown are two sides of the same coin. The first viewpoint is that of the Creator, the second, that of the creature. Both are true; there is just a superior/subordinate relationship between the viewpoints. God's primary perspective is that He executes judgment. Man's subordinate viewpoint is that he is reaping what he has sown, paying the wages of sin - death.

So, when does the fat hit the fire? Any time now. The "80-20 Rule" is already activated. To be precise, judgment is already underway; we as a nation are reaping what we have sown. Once the "80-20 Rule" has kicked in, as it now has, we pass the point of no return. There is no longer a turning back by way of repentance, revival, restoration, reformation and reconstruction until after judgment has ravaged the society, save a miracle.

Many will ask, "Just what is this '80-20 Rule' which guarantees impending judgment, which ensures a people have passed the point of no return?" Actually, it's a phenomenon from the world of economics, from collective human action, and from markets. For example, in business, 80 percent of a business's profits will usually come from 20 percent of its clientele. Likewise, 20 percent of a business' customers will cause 80 percent of its problems. Eighty percent, too, is the cut-off point beyond which optimization becomes impossible, and the amount of added time, effort and money to increase the return becomes prohibitively expensive, exponentially so as one approaches 100 percent. Put differently, it is not all that difficult to fall under the confines of the first standard deviation of the bell-shaped curve. But by the time one has taken the time, expense and effort to reach the second or third standard deviation, the cost to maximize (as opposed to optimize) requires fearful sacrifices.

In trading markets, the "80-20 Rule" applies via the application of the theory of contrary opinion. Specifically, when better than 80 percent of investors become bullish (positive) on a stock or commodity, inevitably that stock or commodity will either accelerate up exponentially, blow off and then collapse, or it will top out at that point (just above 80 percent) and turn back down. The same principle applies when investors become too bearish (negative) on a specific market. When 80 percent or better of all investors are negative on a stock or commodity, that market will either accelerate down in an exponential way in a panic decline to exhaustion, or it will at that point (just after negativity reaches 80 percent) bottom out and turn back up. Either way, the point applies: Once you have passed 80 percent consensus of collective human action or opinion, a blow-off and/or a trend change is imminent. We have reached this point in American society. God's judgment, reaping what we have sown, followed by a trend change, is all but a given. It would take a miracle for it to be otherwise. Is there a biblical basis for a miracle? Has the U.S. sought God's favor and mercy by its fear of the Lord, prayer, obedience and repentance?

Today, 91 percent of Americans routinely lie. This should not be surprising. According to James Patterson's book, "The Day America Told The Truth," only 13 percent believe in all Ten Commandments. This is despite the fact that Century III Foundation of Oakbrook, Illinois has found better than 80 percent consensus among all races, religions and sexes, that the Ten Commandments are a solid basis for a "common good" legal system. Thus, it should come as no surprise that 84 percent of Americans today are what the Bible calls "lawless." Fully 84 percent of Americans today say they have become a law unto themselves.

What is God's standard for impending judgment all the way from Deuteronomy, through the prophets of the Old Testament, into the New Testament, including Jesus' comments, the epistles and Revelation? LAWLESSNESS!

Need more evidence? The Bible makes it very clear that worshiping the creation rather than the Creator invites His wrath. The August 2, 1991 Wall Street Journal, in a front page article, declared, "Eight out of ten Americans are environmentalists." Environmentalism is a pagan, witchcraft-based religion of idolatry which worships the creation instead of the Creator. It is basic to the New World Order. Environmentalism has linked itself with goddess worship, too. Starhawk, a priestess in the movement, stated, "...human beings are meant to be integrated with nature." The Christian concept of man as a steward of the earth who has dominion over fallen nature is alien now to 80 percent of Americans. The ancient pagan concept of unrestrained Mother Earth, replete with her characteristics of conflict, chance, cycles, poverty and death, is with us in full force today. That sounds like judgment. The signs in the heavens as they impact the earth over the next few years ensures judgment.

That's not the end of it. The culture's emasculation of the biblical patriarch in his primary role as protector of home and country is all but complete. Newsweek reported that 79 percent of Americans think women should be eligible for combat, with only 18 percent opposing women in combat. Further, a 1991 Gallup poll revealed that less than 10 percent are committed Christians, and most of them are not knowledgeable regarding Christianity.

It should be obvious that whether one looks at the "80-20 Rule" in terms of violation of the Ten Commandments, environmentalism, or degradation of the biblical patriarch, this country is past the point of no return. Judgment is at hand. We are about to reap what we have sown. But take heart. It also means that a trend change is close at hand.

There is yet another method which confirms the imminent judgment of God. Modern science has verified, through study in the infrared light range, that everything is an antenna. This means all of us are infrared antennas, whose shape and substance, thoughts and emotions, determine the frequencies we emit and attract. In other words, to put it in simple terms, we get back what we give off. We attract what we emit. We reap what we sow. The Eastern religions have long had a warped version of this truth which they call karma.

In this light (infrared), just what is the U.S. giving the world? What are we giving off? Clearly, we are the world leader in promoting, by practice and example, death. Abortion comes immediately to mind. Even the symbol on our Federal Reserve notes is the same infrared antenna that existed between 600 B.C. and 200 B.C. among the pagan Carthaginians who sacrificed their children to the goddess Tanit and her consort, Baal. So, it is no wonder we sacrifice our children, too. Further, since the U.S. dollar (Federal Reserve note) is the world's reserve currency, the world follows the U.S.' example. A Federal Reserve note is a debt. One of the root meanings of the word debt is death.

But that's not the end of the death which the U.S. exports today. We're the largest exporter of debt. The external debt of the United States today exceeds that of all other nations combined. Plus, the

federal debt is increasing at an exponential rate and will hit $10 tril-
lion by 1998. The federal debt is increasing by $1 billion every 10
hours. Total consumer debt is 96 percent of personal income.
Again, a root meaning of the word "debt" is "death."

That's not all. One of our largest exports is entertainment, TV
and movies, issued by Hollywood. "Holly wood" is the wood used
by witches in casting spells, making magic wands, etc. It is therefore
no accident that a major theme of Hollywood, which is exported to
the rest of the world, is death - violence - passed off as entertainment.

Then there are the weapons of death. The United States is the
world's largest arms supplier at 45 percent, more than doubling its
sales to Third World nations in 1990.

We also export dead food, by exporting the American fast food
diet.

In summary, whether we're talking about the export of Federal
Reserve notes which symbolize debt (and indeed stand for death), the
export of death as entertainment (from Hollywood), the export of the
weapons of death (world leader), dead food, or setting the example
for the world in abortion (death), it is very clear that what we are
emitting and signaling to the rest of the world is DEATH.

We get back what we give off. We reap what we sow. The
wages of sin are death. Therefore, God's judgment of death to this
country would be nothing more than a logical response to what the
nation has asked for. And since we have passed the point of no
return according to the "80-20 Rule," we should expect death to be
impending and as comprehensive as the nature of our death-based
exports. As a nation thinketh, so it exporteth, so it is.

Precluding any last minute chance for mercy is the prayer of the
persecuted church in China and the former Soviet Union, as well as
in the Third World. These churches pray for persecution of the
church in the United States. Why? Because the church which is
grounded, established and rooted in the Lord Jesus Christ elsewhere
in the world, the church which has been truly tried by fire, sees the
church in the U.S. today as irrelevant, misguided, reprobate, apostate,
reversionistic, having conformed to the world. Therefore, for the
American church, it's back to basics time. There's no time to waste.
Fear of the Lord is primary, leading to obedience, resulting then in
provision, mercy and protection. It's time for forgiveness, righteousness, restitution and holiness; the church - the non-bloodline spiritual
family of God - praying, fasting, worshiping, studying, obeying and

meeting each other's needs just like members of a natural family. This way the empowerment of the Holy Spirit and the protection of the angelic forces can be released on His justified and sanctified body. This way the church can be a witness to the world by not conforming to the world.

It is no accident that so many have been called out of the United States of late to evangelize and be active in Christian missions elsewhere around the world. U.S. sinners are in the hand of an angry God today. God often scatters His people before impending judgment.

THE TEN COMMANDMENTS

(FROM AN OPEN SYSTEM/SUPER-NATURAL/KINGDOM OF GOD PERSPECTIVE)

The first four of the Ten Great Commandments which God gave Moses have to do with the kingdom of God - i.e. the supernatural, the quantum realm of physics, the metaphysical. The last six Commandments concern the operation of the kingdom of God on earth. These commandments are about applying God's laws of love and liberty to promote the balance between the individual and the collective, between the many and the one so there is peace, prosperity and progress on earth. The laws are all negative, informing man of what he cannot do, leaving the rest of life free. This maximizes man's freedom.

The First Great Commandment of the Ten requires that there be no other gods before the One Great God. It is He who is the ultimate balance between the one and the many, the perfect unity between yin and yang. He reconciles everything as the Great All-in-All, as infinite vectors from zero point energy create the collective unity, much as one ball of a dandelion gone to seed is created by the many individual seeds. God is distinct from and above His creation even though He interacts with it. There is a gap between God and man which only Jesus Christ fills. He is both the first and the last - alpha and omega - with all other gods in subjection to Him and to the degenerating laws of nature, as manifested by conflict, chance, cycles, poverty and death.

The Second Great Commandment of the Ten requires that there be no graven images. This insures that man does not confine God to time and space or assign any limits to him. A fabricated image would thus wrongly attempt to intertwine God with His creation, who always maintains the Creator/creature separation. Again, there is a distinction between God and His creation, with Jesus Christ being the unifying bridge and force. God is loving, living, sovereign, just, unchanging, perfect, righteous, purposeful light; He is all powerful, all knowing, all present and cannot be understood in terms of an earthly image.

The Third Great Commandment requires that God's name not be taken in vain. Words have power. It was God's living, spoken words, His creative energy, that created this fantastic earth. A supernatural God cannot be profaned and degraded in profanity by His creation. He is the potter and we are the clay. When man takes God's name in vain he creates a curse for himself since he will get back what he gives off. Besides, taking God's name in vain is a major sign of rebellion. Rebellion was the first overt act of sin by Satan against God. It was Adam and Eve's first sin, as it is the first sinful act of a wife against her husband. God considers rebellion as the sin of witchcraft.

The Fourth Great Commandment requires that the Sabbath Day be remembered and kept holy. This is man's day of rest. A day of rest is vital to man's welfare long-term. Dr. Peter Rothchild, personal physician to the King and Queen of Spain, has pointed out that this sixth day sabbath rest is key in quantum physics also. The quantum pulse is a 6:1 pulse. This means in order for continual progress to be made, man must work six days and then change his activity, and rest, the seventh day. Otherwise, he deteriorates into entropy. It's only when we rest on the Sabbath Day and keep it holy, that we can overcome the Second Law of Thermodynamics - entropy - and move instead into what God intends: His kingdom come, His will be done, on earth, as it is in heaven. If we keep the Sabbath, we can grow and progress into His supernatural realm. If God decided to rest after He created the world in six days, why are we not to do likewise?

The Fifth Great Commandment requires us to honor our fathers and mothers. This not only ensures long life (Ephesians 6:2-3), but it also ensures respect for life and authority. When an individual does not honor his father and mother, he is literally at war with his life force, his genes, and with his subconscious programming. He is also at war with the basic authority over his life. This will lead to a shorter life. Not honoring one's father and mother, the first unit of authority for each of us, is a sign of rebellion. It insures our destruction as we reap what we sow.

The Sixth Great Commandment is to not murder. All of us have the right to life. Anyone who murders evokes the law of reciprocity: an eye-for-an-eye and a tooth-for-a-tooth. They gets back what they have given off - death. Life is sacred and not to be violated.

The Seventh Great Commandment is to not commit adultery. Adultery is treason against the family, God's basic unit on earth where individuals (yang) voluntarily become the collective (yin). Committing adultery violates the basic bloodline connection that provides support for mankind - the family. It is not without fear and trembling, we note, that in God's Old Testament, that rebellion against one's father and mother - failure to honor them (the Fifth Commandment), murder (the Sixth Commandment), and acts of adultery were all subject to the death penalty. In the New Testament, God's Law of Liberty is based on obedience to His Law-Word. Under paganism, liberty was seen first as sexual promiscuity.

The Eighth Great Commandment is the commandment to not steal. Property rights are human rights. Without property for our person in the form of food, clothing and shelter, we cease to exist. Therefore, when one is deprived of one's property, one is deprived of one's life. Life equals time equals energy equals property. So stealing is akin to murder, because property rights are an extension of personal human rights. Moreover, stealing violates the basic governmental, religious, and economic instruments which God intends for man to use to interface with his fellow man - covenants and contracts.

The Ninth Great Commandment is to not bear false witness - not to say things that are untrue about your neighbor. A false witness in or out of court damages another individual's person, reputation and/or property. False words damage the countenance/aura/electromagnetic field of an individual. This damage to his energy system in turn damages his physical system. Satan is the father of lies, just like he is a thief and a murderer. This commandment, much like the commandment not to steal or murder, sets mankind's feet on a godly path and moves him out of the character of Satan.

The Tenth and final Great Commandment is to offset envy. We are not to covet anything that belongs to another. Envy is destructive because it says in effect that you have something I want, that I know I can never have, and therefore I will destroy what you have. Envy ravages wealth and stops initiative, change, growth, advancement and progress. Institutionalized envy, such as welfare, is particularly insidious since it grows like a cancer, consuming the fruits of production until there is nothing left to sustain it. Envy ensures the decline of man's individual and collective well being.

(One of the most extensive works on The Ten Commandments and biblical law is R. J. Rushdoony's "The Institutes of Biblical Law," Ross House Books, P.O. Box 67, Vallecito, CA 95251.)

SECTION E
CHRISTIAN LEADERSHIP

CHRISTIANS IN A PAGAN SOCIETY

A hallmark of a pagan social order is a secular humanistic state playing god by making its own laws and holding them up as ultimate. This is what exists today in most of the world, including the United States. By contrast, a hallmark of a Christian social order is an emphasis on self-government and upon the development and use of the contract and covenant, which increases individual freedom.

Given these differences, how does a Christian best cope in the pagan, humanistic legal environment in which he finds himself today? He copes by becoming a mature Christian, possessed of good character, covenanting and contracting faithfully. Why? The pagan state, as a substitute god, tries to legislate perfection. The only way the Christian can escape the state's oppressive legal web is to already be mature in Christian character and to consistently covenant and contract to be perfect. Put differently, to maximize personal peace, freedom and prosperity under the oppressive hand of the state, we must operate in a mature Christian manner.

The pagan state tries to force moral perfection upon its people from the top down, from the "outside in" through collective bureaucratic and other legal pressure on the individual. God's way is to work from the bottom up, from the "inside out" through the power of the Holy Spirit and His Law-Word, to achieve moral excellence. The pagan state wishes for its subjects to behave like mature Christians, but under the sovereignty of the state as god. So ironically, the best way the Christian can cope under this alien system is to behave maturely. This is the lesson taught to us by Joseph in Egypt under Pharaoh and Daniel under Nebuchadnezzar in Babylon.

Under the pagan, humanistic government today, the laws and regulations are so comprehensive that we are almost required to be perfect (or a slave) to live within the law. Over 200 pages of regulations are placed by U.S. federal agencies in the Federal Register every day. The United States has 90 percent of the world's lawyers. Fully 96 percent of the civil lawsuits filed in this world today are filed in the United States. To live successfully in the United States today is to walk through a legal mine field. Only if a Christian truly has the character to deal justly and mercifully with his fellow man in a mature way does he have a hope of avoiding legal assault. Only if a Christian covenants and contracts with a servant's heart and performance does he have a prayer of avoiding lawsuits. The only way to escape the computerized jungle of bureaucratic paperwork and control which incessantly flows from the federal government is to covenant and contract verbally. This means the pagan state is again forcing us back to the ultimate in Christian character and contracting: "A man's word is his bond."

The problem long-term, of course, is that the pagan state's system does not work. It inevitably breaks down because it is parasitic and not godly; it does not operate according to truth. When men are good, moral and self-governing, external laws legislated by the state are unnecessary. On the other hand, when men are immoral and evil, legislated state laws, regardless of their ever-increasing number, are ineffective - they simply do not work. Evil men break and/or ignore the laws.

This is what we are facing today, the breakdown of the civil government's legal system. Men are not good, moral and self-governing, so they are ignoring and/or breaking the laws of the secular state. The underground economy in the U.S. exceeds $400 billion annually. One out of every 65 men in the U.S. spends time in jail. These facts shed light on the bankruptcy of the pagan-state system and the efficacy of the only system which works - the Christian self-governing system. It is this reality, this recognition of the bankruptcy of the state and the operational truth of the Christian governmental order, which results in the pagan state's wrongful persecution of the Christian community. Christians are not abused when the state is still hopeful it can successfully compete with the Christian system. Rather, Christians are persecuted when the breakdown of the religious, philosophical, legislative and economic systems of the pagan state becomes obvious. This is the lesson of the prophets, Jeremiah in particular. It is also the communication of Jesus Christ in the gospels. It is further the experience of the early church in Rome. It is only the immature, culturally conforming, irrelevant antinomian religious community which is left alone by the pagan state. Why shouldn't it be? It is lukewarm, and part and parcel of the total cultural collapse. It is only the mature Christian community, operating contrary to the "traditions of men," which suffers persecution as the pagan system founders. For it is only this community whose example illuminates the failure of the state and convicts it of its sin. This was the case with the Russian church as the Soviet Union collapsed. So, while the religious community-at-large suffers generally due to the legislative error of a pagan state, it is only the mature Christian community which is specifically targeted by the state for persecution.

The worst is yet to come. There are few signs of a national revival leading to a reformation in the culture-at-large. Ironically this means that the more righteous in character and covenanting the mature Christian community becomes in the United States today, the more it will be persecuted. After all, self-governing Christians are at the opposite end of the spectrum from a federal government intent on establishing a New World Order.

Up until this point, a Christian man has been uniquely able to walk through the legal mine field planted by the pagan state. For up until now, the state has believed it could successfully compete with and beat the Christian competition in producing a better man and bringing about a better world. Now the evidence of its failings is increasingly widespread. Concomitantly, seeing that a mature Christian community is the only one which can succeed without special favor under a pagan state, the state now lashes out in vindictive injustice. This is what the federal and state government's attack against the superior Christian schools is all about.

This then is what it really means to "suffer for Christ's sake." Mature Christians who covenant and contract with justice and mercy, applying God's Law-Word to every area of life, are light and salt in a dark and dying world. The dying pagan state loves darkness more than light. So it oppresses the mature Christian community. This is the essence of the important lesson Jesus taught in Matthew 5:11-16. It is a lesson which mature Christians had better take to heart today. Only on a just legal playing field is the Christian system allowed to demonstrate that it can produce the greatest peace and prosperity for both the believing and unbelieving community alike. By stark contrast, under the decaying state of today, the greater the demonstration of Christian character and covenantal faithfulness, the greater the unjust persecution. Put simply, we're back to Egypt, Babylon and Rome.

The wheat is being separated from the chaff. The remnant is being matured by fire. As Christians who seek to apply God's Law-Word to every area of life, we had better put on the whole armor of God and work together as a peaceful, cooperative Christian army if we are to meet the challenge of "Onward Christian Soldiers!"

BIBLE TECHNICIANS
AND ESCHATOLOGY

Undoubtedly, one of the most difficult categories of Christian believers to reason with are Bible technicians. By and large, these men
love the Lord and know their Bibles backward and forward. They
can rattle off Scripture and often quote it verbatim for hours on end.
But when you get two Bible technicians together who have spent
their lives doing nothing but devouring the Word and only the Word,
well, it's hard to believe that any two men who believe and know the
same Book could go at each other with such intense disagreement.

Religious intellectuals, professional theologians, primitive Baptists and conservative Presbyterians rank high up on the list of Bible
technicians. The problem with Bible technicians, who know the Bible and only the Bible, is that they miss a significant portion of
God's truth. The Bible, as the infallible Word of God, speaks truly
wherever it speaks. However, it does not speak exhaustively. The
Bible is an outline, a rule book, a law book. We have to begin with
the Bible and take it presuppositionally to God's creation, to the facts
and scientific principles of His created world, and then bring that
knowledge back to the Bible to achieve a complete understanding of
God's truth. It is with this synergistic integration that Bible technicians often go awry. They know the Bible to the exclusion of all
else, failing to recognize that "all else" helps us understand the Bible
and God's purpose for our lives.

Does the understanding of Hebrew and Greek - the original languages in which the Bible was written - help us to better understand
the Bible? Of course. How about the work of biblical archaeolo-
gists? Sure. Church historians? Yes. How about Christian economics, church history or just learning from experience? Of course.
How about studying under mature Christians who work in different
occupations, who come from different cultures and walks of life?
Cannot all this be spiritually enriching? Yes.

Most men, whether believers or unbelievers, are not fools. Men
usually believe something because they have come to learn that it
works or is true, at least partially. So, we all have a lot to learn from
almost everyone. This is why Christian men who have well-rounded
experience and who have read extensively outside of just the Bible
itself, can bring such insight and wisdom to bear on the Word of God
and how it applies to all areas of life. Such men have something

other than an "egghead" narrow technical perspective, which brings balance to man's understanding of what God has to say regarding both His Word and His creation.

We have all heard it said, "You can use the Bible to prove almost anything." For the most part that's true, particularly when an isolated verse is taken out of context. The Bible can indeed be used to prove almost anything. But the Bible, because it reflects a balance between the one and the many and also gives us never-changing principles to be meshed with the ever-changing facts of God's creation, requires us to exercise discernment. It takes discernment to rightfully divide the Word of Truth and apply it in the creation. It takes humility to be able to hear and discern what the Holy Spirit has to say with regard to which part of God's Word applies to a particular set of unique circumstances.

This brings us to eschatology, an area which often divides Christians who have most everything else in common. True enough, man's view with regard to the future and end-time things will influence (and rightfully determine) his actions in the present if he is logically consistent. And since the Bible is one-third prophecy, eschatology is important. But it should not be a basis for lack of fellowship with other Bible-believing Christians. The fundamental issue is, "What think ye of Christ?" In this essential area, there must be unity, agreement that Jesus Christ is the God/man, Who was born of a virgin, lived a perfect life, died for the sins of His sheep, was resurrected from the dead, ascended into Heaven, and now is seated at the right hand of God the Father, from where He rules and we follow. But in nonessentials there should be liberty, and in all other areas, charity.

We all have imperfect knowledge because none of us knows everything about the mind of God and His Word or the integration of how everything fits together in all areas regarding the facts of God's creation. We are therefore best served by first being humble personally, and then tolerant toward our fellow believer, and gracious and merciful toward the unbeliever. This perspective is too often lacking among Bible technicians.

When it comes to prophecy and eschatology, of the three main positions, the classic pre-millennial perspective is the general view that at the end of a period of tribulation, Christ will return and man will then be "raptured" into the heavens. Briefly, the a-millennial perspective is that the kingdom of God gets better and better over time while the kingdom of Satan gets worse and worse over time. There is an ever-increasing division between the sheep and the goats.

The a-mil viewpoint is not widely held. And lastly, the revival in our day and age is that of the post-millennial perspective. Post-mil adherents maintain that Christians will progressively exercise dominion over the earth, geographically, in the nations, but first in people's minds, hearts and lives, and then in all areas of life, until Christ returns. At that time the kingdom will be His.

Not surprisingly in our irresponsible, short-term oriented and escapist world, none of these three classic eschatological views are largely advocated by so-called American Christians today. Most instead hold to the perspective of a "pre-tribulational rapture." For these "nod-to-God" Christians, salvation is just an easy "eternal life and fire" insurance policy; all gain, with no pain, and no responsibility - no priesthood on earth, no discipleship, no stewardship; just sign on the bottom line. Bow, smile, wink, give an acknowledgment some Sunday, walk an aisle and it's all tied down. Heaven is assured. Christianity is wrapped up in a quick, easy, neat package. Whatever happened to the biblical perspective found in Acts that Christianity is "The Way"? Christianity is a way of life, not a religion.

Back to the three classic perspectives. It seems that the pre-mil perspective is a short-term one, particularly the popular pre-tribulational rapture doctrine going around today; that the a-mil perspective is an intermediate-term view; and that the post-mil perspective takes the long-term view. In keeping with the fact that the principles of God's Word all require man to take the long-term view because God is eternal, we probably would be best served by gravitating toward the post-mil perspective. But there are many good Christian men who capably defend all three perspectives - men who make solid logical arguments from the Word of God.

From a pre-mil perspective, as long as Christians are not occupying and exercising dominion, or being stewards or discipling the nations comprehensively around the world, mankind will continue to make the same mistakes he has made in the past. In other words, historical cycles of human action will repeat. So, even if end-time prophecy was in fact first fulfilled in the early history of the church, as many post-mil scholars hold, it does not mean that situations similar to those early times will not come around again. As long as mankind does not occupy comprehensively and move forward in history according to God's linear plan, as long as we are slaves to human action cycles, what goes around comes around. This is why some of the well-meaning pre-mil scholars of today see parallels in contemporary human events with already historically fulfilled scriptural prophecies. The similarities do exist. We are indeed entering effectively another time of tribulation for mankind. Historian Arnold Toynbee called it our "time of trouble." Different words, same meaning.

And truly today, from an a-mil perspective, as the lines are increasingly drawn between good and evil, men who stand for the kingdom of God are becoming more clear-cut and faithful in their Christian walks and lives, while evil is becoming more evident, perverse and reprehensible also. The sheep and the goats are being clearly divided. There is truth to the a-mil perspective that the kingdom of God is more peaceful and life-oriented in all areas while Satan's kingdom is becoming more violent, decadent and death-oriented. This struck home to me when I ministered in Australia in the 1980s. There the division line is more apparent, as it is also in many Third World countries. It seems that the more difficult the situation for mankind, the more openly humanistic the government, and the more harsh man's economic conditions, the greater the delineation between good and evil. We are in the early stages of one of these harsh eras now in the West. (The a-mils believe that the longer history progresses and the greater the division between good and evil, the more imminent Christ's return.)

Finally, what about the post-mil position? Economics is made up of basically two factors, land and labor, things and people. If we look at these two factors alone, using the example of child-rearing (labor) and technology (land), we must conclude that things over time are getting better. Overall, child abuse and child abandonment are not anywhere near what they have been in centuries past, thanks to progressive Christian culture. Even a cursory study of the history of child-rearing reveals this important truth. Furthermore, we are no longer in the Bronze Age, the Copper Age or the Iron Age. Technology is exploding. The technological potential for peaceful Christian dominion and stewardship of the earth exists today as never before. Moreover, men are increasingly using technology for better and better purposes - or for more evil purposes. But the point is, progressive dominion and stewardship in terms of both people and things do exist. It's an indisputable fact. This is what secular thinkers such as Herman Kahn and Alvin Toffler see. It is what the New Agers, despite their Eastern religious inclination, understand in an evolutionary way.

This hopeful long-term vision of the future is what the New Agers, as environmental dupes of the New World Order, work toward. Who in their right mind is willing to work for something when they know they can't win, at least with any sustained motivation or hope for victory long-term? This is what the post-mils and

New Agers have in common, an eschatology of victory. So, they are locked in a life and death struggle - Satan's kingdom or God's?

One of the determining questions of eschatology is, "What on earth is Satan working to achieve?" Which eschatological world view is Satan/Lucifer attempting to counterfeit? Satan, after all, is the great deceiver, the great liar, the great counterfeiter. He comes disguised as an angel of light even though he is not one. (God is light.) Is Satan trying to counterfeit pre-mil, a-mil, or post-mil?

If we begin with man's two basic, diametrically opposed religious options, the sovereignty of God or the humanistic sovereignty of man (Satan), we can then begin to see how all of life falls into either of these two camps. When considering the subject of origins, what immediately springs forth from the sovereignty of God is creationism. What emerges from the sovereignty of Satan (man in his humanistic religion) is evolution, and evolutionary humanism. So, as soon as we establish the abstract religious base of secular humanism versus the sovereignty of God, we immediately next move to the factual earthly base and the perspective of either evolution or creation respectively. Evolution is Satan's great counterfeit to God's plan for redeemed men under Christ to progressively work for the restoration of the earth to a garden.

What is the essence of evolution? That things are getting better and better over time, that we are "evolving." With which Christian perspective is evolution most closely aligned, attempting to counterfeit? Post-millennialism, the concept that Christians will make the world better and better over time until Christ returns. Satan's counterfeit evolution, is attempting to substitute itself for the post-mil reality. The New Agers are close to being on track. They have just bought truth with a deathly satanic warp. Therefore, witchcraft-based, New Age environmentalism is basic to establishing the Luciferian New World Order.

What do people say when things get better and better over time in the secular world? They say things are "evolving." What word, what terminology, should Christians use? Christians should say that things are "progressing."

Finally, from a motivational perspective, God is no dummy. It would be perverse and cruel on God's part to have His Son and our Saviour, Jesus Christ, pay the awful price for eternal salvation on the Cross, win the victory over sin and then leave us, His priests, ambassadors and stewards, here on earth to work for a losing cause. Sure, we are rewarded according to our works, our stewardship and our use of the tongue (Matthew 12) eternally. God understands the principle of incentive, eternally. In fact, he invented it. Men work for benefits and out of love. This is why the Christian free market works and the economics of communism was such a dismal failure. There is no incentive to work under communism. But Deuteronomy, Proverbs, the Gospels, James and the "Little Johns" make it abundantly clear that man is rewarded in time and on earth for being a faithful priest, ambassador and steward. Men who have put it to the test and proved all things affirm that Christianity works in the here and now. This is what made America great. Government is always religion applied to economics.

Other men, believers and unbelievers alike, emulate success. This is the reason that there is a successful company in the marketplace, with a new product or service, other companies quickly spring up to copy it. This is also true, or at least should be, if Christians were doing things correctly/biblically. Believers and unbelievers alike would emulate the Christian "Way" of life.

For an unbeliever, this is what common grace is all about. He cannot live a better life in his pursuit of "personal peace and prosperity" than under a Christian system. (The Bible, of course, teaches that unbelievers have an often unrecognized death wish which propels them toward destruction.) Again, in the case of the Christian free market, where men are free to covenant and contract for the exchange of goods and services, whoever serves best, wins. A Christian will serve best because he first loves God, he is obedient to God and has the heart to serve his fellow man. As a by-product he wins. An unbeliever with an unregenerate heart will serve because he is required to do so before he can benefit himself. The motivation is clearly different - which is why God judges the heart - but either way, the end result is the same. It's a win-win transaction. The sun shines and the rain falls on the good and evil alike. Just as success on earth requires a Christian operating methodology for believers and unbelievers alike, common grace means that men, in their time on earth, benefit under an implemented Christian world and life view like under no other system.

So, logically, it follows that whether the spiritual blinders fall and men have regenerated hearts or men simply seek their own economic self-interest over time, the post-mil perspective bears fruit.

The information explosion globally and the use of computers makes this an even greater probability. We are closing in on the fulfillment of a peaceable kingdom. Any free market economist will confirm that in an environment of perfect information, competition (conflict) could cease to exist. Perfect cooperation should result from the perfect dissemination of perfect information. We are moving more and more toward this reality all the time. The information explosion and the global utilization of computers is an earthly example of how God is in the process of unifying all things unto Himself. Communism, a brutal atheistic, political and economic system, has now been defeated worldwide, philosophically, morally and economically, by the information-based market economy. All other collectivist, bureaucratic governments are feeling the same pressure. The next shoe to drop is a global revival leading to comprehensive reformation where men's hearts are changed - in other words, a massive decentralization.

We are part of an overall process on earth in which God wins. Jesus Christ has had all authority ever since He ascended into Heaven and sat down at the right hand of God The Father. Now His kingdom and rulership are being progressively established on the earth. This is the end goal of the Gospel, the "Good News." We may even win in our own lifetime and, if we don't because of the ups and downs in God's progressive spiral plan for history, then He rewards us eternally anyway. It's win-win for us. That's positive. That's motivational. That's truth. We therefore have motivation to disciple the nations. May we therefore occupy until Christ comes. May we therefore pray and work that, "Thy kingdom come, Thy will be done, on earth as it is in heaven." And, we don't have to be Bible technicians to figure all this out.

THE CRISIS
IN CHRISTIAN LEADERSHIP

In the 1980s, the Associated Press headlined, "Oral Roberts: Money will Keep Me Alive." The August 3, 1987 Time magazine cover story was, "God & Money, Greed, Secrecy and Scandal: An Inside Look at Jim and Tammy Bakker's Bankrupt Empire." It is no longer God versus mammon or Christ's kingdom versus the world's system. It is religious Christianity with the bowed head and bent knee before the altar of mammon. The evil triumvirate of money, sex and power found its completion with Jessica Hahn moving into Hugh Hefner's California Playboy mansion.

So much for the headline grabbing stories that depict what passed for Christian leadership. But away from the neon lights, the backwaters of Christian America's leadership are equally stagnant. Today some incorrectly teach that God is just a magic genie, who can be called upon when one wishes to receive the desires of one's heart. Some preachers are, quite bluntly, simply entertainers, locked into the "star" system. Active support of atheistic collective socialism proliferates elsewhere among the clergy. Meaningless tradition, making Christianity literally a religion that is indeed the "opiate of the people," dominates in far too many quarters of "men of the cloth." Religious schizophrenia, where the spiritual and physical aspects of man are severed, is characteristic of many religious leaders who are submerged in pietism. Others promote psychological humanism, while some are legalistic, some lawless. And then there are those who are locked up in the monasteries - the never, never land of religious symbolism, offset by those wallowing in emotion.

As a result of all these leadership failures, the 20th century American Christian church has been routed by the enemy. Witchcraft-based, Mother Earth, environmental, New Age, Luciferian humanism is more consistent. The American Christian church is in crisis. It is first and foremost a crisis of leadership because where the shepherd leads, the sheep will follow. Too often today, the shepherds are lost, inept, and/or poorly trained.

In I Timothy 3 and Titus 1, we find the job requirements for becoming president of a company, for becoming chief executive officer of a Fortune 500 corporation. Oops, that's not entirely correct, is it? I Timothy 3 and Titus 1 lay out the requirements for becoming a bishop, for leading God's people. What's the point? Simply this:

the requirements for heading up the church are identical to those required of leadership in a successful organization in the so-called "secular" world. Is this the way Christian leadership is installed today? By no means. Small wonder then, that the church and Christendom is in crisis and beaten down by the enemy. Its leadership (shepherds), in far too many cases, have not even met the basic biblical requirements for their positions!

Just take a look around at the successful masculine leadership in all walks of life, which exhibit both spiritual character and professionalism in their callings. Such men have proven themselves previously, and thereby earned the right to head up their organizations. The president of a company, the chief executive officer (CEO), is a man who is generally blameless. Surveys in Fortune magazine reveal overwhelmingly that the CEO is the husband of one wife, having in most cases been married to his original wife for 20 years or more. His children have been brought up understanding authority, in the fear and admonition of the Lord, as it were. Therefore, his children are not accused of deception or insubordination. Further, the president (CEO) is a good steward. In other words, he is a good economist. He understands the practical working out of things. He is not all "pie in the sky, by and by."

He is not self-willed. He works for the good of the organization overall. As a leader, he serves. He meets the needs of others, promoting them rather than himself. His eye is upon accomplishing the objectives of the organization, not feeding his own ego.

As president (CEO), he is slow to lose his temper. His anger has to build slowly over time to the point of righteous indignation before it is released. He is mature. He has seen most of the challenges and aggravations before. He realizes that life is the "martyrdom of pin pricks." So he is stable and steady in all challenges. He does not ride the emotional roller coaster of feast or famine, of success or failure, of fear or greed. He does not give in to every whim of management theory which regularly snags the business community. He knows what works. He has proven all things. Thus, he moves forward toward the organization's objective.

His confidence, his spiritual maturity, his character and his professional competence mean that the details of life do not overwhelm him. He concentrates on the important, rather than on the urgent things of life. So, he does not attempt to escape the problems of the day by being given to wine. He has no frustrations to be vented with violence. In fact, he is not violent. He takes things as they come, a day at a time. Realizing that making money is a by-product of first doing things correctly, he is not greedy for money. Making money takes care of itself when his company professionally provides the needed goods or service.

Recognizing the principle of "synergy," that the whole is greater than the sum of its parts, the good CEO concentrates on the character development and professional development of his subordinates, so that they all voluntarily work better together as team members toward a common beneficial objective. He is not threatened by those beneath him. He is hospitable to those who are under his authority, as well as to his customers and strangers in the land. He attempts to live peacefully with all men. He is the servant of all.

The president (CEO) loves what is good, having been tested by the triumvirate of evil (money, sex and power) on his way to the top. He has overcome such evil. He is rational, sober-minded, has a strong sense of justice and does what is fair and good. Disciplining both his thoughts and his tongue, he is self-controlled. He carefully chooses and measures his words. He holds fast to that which is good. He realizes the importance of balance, and so he is temperate in all things. His behavior is exemplary and because of his wisdom, he has earned the right to teach those under him. He has learned that quarreling accomplishes nothing, and that "a man convinced against his will remains unconvinced still." Therefore, he "speaks the truth in love," gently. He is a proven veteran who has found his fulfillment in the humility and service of leadership. Accordingly, he has earned the respect of his peers.

Question: How many Christian leaders today measure up to these lofty qualifications, to these high standards? The best of the world's non-church organizations demand these qualifications of their leadership, why not the church? Isn't the leadership of the church supposed to be "the best of the best"? Where are the "top guns" of Christian leadership?

I Timothy 3:6 warns us specifically that a bishop (a church leader) is not to be a novice, because a novice falls victim to pride, the same mental attitude sin that tripped up Satan. Pride, by definition, is not humble and does not serve. Pride is a self-promoter. And yet, the primary criterion for leadership in Christ's kingdom is the requirement of service. Jesus Christ, the greatest leader of all, informs us in Matthew 20:28 that He came not to be served, but to serve! His unequaled service to mankind in turn earned Him the right to sit at the right hand of the Father where He is given all power in heaven and earth. Jesus was tested in all things before He earned His exalted position of authority. Isn't Jesus Christ our example as well as our Savior? What then can be said for proud, selfish, unserving, self-promoting Christian leadership? Sadly, not much good.

Luke 16:11 instructs us that if a man has not been tested and proven faithful in the little things of this world and then particularly the big things like money, who in their right mind will trust him with the riches of Christ's kingdom? Supposedly, no one. And yet, so-called American Christian "leadership" today is saturated with men (and women, God forbid) who do not know the first thing about being faithful in the little things, much less the awesome challenges of mammon. Far too large a percentage of American Christian leadership today could not pass the qualifying exam of I Timothy 3 and Titus 1 if their lives depended on it, which in a very real spiritual sense, they do.

Small wonder we get so many "airheads," so many "sky pilots" as religious leaders. Their heads are so high in the clouds, removed from proven common sense reality, that they are no earthly good. Far too many Christian religious leaders have to go through life learning the hard way, because they have never been apprentices as required by Scripture. They have never met the biblical requirements for leadership, either. Only after they have slaughtered enough sheep do they learn a lesson or two. So, only by the time they are too old to set a bad example, have they finally learned enough to give good advice and lead.

What three things, more than all others, ruin a man in his climb to the top in his so-called "secular" calling? Money, sex and power - the triumvirate of evil. What three things, more than all others, ruin a church leader and bring about his downfall and humiliation. Gold, gals and glory. Well, gold, gals and glory are the same thing as money, sex and power. Gold equals money. Gals equal sex. And glory equals power. The point is, if we did things correctly and selected our leadership according to the way God told us to in His Word, we would select only proven leadership, men who had been successful in both their homes and their callings according to the requirements of I Timothy 3 and Titus 1. These men, before they were qualified to become Christian leaders, would have already passed the test of pride as represented by money (gold), sex (gals), and power (glory) in their march to maturity in life. Such men, mature in their character, successful in their professional callings and proven in leadership, would be able to both set a good example (serve) and also effectively lead Christian organizations. In church history, the Episcopal church rose to greatness by selecting its leaders precisely in this biblical manner.

The Lord Jesus Christ knew exactly what He was doing when He chose His disciples from the real world, from out of their successful secular callings. He chose men who had already been tested by the lust of the flesh, the lust of the eyes and the pride of life. Jesus chose as His disciples men who already knew how to serve, to covenant, contract and lead. It was no accident He shunned, and in fact had His greatest confrontations with, the religious leaders of His day. He would have the same conflicts with most of the so called "Christian" religious leaders of today.

There is truth to the adage that wisdom comes with age and experience. It is the testings, the trials of this world, which mature faith, character and professionalism. We learn much of the true richness of wisdom from the old patriarchs and the old prophets of the Old Testament. But, it is unfortunately all too true today that too many of America's old religious leaders have grown up in protective church bureaucracies where they have been insulated from the realities of life and the practical challenges to the kingdom. So, they are often captured by frivolous illusions, leading to strong delusion. Further, it is even more true that the "young turks," who are eager to "make a name for themselves" among God's people, have no business in authority or positions of leadership. They have not served their time as apprentices. They have not met the job requirements of I Timothy 3 or Titus 1.

From working at the highest level in both the business and religious community, I can say beyond a shadow of a doubt there is more backbiting, backstabbing, fights for power, greed, hoarding, selfishness and pettiness among so-called Christian religious leaders than ever existed in my experience in the business world. The reason is that immaturity in both character and professionalism permeates religious leadership. Church leadership has not gone through the biblically required proving grounds necessary to handle such an exalted position. Small wonder then that it fails. It is unqualified.

The 1987 media-promoted scandal about Christian religious leadership in the United States found specific Christian leaders to be anything other than blameless. Adultery and fornication problems are rampant in the ministry-at-large, not to mention the explosion of homosexuality. The children of preachers are notorious culturally for being hell raisers. How many bishops, how many overseers, how many church leaders are good economists? Next to none. And yet

Titus 1:7 makes it very clear that a bishop is to be a steward of God. The word "steward" is the same word in the Greek from which we derive our word economics.

Far from being temperate, gentle, and not quarrelsome, today we find many young, unqualified, Christian religious leaders who have their own agenda, who are building their own self-willed empires and fiefdoms. Some of these men, in their doctrinal arrogance, are quick-tempered, given to the vicious use of their tongues and plagued by low self-worth. They are not interested in "playing rhythm guitar behind Jesus." They want to be "the lead singer in the band," today! Not having their self-worth established in a godly way, first from a relationship with God, then by the building of the kingdom of God within themselves, and then in the working out of their calling whereby they serve their fellow man, they instead inflict their inadequacies upon the naive, trusting sheep under them. In this mutually co-dependent parasitic relationship, these wolf-like "shepherds" suck and draw the approbation from the sheep they are supposed to shepherd. This ungodly need for approval not only makes them vulnerable, but also renders them unable to truly serve the sheep over whom they have been given charge.

How can a man serve when he is taking? So, as these splendorous birds strut and prance before their gullible audiences, it is no accident that their low humanistic self-worth radiates the pride of a novice and the delusion of grandeur which comes with it.

The unproven character of ungodly church leadership is also too often today marked by drunkenness, drug abuse, unbecoming outbursts of emotion, temper tantrums, subjectivity, relativity, instability, doctrinal heresies, a tendency to see oneself as above God's law or as the exclusive spokesman of God's law, and being viciously critical of other men in the kingdom.

If power and sex don't do such men in, then money brings about their demise. The exposure of despicable greed and covetousness in American Christianity in 1987 rightfully alienated both Christians and non-Christians alike. Weak men must draw to themselves trappings from the world system in order to feel important, in order to boost their humanistic self-worth. Thus, we are plagued with the religious Walter Mitty types, secretly desiring to have material possessions and social applause. This is evil and ungodly.

Judgment begins at the house of God. It begins with leadership which is called to be accountable. Judgment of Christian religious leadership in this country began in 1987. The demise of the U.S.

dollar and the now clearly evident ineptitude and corruption of U.S. politicians ensures that a religious, governmental and economic judgment is underway. How could it be otherwise? Government is always religion applied to economics.

As our myths, illusions, and prideful and ungodly foundations are shaken, religious Christian leadership in the United States will increasingly be called into question, brought unto judgment and repudiated. Slumping financial contributions are already votes of "no confidence." The foundations have to be shaken. When the godly standards for American Christian leadership are finally reestablished (probably after a purge, and possibly a persecution), then Christ's kingdom can once again move forward in this nation. Then there will be harmony and truth, and not the hypocrisy and lip service so evident today. The "false ways" of Christian leadership in this country today must be cleansed. We need more tentmakers like Paul, who was not a burden to his people. We need more businessmen like the Good Samaritan who served his fellow man when religious leaders failed to do so.

GENTLEMEN

As men go, so goes a nation. Collectively, men are physically stronger than women and categorically more logical - left-brain oriented. They also have more control over their bodies. When push comes to shove, these two male characteristics carry the day. We never hear of cowardice being attributed to women. This is why both Israel and the old Soviet Union have jettisoned the fanciful idea of having women fight in combat. Their male soldiers ended up in a protector's role, unnecessarily risking their own lives to the detriment of the military objectives. I remember during Vietnam when I went through Air Force survival school near Spokane, Washington, the three women who went through training with us (including POW camp) ended up in the fetal position, nonfunctional.

Nations and societies are not special when men rule, only when mature Christian men rule. Only mature Christian men, "gentlemen," can provide the correct balance of justice tempered with mercy, of law and love, of severity and kindness. Going back to Adam and Eve, the natural sinful tendency of men is to be irresponsible, response unable, and for women to be dominant. When these two ancient male and female sin complexes are maximized, a society is in an accelerated decline. Men and women both self-destruct. For example, the purpose of a civil government is to enforce contracts, prevent fraud and protect its citizens against all enemies, foreign and domestic. Other activities by government, as economic history consistently demonstrates, result in a curse on the people long-term (I Samuel 8).

In the United States today, the collectivist mindset (feminine/yin) has encouraged government to expand beyond its limited rightful functions of providing for the common defense and enforcing contracts. The expansion of the federal government's "butter" programs (health, education and welfare) has accelerated since 1920. Previously, even though only men voted, it was understood the vote was cast by the man for the unified household, providing the proper balance of law and love. Women understood they were the power behind the throne and that their hand, which rocked the cradle, ruled the world. Today, there is no one behind the throne in too many cases, and/or the throne is abandoned. And the hand that rocks the cradle today is a day-care worker.

The natural tendency of men to become irresponsible means that their logical, law-based, God-given sense of justice is by nature tuned into mercy. Men intuitively understand mercy. By contrast, when women become involved in the law, they tend to either lose their sense of mercy and become hard (which is why women don't generally like working for other women), or they will carry their nurturing instincts to an extreme. The latter leads to the civil government becoming involved in economic functions (health, education and welfare) and in a short-term orientation of the law. Both are contrary to God's law and will. All of God's laws have a long-term orientation. The functions of health, education and welfare are the responsibility of the nuclear family, the extended family and the local church primarily, as well as voluntary charitable organizations. These separate responsibilities in turn provide a powerful check and balance between these autonomous institutions and civil government. As responsibility goes, so flows power (I Samuel 8 and Revelation 13).

When Adam became irresponsible and sinned, letting Eve dominate him, at least three things occurred: 1) the covenant with God was broken; 2) lawlessness and death entered into the creation; and 3) secular humanism sprouted. So the second Adam, Jesus Christ, had to perfectly keep God's law, humbling Himself unto total obedience and thus fulfill and restore the covenantal relationship between man and God. Jesus Christ was the first true gentleman. In like manner, when men are covenant keepers, obey God's law and humble themselves under God's authority in their homes, local churches and callings, a Christian culture can take root and flourish. When mature Christian men, gentlemen, rightfully fulfill their godly responsibilities, there is very little left for a civil government to do. Civil government effectively becomes irrelevant. A peaceable kingdom replaces it. But unless Christian gentlemen rule compassionately in their homes and churches particularly, chaos will result in the nation.

A Christian culture is impossible to develop in a society which has an evolutionary rather than a creationist perspective. Creationism is the natural out-working of God's sovereignty. Evolution is the natural out-working of satanic humanism. In an evolutionary-based culture, men will move toward extremes and either become macho, in a survival-of-the-fittest manner, or they will become wimps, dominated by women. They will not be gentlemen. Men will accordingly miss the balance of doing justly, loving mercy and walking humbly with their God.

The John Wayne culture of the 1950s through the mid-1970s greatly accelerated the macho perspective. Thus, when men read, "Christ wept," they tended to close the Book. The belief of far too many men was that if "Christ wept," He is not a "real man." Jesus

Christ would not play on the NFL circuit. The fallout too often is that the churches are left to women, steel magnolias at that. Some poor pastor, lacking supportive, balanced, mature male eldership, is eventually run ragged and burned out by women's money and dominance. And some poor pastor's wife is too often pulled a dozen ways at once, if not slandered to ribbons.

God's laws line up with the nature of His creation. For this reason, God assigned men's tasks to be commensurate with their created abilities. In the Old Testament, all authority was given to the patriarch except for the execution of a member of his own family. But even here, he could put a rebellious child out for the community-at-large to stone to death. No one had more authority in the Old Testament than the patriarch of the family. In the New Testament, the instruction in God's law, the application of God's law and governing responsibility of God's law is assigned to men as elders in the church. The requirements of eldership for men are stiff. To be an elder, a man must be tested and proven in the things of the world (Luke 16), exhibit proven broad-based maturity as a Christian man (Titus 1), and have either a proper wife or responsibility for not more than one wife. In other words, he has to be a complete gentleman.

Women seeking "equal rights," rather than an equitable situation, eventually exhaust themselves in head-to-head competition. In polls taken today, women confess they were better off before they were liberated. They had more respect, were more cherished, had more leisure time, less stress. Their children, deprived of the security and love only a mother (now absent) can give, enter adulthood with scars and are motivated by unrealistic needs and unrecognized drives. On a broader scale, the economic/political functions of society degenerate as a feministic agenda is continually thrust upon the federal government. The federal government reaches the point of fiscal exhaustion in its efforts to provide totalitarian control, eliminate all risks and provide total security. The maternal governments of Latin America are a perfect example of this. And when they fail, they turn macho. The voters there run like lemmings from one extreme to the other, missing the Christian balance of law and love, which comes with mature masculine leadership - the anchored, grounded, light-filled male vector.

Just as God's plan for man is anchored in His word, of which Jesus Christ is simultaneously the person, fulfillment and example, a society is anchored in the lawful obedience of men to God. Colossians 1:23 speaks of the importance of being grounded and steadfast, continuing in the faith and not falling away from the hope of the gospel.   Mark 4:17, in Jesus' parable of the soils, declares that if believers have no root in who they are in God, they cannot endure. Trials, tribulations and persecutions precede a fall if gentlemen have no root in their identity grounded in Christ.

When the stormy winds of crisis blow, it is men who provide the grounding and the root to persevere in the home, in the church, in a business, in a community, in a military situation and in the nation. French historian Amaury de Riencourt demonstrated that civilizations dominated by women yield readily to male dictatorships in times of crisis. Steven Goldberg's book, "Why Men Rule," makes an excellent case. The United States today finds itself in a position much like Rome before the Caesars and like Germany prior to Hitler, according to Peikoff's "The Ominous Parallels." The dark, chaotic, collective, feminine matrix implodes, giving rise to a macho politician.

In our nation today, overwhelmingly, families that live below the poverty line are headed by women. It was the destruction of the black family and particularly the black Christian father that destroyed the black community.   Black economists Walter Williams and Thomas Sowell have documented this sad truth. Youths involved in drugs or who are criminals are from broken homes and single-parent families, predominantly headed by women.

There is an important balance, however, once a male-based, grounded, lawful root is established. Coming together as a family unit, men and women, the "many," become "one" flesh. The law and love characteristics of God are joined together in this union between a man and a woman. But men have primary responsibility and, therefore, authority. Indeed, going all the way back to both Christ and Adam, if a man does not provide for his own, especially for those of his household, he has effectively denied the faith and is worse than an unbeliever (I Timothy 5:8).

Men are commanded to provide for, defend and instruct their families, and love their wives as Christ loved the church. Mature Christian men, being grounded and having a root in themselves, have the ability to give and serve, to cherish and exemplify the fruit of the Spirit. They are gentlemen. God's authority given to men is to be exercised with love. Without love, male authority moves toward tyranny. Leadership by inspiration sours to dictatorship by fear where love fails.

Christian gentlemen provide not only a protective and secure umbrella for women, but also an opportunity for them to fulfill their dominant, right-brain, holistic, nurturing capabilities in the home, the local church and community. Additionally, such men provide the fertile environment necessary for women to develop their economic and business talents, from whence they can finance the health, education and welfare needs of those they touch (Proverbs 31). Thus, godly women see their "butter" agendas fulfilled in business, not government.

Women who are not provided a godly loving anchor by a grounded male root too often end up carrying their energy too high in their physical bodies. They cannot "settle down." Indeed, the widespread affliction of Epstein-Barr Virus (EBV) in women and reproductive problems are often a function of not being properly grounded. Women, after all, are still "empty vessels." They are first and foremost receiving units as infrared antennas.

Men in the world today know little of what it means to be a gardener, to live quiet, peaceful lives of service to their families while fulfilling their calling. Men are by and large not grounded; they have no root in themselves. Thus, they have no long-term anchor capable of stabilizing them or their families when the stormy winds and challenges of life come. As the empty vessel, women accordingly suffer even more during hard times. And women aggravate their status by being rebellious. Plus, in today's world, without a Christian fatherly example or a rich marital experience, women have no frame of reference for what it means to find fulfillment in their husbands' lawful and merciful spiritual leadership and calling. Too many women have never known a gentleman. The result, symbolically evident by short hair, is stiff-necked, cold, hard, and angry women, a fast track to burn-out and exhaustion, not to mention witchcraft. Few and far between as the examples may be, the most fulfilled men and women today, both Christian and non-Christian alike, are men and women in a marriage who work together in the family and in the family's calling/business. This is the basis on which the early Puritans established this nation.

Men are not gentle by nature, at least until they become older and their estrogen and feminine core kick in. By nature, they either become macho (evolutionary survival of the fittest) or wimps (irresponsible). The concept of a "gentleman" is a Christian concept. Men become gentle when they are rooted and grounded in humble, covenantal obedience to God's law and manifest maturity by love as the fruit of the Spirit. Gentlemen flow inescapably from Christianity, from a broken and humbled heart and spirit unto God. It is therefore no surprise that Christianity has degenerated in Western civilization, as gentlemen have become more scarce.

TOWARD A GODLY
CHRISTIAN HOME

It is a struggle for a Christian man and woman to create and maintain a Christian home in our day and age. Everything from all sides works against it.

Most Christians today are products of the secular humanistic public school system, the public universities, tradition-drenched Christian denominations, and are also bombarded by the anti-Christian mass media and Hollywood. Thus, we have to start from ground zero and reprogram. Swimming against the tide of an ungodly culture is an awesome task. The power of grace is mandatory, along with some basic applications of biblical law.

Christian children have great difficulty understanding why they are required to be different from other boys and girls. The Christian way of life is such a minority lifestyle these days in the United States. The tremendous peer pressure brought to bear upon today's Christian youths - the ridicule, the sarcasm - all bring a tremendous desire to conform. The more ungrounded the home, the greater the desire to conform to the culture. If Christianity is not made to make sense and seen as fair by children, made logical and brought down to reality on a day-to-day basis, if there is not a united Christian mother and father who apply it consistently - the probability of rebellion by children in the Christian home is increased substantially. For this reason, it is helpful to boil Christianity down to four operating rules which govern the family. Children can grasp, understand, appreciate and operate under these guidelines. So, they are effective. These four principles make God real, practical, fair, loving, gracious and meaningful in children's everyday lives. Further, the rules work (as do all of God's laws), so children are not in conflict or religiously schizophrenic, as are so many Christian youths these days. Children can understand when God is served, everyone wins, including them.

These four rules for the household are:

1) discipleship; 2) stewardship; 3) redeeming time and tongue; and 4) giving before getting.

Children can learn discipleship when they have observed, been taught, and have experienced what it means to be disciplined. From the activities they enjoy, such as gymnastics, hiking and working hard to make their entries winners at the county fair, they can learn what it means to practice discipline. To them, being a good disciple also means obeying the instructions of the coach, whether coach be father, mother, the gymnastics teacher, the hiking instructor or ultimately the Lord Jesus Christ and His Law-Word. They can also learn that disobedience means unpleasant consequences. They know that being a good disciple means work, often unpleasant work (dishes), school work and short-term pain for long-term gain. It means being consistent and organized, both in one's personal life and one's work (calling). When one is self-disciplined, one can be a disciple.

The children can learn, too, that nothing is free in life, not even eternal salvation. Jesus Christ had to pay the price for it. Being disciplined and being a good disciple is manifest by being a good steward. What God has given us for stewardship is precious and is to be given appropriate care. This means being personally responsible for material things in addition to being self-governing. Children can learn they are held responsible and accountable as stewards for their appearance, for good grooming, for cleanliness, for their clothes, their rooms, their schoolwork, their livestock, their toys - for any and everything that involves them personally. Plus, they have a duty to the family and to family chores. Being a good disciple means being a good steward.

Next, children can learn how precious both life and time are. They can understand that time is the only resource we all have, the one aspect of life where we are all equal. We all have limited time. Therefore, time is to be valued and used productively. Time is to be redeemed; it must not be wasted. Just as at the end of the day the discipleship and stewardship requirements are to be reviewed, the child should be required each day to justify the way he spent his time during that day. This is just good management - responsibility and accountability in a feedback loop. It is necessary for success in a business; it is also necessary for success in a family. It is a requirement for success in any enterprise, including Christianity.

The taming of the tongue is an ongoing challenge. The requirement to bring every thought into captivity to the obedience of Jesus Christ comes down to the children not only examining what they are thinking and feeling, but also governing what they say. At the end of the day, each child's words and comments are to be reviewed as to whether or not they spoke out of a godly or an ungodly heart, mind and tongue. (This critique is a summation of correction administered throughout the day.) Instruction and discipline (to make better disciples and stewards) is then provided as necessary. All this is done in a loving manner, with the clearly stated purpose of gently molding the character of Christ in children for the long-term benefit of all concerned.

Finally, rather than competition being emphasized, the program of the Prince of Peace, that of cooperation through covenant and contract is to be stressed. Children should be required to give before they get. They must serve before they receive. Work comes before play or rest. This is the way both God and the moral free market work. Men must serve, produce, and contract successfully before they receive. The earlier this lesson is learned the better. It is the basis of establishing harmony, not only in the Christian home, but also in society-at-large.

These four principles provide the basis for teaching practical, applied Christianity and dominion and stewardship to children in the home. While undoubtedly these four rules/principles do not capture all of applied Christianity, they do optimize it for children. Discipleship, stewardship, redeeming time and tongue and giving before getting, provide broad coverage for the integration of spiritual and earthly truth, apply and resolve the problem of the one and the many, and provide harmony between spirit, people and things. It is win-win-win. God is served. Our fellow man wins. And the children win. Plus, it's all sealed with a KISS: Keep It Simple Stupid! Children can remember four rules. Moreover, most of whatever else they are taught in Christian curriculum or in church can be pigeon-holed into one of these four rules.

Continued reinforcement of these four biblical avenues of instruction, under the umbrella of a biblical patriarch (Father Knows Best), with appropriate delegation to a like-minded helpmate/mother (Proverbs 31 woman), provides the balance to both speak and teach the truth in love to children. When children are trained in this way - particularly in the formative years of ages one through 10-12, when the children's subconscious delta, theta and alpha rhythms are being programmed - then when the children are old, they will not depart from this instruction. They will have a grounded root in themselves, in Christ, which will successfully carry them through life.

Christian activists today focus on national reform. We need to first get down to basics, to get our priorities straight. God, the Holy Spirit, needs to change our patriarchal hearts and heads so that our character is changed. We need to become convicted by the Holy Spirit to the point of behavioral change by God's Law-Word. When our character is altered and becomes more Christ-like, then our disciple and stewardship responsibilities will be correctly manifested by example. (Children learn best by example.) We will more readily redeem time, tongue, and give before we get. There will be peace and harmony in our homes. When there is productivity, organization, and peace and harmony in our homes - there will be a basis, by example and habit pattern, for harmony in our churches, communities and nation.

SECTION F

CHRISTIAN GOVERNMENT

GOVERNMENT IS RELIGION
APPLIED TO ECONOMICS

Unquestionably, the physical, institutional separation of church and state has historically been vital to the maintenance of freedom, prosperity and the protection of the rights of individuals. Indeed, a republican form of government is dependent upon the dispersal of power which comes with the institutional separation of church and state. Men cannot handle a concentration of power. Power corrupts and absolute power corrupts absolutely. The men who run the government must be different from those who run the state.

On the other hand, it is equally important to realize that in the abstract realm, the realm of ideas, that separation of church and state is impossible. In fact, in all societies government is, inescapably, religion applied to economics.

From religion comes our ethics and morality, and our ideas about right and wrong, good and evil. Government enacts these religious ideas into law, which forms the rules that in turn frame the arena of economics (human action). The law-giver of any society is always the god of that society. This means that in order to harmonize abstract principles with concrete reality, the clergy of a country must actively critique and petition the lawmakers of a society if the religious, legal/governmental and economic will of the people is to be fulfilled.

Furthermore, the centralization or decentralization of responsibility, law and power determines the prosperity or poverty of a civilization. Indeed, close at hand, we can witness the difference between the prosperity of the United States and the poverty of Mexico, stemming primarily from the differences between the centralized religious, political, and economic systems which dominate Mexico, versus the decentralized institutions which have historically governed the United States.

Assessing economic reality from the standpoint of political legislation and religious principles, we know that prosperity also comes when market freedom and harmony exist in a society. Political freedom comes when men are self-governing under God and responsible for themselves, their families, and the health, education and welfare of their community, as implemented by the private sector, local charities and churches. Bureaucracies, on the other hand, grow in a vacuum of irresponsibility. They are always expensive and wasteful, regardless of their institutional brand. Therefore, the greater the irresponsibility of the people, the greater the growth of bureaucracies and the less general freedom and prosperity. This is also true regarding national defense. A well-armed militia and a solid civil defense system go a long way toward securing freedom and prosperity.

Next, harmony comes to a society that first asks and then resolves the ultimate political/religious/economic question: How do we resolve the conflict between individual rights and group rights? Because we have no religious consensus today, it follows that we also lack a political consensus. Therefore, conflict reigns. Economics gets torn asunder by special interests.

It is economic cooperation, the specialization and division of labor leading to trade, that results in harmony and prosperity in an economic system. But such a system rests upon the integrity and morality of a contract-honoring citizenry which in turn is based on a political and religious consensus. A contract is a religious/moral, legal and economic document.

The laws which govern a society's economic system must be geared toward insuring the balance between individual and group rights. Both must coexist simultaneously, with individuals creating groups/organizations. But, today we are violating most of these harmonious, economic, political and religious principles. Small wonder then that we are becoming a poorer, debt-burdened people. (One root of the word debt is "death.")

The religious principle which captures the essence of the ultimate political and economic question is found in Christ's Second Great Commandment - to love our neighbor as ourselves. This balances the rights of the individual with the rights of the group by providing a balance between self-interest and service. It is only when we see our self-interest being advanced by service, when we first serve our fellow man and as a by-product are rewarded, that we simultaneously meet both the needs of the group and those of the individual. This is a win-win-win transaction, producing harmony and prosperity for the individual and for society, as well as fulfilling the will of God. When men operate under such principles, the enslaving, expensive, wasteful bureaucratic institutions which dominate wither away and die. They become unnecessary.

People get the government they deserve. We reap what we sow. As a founding father, William Penn put it, "Men must be governed by God or they will be ruled by tyrants." Put differently, when law does not come from God, it inescapably comes from men who are eventually corrupted by the likes of money, sex and power.

God's Second Great Commandment (effectively the Golden Rule), which He restated from the Old Testament law, must be our guiding principle, both individually and corporately. It is religious in essence because it is a statement made by God Himself. It is governmental, because it is a command which specifies a rule/law of behavior. It is economic because it governs human action in a contractual/covenantal way between individuals and society. It is epitomized personally in Jesus Christ who is, for Christians, the High Priest (religion), the Law Giver and Judge (government), and Creator/Sustainer of the universe (economics). It is no accident that Satan's three temptations of Jesus were governmental, religious and economic.

THE FUTILITY OF A POLITICAL SUPERSTATE

In a truly Christian nation, it shouldn't matter much who is elected president. In a godly nation, the president simply would not have all that much to do. Why? Christian government is primarily and foremost self-government. When a man is self-governing, he does not need to be externally governed by politicians, by government bureaucrats or federal judges. Self-governing husbands and wives in families teach their children to grow up and be self-governing. Schools, local churches, local businesses, and local communities also emphasize the development of character, humility, responsibility, duty, empathy and the contractual productive activity of an individual in a godly social order. This way, by the time power eventually trickles up to the top, there is very little left for the president. The fact that the United States now has 83,237 separate governments, 504,408 elected officials, plus millions of bureaucrats is testimony to our ungodliness.

Throughout history, nations have raged and warred against God's self-governing law and His kingdom. Today, ambitious politicians, empire-building bureaucrats and god-like judges prefer for individuals to be irresponsible and anything but self-governing. This way the politicians, bureaucrats and judges cannot only justify their existence, but also accrue more power. If the people of a nation remain child-like and do not grow up from milk to meat, or if they remain as natural men and women who follow the path of least resistance, just like nature, then someone will rule over them. Power-hungry politicians, bureaucrats and judges are all too glad to fill this void in an abusive way, as I Samuel 8 and Revelation 13 teach all too clearly, and as Nobel prize-winning U.S. economist Bachman confirmed. Such a pagan, non-Christian approach does not work long-term because it is contrary to God's law and because civil government is a parasite. It is therefore illogical, impractical and economically bankrupt.

The nature of Satan's kingdom and the nature of sin, is that of a short-term orientation, which is based upon both conflict and death. These are key characteristics of a pagan, bureaucratic governmental system. Bureaucracies thwart progressive non-traditional change. They squelch progress. Government-imposed laws solve problems only temporarily in an attempt to take away the short-term pain necessary for long-term gain. The result is that government creates much greater pain and more problems in the long run. The destruction of the black families in the inner city, thanks to the federal government's welfare programs, is an excellent case in point. (See Charles Murray's book, "Losing Ground." Also important in this regard are the works of black economists, Dr. Walter Williams and Dr. Thomas Sowell.)

Next, the very nature of redistribution of wealth through taxation is, by definition, economic class warfare - in other words, conflict. No one would allow their wealth to be seized if it were not for the not-so-subtle threat of government force. If people wanted their wealth redistributed, they would simply give it away. That's what Christian charity is all about.

Civil government is death-based. Both "guns" and "butter" programs - the military and welfare - have their roots in conflict, and ultimately in the threat of death. The power of the state is the power to destroy. The growing parasitic bureaucratic fascism which is increasingly strangling this nation today must be seen for what it truly is: ungodly! It incorporates key traits of sin - short-term orientation, conflict, and death. It encourages people to be irresponsible and undisciplined, rather than disciplined Christian disciples. The bureaucratic welfare state encourages people to take rather than to give and serve, contrary to Christ's Second Great Commandment. It rewards individuals who remain as natural men and children, and discourages them from growing up to be mature stewards. It encourages the citizenry to nurse economically and legally at the breast of the federal government, feeding on milk rather than meat. And the president rules over this occult empire with the latent power of an absolute dictator, courtesy of his Executive Orders.

Because Jesus Christ is the ultimate God-Man, we have in Him all we need by way of a president - a King, a Lord, a Priest and an Economic Creator/Planner. Therefore, because all governmental, religious and economic power accrues to Him Who rules over His creation, He can therefore delegate and decentralize governmental, religious and economic power on earth to individuals He chooses. This means that a major issue on earth is power. It's Christ's decentralized kingdom, beginning with each of us as individuals, versus the centralized power of the political superstate. Ultimately, Jesus Christ delivers the kingdom to God the Father when He puts an end to all rule and all authority and power (I Corinthians 15:24). Therefore, it follows that the nature of the religious system active on the earth determines who accrues governmental and economic power. If Christ rules, where the Spirit of the Lord is, there is liberty. True liberty always walks on two earthly legs - one leg is economic, the other is political. If a man is not free economically, he is not free. Someone else determines how he spends his time - when, where, with whom, doing what, for how long, for how much. If a man is not free politically, he is not free either. No one seriously argues that the subjects of the former Soviet Union were anything but slaves. They were not free because they were not free politically.

Jesus Christ delegated power to us individually and thereby de-centralized power on the earth. He gave us religious power as be-liever-priests. He gave us political power as self-governing men and women who are ambassadors for him and kings in our own right. And he gave us economic power in our commission to be stewards of the earth. This individual power, coupled with the institutions of the family, the local church and those of the local community, wrap up nearly all remaining power, leaving very little at the federal level. From this Christian perspective then, it really should not matter all that much who is elected president. In a properly ordered Christian nation, the president would indeed have very little to do. He would have no health, education or welfare responsibilities, no "butter" programs to budget or administer. Such would be taken care of at the individual and the local community level by the family, the ex-tended family, the local church and the local community. The Bank at Mondragon in Spain has shown us the way economically, finan-cially and socially in this regard, also. The president would also have few judicial or legislative responsibilities, only ensuring that the principles of the law of God were correctly applied in situations which arose in the nation. Even in the area of the military, as com-mander-in-chief, the president's responsibilities would be substan-tially reduced by self-governing men and women, who maintained the responsibility for their own defense through their local militias, as existed in early America and as operate in Switzerland today.

The fact the president of the United States today has tremendous power is a direct indication of the un-Christian nature of the nation. In fact, from this observation, we can glean a general Christian prin-ciple: the greater the bureaucracy of a nation, the greater the power of the chief executive, the greater the judicial and legislative power centralized at the federal level, the more ungodly the nation.

The subsequent truth is that an ungodly, pagan, bureaucratic, cen-tralized federal system does not work long-term. Sin is, by defini-tion, error and is death oriented. (The wages of sin are death.) So sin is a loser. Such an error-racked system as we have today can only, inescapably, in logical cause and effect fashion, reaping what it has sown, go bankrupt. Increasingly, interest alone on the federal debt is working toward becoming the largest item in the budget. (It is third presently.) This is the road to economic and financial ruin, revolution and anarchy, and finally totalitarianism.

Pouring salt in the wound is the hard fact that laws legislated by civil governments simply do not work long-term. Indeed, while all laws are legislated morality - because all laws are the legislation of religious ideas about right and wrong and good and evil, at the same time, such legislated morality is unworkable. When men are good and godly, they are self-governing. Therefore, laws legislated by civil governments are unnecessary. Men live first and foremost by Christ's Second Great Commandment, by the covenant and contract. On the other hand, when men are evil and ungodly, laws legislated by civil governments are broken and/or ignored. So it's Catch-22 for the pagan, bureaucratic, centralized, federal government. In order to maintain its power, the federal government must keep its citizens in a sinful state - as children, irresponsible and conflict-ridden. The nature of such brats, however, is that they are economically non-productive long-term. Plus, they cheat, lie, murder and steal. The citizenry must be productive and honest if the federal government is to sustain itself through taxation.

Also, by encouraging its subjects to remain as undisciplined and emotional brats, the federal government ensures that its laws will be either ignored and/or violated. Brats don't behave. They are lawless. So, the federal government's bureaucracy and courts increasingly find themselves at war with their own people, forcing the bureaucracy to grow, building the basis for an eventual revolution against the government. Long-term, the ungodly centralized political system is a loser economically and politically, because first it is a loser religiously.

The final tragedy of this governmental ungodliness is that an unjust, ungodly, bureaucratic, centralized pagan superstate consumes its people and its resources as it attempts to survive its own death throes. The parasite consumes the host. We should expect as much. All gods demand tributes and sacrifices. This is the lesson of ancient Rome, Hitler's Nazi Germany, and the Soviet Union, who were anything but "Big Brothers." They were all collectivists, "Big Brothers" who failed. So, when we see the massive accrual of power in our country at the federal level, with the excessive emphasis on who is elected president, we know we are very close to reaping the ungodliness we have sown.

Civil government is simultaneously a parasite and a predator of its people. God Almighty is neither. God is love. He serves. Every good and perfect gift comes from above. The God of the Bible extracts far less from His people than do the minions who run a political superstate.

COMMUNISM AND THE NATURAL MAN

Nature follows the path of least resistance. Accordingly, so does the natural man. He takes the easy way out. This is why the world today is slipping so readily into the fascism of a New World Order. International fascism promises the easy way out, the path of least resistance. "From each according to his ability, to each according to his needs," through stocks, multinational banks and corporations in collusion with government. This is just like in the 1987 hit movie, "Network." The deception of the New World Order is that it attempts to trick men into thinking they are free, when in fact their freedom is akin to a goldfish swimming in a bowl. This is the illusion of freedom and individualism, when it is really slavery and disguised collectivism. The fruit of this deception, however, is the reality that it does not work. As an economic system, it has failed miserably in the Soviet Union, Red China, North Korea, Vietnam, Zimbabwe, Sweden, and as of late, in France. In these communist/socialist states, preludes to international fascism, men are frustrated because they cannot better themselves and thus are given to civil unrest, alcoholism, job absenteeism, drug abuse and wife beating.

Slavery today is slavery to the civil government. Slaves are neither happy, free, prosperous, nor responsible; nor do they make good stewards. By radical contrast, Christians are called to take dominion over the earth exercising their God-given stewardship authority as service-minded leaders. The result is that mature Christian men and women are happy, free, prosperous and responsible. The degree to which Christian stewardship is not practiced results in civil government filling the vacuum of irresponsibility, the vacuum of unbelief, with free men becoming slaves. This is why the Bible condemns the natural man: "But the natural man receiveth not the things of the Spirit of God: for they are foolishness unto him: neither can he know them, because they are spiritually discerned". - I Corinthians 2:14. So, we have a clear-cut difference between the "human action" of nature's (Satan's) slaves (collectivism) as opposed to God's born-again free men (individualism). A man's actions, a man's works, testify of his spiritual fidelity or infidelity. This is why a criterion for assessing a man's Christian edification in early America was the quality of his workmanship. This standard was in keeping with James 2:17, "Even so faith, if it hath not works, is dead, being alone." There are too many "words" today from religious and political leaders and typical Christians, not backed up by, or inconsistent with, their actions. We should evaluate them accordingly, being "wise as serpents, and harmless as doves." - Matthew 10:16.

In a very real sense, there is no such thing as a free market. Absolute freedom results in anarchy which men never tolerate for long. Men need boundaries. Men always wrestle for the balance between law and freedom. Therefore, freedom and the free market are bounded by the laws of some system. Laws are simply the enactment of some religious ideas about morality and ethics. Therefore, all governments are the establishment of religion, as their laws frame the economic marketplace.

Collectivism, as represented by communism/socialism, is an economic failure everywhere. Our politicians who enact socialistic/fascist laws that are contrary to God's laws are likewise guilty of the same offense. Economic prosperity is a by-product of obedience to God's laws and commandments, being the result of good stewardship. He has given us the laws, the rules, to frame the economic marketplace that lead to prosperity. So why do men gravitate toward various forms of collectivism, when it is an acknowledged failure? Because the natural man wants something for nothing, for the government to steal another man's productivity and feed him for free. It is man's nature to be irresponsible.

The good news, however, is that when Christian spirituality and God's law are finally linked with the economics of God's creation, recaptured from Satan's realm, the world will experience an explosive Christian revival. When the veil of deception which blinds the natural man is lifted and he realizes that God through Jesus Christ has not only provided for his eternal salvation, but also has a perfect plan for him individually in time, which is consistent with his own long-term self-interest, the unity and the love of God will be manifest to the world in a way heretofore unseen. God will not only receive the glory resulting in praises uplifted to Him by man, but also Satan's proud and selfish rebellion will be revealed for the sin/error it is. Satan then will be totally condemned by an honest man's free will and joyful acceptance of both God's eternal and temporal provisions. Only hardhearted rebellious man will persist in his love of death.

We are told in John 10:35 "scripture cannot be broken." So, why do Christian free men back off when the collectivists point to portions of scripture which appear to be communistic? Sadly, this is due to the fact that too many Christians do not correctly understand the whole council of God and, furthermore, too many of God's people are still blinded by their culture. So, they pick and choose the passages from God's word which fit their personal biases. This is an age-old problem, one which the apostles clearly faced in early church history.

Let's examine the Bible passages which collectivists, like socialists, fascists and communists, misuse to support their position. By pointing out their error and deception, we strengthen the case for a marketplace of freedom, bounded by God's laws - Christian free enterprise!

Collectivists first point to the apparent communism of Matthew 14:16-21 and 15:32-38; Mark 6:36-44 and 8:1-9; Luke 9:12-17; and John 6:5-13. These are the gospel accounts of how Jesus took the loaves and fishes, blessed them and distributed them among the masses, so that all ate until they were filled. The excess loaves and fishes which were then regathered were greater than the original amount distributed. It is this "sharing" function that the collectivists point to as an example of communism - "From each according to his ability, to each according to his needs."

Partial truth is also partial error. Error - to miss the mark - is sin. Here's where the communists have missed the mark: First of all, the rules of conduct for men with men is different than the rules of conduct for God with men. Jesus was the human incarnation of God. In the distribution of the loaves and fishes, He miraculously created all that was needed to feed the masses, plus an abundant excess. This proved His lordship over creation. Jesus' miracle was testimony of his deity. John 6:14 states, "Then those men, when they had seen the miracle that Jesus did, said, this is of a truth that prophet that should come into the world."

A sovereign God does what He will with His creation. We see this type of provision in the Old Testament in Exodus 16, where the Lord provided manna from heaven. God's provision for man in the economic realm is of an entirely different flavor than man's interaction with man. Collectivism confuses the two, but then again, collectivists try to play God, so it is no accident that they would confuse this issue.

Collectivists ignore Genesis 3:19, "In the sweat of thy face shalt thou eat bread." They also ignore II Thessalonians 3:10, "For even when we were with you, this we commanded you, that if any would not work, neither should he eat." Christianity puts the responsibility on the individual, and specifically the man who is head of the household: "But if any provide not for his own, and specially for those of his own house, he hath denied the faith, and is worse than an infidel." - I Timothy 5:8.

Secondly, with regard to the loaves and fishes, we see that Christ was dealing with His own people, literally His followers. This economic distinction between believers with believers (the church today) versus believers with unbelievers (charity today) regarding "sharing" is also clearly made in the Old Testament, where debt between borrower and a lender - both of whom were believers - was to be charitable. There was to be no interest or usury charged on debt between believers. By contrast, a loan made by a believer to an unbeliever is not commanded to be charitable. In this case, usury (or interest) can be charged.

The next scripture which the collectivists turn to in an attempt to support their flimsy assertion that God's word supports collectivism are found in Acts 2:44-46; 4:32-37 and 5:1-11. These scriptures in Acts discuss how believers held all things in common, having sold all their possessions, then providing to each person what he needed. Here again there is apparent communism, the sharing of all things equally. But, there are two points in these scriptures in Acts which the collectivists either carelessly or purposely overlook. And, both of these points obliterate the collectivists' case. These two points are: 1. In Acts we are dealing with the body of believers, interaction among believers, the church, not interaction between believers and unbelievers. What we see here in Acts is effectively the charitable responsibility of the local church! Are we all one body in the world today? Of course not. Should we all be one body in the local church? Most certainly. Are our tithes, gifts, and offerings to the local church held in common, where "from each according to his ability to each according to his need" economic goods and services are dispensed? Of course. To whom much is given, much is expected. The local church is the limited fellowship by which this spiritual union of the body manifests itself in economic communism. But again, church membership is voluntary. In the local church, we are members one to another with separate functions, united in the body of Christ as a body of believers. Just as the food we eat individually is dispensed to the parts of our own physical body which need it, so too are the economic receipts of the local church dispensed among the members of its body, the body of Christ, Christ's believers, according to need. Scripturally, charity begins with the family, then extends to the local church, and finally to the local community. It is only when men are irresponsible in these three God-selected decentralized areas that civil government then fills the vacuum of this irresponsibility and wrongfully takes on the role of charitable distribution. 2. Notice that this common sharing in Acts was voluntary. Discipline only came when the voluntary covenant was violated.

In all cases worldwide, historically, collectivism is based upon force, upon coercion, unlike Christianity which respects the free will of man to share and give. Collectivism runs roughshod over man's free will and forces economic contributions for the "common good." The difference between Christian, free will, economic offerings and forced, collectivist, economic redistribution is literally the difference between light and dark.

Collectivists don't have a leg to stand on when it comes to buttressing their case from God's Word. It is only by ignoring 1) the deity of Jesus, 2) the difference between God's economic relationship with man as opposed to man's economic relationship with man, 3) the difference between economic interchange among believers versus economic interaction between believers and unbelievers, and 4) the difference between freedom and coercion, that allows collectivists to make the spurious case that collectivism is validated by scripture. Collectivism is a system of the natural man, antagonistic to God's plan for His people, being very clearly a Satanic counterfeit of the voluntary sharing among believers. Christian fellowship leading to voluntary redistribution of wealth is a far cry from the evil, coerced, envy-based, centralized collectivism which exists politically in the fallen order of today's world.

However, until Christians include economic dominion and stewardship as part of their holy responsibility to redeem the time, to occupy until Christ comes, to disciple all nations, and in their priesthood bring about the restoration of all things, we will leave the basis of physical life itself under Satan's dominion. We dare not do this. We Christians must overcome in the area of economics, for religion comes down to economics.

Believers need to be faithful in the little things first. Then, in their day-to-day lives, they can multiply their talents and build up a surplus and inheritance, their first fruits so to speak, to provide for their families and to give to the local church as the church has need.

Only Christian-based free enterprise produces surplus. Collectivism, as practiced by the atheistic former Soviet Union, does not work. Before the communist revolution, Russia used to be an exporter of foodstuffs. The godless Soviet Union that Russia then became sunk to the position of becoming a net importer of food. Previously, when the Soviet Union did allow free enterprise to flourish, such as in private gardens (which occupied less than three percent of the agricultural land in the former Soviet Union), those gardens produced over a third of all the fruits, vegetables and poultry raised.

God's Word requires us to be discerning. We must continually learn, recapture and apply the changing facts of God's created order, in light of His perfect and unchanging Law-Word. We must seek the guidance of the Holy Spirit to give us correct judgment in our working out of this union between the eternal abstract and the physical concrete. Then we will experience the fulfillment of Romans 8:28: "And we know that God causes all things to work together for good to those who love God, to those who are called according to His purpose."

SECTION G

CHRISTIAN ECONOMICS

WEALTH FOR ALL

In an honest, open, Christian economic system, which is similar to New Age quantum physics, earning a living would not be a primary consideration for most folks. At first blush, this appears to be an absurd statement. However, when we consider the open system perspective, as well as economic history, this statement becomes credible. In the modern era, in a true Christian economic system, the average working man or woman, given today's high level of education, and technology available, would have to work only approximately three months a year to earn the income necessary to meet his/her annual economic requirements and live debt free. Looked at differently, we have worked very hard to get into the economic mess (debt/slavery) we endure today.

We live in a debt-based, closed money system rather than an open, honest, free market, Christian kingdom, quantum money system. Under the Christian system, money is earned into existence rather than created as debt as it is today. (One of the root meanings of the word debt is death.)

Have you ever noticed all those beautiful and intricately designed cathedrals, and other magnificent edifices of architecture, which exist in old Europe? Have you ever asked yourself how ordinary men and women, craftsmen of that day and age, had the time and resources necessary (minus our technology) to create such beautiful works of art that have lasted for centuries? Why don't we have that kind of time available to us today? We certainly have superior technology. Why do we have to scramble to earn a living and they did not? What about all the beautiful old train stations, churches, and court houses which were built in 18th and 19th century America? Why don't we have similar works of art today? Where are the craftsmen who have the time, care and leisure to produce such wonderful works and still earn a decent living? What happened between then and now? What has changed economically?

It all comes down to what makes up an honest and open Christian, (quantum physics) economic environment, which is missing today. Did you know that the so-called Dark Ages, the Middle Ages in Europe, were called the Dark Ages because there weren't government bureaucracies around to keep records? Such times proved to be some of the most prosperous times in history for the common working man, just like in early American history. America was the land of opportunity, and with the seizing of that opportunity came economic security in the land of the free and the home of the brave. Great economic advancement occurred, as I've discussed in detail in my earlier books, "Wealth for All" and "No Time For Slaves." In the so-called Dark Ages, the European Middle Ages, the average "peasant" worked only about four months a year to meet his annual economic requirements, enjoyed regularly at least four courses at each meal and lived debt free. He wore silver and gold buttons and buckles on his coat and shoes. He was not taxed nearly as heavily as we are taxed either. In fact, Americans today are taxed more heavily than the Pharaoh of Egypt taxed the Hebrew slaves of the Old Testament of the Bible. Moreover, under an honest, Christian, economic system, new technology would increase the number of jobs rather than eliminate them, as is the case today.

How do we recognize an honest, Christian, economic system? We study the real thing. Then we can easily recognize the counterfeit. It is really no different than a U.S. Treasury agent being taught to recognize a counterfeit U.S. one hundred dollar bill.

It has been established globally that an initial investment in agriculture, generally, in an emerging developing economy, returns five to seven times its investment regardless of race, religion, culture, creed or location worldwide. Why is this true? Agriculture is where abundant free energy from the sun is transformed through photosynthesis into matter by way of crops and the grass and grain that livestock eat (Mark 4:28). These commodities in turn can, and historically were, monetized and used as money. For example, a farmer could plant wheat and from his wheat crop issue wheat receipts which were honored and served as money. So, too, with any other commodity, including gold and silver.

The point is, where there is unlimited energy (as there is from the sun), there are potentially unlimited commodities which can be produced (crops and livestock), and these commodities in turn can be monetized. Therefore, because there is unlimited energy, there is potentially unlimited money and wealth - wealth for all. So, when there is an abundant harvest and livestock which reproduce, there is normally, in an honest, open, Christian, quantum economic system, a higher standard of living with falling prices. There is subsequently also full employment and an increasing need for labor, indeed a perpetual shortage of labor, because a Christian economic system fosters the creativity which yields new products and services, improvement of old goods and services, and general progress. There is more leisure time among those who have met their annual economic needs, as well as more discretionary income, that can be spent for services which are labor intensive. This is why wealthy countries import foreign labor, such as the U.S. does of Mexican nationals for domestic household help and crop harvesting. Moreover, as a country becomes more wealthy, people are able to better develop their God-given talents. This allows them to be increasingly creative and productive, so their re-creation is the joyful development of their talents. This is fun.

In such an economic system, what happens by and large, is that each individual ends up primarily developing his talents in the specialization and division of labor, which he offers by way of goods or services in the marketplace. There is also plenty of honest money circulating to support the upper levels of mankind's creativity - the arts. Thus, "the arts" find their greatest support in honest, open, free-market, Christian quantum economics as does environmental integrity. Poor countries, like those in Africa, and big bureaucratic countries, like the former Soviet Union, cannot afford the expense of environmental integrity.

Basically, there are only two parts of the economic equation, land and labor - in other words, things and people. People are more important than things because people make, use, abuse, preserve and destroy things. Therefore, the greatest investment of any economic system is in its people and their creative, self-governing capabilities. This way the economy can expand harmonically and the civil government is limited. When folks can self-finance their own creative economic efforts, they don't need a typical job. And when folks govern themselves, they don't need a civil government to rule over them. As folks develop in their unique God-created talents and become more self-governing, they are more productive members of society economically, as well as more socially cohesive.

This talent discovery and self-governing training of a child begins in the home during the first 12 years when the subconscious of an individual is being programmed in the delta, theta and alpha rhythms of the brain which carry 98 percent of all people throughout life. "Train up a child and when he is old he will not depart from it" declares Proverbs. This is reinforced by the biblical laws of love and liberty, taught by the family and church on the local level.

Both the local family and the extended family are voluntary social safety nets created by individuals, through bloodline connections. Members of families ("the money") enter into the family covenant with one another and become the "one" or the collective. In like manner, the church is a collective, whereby individuals voluntarily come together in the non-bloodline spiritual family to meet each other's needs. Thus, the local nuclear and extended family, the local and extended church, backed up by the local social, school and business community provide basic safety and social nets which fulfill man's collective needs, offsetting the tyranny which inevitably results from the centralization of a power in a federal government and its social services.

There are only two ways in which a society can be organized, from the top down or from the bottom up. If a society is organized from the top down, inevitably, civil government, a collective economic parasite, ends up playing the role of god. This is the maximum distortion of reality: a parasite, civil government, playing the role of god. Such a government, when it is fully manifested, consumes its host, "we the people," and destroys society. Anarchy results. Time after time, history has demonstrated that centralized federal governments, like Rome's, Hitler's Germany, the Soviet Union, and many others, have fallen. Their money becomes worthless. Worthless money leads to revolution. How much better for a society to be organized from the bottom up, with the focus on individual development, individuals who voluntarily form collectives through the use of covenants and contracts. After all, the covenant/contract is the complete individualistic governmental, religious, and economic document. It is governmental because it is legal, defining the parties, the rights and duties of the parties; it is no better than the morality of the parties to the contract and, therefore, is religious; and finally, it is economic, because it specifies the benefits and the penalties available to the parties. This covenantal/contractual system is effectively what existed in early America. It made this country great, the most free and prosperous country on the face of the earth. We are a far cry from this today.

There are only two ways wealth can be obtained. It can either be earned or it can be unearned: gifted, inherited or stolen. Thomas Jefferson was correct in stating there should be a natural aristocracy where primarily wealth and power are earned. This is an incentive for people to be productive and service oriented. Unearned wealth, unless it is gifted or inherited, is by default theft. Unearned wealth (theft) results in conflict in society as the wealth of some parties is taken involuntarily and given to other parties. Conflict is never the basis for economic productivity. Economic prosperity requires a peaceful environment. Moreover, property rights are an extension of human rights. Therefore, when property is taken from an individual, his life is taken from him in effect. Life equals time equals energy equals money equals property. Where would any of us be if we had no clothing, no food, no shelter, and in today's society, no money? We would be destitute or eventually, even dead.

All of us have only one thing in common, time. Here we are all equal. Time is not only precious, but is also limited. How a person chooses to spend his time determines what he makes of his life. When we work and produce goods and services, we are spending our life. Therefore, our life equals our time, and our energy, and our money, and our property. If someone takes our property from us without our consent, he is taking our life, our energy, our time, and effectively our money - the goods and services we would have purchased with that money. This is wrong. It violates God's law. One of The Ten Commandments is, "Thou shalt not steal."

Let's now look at the major contributors to creating wealth for all in an honest, open, Christian, quantum, economic system that produces universal peace and prosperity. They are:

(1) Self-governing, re-creative individuals who covenant and contract with each other, take the long-term view, serve before they receive, operate with humility and responsibility personally, and with empathy and duty toward their fellow man. This perspective considers that man as an individual (yang - masculine) is the ultimate resource, who with character and professionalism, can maximize his productivity. This was captured in early American history by what is called the Protestant Work Ethic. It is activated by the covenant and the contract - the basic governmental, religious and economic documents. By taking the long-term view, individuals apply every biblical principle, all of which require the long-term view. God is eternal, so the closest we can come to being God-like is to take a long-term view. In doing so, man serves his fellow man, thereby pleasing God, and consequently serving himself. Taking the long-term view, serving before receiving, and operating with humility and responsibility, empathy and duty, balances the rights of the collective one (yin - feminine), with those of the "many," or individuals (yang - masculine). This is The Golden Rule and Christ's Second Great Commandment applied.

(2) Free, unlimited, new wealth from the sun, through the process of photosynthesis, transforms unlimited energy into unlimited matter, which can then be used as money or monetized. Commodities monetized means unlimited money, and therefore potentially unlimited wealth. Commodities not only include agricultural commodi-

ties, but also the monetization of the likes of oil, gold and silver. Gold and silver have historically always been real money. Precious metals are the only money which are not simultaneously someone else's debt/liability. They stand on their own. They meet the biblical standard of a just weight and measure.

(3) The specialization and division of labor which leads to trade, as Adam Smith discussed in his classic book, "The Wealth of Nations." With this we have an explosion of prosperity. People are more productive when they do what they have been created to do, which is what they truly like to do. They fulfill their destinies. They then trade their creative productivity with others. This is a peaceful cooperative process whereby people need and appreciate each other.

We are all equal in the eyes of Jesus Christ, but it is our created inequality that makes us unique and special. It is the fact that we are unequal and have something to trade and/or learn from others that means we need each other, and this results in the peaceful activity of economic trade. Individuals are unique, creative, necessary and important when their individual God-given talents are developed, and when they trade the output of those creative talents with their fellow man. As a result, cooperation exists. Literally, the peaceable kingdom of God results.

(4) Technology which results from the investment of capital (savings), and the discovery of new applications for God's natural resources. In the Information Age which we have recently entered - with computers, computer robotics, computerized capital equipment and the like - we are already observing that the greater the information in any system, the more quickly competition transforms into cooperation. With technology, we can produce more, better, different goods and services with less effort, less energy, less resources, in less time. Technology helps make life more effective and efficient. It frees up man for a higher and better use of his time in an open, honest, Christian economic system. Just think what the Middle Age entrepreneurs, who worked with water wheels, horse collars and, by our standards, crude technology, could have accomplished with their honest, open money system if they had our technology. Look at the beautiful cathedrals they built back then. What could we do today, given an honest, open, Christian, quantum system of economics? It would literally bring about the stewardship of the entire earth which the Bible commands. It would work to usher in the kingdom of God on earth.

(5) Inheritance. If we consider all the wealth each family would accumulate over time in an honest, open, Christian economic system,

only taxed to a very limited extent by the civil government, and then primarily for the purposes of defense, justice and enforcing contracts, each generation would inescapably be richer than the one which preceded it. With biblical inheritance not being taxed, and there being effectively only one civil tax - a national sales tax - each generation would have a huge capital base (from inheritance) from which it could begin its economic development anew, not to mention having its own in-house established social and safety nets. The tithe (tax) to the local church finances the health, education and welfare needs of the unfortunate at only one-fourth of the cost of a civil government's bureaucracy.

(6) God's Law, which frames the rules of the marketplace. Biblical laws rightly applied are the laws of liberty and the laws of love. Such are based in covenant and contract, and include restitution for violation of another's human or property rights. Biblical law, rightfully applied, maximizes the boundaries of freedom for the maximum number of individuals, and balances the rights of the individual (yang - masculine) with the rights of the collective (yin - feminine), so there is harmonious and peaceful personal interaction. Taught and applied on an individual level to the young, so an individual is primarily productively creative and self-governing throughout life, the application of biblical law to a society prevents the piles of bureaucratic regulations and unjust court decisions which enslave man.

Biblical law also establishes city versus rural country, social and lifestyle harmony, by limiting absentee ownership of land, by requiring open system, honest money to be created in the rural country. It also offsets the slavery of conflict, chance, cycles, poverty and death of fallen nature which naturally flows to entropy - the Second Law of Thermodynamics. (Limited absentee ownership of land exists in Switzerland and Bermuda today.)

The Christian real estate economic system is a far cry from the ruthless absentee ownership of land of today, by which large corporations, wealthy individuals, and the federal government buy up the countryside and leave native farmers, ranchers, and small communities destitute, not to mention driving up the prices of land in these rural areas so that individuals who wish to relocate from the city and make productive use of the land's resources are financially unable to do so.

The Christian economic system is also a far cry from federal and state government involvement in the economy, which while providing a short-term benefit, creates a long-term curse, as bureaucratic inefficiency, economic distortions, corruption, and high costs result. It has been well said that bureaucracy is the greatest institutional manifestation of human evil.

Then there is the debt (death) of dishonest money, of fiat, fractional reserve banking, with its never ending compound interest on debt which exhausts man. The Federal Reserve, which runs the money system of the United States, creates money out of thin air, resulting in a debt, which "we the people" owe generation after generation until we're busted. The Federal Reserve is not even a federal entity: it is a private corporation which runs the nation's money. Wouldn't you like to own the nation's money machine? Well, a number of big banks do just that.

It is the creation of credit (debt), and the contraction in the use of credit (debt), that causes the business cycle of boom and bust, of inflation and deflation. This, in turn, causes the destruction of the middle class - not to mention the general misery that all this causes - enriching a few at the expense of many. Such a destructive money system is very detrimental to productive, long-term planning. It promotes speculation and penalizes hard work and thrift, as well as morality. Thoughtful Austrian economists have written that with the debasement of a nation's currency, its morality fails, also. By contrast, under an honest, open, Christian economic system, there are no cycles of boom and bust, but rather steady, reliable growth over time, resulting in lower prices and a higher standard of living.

What type of individuals does this debt system foster? Individuals who either depend upon others (parasites) or prey upon others as predators. The civil government as an economic parasite encourages its subjects to take the conflict-ridden, short-term view; it encourages people to take before they give, to operate with pride and irresponsibility personally, with no empathy or duty toward others. Such action increases the role of civil government as referee in the economic arena. The Evolutionary Golden Rule kicks in which is win/lose short-term and lose/lose long-term. This is in sharp contrast to the open, honest, Christian kingdom economic system which is win/win/win/win. Individual man wins, collective man wins, God wins and the environment wins. Needless to say, there is lack of true character and professionalism under a non-Christian economic system.

An honest Christian system is built from the bottom up, beginning with individuals and families in agriculture, small businesses and industry, followed eventually by large industry. These are the "goods base" on which every society must be built to be stable long-term. From this base, personal and information services can be built. Demand for real estate and the civil government are bridesmaids that are dependent upon the health of these other, more basic sectors of the economy.

The more diversified and decentralized the economy, the more prosperous it is and the more it can withstand manmade and natural assaults. Cities have historically been slave centers, marked by debt money and the exploitation of the masses by the few. We have been living in frozen world cities for the better part of the 20th century, defacto slavery.

Contrasting the city versus the country, the city is vertical in its architectural and human organizational structures. It is collectivistic and, therefore, is feminine or yin (dark). Cities incline people to become either predators or parasites. The city is its own human jungle where survival of the fittest occurs. It is labor intense with many wage slaves. However, it provides for the specialization and division of labor and the development of technology.

The rural country is horizontal, lateral, in its human and organizational structures. It focuses more on the individual, which is masculine or yang (light). It is more freedom-oriented, like farmers, ranchers or mountain men historically. It works with covenants and contracts, where humans are the basic ultimate resource. It functions according to both the spiritual and physical golden rules. The Spiritual Golden Rule is, "Do unto others as you would have them do unto you." The Physical (Monetary) Golden Rule is, "Whoever has the gold, makes the rules." God and gold rightfully go together. Historically, gold has always flowed to areas of real productivity (life). Today, gold is flowing to the Asian Pacific basin nations. China is predicted to be the next great civilization in the 21st century. Gold is produced in the rural country. It is also where the land is, and where commodities are produced - commodities which can be monetized.

Two principles established between the city (yin - feminine/collective) and the rural country (yang - masculine/individual) bring balance, harmony, peace and prosperity. These are presented below:

(1) Strictly limiting absentee ownership of land. This promotes a spirit of community and turns the world into a garden rather than a wilderness. No man or organization should own more land than violates the spirit of community or more than he is able to turn into a garden. People need to experience the effects of their actions on people and the environment, and this is possible primarily if they own land and work where they live.

(2) Allowing the rural country to be the primary and nearly exclusive creator of money through the monetization of commodities, the issuing of receipts for commodities, or computer entries as money representing actual commodities. Free-market money - honest Christian, quantum money - is produced in the rural country. People flow to money. Where the money is found, so are jobs. Thus, under such an honest, open, Christian quantum economic system, the money and jobs would be in the rural country. This would lead to a mass exodus from the cities, a decentralization of society, and the greater positing of religious, political and economic power in the individual as the decentralization occurred. Thus, man would become more God-like. God as Father, Son and Holy Spirit, is three separate individuals (masculine) who come together in covenant voluntarily and co-exist as One (feminine). In God's eternal realm, the one and the many, the feminine and the masculine are balanced and co-equal. But here on the earth in time, because we are linear and making progress toward perfection, the many individuals (masculine) voluntarily through covenant and contract become the collective one (feminine).

The answer to the economic question of our day - why the technological advances in communication, transportation and other technology have not naturally led to decentralization rather than centralization in our society - is that we have not strictly limited absentee ownership of land and allowed the rural country to be the primary, and probably exclusive, creator of money. Under such an open, honest, Christian, free-market economy, every man would live under his own vine and fig tree. We would thus see the fulfillment of "thy kingdom come, thy will be done, on earth as it is in heaven."

In the United States today, as the late Dr. Iben Browning documented, 88 percent of the population claims to be Christian. Since government is always religion applied to economics; and since we live in a democracy where supposedly the individual has power; and since in this nation, 88 percent claim to be Christian; we should have a Christian economic system, and a Christian civil government.

Dr. Browning also demonstrated that historically, the per capita income in Christian societies - particularly Protestant Christian societies which focus on the individual - is at least six times that of Roman Catholic countries. There is even greater spread in per capita income between Christian and non-Christian social orders, particularly social orders which have not adopted common grace, basic, Christian economic principles.

As should now be apparent, it is a lie that "economics is the dismal science." Economics today is dismal because it is captured by a fallen debt (death) based system. It is a lie that we live in a world of limited natural or human resources. There is unlimited energy, and, therefore, potentially unlimited natural renewable resources, not to mention the discovery of new and better ways to use resources. It is a lie that we have too many people on this earth, as has been clearly demonstrated by the Austrian school of economics and by other Christian economists. In an open, honest, mature, Christian economic system, there are never enough people to do all the work which needs to be done. Christian men and women are the ultimate resource. It is a lie that man has unlimited wants. The very nature of mature, productive man is to forego instant gratification and save for investment and for deferred gratification. This has been the hallmark of progress throughout mankind's history. It has always been those people who have taken a long-term view, who have saved and invested, who have become the upper class of any society. This has resulted from individuals limiting their wants. Progress only comes with disciplined limitation of one's wants. This is Christian discipleship applied to economics. Indeed, it can be successfully argued that true joy results from having peace with limiting one's physical/economic wants.

We live on the threshold of the greatest economic opportunity ever available to mankind, if we will first seize the moment spiritually. Religion always comes down to economics, just as faith comes down to works. As a man believes, so he thinks, and so he acts economically. "Human action" is the definition of economics, according to the great Austrian economist, Ludwig von Mises.

Even the biblical sabbath fits into this equation. As Dr. Peter Rothchild has demonstrated, the kingdom/quantum pulse is a 6:1 pulse. In other words, in order to make real progress, in order to prevent chaos, there needs to be a rest after six impulses of activity. So, when we work six days and rest the seventh, we recharge ourselves according to the laws of quantum physics (the kingdom of God) to be more creative, productive and make consistent progress in our economic lives.

We have nothing to lose but our chains and poverty, with freedom and wealth to be gained. The creation groans, awaiting the manifestation of the sons of God, as environmental integrity is a by-product of wealth for all.

FAITH AND VOCATION

The November, 1983 issue of Psychology Today featured an interview with Dr. James Fowler entitled, "Stages of Faith." In that interview Dr. Fowler stated, "There is a theological conviction underlying this whole work, a conviction I call the sovereignty of God. Correlated with this is my conviction that the human vocation - the authentic end of being a person - has to do (whether we know it and acknowledge it) with finding ways to relate properly to the Being at the heart of the universe."

Psychology Today is a not a Christian magazine. Dr. James Fowler is professor of the theology of human development at the Candler School of Theology at Emory University in Atlanta, Georgia. Fowler earlier had been on the faculty of Harvard Divinity School.

What is important is that Fowler's book, "Stages Of Faith," links faith directly with a man's vocation - his calling, or work. This is religion coming down to economics! This is the very essence of the meaning and purpose of this life which lies at the very heart of Christianity. Man is put on this earth - once born again and redeemed - to work, to discover his vocation, to carry out his calling, and thus accomplish God's purpose for his life. This is re-creation. By contrast, pagans emphasize leisure with sensual pleasure being primary. Work in this pagan context is a means to provide that end, leisure.

Man cannot give God anything. God is sovereign, the Creator and owner of everything. God instead gives to man, beginning with Jesus Christ and carrying through to man's calling. So, how does man please a God who is and has everything? Man pleases God by obeying God, by doing the work for which he was created, the work that is intended to serve one's fellow man. Over and over again in the Bible, God tells us that we are to serve Him by serving our fellow man. As a by-product of our contribution to our fellow man, we benefit ourselves. It's a win/win/win covenant and contract.

God designed the three-way win in this manner because there exists a psychological principle, the proposition being, that if someone gives something to someone else which the receiving party cannot repay in some form, shape or fashion, the long-term result will be that the recipient of the gift will return evil for good. The person who cannot repay will effectively repay the loving gift with scorn and hatred to the detriment of the giver. This is why Christian charity is to be short-term only, to help folks get back on their feet. If they don't work, they don't live.

God gave us eternal life when He sacrificed His only Son, Jesus Christ, on the cross at Calvary. We did not earn or deserve this gift from God and there is no way we can repay it. So, what way did God provide for us to circumvent our evil sin nature and our natural psychological tendency to rebel against God and repay evil for His good? Stated differently, how do we reimburse God for His gift of eternal life when it is impossible for us to give God anything? The outlet, the pressure-relief valve, that God has given us is this: because He gave to us, we give to our fellow man. Therefore, the way we give back to God is by service to others (in addition to praise and worship, of course). The Lord Himself tells us in Matthew 10:8, "...Freely ye have received, freely give." The words of the Lord are again quoted in Acts 20:35, "It is more blessed to give than to receive." Those who are given much are expected to, in return, give much. Thus God, in His marvelous wisdom, by admonishing man to give to his fellow man, has not only provided man with a way of pleasing God for what God has given to him, but He also provides for a harmony of interests between all men and God, resolving the individual versus collective conflict between men. When man gives to his fellow man, his fellow man benefits, the giver benefits as a by-product of this service, and the will of God is fulfilled. Again, it is win/win/win. Moreover, the only way an individual can truly develop self-worth, and pass from sorrow to joy, darkness to light, death to life is to follow this heavenly prescription.

Notice further that all of man's responsibilities as a Christian ambassador pertain to service to his fellow man. This is what separates Christianity from all other humanistic religions. All other religions are either an attempt to evolve to become God, an attempt to directly please God, or an attempt to establish man as God. This leads to man's focus being on the eternal realm and on himself. Christianity uniquely upholds a distinctive Creator/creature separation, with man's focus being on his responsibilities in time to his fellow man and to the earth (dominion) as the way of pleasing God.

Repeatedly in both the Old and New Testaments, man's duties are to the land and to his fellow man - land and labor. The two components of economics are land and labor. Thus, the Christian issue is one of economics. The basic instruments of economics are the covenant and contract, which are the bases of God's relationship with man in land and labor.

There are at least 55 million born-again believers in the United States. One-fourth of the population is Christian. One-quarter of the world's population is Christian. If Christians were truly Christian in terms of rightful Christian action, only three percent of the Christian population would be needed to change this nation and the world. This means the church has eight times the manpower it needs to disciple the nations and occupy until the return of Jesus Christ.

II Timothy 2:15 declares, "Study to show thyself approved unto God, a workman that needeth not to be ashamed, rightly dividing the word of truth." Man is to study the Word of God, to become edified in a church body, and to overcome, so that he may be a good workman in time. The purpose of Bible study and the purpose of the church, is not only to worship God and give thanks for all His blessings, but also to train up the believer so that he is a mature self-governing believer/priest who may work in his calling in the real world, thereby serving his fellow man, which is pleasing to God. Christianity is meaningful. It is practical. It is the successful formula for life here and now on His earth.

Now, let's tie faith and works together. When we, by an act of faith, work with God's perfect abstract model of truth (His Law-Word), and then with the temporal facts of His created realm, bring them together for victory, we honor Him. God is honored when we correctly interpret the facts of His creation, recapture them to His glory, and use them in light of His perfect Law-Word. This links man's faith, a spiritual characteristic, with his dominion/stewardship responsibility on the earth, his works. James 2:22 states, "Seest thou how faith wrought with his works, and by works was faith made perfect?" James 2:24 continues, "Ye see then how that by works a man is justified, and not by faith only." Christians are to be active workers, applying the mind and heart-changing tools God has given them in the Bible to His creation!

God's creation is an expression of His essence. The inescapable perfect link between God and His creation is given to us in John 1: "In the beginning was the Word, and the Word was with God, and the Word was God. The same was in the beginning with God, all things were made by Him; and without Him was not anything made that was made. In Him was life; and the life was the light of men." The creation is evidence of God's handiwork. The evidence of man's faith is his willingness to work in his calling to progressively redeem from the curse both himself and God's creation, both labor and land, the two parts of the basic economic equation. God's law frames his natural and moral creation to bring all things into harmony.

We are born into this world with a sinful nature, we are not perfect, we are flawed. This is another way of saying that man makes mistakes and has naturally an animal nature - he is a fallen natural man. When man is "born again" through faith, filled with the Holy Spirit, and growing to maturity, the labor side of God's plan is activated so that he can go to work with his developed talents in the creation, the land side, and reclaim it from wilderness to perfect harmony as once existed in the Garden of Eden. First men and then the land are to be recaptured from Satan's fallen cursed chaotic order to God's harmonious glory and perfection.

Will we ever accomplish this perfectly? Of course not. We are all sinners and we all make mistakes. But there is our assigned goal, work and objective. When we are successful in time, we are rewarded in time and eternally. We do reap what we sow in time, in terms of the recaptured creation, on earth, as well as eternally. As we grow individually, we extend our occupation throughout the creation. As we grow to be more Christ-like, so too is the creation more Christ-like, more in harmony. The opposite is true for the pagan. When man is wild, so is nature a wilderness, subject to environmental abuse. Since man was given dominion/stewardship responsibility over the earth, as man goes - so goes the earth.

Dr. Fowler's "Seven Stages of Faith" reflect this Christian growth. Stage one he calls Primal Faith (Infancy). Stage two is Intuitive-Projective Faith (Early childhood). The third stage of faith is Mythic-Literal Faith (Childhood and beyond). Stage four is Synthetic-Conventional Faith (Adolescence and beyond). Stage five is Individuative-Reflective Faith (Young adulthood and beyond).

Now notice the sixth and seventh levels of faith according to Dr. Fowler. Are they harmonious with the paradoxes and apparent contradictions, the Truths-In-Tension (TNT), that appear in scripture - which, in a mature believer, are reconciled to the total harmony of the character of God Himself? Yes. Stage six of faith is Conjunctive Faith (Mid-Life and beyond). Stage six of faith, "The embrace of polarities in one's life, an alertness to paradox, and the need for multiple interpretations of reality mark this stage."

Stage seven of faith, the final stage, is Universalizing Faith (Mid-Life or beyond). "Beyond paradox and polarities, persons in this stage are grounded in a oneness with the power of being. Their visions and commitments free them for a passionate yet detached spending of the self in love, devoted to overcoming division, oppression, and brutality."

I John 4:8 tells us that "God is love." Romans 13:10 admonishes us: "Love worketh no ill to his neighbors: therefore love is the fulfilling of the law." In other words, there is intended total harmony between God, His love, His creation, becoming Christ-like and work, between spirit and matter, between faith and vocation.

HUMANISM ON THE JOB

A Media General/Associated Press poll indicated that 91 percent of Americans like their jobs. But what they like most are the people with whom they work and the work itself. In other words, the "spiritual" benefits are the main reasons Americans like their jobs. This is not surprising since man is primarily a spiritual being, "made in the image of God."

Lower-rated reasons given why American adults like their jobs included money, hours and company benefits. These things speak to man's nature as a physical creature, "formed from the dust of the earth."

It can be seen from these poll findings and Scripture that emphasis on a materialistic lifestyle is not only contrary to God's law, but also to what people themselves say motivates them. It is contrary to our own perceived best interests. God's law and man's interests are in harmony when work is handled biblically.

Christianity focuses on how man best serves God by serving his fellow man (economics). While the Old Testament dwells on the "land" factor in the land-labor economic equation, the New Testament in large part focuses on the importance of man's work (labor) and his relationship with his fellow man, the very two things which men say today still brings them the most satisfaction on the job. So much for the decadent promise of dialectical materialism, the basis for the communism and socialism which infected the world economy, including America's, so deeply in the 20th century.

For years, business struggled to motivate employees. Nothing seemed to work. Americans for the most part remained, "wage slaves." Why? Because the problem is ultimately "spiritual," a perspective modern business is just beginning to recognize. Dr. Frederick Herzberg, writing in the Harvard Business Review, traced out the sad history of attempts to motivate employees. Management has tried nearly everything, including negative physical and psychological sanctions, as well as positive incentives such as reduced hours, higher wages, fringe benefits, human relations training, sensitivity training, communications, and employee counselling. None of these has worked. True enough, if "creature" factors - job security, good job status, good relationships with subordinates and supervisors, a satisfactory salary and work conditions, and a solid company policy and administration - are maintained, job dissatisfaction is avoided. But the factors which bring satisfaction on the job include achievement, recognition, the work itself, responsibility, advancement and growth. These are the "spiritual" factors.

It is the satisfaction of spiritual needs which motivates man; in short, giving employees challenging work in which they can assume responsibility. This is the answer for those who struggle with the management tools of organizational theory, industrial engineering, and behavioral science. Today, the focus is on job enrichment, which is well and good, once the foundation is established. Unless men build upon God, they labor in vain.

Sadly, rebellion against authority, the first active behavioral consequence of humanistic pride, is ever present on the job. The Media General/Associated Press poll indicated that only 3 percent of working Americans like their jobs because they like their bosses. This is confirmed in research by Boston University's Donald Kanter and Philip Mirvis as reported in The Wall Street Journal (Feb. 10, 1987). Fully 78 percent of American workers are suspicious of management, developing an "us-against-them" syndrome that interferes with their performance.

Ironically, here, too, most of these workers are satisfied with their jobs, their pay, and their opportunities for promotion. They also cooperate with their fellow workers on the job. They have just never learned (perhaps were never taught) the discipline of discipleship, or the apprenticeship of stewardship, or the importance of being under authority. Therefore, just as management overlooks the spiritual base in motivating employees, employees frustrate their own interests by their pride and their failure to be disciplined under authority.

Questions: Given this distrust and disrespect for authority, just what will happen when the next recession hits and if unemployment soars above 10 percent? What happens when the debt pyramid collapses? Our American standard of living cannot be sustained long-term by debt, particularly since we have lost our industrial and technological edge to the rest of the world and our wages are uncompetitive globally.

If management is going to successfully motivate employees, it must meet the basic "creature" needs. But more importantly, management must focus on the primary "spiritual" needs of the workplace. Employees, on the other hand, must be good disciples, good apprentices, obedient to authority, like Christ taught his disciples, before they can become good stewards and truly good workers.

COMMON GRACE IN
THE FREE MARKET

The doctrine of common grace holds that God's laws have an inescapable and comprehensive application throughout His creation. One of the arenas in which common grace operates is economics - including that crucial component of economics, man's labor.

God in His grace has made it possible for prosperity and peace to be the common or general experience of mankind. The mechanisms for this result are the biblical laws of covenanting and contracting - the foundations of the free market. Biblical covenanting and contracting, the securing of just, mutual self-interests, are a divinely devised pattern for relationships that will perform with common and predictable consequences in any culture.

The prosperous results of free-market contracting were once brilliantly visible in the biblically-based economy of the United States. Today, free-market "miracles" are also being performed in the non-Christian cultures of Hong Kong and Taiwan, and they are operating with fantastic results in South Korea.

Why is this so? It is because contracting - a biblical instrument - creates consistent results under God's common grace. The Christian in the marketplace understands The Second Great Commandment and The Golden Rule - that if he is to reap the economic benefits (self-interests) of unfettered enterprise, he must grant equal freedom to his fellow man. A non-Christian in the marketplace may begin as ruthless, greedy and selfish, but if he hopes to profit from any economic contract he has made under commitment to a free market, he, too, must learn first to serve. He, too, must follow the Second Great Biblical Law and The Golden Rule.

If men want peace and prosperity on earth, they must operate therefore according to the godly free market under common grace. All sane men do want peace and prosperity in their efforts, as Solomon observed: "There is nothing better for a man than he should eat and drink, and that his soul should enjoy good in his labor." - Ecclesiastes 2:24 and, "So I perceive that there is nothing better than that a man should rejoice in his own works, for that is his heritage." - Ecclesiastes 3:22.

Too many men continually fail, in our modern age, to pursue this "natural" inclination through free-market principles. Why is this so? One principal reason may be that our societies have fallen for the deceit of the god of the age - this state. It is no accident that the state is so widely at war against the free market. Free contracting minimizes the functions of the civil state. When men are free, they are self-governing - needing civil government only for the purpose of enforcing contracts, preventing fraud and providing for the common defense against threats to free action. The unbeliever and immature believer are spiritually blind to this and thus are prone to opt for the economic security deceitfully promised by the state. Moreover, Christian covenanting, rightfully applied, helps create the social safety net, met expensively and inefficiently by government bureaucracies.

The key to the common-grace free market is an understanding of godly political and economic institutions for a nation. Such an understanding within a populace will produce spiritually mature leaders for these institutions. This will not come about, of course, without spiritual renewal, reformation and Christian reconstruction. Christian maturity is vital to the common-grace free market, and the peace and prosperity which it inescapably generates. Contractual morality undergirds the free marketplace. Work - broadly defined as all economic enterprise - will then become the blessing it was intended at creation to be.

Again, as Solomon observed of working men: "I know that there is nothing better for them than to rejoice, and to do good in their lives and also that every man should eat and drink and enjoy the good of all his labor - it is the gift of God." - Ecclesiastes 3:12-13.

THE TIME VALUE OF MONEY

People are more important than things because people create, use, abuse and destroy things. Furthermore, when people are treated as more important than things, there tends to be harmony and coop- eration in a society. What usually follows is more voluntary sharing, justice and collaboration concerning things. This cooperation - cove- nanting and contracting - in turn creates more prosperity, more things. So prosperity long-term for any society rests upon having its priorities straight, placing its primary emphasis on people rather than things (and money).

This emphasis on people rather than things is the essence of why the Bank of the People's Labor at Mondragon, Spain has been so successful long-term. No business failures; no loan failures; the highest productivity in all of Spain, the highest profitability (nearly double that of its competitors), and the highest morale and innovation ratings possible - all characterize Mondragon. Success there has been achieved in all areas. Success is a by-product of doing things correctly. Ultimately, ideas do have consequences. Religion comes down to economics.

Critical to the achievement at Mondragon, although unstated and possibly unrecognized even by these people, is that they have estab- lished their priorities on people systems and effectively checkmated the natural inclination to focus on the time value of money with its compounding effect. The compounding of money in a fractional re- serve, debt-based, interest-sensitive society, such as ours, inevitably leads to a focus on things (and money) rather than people. The rea- son for this is because the challenge of compounding is a challenge which no individual or society can meet or beat long-term. The compounding of interest, money earning money on money, is relent- less, ruthless, and eternal, unforgiving of mistakes and eventually is exponential. By contrast, men do make mistakes, need rest, do not forecast the future perfectly, make poor use of human and natural re- sources and are fortunate if they can simply achieve arithmetic economic growth. Therefore, it is no surprise that the slave-like god of debt money and compound interest eventually forces all to bow at its altar. As men are forced to serve this god of money (mammon), inescapably then money (and things) become more important than people.

Human nature has not changed. We should hail back to the sound advice given us by the Hebrews of the Old Testament, the

Greeks, the great Christian teachers of the Middle Ages, and the Founding Fathers who built this country. These wise men warned against and often outlawed fractional reserve debt money, compound interest, usury and paper money. They spurned debt generally. They found reprehensible the concept of money earning money on money - compound interest. And they were prosperous.

The bottom line is this: If a people in a society are to be prosperous, peaceful and happy long-term, the economic structure of society must establish people as superior to things. But in order for this to occur, a society must establish the rules (boundaries) of monetary law. Such monetary law must first and foremost include the prohibition of fractional reserve debt money, paper money that is not backed by commodities, and the compound interest factor, whereby money earns money by simply being money. Strict limitations on the nature and length of debt itself are also important. Such prohibitions forbid non-productive financial activities, such as we have seen run rampant in recent years by way of junk bonds used for leveraged buyouts, mergers, greenmail, and the weakening, dismantling and sell-off of productive business corporations. Such prohibitions are the only way to establish the correct priority of people over things.

Since people are indeed primarily spiritual beings, made in the image of God, then they are eternal. Therefore, people are more important than things (and money), which are temporal. Hence, the very concept of the time value of money as eternal, as always producing more without end, is a travesty, as debt-based society after debt-based society has demonstrated time and time again down through history. These nations have crumbled and disappeared, having first rotted economically from within. When a people focus on the time value of money and such things as discounted present value, as our social order so totally does today, it has bought the lie of money as a god. It has elevated money and things to a more important status than people. It has relinquished its freedom and prosperity in exchange for a walk to exhaustion on the ever increasing angle of inclination - the treadmill of compound interest.

Additionally, children become a curse rather than a blessing. Children are expensive, so they are sacrificed to the god of debt service. It isn't coincidental that with the increasing debt load in a society, there is a concomitant increase in abortion. A people who do not reproduce themselves and who murder their young, by definition commit suicide long-term. Thus, the time value of money inescapably destroys mankind. It is no accident that one of the root meanings of the word debt is death, just as the root meaning of the word mort, as in mortgage, is also death.

To hold as absolute the concept that life is time and time is money, is to equate life with money. Then money and things can become more significant than people, and conflict over money and things accelerates bringing about poverty, not prosperity, and the society begins to die. The result long-term is less things for less people. So, unless there are laws which tie money to man's real, finite world, establishing it as a commodity or a representative thereof, there's no hope for cooperation triumphing over conflict, for viewing people as more important than things, or for escaping the long-term exhaustion and bankruptcy resulting from the tyranny of the time value of money.

The love of money (greed/selfishness) is the root of all evil. Evil is 180 degrees out of phase with life. God is life. It is not coincidental that live spelled backward is evil and that the root meaning of the word debt is death. Debt money is death-oriented and evil, not live.

A BANK MEN CAN BANK ON

Tucked away in the Pyrenees mountains of northeastern Spain, nestled in a long-persecuted area known as the Basque, lies the all but unknown village of Mondragon. Establishment forces have many times attempted to oppress the people there. For example, during the 1920s, many Basque towns and villages were active in the Spanish anarchist movement. The people went so far as to eliminate government money from their villages and replace it with a simple barter system. Not only does this financial action show the fierce independence and rugged individuality of the area, but it also demonstrates that these people had some idea about what real money and honest economics are all about.

The Basque stood and fought against Franco. When Franco achieved victory, he outlawed their language and required them to speak Spanish. All this did was reinforce the solidarity and community spirit of these hardy people.

In 1941, a Catholic priest who had fought in the Spanish Civil War, Father Jose Maria Arizmendi, was assigned to Mondragon. Father Arizmendi, understanding that faith without works is dead (James 2), began implementing social and economic systems at Mondragon that proved indeed that religion does come down to economics (human action). Since the Roman Catholic Church had never officially supported either capitalism (individualism) or socialism (collectivism), Father Arizmendi sought to pull the best from both systems for use in his development plans at Mondragon.

It is not surprising that this priest was successful. For, since debt capitalism emphasized radical individualism and socialism stresses radical collectivism, if the strong points of both systems could be harmonized, then the basic problem of humanity is resolved. In other words, how do we balance the rights of individuals with those of collective society?

Despite half a century of success, Father Arizmendi's work at Mondragon only recently came to light with a BBC-produced film entitled, "Mondragon: An Experiment." Perhaps the most knowledgeable individual on Mondragon in the United States is Dr. Terry Mollner, who authored, "The Mondragon Cooperatives and Trusteeship" (Trusteeship Institute, Inc., Shutesbury, MA). Dr. Mollner also wrote a short summary of the history and results of the Mondragon economic experiment for the April 1986 issue of Green Revolution

(R.D. 1, Spring Grove, PA 17362). The facts which follow concerning Mondragon are drawn largely from Dr. Mollner's work.

The linear sequence from the abstract to the concrete runs as follows: religion - philosophy - creative ideas unifying thoughts with matter - work - material achievement (economics). In structuring both his worker cooperatives and the bank at Mondragon, Father Arizmendi struck the right chord in human nature because he applied a correct religious/philosophical principle. The maxim is that harmony (leading to material achievement) results when the rights of the individual (capitalism) are in balance with the rights of collective society (socialism/communism). Small wonder then that his economic experiment is successful. Thoughts precede action. Ideas have consequences. Religion comes down to economics.

The strengths of pure capitalism are its emphasis on individual character development, professional performance of a task, freedom, incentive to work, the primary use of the contract which permits bottom up growth horizontal relationships (equality), and finally, when correctly formulated, that self-interest is only actualized as a by-product of first serving one's fellow man. The worst of warped capitalism - dog-eat-dog evolutionary conflict for the survival of the fittest; OPM (debt financing with few becoming prosperous at the expense of others); debt; fractional reserve money which is not a commodity; and competition for the purpose of win/lose - is discarded.

The worst aspects of communism/socialism are also discarded - forced cooperation and communal activity (slavery) enforced top down by a militaristic, oppressive bureaucracy; no individual incentive to be productive or to work; and no individuality which allows the development, expression and free use of an individual's unique God-given talents. The best of communism/socialism is retained - the idea that workers should be the owners of the means of production (if they earn it). The emphasis is on cooperation, harmony and community spirit - the greatest good for the greatest number, not at the expense of killing individualism, but instead created by individualism, since balance must be maintained.

While no student of economic theory, Father Arizmendi stumbled upon the reality that economic prosperity only flourishes long-term in an environment of cooperation rather than conflict. (Competition rightfully implemented short-term is only for the purpose of serving, not to create a win/lose situation. If conflict produced economic prosperity, there would be no such thing as flight capital where conflict exists. Instead, people would invest in Lebanon, Nicaragua,

Iran, Iraq, Bosnia, etc.) Father Arizmendi, because he was a priest, captured this cooperative idea in terms of love - a primary characteristic of God. God is love. Because of God's love, he effectively reasoned, people are more important than things. Furthermore, when and where there is love between people, they treat things differently than where conflict exists. Where there is love, there is more voluntary sharing, justice, and give and take - more cooperation concerning things. Where there is not love, however, where conflict reigns between men, things become a catalyst for even greater conflict. Instead of sharing - hoarding, envy, theft, suspicion, injustice and greed exist. Things become more important than people in a conflict-ridden society which lacks love.

Matter exists in time and space. On the other hand, people and their relationships can transcend time and space. Therefore, people are more important than things. With this handle on economic reality, Father Arizmendi set to work establishing systems that emphasized people over things.

The final point of progression of Father Arizmendi's work, the crowning glory of his economic experiment, is the Caja Laboral Popular ("The Bank of the People's Labor"). This bank, headquartered in Mondragon, is active in nearly every village throughout the Basque region of Spain. This cooperative bank has 120 branches, and is both a custodian and investor of the deposits of nearly 400,000 families. This is incredible for a bank founded in a church basement nearly 40 years ago (1958).

This bank has a clearly defined objective: to create worker-owned jobs for the community. In its purpose, The Bank of the People's Labor has given incentives to individuals to work and also become owners of the means of production for the purpose of serving their fellow man, and as a by-product, serving themselves. It all began with a man who was first seeking to serve God. As a result, the Mondragon bank has a 100 percent success rate at forming industrial cooperatives and making loans. It has experienced no failures. By contrast, in the United States, only one out of 10 new businesses will survive the first five years. But then again the emphasis in the United States is different. The investment philosophy and approach of the Mondragon bank is to invest in people, not things, because people can become the ultimate resource rather than being predators or parasites in society.

The investment priorities of the Mondragon bank are: 1) workers; 2) managers; 3) the goods or service to be produced; and 4) capital/money. This is just the opposite of what exists under the Western debt capitalistic system today. In the West, emphasis is primarily on capital, then the goods or service, then management and finally, workers.

Ironically, Western debt capitalism and communism both stress the development of capital (things). Dialectic materialism - the idea that economics is the motivational root of all of man's actions - is basic to communism. But because capital (money) is effectively stored energy or stored labor, we inevitably get back to the character, professionalism, incentive and work habits of people as primary for producing things, or for making money. So today in the West, we are reaping what we have sown. As a consequence of elevating things above people, we are now under economic, political, social and spiritual distress. Only two percent of Americans are financially and economically self-sufficient at the age of 65, while 96 percent are flat broke, being dependent upon shaky pensions, the nearly bankrupt Social Security system, or friends and family, to stay alive economically. Then we have the technically insolvent federal government ($5 trillion debt) and the pitifully weak U.S. dollar. We are effectively in Chapter 13 bankruptcy as a society.

Debt capitalism does not produce the greatest good for the greatest number. Far from it. Only two-tenths of one percent of all Americans are millionaires. Only 15 percent of Americans are capitalists. The bureaucrats who produce nothing constructive consume our wealth, if the international banks don't give it or loan it away first. Moreover, only three percent of the U.S. population owns 85 percent of the private land in the United States. This is worse than in El Salvador. In California, only 1 percent of the population owns two-thirds of the private land.

Our sad state of affairs is readily seen by the fact that the largest sales in U.S. drug stores are for: 1) Mylanta; 2) Anacin; and 3) Bayer aspirin. In dollar amount of sales in U.S. drug stores, No. 2 is Anacin, No. 3 is Tylenol, and No. 4 is Advil. The bankruptcy of our governmental, religious and economic systems is literally giving all of us a collective headache. The cancer death rate is up 8.7 percent. We are effectively gripped in the momentum of a downward death spiral. Further reflecting this death spiral, the United States ranks first globally in military expenditures, and leads the world in military technology, military bases globally, and nuclear warheads and bombs.

Of course, it was worse under communism, the ultimate collective. There the bureaucracy was far more extensively developed.

(Bureaucracy is the greatest institutional manifestation of human evil.) The greatest economic class distinctions in the world existed in the former Soviet Union. The high ranking members of the Communist Party and their obedient bureaucrats lived like kings, like gods, while the masses of people stood in line to buy toilet paper. Furthermore, every Russian woman on average had six abortions, while Russian men drank themselves to death. The eyes of the people of the former U.S.S.R. showed no sparkle of life. Reflecting this, the former U.S.S.R. ranked 44th globally in life expectancy and second in weapons' expenditures. The U.S. and the former U.S.S.R. together, with less than 11 percent of the world's population, accounted for 60 percent of global military expenditures, 80 percent of the weapons research, and 97 percent of all nuclear weapons. It's a miserable life at either evolutionary extreme of individualism (debt capitalism) or collectivism (communism).

Because Mondragon has discovered rightfully that people are more important than things, the Mondragon bank invests first and foremost in people. The Mondragon bankers figure the goods or service produced will be self-perpetuating in time. If the investment is made in the right people, and people can work cooperatively, professionally, effectively and efficiently, then the bank and business can always change the goods or service produced to meet the needs of the marketplace.

Because of this philosophy of people being the primary investment, the bank is a cooperative one in which the people themselves have a stake. The result is the entire community is business-oriented and backs the bank and the businesses it creates. The workers, managers, owners, consumers and bankers as owners of the means of production are all one and the same, or at least closely tied to one another. People in Mondragon are literally investing in themselves. Business is a blessing at Mondragon, rather than the curse it has too often become in the West.

Furthermore, the bank backs the people and their businesses when they get into trouble. Why shouldn't it be that way? The people are simply backing themselves. In fact, the bank makes a commitment to both the people involved and the business to back them until they succeed. If the goods or service produced has to be changed, so what? It's changed. People are more important than things. People produce things. Therefore, the primary investment is in people! You can desert the thing, but not the people.

If a business falls on hard times or is struggling, the bank's entrepreneurial division has a policy of lowering the interest rate on loans to these worker-owned cooperatives as business gets riskier. This is a long-term view. Short-term pain for long-term gain has always been necessary for success in any human endeavor. At Mondragon, the voluntary attitude of all for one and one for all supported by incentives, maintains balance because workers, managers, owners, the bank depositors, the bank and consumers are all one and the same. Everyone has a vested interest in seeing that every worker-owned business is ultimately successful. This further provides life-time job security, even though the business itself may change by way of new or different goods or services, depending on what the market demands. Crisis management is thereby also avoided. Stress is minimized, if not mostly eliminated.

If these people had honest, free-market money, based in some ultimate physical reality, such as they effectively did during the Spanish Civil War, the sky would be the limit economically.

Can we as Americans imagine an economic and financial system where our investments are secure, our savings are indeed safe and growing in real terms, without inflation or deflation, where workers do not have to worry about absentee ownership, new management, being fired, transferred, or losing their jobs due to a plant or business closing?

Just how does a business get started at Mondragon? First of all, a group of men (friends) voluntarily get together and decide they want to start a new business. So people who already have a covenantal and often contractual relationship with one another (love), get together and decide to work together (things/money). Thus, spiritual and economic realities are in basic harmony. Each member of this business starter group has to put his money where his mouth is. He is required to have a financial stake in the venture, to be a true capitalist. Each member loans the business some of his own capital. Therefore, the individual group members are literally at risk. Then they go to the bank.

At the Mondragon bank, the bank's entrepreneurial division interviews the business starter group regarding their request for the bank's assistance. The bank's first priority is to determine if there is truly a loving bond and solid relationship between the various people in the proposed business start-up group. This is the foundation for the new business - people and love. If the bank is happy with both the character and covenantal relationships of the group members seeking to start a new business, the bank then joins into a contractual partnership with the business on behalf of its depositors, for the purpose of creating this new worker-owned cooperative.

Both the bank and the group desiring to form the new business are committed to work and provide capital until the business is running profitably, effectively and efficiently. Everyone has a stake in the venture, both short-term and long-term. The investment is by way of both people and capital, with the priorities being in that correct order, followed by things or service.

Next, democracy comes into play. The business start-up group meets by itself and chooses one of its members to be the manager of the new business. Important long-term strategic planning commences. This elected manager is required to spend two years working with an expert of the bank for the purpose of developing both a plan for the business and a community development plan. Thus, the goals of the individuals of the business group are required to be in harmony with those of the community generally. Community considerations such as housing, parks, commercial development and other community services are considered.

When all this is eventually accomplished, the decision about which goods or service are to be produced is finalized. This product or service must be determined to be in the best interest of the people of the community long-term before the bank will finance it in partnership with the business group. In other words, the people are deciding with their own money what they really want in the marketplace and their community. Consumer preference is effectively sovereign by determining producer investment.

Now, practically speaking, the process is not all this cut and dried. The group of friends who decided they wanted to work together and form a business to serve the community (and as a by-product meet their personal needs), had a good idea initially about what goods or service they wanted to produce before they got into partnership with the bank and established their worker-owned jobs. The members of the group came together, bringing their strengths of character, commitment and specialized professional skills, to furnish a particular product or service. It is how they will use these skills, let us say in electronic technology, which is decided last of all.

An extensive market study is conducted to determine the true needs of the community. In fact, everything that makes for a successful business is carefully covered at Mondragon. Most businesses fail due to insufficient capital, poor accounting, inadequate and inept management, labor problems, no strategic or tactical business plan, no marketing plan, and goods or a service produced which is not desired by the marketplace. All of these problems are solved going in, to the maximum extent possible, before the business ever gets off the ground at Mondragon. No wonder Mondragon has a 100 percent success rate; they are doing everything right. Success - making honest money - is a by-product of doing things correctly.

The bank's entrepreneurial division has two bank worker-owners who are involved full time in identifying new products needed by the community which require new businesses to produce them. The emphasis is thus clearly on research and development, and production over and against consumption. This is true, progressive capitalism. Furthermore, down the line if the manager is found to be incompetent, he is demoted back to the group and a new manager is chosen. He is not fired, just demoted. If the product or service is found not to be viable, a new product or service is developed, even if it means new, expensive capital equipment has to be purchased. So, excellence in both people and product are demanded at Mondragon. Incompetence and failure are punished in their own careful, loving way. These Mondragon cooperative businesses stress both responsiveness to the marketplace by way of consumer-demanded goods or services, as well as excellence in individual productivity and management. Small wonder the bank has never suffered a loan default.

Mondragon, with its primary and correct emphasis on people, finds group strength is a function of individual strength coming together voluntarily in a loving and supportive atmosphere. Individuals meet both their love and money needs by voluntary, contractual exchange (with incentives for hard work). They also "find themselves" by losing themselves in their service to their community. Thus, the balance between their individual self-identity and the community's collective identity are in balance. Harmony, peace and prosperity inescapably have resulted.

From 1958 to 1986, the Mondragon Bank of the People's Labor produced 20,000 worker-owned jobs and over 100 cooperative businesses. Eighty-six of these cooperatives are industrial enterprises. These industrial enterprises produce everything from home appliances, such as toasters and refrigerators, to tools, such as sophisticated die presses, down to plastic rulers.

These eighty-six cooperative industrial enterprises are the top producers in all of Spain. Their productivity per worker is also the highest in that country. Their profitability is nearly double that of their competitors. An independent study by the Anglo-German Foundation for the Study of Industrial Society found that the management of these cooperatives (which was chosen by the group of owner-workers and approved by the bank) to be some of the most aggressive and innovative ever witnessed by the Foundation's staff. Needless to say, these worker-owners were also found by the Foundation to be highly motivated and fulfilled by their jobs. ...If we do things right, things usually turn out right, given justice and honest money.

Projects other than industrial ventures have proven successful as well. There are pre-order and storefront-type food cooperatives which have been successfully established. A consumer cooperative, Eroski, has 120,000 members and 72 stores throughout the Basque region. Some are small mom and pop-type operations. Others are more like Kmart. Additionally, there are six agricultural cooperatives, 14 housing cooperatives, 43 cooperative schools, and four separate cooperatives which provide services to the other cooperatives. These four service cooperatives are the bank itself, a technical research institute, a League of Education and Culture (which has a technological division, a business and professional school), and a social security and medical cooperative. In other words, the people through their work and productivity in their own businesses, and through their own bank, have financed their own health, education and welfare needs. Government involvement is not only unnecessary, it is totally unwanted in creating the social safety net.

Can we imagine the results of totally eliminating the civil government's involvement in economics, and in the health, education and welfare of the nation? The Department of Health and Human Services is the largest item in the federal budget. The simple people of Mondragon are telling us that such civil government involvement is completely unnecessary, not to mention the fact that HHS primarily serves the bureaucrats and does not really meet the needs of the people whom it purports to serve. Civil government instead literally becomes what it should be, a service for which the people contract (a constitution), for the limited purpose of providing for defense against all enemies foreign and domestic, for putting down insurrections, revolutions and riots, and for enforcing contracts. Civil government has no legitimate function in economics, in the areas of the production, distribution, or in the use of resources.

Give these tough-minded people at Mondragon their own high-tech self-defense militia, which they would naturally gravitate toward anyway, along with a good civil defense, and no power on earth could challenge them.

There is an aspect of the Mondragon worker-owner program with which I take issue (in addition to their lack of free-market, honest, commodity money).   The salary scale among the worker-owner group business cooperatives is restricted.   No worker-owner can receive a salary greater than four and one-half times that of the lowest paid worker in the worker-owned business.   While this keeps economic equity (and therefore real power) balanced in the community, it would seem to come at the expense of maximizing individual incentive long-term.   (But at the other extreme, the salary ratio from the highest to the lowest paid worker in the United States today exceeds 100 to 1.)   Furthermore, because the lowest salary paid is only slightly above minimum wage, the highest salary paid at Mondragon is significantly lower than the salaries paid to men who work in the more conventional business sector.   However, because these Mondragon workers are owners of the means of production, the worker-owners' share of profits usually makes up for the lower salary.

It would seem that the percentage of the profits and dividends paid by the business each year should be in proportion to the contribution made and, therefore, include the salary earned by each individual worker-owner.   In this manner, a natural aristocracy would arise.   Those who earn more will be those who produced and therefore served the most.   Who could argue with this?   An individual who has worked and produced to provide the greatest good for the greatest number is entitled to the greatest reward.   Additionally, a buyout arrangement between worker-owners and/or the bank would quickly resolve any irreconcilable personal differences between men in the business, or facilitate a job change if desired.

Given the example of Mondragon, it becomes clear how we in America have lost our way.   The destructive and death-rendering consequences of our era are all around us - in our families, our health, our communities, our economic and financial systems, our jobs, our governments, our legal system, our medical bureaucracies, our educational institutions, our military-industrial complex, our labor unions, our courts and in our religious institutions.   We are individually and collectively caught in an accelerating death spiral.   But there is hope.   We are not dead yet.   Our heritage is that of the greatest spiritual and economic freedom the world has ever seen, given to us by God-fearing, self-governing men.   Mondragon has the abstract and concrete solutions.   We have the spiritual and economic answers necessary to put our national house back in order.   Furthermore, we have the technology necessary to achieve these desirable ends.   The only question is whether we have the faith, the individual and national character, and the will to go to work to change things.   If we do, then a glorious future awaits us long-term.   If we do not, then we will effectively, by our sins of omission and commission, commit suicide. We shall die.

The choice is ours. The two paths available are clearly before us. One is easy short-term, but brings death long-term. This is the path we are on presently. The other path is painful short-term, but brings abundant life long-term. We will reap what we sow. The people at Mondragon were worse off than we are now when they got started. They turned things around. Can we do any less?

MONDRAGON: FINAL REFLECTIONS

Human action is never static; we are either building up or we are tearing down. Anytime we're coasting, we're headed downhill. We are always acting either constructively or destructively. Sadly, destruction tends to come naturally. That is the curse, the law of entropy, the Second Law of Thermodynamics.

There is nothing quite like a crisis to bring out the true character and mettle of a society. A people's spiritual values, the laws which stem from these religious roots, and the individual and collective behavior patterns taught and applied, largely determine whether, when the pressure is on, a people will pull through together during tough times or self-destruct by turning on each other.

In this sense, people reap what they sow. They cannot for long act contrary to their religious beliefs, mental perspectives, internalized laws, cultural indoctrination and habits, for when the pressure is on, most people react automatically.

Of course, individuals need to have basic physical stamina, with the vitamin and mineral base of live, nontoxic (enzyme-rich) foods and pure water in their diet if they are to have the energy to persevere. The quality of the food not only determines whether the advanced (cerebrum) or primitive (limbic) brain centers are used, but also how well the immune system and the brain interact. (Stress is simultaneously mental, emotional and physical.)

If individuals are taught the principles of humility, empathy, responsibility and duty, a long-term view, the necessity of short-term pain for long-term gain, the importance of service before reward - and if these values are worked out in time in bio-regional communities - then there is an individual who can bring strength to the collective. Such an individual is in harmony with himself, God, his fellow man, and the creation. He understands the balance between love and economic self-interest, and his need to be a good steward of the earth. He is a resource, an asset to society, rather than a predator or a parasite.

A healthy society will be decentralized, architecturally and structurally, applying in the agriculturally-based social order the contract and the covenant. The religious, governmental and economic nature of the contract establishes a fair balance (equality) that creates a working unity in the face of inherent differences (inequality). The contract is the only economic instrument that fosters a situation in which disparities are appreciated as indispensable. For without the contract, there would not be a way to make use of the naturally occurring division of labor so necessary for the development of resources and the improvement of life. The contract establishes the worth of the individual and unity amid diversity. Self-interest, incentive, and risk-assumption are part of a balance between duty and service, of human need and security. People are correctly seen as more important than things, as the ultimate resource, because people determine the use of things. Thus, in a sense, people are like-minded, and this unity of love is created socially.

The constitutional contract with government works its way back to its roots in an individual, through the church (God's non-bloodline voluntary communal body), and the extended and nuclear bloodline family. Ideally every man can then, in effect, live under his own vine and fig tree, eating primarily fresh foods which have the same magnetic charge as where he resides. Blessed with pure air, soil, and water, a man has the necessary nutrients in his body to live in peace physically.

None of the above characterize our society today. Therefore, reaping what we have sown, our society, particularly our cities, will have difficulty meeting the challenge of the next comprehensive crisis.

In early America, 90 percent of Americans owned and worked the land in a horizontal, decentralized, contractual and covenantal fashion. Today, farmers make up less than 3 percent of our population. In 1800, less than 2 percent of free Americans worked for someone else. Today, 95 percent of Americans work for someone else usually in a vertical bureaucratic hierarchy. Some 80 percent of our people live in the cities, too, and are dependent upon government in some fashion. Our society is built vertically. Vertical is bureaucratic and historically limits freedom.

Debt capitalism is Orwellian. Capitalism (savings applied) requires short-term pain for long-term gain. Savings (capital) must be accumulated from the past and in the present for investment in the future. Debt, on the other hand, involves short-term gain with often no consideration for the long-term pain it brings through compound interest and slavery. Debt is a form of slavery. Debt is borrowing from the future by mortgaging the past to consume in the present. It is the antithesis of equity capitalism/free enterprise. How can our people not be in conflict personally when our basic system of economic debt capitalism is intrinsically a contradiction?

Debt capitalism, which focuses on the evolutionary radical rights of the individual, puts man in conflict with his fellow man, elevates the destructive principle of the survival of the fittest, and has led in its true evolutionary perspective to the emphasis on things rather than on people. Communism, on the other hand, with its radical focus on the collective masses - with its power-endorsed, top-down bureaucracy - not only destroys the individual building blocks of society in terms of character, initiative and family, but also puts its emphasis on things rather than people (dialectic materialism). Looking at the two extreme political/economic options of evolutionary communism and debt capitalism, it is clear that either way the outcome is top-down, vertical, bureaucratic domination. Both by the very nature of their impositions are conflict-ridden. And when the two join forces, as they are already doing in Hegelian synthesis of bureaucratic socialism, the world's ultimate coup will be completed. We will have the New World Order of atheistic bureaucratic socialism/fascism. Yet, the hope that Mondragon represents is that there is an end to the march toward this abomination. When the people who truly earned it are the owners of the means of production and when individual incentive is made possible through service and equity-based, non-debt capitalism, conflict is neutralized and the balance between unity amid diversity, between the one and the many, is achieved.

Worker-owned businesses in this country have done far better, especially during crisis, than other types of debt capitalistic ventures. The work of Dr. Tom Peters in the area of effective business management principles has confirmed this truth. For example, where employee stock ownership plans (ESOPs) exist, businesses are more productive, more competitive, marked by higher profits, better employee morale, and less absenteeism. The business is seen as a family. The family is the basic social unit of society, one place removed from the individual - whether it is the nuclear family, the extended family, the spiritual family in the local church, the economic family in the local business, or the political family in the local community. Man's need for love, his spiritual need for family, is often as high a need as his need for economic sustenance - sometimes higher - as in newborn babies who require affectionate touching.

The reason the banking experiment at Mondragon, Spain has been successful for nearly four decades is because people found the correct balance between individual rights and collective society. The conflict between radical individualistic capitalism and collective communism was resolved at Mondragon. Individual needs were harmonized with those of the community. Additionally, leadership was earned, and was local and accountable.

The crisis of persecution brought out the best in the people at Mondragon. They did not self-destruct. They created a system that's a shining example for us all.

In other areas, too, facsimiles of Mondragon have sprung up independently. For example, in 1940, Poland began an investment trust which operates effectively just like the bank at Mondragon. Over 175,000 people work in Polish cooperatives. Both the Poles and the people in the Basque region, without knowledge of each other, set up almost identical systems. This gives us a sense of hope. Are we about to see the hundredth monkey syndrome manifest itself as we purge the errors of this age and the foundations of our culture are shaken? The radical individualism of debt capitalism and the radical collectivism of socialism and communism are both dying. Furthermore, their focus on things as more important than people will accelerate their death in a world caught in comprehensive crisis.

When things are more important than people, conflict is inevitable. Conflict then becomes the determining factor in deciding how to divide the economic pie. However, when people are more important than things, where spirit is more important than matter, there can be like-mindedness and love. Common ground is sought. This common ground established the basis for cooperation and the just and merciful division of things in collective society without destroying the initiative of the individual. The contract (law) then, in accomplishing this, becomes the primary instrument of love. Such is next to impossible where the time value of money rules (compound interest).

Mondragon has proven that it can outperform both socialism/communism and debt capitalism. We know a people and a society by its fruits and its works. The fruits and works of Mondragon, in terms of the spiritual, mental, physical, emotional, governmental and economic health of its people, slam dunk both fault-ridden debt capitalism and communism/socialism/fascism. Furthermore, the consistency in Mondragon between means and ends, between process and goals, is a shining light of truth which illuminates the inconsistencies and contradictions of both debt capitalism and communism/socialism.

The United States is now a class-structured society as the middle class has been progressively destroyed under debt capitalism. The former Soviet Union, far from bringing about the classless society promised by Marxism, was one of the most class-structured societies in the world. Position there was not based upon merit or service, it was based upon status in the party, in the bureaucracy. The fruits of communism therefore confirm the error of Karl Marx. The end cannot be different from the process, from the means, and maintain its integrity and validity long-term.

There are essentially two aspects of real power: 1) being able to act effectively to accomplish what you want; and 2) not being under the control of other people, but instead cooperating with other people. Both of these are achieved at Mondragon.

People's Express almost got it right in this country, with the company organized as worker-manager teams without supervisors. Low salaries but generous profit-sharing plans and stock dividends provided for both individual incentive and group cooperation.

When a corporation decides to enter a new product market, it is coming close to duplicating Mondragon. The corporation already has established its primary investment in people, in its management, staff and workers. Capital, accounting, marketing and feedback systems already exist. So, "pick a product."

The May 1987 issue of Inc. magazine, in an article entitled, "Every Worker An Owner?", pointed out the advantages of ESOPs. This is perhaps as close as we have come in the United States to the successful experience achieved at Mondragon. This Inc. magazine article documented that companies with high degrees of employee-ownership outperform similar-size competitors. They also expand faster than they did previously.

Knowledge of how to run ESOPs and other worker-owned collectives in this country is widespread, but it is so contrary to cultural norms that existing ESOPs are few and far between. It may take a crisis to establish them, in institutions similar to the bank at Mondragon.

The Trammell Crow Company caught a glimpse of this people principle in its early years. It became the largest real estate development company in the country partly because it provided its leasing agents and staff personnel with the individual incentive of owning a piece of the action of the projects developed. This fostered a system of checks and balances with power in the local offices offsetting activity at the central Dallas location. This arrangement worked well because entrepreneurs primarily were hired since real estate development is, after all, an entrepreneurial business. But debt caused this company grief.

What are some of the specifics, the technicalities, incorporated at Mondragon, which have made it successful? Each division of 20 to 50 worker-owners conducts at least a monthly work Group meeting to discuss any and all issues. Management and their Social Council representative are part of the Group. This numerical division of 20 to 50 is important. Studies in large churches in the United States have indicated that most people never get to know more than 20 to 50 members of any congregation. The more successful churches have accordingly divided up their larger church into these smaller numerical units.

At Mondragon, worker-owner Group members elect a representative. This representative then meets with all the other representatives of the worker-owner businesses in the Social Council. The ruling Board has delegated to the Social Council all the worker issues with which unions are normally concerned - salaries, safety, fringe benefits, job descriptions, etc. Furthermore, the Social Council is responsible for deciding to which charities 10 percent of the annual company profits will go (a tithe).

Every worker-owner can be involved in managing every aspect of the business. All worker-owners have one share of voting stock. Therefore, they all have equal power. Management and labor are distinctive, but both of them fall under the umbrella of the cooperative, and both are subservient to the Board. This assures total integration and coordination. If the Board, for some reason, should fail in its task, then the General Assembly of all worker-owners, which wields the ultimate power within the cooperative, can overrule the Board. This results in total accountability at all levels. A member of the Group who has also been elected to the Board may also participate when it comes to the more mundane worker-owner matters.

Each cooperative (worker-owned business) elects representatives to the Association of Cooperatives. This Association elects the Board of the secondary cooperatives which include the Bank at Mondragon, the Research Institute, and the Insurance and Social Security institutions. However, the main focus of the Association of Mondragon Cooperatives is to create worker-owned jobs. This primary objective of the Association of Cooperatives enhances current worker-owner job security which gives the current worker-owners an incentive to be enthusiastic about automation. The worker-owners are equity capitalists. For this reason then, the cooperatives at Mondragon have moved aggressively forward in robot development. The worker-owners realize that their jobs are not threatened by automation and progress, and that new jobs are being created in which they have a stake. Thus, the worker-owners enthusiastically embrace computerized automation which eliminates repetitive jobs, dirty jobs, and increases the productivity and the viability of a product produced for the international marketplace.

This also means the worker-owners at Mondragon can be progressive and embrace change, even if it eliminates their own particular job, because they own the business themselves. They are not threatened. New jobs are being created for them, and as a member of the Mondragon cooperative, having a job is guaranteed for life.

The civil government has no involvement in this process. No worker-owner in the Mondragon cooperative is ever dependent upon public assistance. The purpose of the cooperatives is to contribute to the needs and development of society, which means the health and welfare of the individuals within the cooperative society. Beautifully then, each worker-owner in the Mondragon cooperative has the incentive to provide for himself and simultaneously serve society. It is unity amid diversity personified, producing social harmony. It is the balance between the one and the many, between individual and the collective.

What do the Mondragon cooperatives do with their profits from their businesses? Presently, 70 percent of the profits are distributed among the worker-owners. This distribution is based upon an earned salary scale, as well as the number of years an individual has been involved with the cooperative. Thus, individual productivity is balanced off with time commitment to economic society in the profit distributions.

Moreover, the profits are not cash distributions. Instead, they are allocated to the worker-owner's internal capital account, where they are regarded as a loan by the worker to the cooperative. Therefore, the worker-owner becomes an investor, an equity capitalist, by way of investment in both his own business and the community-at-large.

The worker receives dividends each year in cash just before Christmas. Interest is paid annually on his internal account. As the worker-owner's investment in a cooperative increases, the cooperative re-invests his profits to create more worker-owned jobs, more profits, more dividends, and more job and financial security for the worker-owner. This methodology is very important. It allows newly-formed cooperatives to receive uncollateralized capital at low interest rates. In the West, this start-up capital is normally the most difficult and expensive capital to borrow, with the lack of sufficient capital being the primary cause of failure for most new businesses.

What happens if the cooperative for one reason or another ceases to exist? The remaining amount of funds, which is collectively owned, is given to charity and managed for the general welfare. There is, therefore, no owner or banking incentive at Mondragon to arbitrarily bankrupt businesses, to go out of business, or to cash out of a business which is profitably providing a needed social good or service. Only those businesses which really have no hope and should be liquidated are, in fact, liquidated.

The worker-owner does have use of his portion of his 70 percent of the profits if he needs it. This 70 percent capital account can be used as collateral at the bank for a personal loan. On this personal loan, the interest rate which is charged the worker-owner is only 1 percent or 2 percent above what he is earning via the cooperatives' use of this capital in the new job creation process.

Compare and contrast what the Mondragon worker has going for him - a rich life individually and socially, a productive, profitable and economic life - to that of his American counterpart. The Mondragon worker-owner has job security, tenure, financial security, a say in all aspects of his business where he is a worker-owner, a voice financially and personally in community affairs, a sense of belonging, and the incentive to be progressive, creative, and productive. He experiences the excitement of personal involvement with his own (and the community's) bank, research institute, insurance program and social security system. He is an investor, a consumer, an important individual with dignity, and yet at the same time, he is encompassed by a strong sense of belonging as a significant, loving member of the community. He has it all - love and money, heaven on earth - "thy Kingdom come, thy will be done, on earth as it is in heaven."

When we see what has been accomplished and proven at Mondragon, Spain for nearly 40 years by way of the answers necessary to meet both the love and money needs of man, the answers that already exist with regard to meeting individually and collectively man's biological, safety, social, and self-fulfillment needs, and then compare it to what exists in this country today, we have reason to work for constructive change.

We Americans are a proud, stubborn people. We are devoid of love, as we war with one another over everything, filing 96 percent of the civil lawsuits in the world. "Who do you know in Idaho? Does anyone there know you? Who do you know who lives next door, or is he a stranger too?" sing Killough & Eckley. We are dead spiritually. We declared some 25 years ago that "God is dead." We are impoverished economically. Everything we own today is in hock, in debt. We, as a nation, with 75 percent of us dying from heart disease and cancer, are physically depleted. The average American on the standard American diet (SAD) is overfed and dangerously undernourished as we eat stale, lifeless foods produced from poisoned air, soil and water. We live in dead cities of glass, concrete, asphalt and steel, and thereby miss the life-giving diamagnetic charge so necessary for our peace and tranquillity, which is provided only by the trees and plants of God's Good Earth.

The colors blue and green, which are so vibrant in a decentralized "vine and fig tree" agricultural economy, are vital to our spiritual and physical health as their wavelengths impact and nourish our pineal and pituitary glands. All this is missed in the cities - the heart of our civilization.

Oswald Spengler was correct. Our civilization peaked nearly 100 years ago with the rise of world cities. City-produced chemicals have brought rampant toxicity to the countryside. Undertakers tell us it takes a third less embalming fluid to preserve us. We are therefore already one-third dead. We only await our final burial.

Seen in this light, the American emphasis on looking good is a sad, cruel joke. What we need is radical surgery on our hearts (figuratively speaking) to begin anew. We need a spiritual, mental, emotional, and physical individual and collective renewal. But such seems not about to come until we suffer much pain, until the system comes crashing down on our heads and our cities die. The sun of that sad date is already setting. For the sun of love, joy, peace, patience, kindness, goodness, faithfulness, gentleness and self-control has long ago set and departed from the American urban spirit.

AN ANSWER TO THE UNANSWERED ECONOMIC QUESTION

Advances in both communication and transportation today should effectively lead to decentralization and widespread GDP over large geographic areas. However, such is not the case. An answer to this dilemma lies in the age-old urban versus rural conflict. This can also be characterized as a vertical (urban) versus horizontal (rural) phenomenon, a collectivist (urban) versus individualistic (rural) conflict. Such a confrontation, a slave (urban) versus free (rural) situation, has to do with a lack of balance between the "labor" (urban) and "land" (rural) parts of the economic equation.

The challenge for any civilization is to maintain its balance between city and the countryside, its balance between its vertical and horizontal institutions, between the tendency toward collectivism versus the rights of individuals, to minimize slavery and encourage freedom. The two parts of the basic economic equation, "labor" and "land," are the essence of man as God created him - "made in the image of God," and "formed from the dust of the earth." Maintaining the balance between urban and rural should rightfully come through decentralization because the advances in the technologies of communication and transportation are in essence decentralizing. So, things really do have to be out of kilter for a phenomenon which should occur - decentralization - to be short-circuited.

The "specialization and division of labor" occurring most conveniently in the city, together with the intellectual aspect of cities giving rise to the development of technology - both of which create and increase wealth long-term - should harmonize with the raw materials and resources of the land found in the rural countryside.

The problem comes when the decentralizing, peace-bringing, prosperity-producing work ethic of the Golden Rule, "Self interest is best served first by service," is replaced by the evolutionary "survival of the fittest" norm. With the advent of applied evolution in Western civilization in the late 1800s, the theological perspective of the collective "one" which was common to all ancient empires and led to the centralization of power in the cities, picked up steam. Because government is always religion applied to economics, evolution was the final link, making possible this unified, natural, unholy trinity of government, religion and economics. As the evolutionary approach to origins was sanctioned for instruction in public schools, power has been increasingly centralized.

There are in this life two "jungles." There is the jungle found in the natural environment, such as in parts of Africa and regions of Latin America. This is the land jungle. It is a geographic area that has not been transformed into a "garden." Today, they call a jungle a rain forest. There is also the labor jungle, the evolutionary city. The city becomes a jungle when man is no longer a God-ruled, self-governing ultimate resource; but instead becomes, in an evolutionary way, the ultimate predator or the ultimate parasite.

When the city becomes a jungle, as it becomes increasingly evolutionary, the city in its survival of the fittest way uses its labor power - manifested both politically and economically - to oppress, exploit and eventually bankrupt the rural countryside. (Man ultimately rules over and determines the use of nature.) This short-term perspective is not to the city's benefit long-term, because the rural countryside is the natural resource lifeline, the umbilical cord, which brings life to the city. The rural countryside can survive on its own because it is self-sufficient with regard to the necessities of life - food, water, clothing, shelter and fuel. The rural countryside is where the sun's free energy through photosynthesis is transformed into matter. The city, on the other hand, is dependent on the rural countryside for these basic subsistence needs. Therefore, when the rural countryside dies, the city cannot be far from extinction.

Military strategists have long known this truth. If you want to totally destroy a civilization, but destroy only its cities and leave its rural countryside intact, the civilization will come back. Why? Because its roots, both resource-wise and value-wise, are grounded in the rural countryside. However, if you destroy a nation's countryside, its cities will wither and die. The subsistence base which supports the cities' fragile life support systems is cut off. This is why it took General Sherman four years to destroy the Old South during the U.S. Civil War. He had to destroy the countryside - its plantations and farms, its churches, its work ethic. He could have marched directly to Atlanta in 90-120 days.

The checks and balances between the city and the rural country are achieved by implementing two key biblical economic principles in the social order:

1) Strictly limiting absentee ownership of land; and

2) Allowing the rural countryside to be the primary, if not the exclusive, creator of money through the monetization of commodi-

ties, the issuing of receipts for commodities, or through computer entries representing actual commodities. In other words, free-market money, honest money, is produced in the rural country.

People flow to money. Where there is money, there are jobs. If the money is created in the countryside, people will migrate to rural areas causing decentralization. However, if the money is created by a fiat currency, fractional reserve debt banking system in the city - with its unlimited compounding of interest as it is today - then people are sucked through the resource pipeline from the rural areas to the city where they are used up like tissue paper. No rural decentralization or dominion of the earth can then occur. There is no subduing of the conflict, chance and cycles of the natural earth. The technological advances in communication and transportation, and the specialization and division of labor, therefore, are not allowed to work in harmony with decentralized, rurally created, honest, free-market money. Few prosper as a result.

With rurally produced, honest, free-market money, rather than having 80 percent of our people live on approximately 1 percent of the land in the cities, 80 percent of our people would instead be geographically dispersed throughout the countryside.

The federal government today owns 42 percent of the land in this country, contrary to the U.S. Constitution. And, according to Town and Country magazine, less than 5 percent of the people in this country own approximately 95 percent of the land held by the private sector. The rest of us are dispossessed.

By strictly limiting absentee ownership of land to small plots primarily owned by seasonal residents; by restricting absentee ownership to less than 50 percent in any major land or capital venture; by requiring at least six months annual residence in an area; and by encouraging instead long-term land and/or capital leases of less than 50 years in the rural countryside; decentralization is further encouraged. Land generally becomes less expensive and more affordable the farther removed it is from the city. This makes migration to the countryside more attractive. The absentee ownership of land - which is also so evident today in economically stagnant Europe, Great Britain, Guatemala and other Latin American countries - is minimized. The status of folks in the rural country would amount to something more than feudal serfs if absentee ownership of land was limited. Government-owned rural lands, with the possible exception of a few parks and wilderness areas, would disappear, too. The federal government would no longer be able to bankrupt the farmers as they are doing today in this country, or starve 10 million to death as the Soviet communists did in the Ukraine in the early 1930s. Government involvement in the economy long-term is always a curse. It follows that all land taxes would be abolished as well.

In many Latin American countries, laborers who work the farms, ranches and plantations are dispossessed. They stay perpetually poor, with no incentives to better their lives. Consequently they tend to be inclined toward communism, while the owners live in the city, not on their income-producing land in the countryside, among their laborers. In Ireland, during the famine of 1847-1849, thousands of Irish literally starved to death. They would stand along the sides of the road, begging for the food which they had produced, as it was being shipped off in carts to be sold by the absentee landlords who owned the property and resided in London.

Today, it has been globally demonstrated that the only workable solution to Third World economic development problems begins with the working ownership of small family farms. The small family farm is the basic land and labor unit.

Absentee ownership of land destroys the spirit of community (harmony), which is necessary for widespread prosperity long-term. It limits personal accountability, which is vital in human affairs. Absentee ownership of land not only prevents men from being held personally accountable for environmental damage and abusive actions to those who live and work the properties, it also alienates the rural country from the city, weakening the nation.

Tenants who work the land have no real stake personally in nurturing and improving the land long-term for some absentee owner. They can't get rich either. This, in turn, leads to such evils as rural land and water pollution, demineralization of the soil, substandard food, and increased toxicity of the environment. Eventually, the rural country is turned into a wasteland, which wrecks the general vitality of the people. The city then dies, too. This is why deserts reign supreme today and the land is depopulated where, formerly, civilizations existed. The vertical bureaucratic city/state empires of long-gone civilizations were noted for their absentee ownership of land. Northern Africa, for example, today a desert, used to be a swamp area. No man should own more land than that amount which he can turn into a garden.

Countries which have strong laws requiring local ownership of land and healthy restrictions on absentee land ownership include Switzerland and Bermuda. We do not have to reinvent the wheel in this matter. We can learn from these other countries.

When the city controls the monopolistic issuance of non-commodity money by special interest groups (banks) through political edict - which in turn tends to allow all wealth to be concentrated increasingly in the city into fewer and fewer hands - it encourages and results in the buying up of the rural countryside, dispossessing the country folk. The rural folk migrate to the city. Then the city has effectively signed its own death warrant long-term. When land and labor die, economics dies. When economics dies, the city, the rural country and the entire civilization dies.

We now know why the advances in communication and transportation today have not led to a decentralization of GDP over a widespread geographic area in this nation. The imbalance of power, brought about by city-created dishonest money and the promotion of absentee ownership of land, has led to this massive distortion.

* * *

"I personally think the notion of the 'city' is becoming obsolete. Cities grew up originally because you had great access to natural transportation. We have a terrific harbor here (N.Y.) - which is also the case in Boston, Washington and other cities that have been around for a long time. Transportation and distribution were a definite need. So you built up a tremendous infrastructure, railroads, ports and terminals, everything else. But now communications, technology and the movement of goods have advanced so far that the whole idea of the city - having this tremendous infrastructure to support the economic activity that is at the center of the nation's prosperity - doesn't make sense anymore." - Michael Aronstein, Barrons, October 23, 1992

* * *

Given the dependent, slave-like nature of the American general public today, it might well take central government's implementation of biblical law initially to provide the incentives necessary to reestablish the decentralization which brings freedom, peace and prosperity to all of society. God took 40 years to let the Hebrew slaves of Egypt die out before their descendants were tough and courageous enough to conquer the Promised Land. How long will it take this nation to turn around?

SECTION H

THE CREATION

THE NATURE OF NATURE

The fallen, imperfect and cursed creation (nature) manifests at least five devilish traits: 1) conflict, 2) chance, 3) cycles, 4) poverty and 5) death. Therefore, when the "natural man" (the "old man") is left to his own unregenerate devices, we find all five of these traits rampant in societies throughout the creation. <u>Conflict</u>, for instance, can range from interpersonal verbal abuse and fist fights, to revolution and war. Next, where God's Law-Word does not rule, the disorder and pain of <u>chance</u> take center stage. Planning becomes impossible. And men have no hope as they are trapped in the degenerative, repetitive, downward spiral of natural <u>cycles</u>, being slaves of the cursed natural order rather than taking dominion over creation. The result of all this is <u>poverty</u>, the desertification of the earth and man reduced to the status of an animal - living just to survive. Man and the earth - and God's other creations - then <u>die</u>. This is why pagan civilizations rape the earth rather than "re-create" it into a garden. The earth degenerates into a wilderness. Pagan civilization has no "supernatural" way to escape this five-fold curse. The biblical curse, scientifically, is the Second Law of Thermodynamics, the law of entropy, of decay.

Nature, both man and the rest of the natural order, needed supernatural salvation from this five-fold death trap. There must be a metaphysical answer to the physical problem. This is what the work of Jesus Christ was all about, and why it was (is) all important. Jesus Christ came from above and outside of nature (supernaturally) to provide both a legal and practical solution, both eternally and temporarily, for both man and the creation's dilemma. Mankind had already proven himself unable to keep the perfect standard of God's law to the detriment of both man and the earth. So, the ransom price, the perfect keeping of the law, was paid by Jesus Christ. This then transformed the eternal curse of the law into a blessing in the temporal realm.

There are at least four basic purposes of the Law-Word that serve to guide us in our redeemed work of "re-creation": First, the Law-Word provides a standard of justice for determining right or wrong, and good and evil. Consequently, all men are then equal under the law - for when the law comes supernaturally from above and outside of nature - men no longer make the law. They instead simply apply the law to the facts of the case. All men are equal under the law since no men are primary lawgivers. Furthermore, since the Ultimate

Authority-Lawgiver (God) is not natural, but rather supernatural, men can spread out and decentralize under this common, supernatural, godly authority.

Secondly and thirdly, in the New Testament, God's Law-Word is called both a "law of liberty" and a "law of love." These two characteristics of God's law are manifested in society and throughout the earth when the law is used correctly. All things in God's creation are finite. Only God is infinite. In other words, all things in God's creation have limits. The very nature of a limit to a finite creation is by definition a rule (a law), a boundary, which defines the nature and extent of activity. For example, the law of gravity presents a limit to physical action and defines how physical action may occur. This is what God's law does. It defines the nature and limits of a specific activity and thereby establishes the balance between the various finite parts of God's creation.

Fourthly, God's law balances out the yang/yin, masculine/feminine, individual/collective, many/one differences. It provides harmony, Truth-In-Tension (TNT), between apparent opposites.

Because nothing achieves this balance better than God's Law-Word, it is called in scripture both the "law of liberty" and the "law of love." It is the "law of liberty" because it maximizes human freedom, providing man with the greatest latitude possible within limits. It is called the "law of love" because it resolves conflict and works to transform both man and the creation into a cooperative peaceful relationship. By contrast, the work of Satan is to limit our God-given freedom by defining what we can do. This is manifested in the United States by the thousands upon thousands of regulations, regularly churned out by unelected bureaucrats which prescribe behavior in all areas of life. The natural consequence of this kind of rule is conflict. Conflict is the inevitable result when men and women are treated like children by the paternal state.

As a result of the outworking of God's Law-Word, the curse of conflict is eliminated and peace and prosperity reign. Because God's Law-Word is certain, the curse of chance is also removed. Men can plan successfully long-term. Also, God's linear direction for history takes hold and cycles move into a secondary subordinate position. Real progress can then be made. This freedom, peace, cooperation and planning in the marketplace lead to prosperity replacing poverty. And finally, life overcomes death. The earth is transformed from a wilderness into a garden. The five-fold curse is removed as redeemed man works through Christian reconstruction.

Since God is life, His Law-Word brings life too, when applied in time to the creation by regenerate men who work as led by the Holy Spirit. Evil is replaced with things live (evil spelled backward). So, the further man is removed from God's Law-Word, the more death-oriented he becomes.

In the 1960s, the United States declared, "God is dead." So, it is no surprise in American society today that we are witnessing the murder of the unborn, the death of the family, the death of the debt (death) based money system, the apostasy (death) of the church, dead food, dead music and the demise of the political, economic and military order. It is insane in a sense. But insanity is the hallmark of the rejection of God's Law-Word. God is perfect logic and sanity, as well as perfect love and life. His Law-Word is the expression of these qualities. The wages of rejection of God's Law-Word are insanity and death. The creation cries out today for the life-giving application of God's Law-Word. Obviously, we have a great deal of work left to do on the "nature of nature."

THE WAR OVER ORIGIN

Down through the ages there has arisen, over and over again, a head-on conflict between the two basic theories of origin - creation and evolution. Both are intensely religious, because both involve assumptions about the ultimate nature of reality. One entails a supernatural intervention, the other natural processes. One involves cause and effect, the other chance. One is personal, the other impersonal. One is Creator-initiated, the other creature-initiated. One is found in the Western Christian tradition, the other in Eastern tradition and atheism. One assumes original order, the other that complex systems arose out of chaotic systems. One is time-limited and historical, the other timeless. One holds to absolute truth and limits, the other to relativity - no limits and no truth. In one, life has meaning; the other, no meaning. One has an open system of life, light, love, supernatural law, liberty, laughter (joy) and a long-term view. The other is a closed system which operates on conflict, chance, cycles, poverty and death. The war is over what is true - creator or evolution.

Because no men were actually present at the time of the beginning, all men make guesses about how the origin occurred. In a scientific sense, since there were no witnesses, and neither can be experimentally duplicated, neither theory can be proven. Thus, any individual who discusses creation or evolution has assumed the role of a religious priest because both theories are inescapably faith-based.

All of man's thinking is ultimately circular. Man can never be totally objective because he cannot learn all things about anything, due partly to the fact that he has a limited mind and limited time on this earth. Belief in creation or evolution is, therefore, the ultimate presupposition concerning physical reality. Now, any of us can believe anything we like as long as the consequences of our beliefs are trivial. We can entertain our illusions. But, when our personal welfare and survival, as well as the welfare and survival of mankind, depends upon our religious beliefs (creation or evolution), our beliefs had better correspond to the real world. Beliefs precede thoughts, and thoughts precede actions. The pen is mightier than the sword in that those who think and reason are also those who plan and lead; those who lead have some underlying beliefs or values which are by definition religious. Our welfare is determined by the model followed by our leaders. The following are two possible origin models:

The Creation Model

Each man is made by the Creator. The Creator has designed each individual for a special, specific purpose in life (destiny), and has given each man the necessary talents to achieve that purpose. Thus, every man must have the liberty to pursue the development and use of his unique Creator-given talents that he might fulfill his destiny in time. To facilitate the Creator's master plan for the human race collectively through men individually, the Creator gave men rules (principles) to live by in the Bible. Utilizing these principles, each individual, by acting in his own self-interest of personal talent development long-term, serves simultaneously each other individual, thereby bringing into harmony the best interests of both the individual and the group, fulfilling the Creator's purpose.

Since each individual has been given specific talents which benefit every other individual, directly and/or indirectly, men readily co-operate in the free market. They contract and covenant with each other for various purposes, so that each party can benefit from the other's developed talents in the production of goods and services.

Government is hired as a decentralized servant of free men to ensure that the Creator's laws for man are enforced for the betterment of all men. Government is the employee, the overhead expense, paid for by free men to protect these free men from internal and external violence. Government also referees and settles disputes in the free market. Man, the spiritual being with a physical nature, is eternal. Government, man's created institution, is temporal and therefore, inferior.

The Creator, in his wisdom, first created man as a spiritual being with a subordinate physical nature. Man's physical nature became primary when Adam disobeyed the Creator in the first economic garden. He fell from spiritual grace, so to speak. But, a loving, sovereign Creator, with a perfect plan, came seeking after him, and provided man with a perfect atoning sacrifice, Jesus Christ, which restored man to spiritual fellowship with the Creator. Man's physical nature could again potentially be subordinate to man's spiritual nature in time, and the economic development of the earth (garden), through the development of each man's talents, could continue. The struggle back, however, is a tough one.

Since man had fallen from spiritual and material perfection in the garden (the first economic world trade center), the Creator knew that man would by nature pursue his physical instincts. He would prey on his fellow man, acting in his own selfish, short-term interests, just like animals do, in a "survival of the fittest" manner. To give fallen, physical, fact-oriented man an incentive to pursue the development of his spiritual nature and gifts given by the Creator, to prove to man in time that His way was the best, He instituted the family, church, nation and free market. For it is with these institutions that men can have their natural self-interest met by possessing the freedom to develop and exercise their talents with the purpose of securing gain for themselves in voluntary collectives.

Men learn that the Creator's purpose for their lives, their own best self-interest, and the self-interests of their fellow man come together in a unified harmony when the Creator's primary, spiritual, principled methodology is pursued.

In keeping with their spiritual nature, men best meet their economic needs by thinking, conceiving, planning and acting creatively on "principle" primarily, and "facts" secondarily.

The creation model moves from perfect economic conditions, to imperfect, fallen, cursed or natural economic conditions, back toward perfection. Perfection, though not totally attainable, is the standard and the goal. This ensures continual human progress. Economic blessing is a result of man's principled development of his individual talents, and his disciplining of his physical instincts. Social harmony abounds then, because not only does man love his work and is rewarded for it economically as he develops his Creator-given talents, but he also readily cooperates with other men who have complementary talents. In this way he is able to provide for his family, thereby enhancing love and security, along with the fulfillment of his basic biological/economic needs. He also voluntarily creates the communal social safety nets.

Finally, in the creation model, man has a sense of the urgency of time. As one of God's creations, man knows he is accountable for how he spends his time on this earth. Thus, Christians are commanded to "redeem the time." Also, as the Apostle Paul wrote, "It is appointed unto man once to die and then the judgment." Our time on earth is linear history, with cause and effect, ending in judgment. This trust instills the fear of the Lord as primary in Christians and gives them a sense of urgency in how they spend their time. By contrast, in the evolution model, the cycles (which are winding down - entropy) - are held in faith by some to be winding upward in reincarnation. But if man gets another go at it, if he gets it wrong this time around and doesn't repent, then the work of Jesus Christ on the cross of Calvary was unnecessary. Put differently, it was a waste for Jesus Christ to die for man's sins (errors/mistakes) if man does not need a savior/atonement/propitiation because he gets another chance at life anyway after he dies, thanks to reincarnation. If there is no judgment and reincarnation is true, then it was a mistake for Jesus Christ to die on the cross to save man. With reincarnation, man does not need saving. He is instead evolving and becoming better and better until he is as God.

So, what gives credibility to the lie of reincarnation? Fallen spirits influence, speak to or indwell various men and women down through history. If a spirit has been associated with, let's say, three people in the 18th century, and then three more people in the 19th century, it would be a small thing for this spirit to communicate this personal history to an individual living in the 20th century and convince (deceive) him/her into believing this was that individual's previous reincarnations. That 20th century individual would have believed a lie.

The Evolution Model

The bottom line issue in the evolution model, as in the creation model, is economic. Religion comes down to economics. But, under the evolution model, man is an animal, nothing more. And like an animal, he is pitted in never-ending conflict and competition against every other man, with the "law of the jungle" reigning supreme. Here, the "survival of the fittest" is the standard and goal. Each individual is continually at war with every other individual, seeking whatever gain and advantage is possible, preying on the weak and vulnerable. The short-term view and "facts" (not principles) are the focus for obtaining this economic superiority. The spiritual, thinking, planning aspect of man is subordinate to, and is distorted into, scheming, plotting, and conspiring to benefit man's animalistic short-term lusts. Widows and orphans beware. It is a "dog-eat-dog" world under the evolution model.

This competition is rooted in a lack of love. There is no room for the likes of love, compassion, giving and charity, only room for money, sex, power, arrogance, taking and exploitation, just as in primitive societies, which are accordingly animalistic, dependent upon a death-based nature. There are no ultimate savings, no economic capital formation, and no tools produced, which would allow the development of culture, technological progress, environmental integrity, health, medical and scientific research, as well as all other forms of social advancement. (Economic savings is a long-term concept, foreign to the short-term, evolutionary, fact-oriented world of animals. When a society shifts from the creation model to evolution, it consumes the savings and capital which preceded it.)

As animalistic evolution increasingly engulfs a social order, men's spiritual natures cry out for protection and relief from the evolutionary terror of day-to-day life. Individuals look to the collective power of civil government, which is the epitome of the evolutionary spiral and the ultimate in the "survival of the fittest," to protect them. Government agrees to do so, but at a terrible price. Government, after all, must and will seek the short-term gratification of its own interests in the evolutionary model. (This is one reason why big governments are continually plagued with corruption and scandals.)

Government, instead of the Creator, becomes the master planner. Individual freedom progressively dies, as government creates more and more laws and regulations in a bureaucratic attempt to harness and control the lawless individualistic, animalistic, evolutionary nature of man. External discipline is substituted for internal discipline (the modus operandi of the creation model).

Government, of course, likes its exalted role as the king of the jungle. Government thus finances wars, revolutions, and joins with powerful financial, business, media, advertising, educational and religious interests to further centralize wealth and power. Government also encourages the teaching (in public schools) and use of the evolutionary model in day-to-day life, in order to continually justify its control over human evolutionary existence.

When this government control is maximized, fascist commerce and politics dominate a society. Commerce and politics are both facts oriented, so the government animal has reached the epitome of its development, backed by high economic interests. Empires and world cities dominate the landscape at this tip of the evolutionary spiral. But eventually reality strikes, and strikes hard. The empire and emperor are found to have no clothes. Government and cities are both seen for what they are - economic parasites, dependent ultimately on the open system spawned in the rural country.

Governments do not create wealth. They can only take it through inflation and legalized theft (taxation), and then redistribute this wealth bureaucratically to the people under them, who demand it in the form of social (butter) programs. This government readily does in order to maintain and justify its power. Likewise, the cities, historically always slave centers, parasitically draw their human and economic resources from the rural country. When the parasites - the governments and cities - are fully developed, the society dies, either from without, as government sacrifices its defense responsibility to its illicit economic function, or from within through revolution, as the common people pull down the government for failing at an impossible task: the production of Wealth for All. Men revolt when they cannot do meaningful work and be paid honest money for it. Men revolt when they receive favors (welfare) which they cannot repay. The parasites - governments and cities - have at that time consumed the host, "we the people."

The deception of evolutionary "progress" is seen for the charade it is - a short-term, superficial, illusionary glorification, leading to long-term destruction and chaos into degeneration. This typically occurs when the climate turns less favorable. The myth is that a phoenix will arise from the ashes in a miraculous way. This is an act of faith.

There are only two factors in the basic human economic equation - land and labor. Together, with savings (impossible under the evolutionary model), they produce capital (tools), which bring about the economic good life. Government centralization schemes can only last while the climate is favorable and the land's production is abundant, allowing the squandering of human resources. When the climate becomes harsh, however, human energy must take up the slack and become efficient, throwing off the wasteful folly of centralized planning. Or, the central government finds a way to eliminate people, such as in a war. If individuals are seen as nothing more than human resources, why can't they be harvested like trees, which are natural resources.

In the evolution model, individual conflict leads to group coercion and slavery by civil government, to the benefit of a few at the miserable expense of the many. This situation persists until the inevitable economic crash, accompanied by the resultant political collapse, followed again by individual conflict, as the pathetic never-ending cycle continues. In the evolution model, human action grinds over and over again on a bloody wheel (cycle) throughout time. There is no real human progress as in the linear progression of the creation model. Real technological breakthroughs are hidden and suppressed by the government. Furthermore, blood sacrifices and inexorable revolutions in the evolution model continue as substitutes for the blood sacrifice of Jesus Christ in the creation model. Revolutions occur when governments are seen for the lie they are - false and inept creators - parasites - who fail to solve basic economic problems because they are religiously bankrupt.

* * *

The theory of evolution goes back to ancient times and is almost as old as creation itself. It was prevalent in the Egyptian Empire, in Greece and Rome, and found its way into Western civilization through social theory and thought prior to its application on the scientific level. Dr. Gary North, in his book, "The Dominion Covenant," elucidates how Darwin's biological evolution followed philosophical evolutionary thought in Western civilization.

In terms of Christian cosmology, creation - the act of a sovereign Creator - is in direct conflict with the cosmology of evolution, because evolution is humanistic and atheistic. As Dr. North further pointed out, Darwinian evolutionary thought is fundamentally Greek paganism. Thomas Huxley referred to Darwinian evolution as "the revivified thought of ancient Greece." And, since it is Greek culture that the United States government today is attempting to emulate and reestablish, it therefore follows that the religious belief of America's ruling elite, that of humanistic evolution, is aggressively antagonistic to Christianity and creationism.

Evolution is and always has been an elitist humanistic religion, accompanying the rise and fall of world empires. Empires and humanistic pride go hand in hand. The ancient empires of Egypt and Greece held to the theory of evolution. The modern world empires of Nazi Germany, the U.S.S.R., Red China and the U.S. are also characterized by their grounding in the religious theory of evolution. Today, in the United States, evolution is the religion of the public schools. (The Supreme Court affirmed it in the 1960s when it established humanism/evolution as a religion.)

Whether we look at the forced slavery of ancient Egypt, Nazi Germany, Red China or the U.S.S.R., we quickly see that the result of the working out in time of the theory of evolution is massive human misery. Because in America we still have the vestige of a Christian creationist culture, we find repugnant the mistreatment of the Israelites by the Egyptians; we are outraged at the atrocities that Hitler's Nazi Germany committed against the Jews; and we are appalled at the violations of human rights and mass murders of Mao Tse-tung in China, and by Stalin and other Soviet leaders in Russia which Aleksandr Solzhenitsyn so graphically discussed in his book, "The Gulag Archipelago." But, consistent with the theory of evolution, these actions by Hitler, the pharaohs, and Chinese and Soviet leaders are justified. Evolution, the humanistic elitist religion, condones whatever actions big government may take valid. Government is the "survival of the fittest," or as Hegel put it, "god walking on earth."

Given that U.S. society increasingly, through indoctrination in the public schools, is captured by the religion of evolution/humanism, is it not logical that actions taken against U.S. citizens will eventually be similar to acts exercised in ancient Egypt, Nazi Germany, Red China and the Soviet Union? After all, our federal government is the "survival of the fittest," too. The federal government is the highest product of the evolutionary spiral, the end result of "natural selection." Thus, according to the "law of the jungle," "might makes right." Therefore, consistent with evolution, the federal government can do whatever it pleases. It is the "god" of our society, the evolutionary "king of kings." And, it is, without a doubt, elitist since the evolutionary spiral allows for only a few to ascend to the top, their ascension justifying their right to dictate to the rest of us. Are not the actions of the federal government against Randy Weaver at Ruby Ridge and against the Branch Davidians in Waco evidence of this?

These elitists are top-level government employees (civil service types), multinational corporate officers and multinational bankers, high-level decision makers in the military/industrial complex, federal judges, attorneys, scientists, social scientists and high-level elected officials. Their right to rule is, of course, supported by the media ruling elite, which reinforces this religious, humanistic, evolutionary, indoctrination process, once the public school's years of conditioning are complete. Today, in the U.S. we have voluntary slavery (wage slaves), debt slavery, and slavery to the state.

Now, it can be argued, and it's true, that the federal government, in an ironic twist, prevents the savagery of the "law of the jungle" and the "survival of the fittest" from being played out to its full, violent fury in society. This is the way the federal government justifies its gigantic existence. Men have never allowed anarchy, the "law of the jungle" and the "survival of the fittest," for long. Men seek law and order. When men do not see themselves as self-governing, with the Creator and His laws as the master planner for their lives, then government, the substitute planner, comes in and fills this vacuum of unbelief. Government justifies its planning and control function by preventing the strong from always preying on the weak, a natural animalistic process under evolution. Fearful men look to government for protection. Under evolution men are insecure, having no rest.

By promoting the theory of evolution (effectively humanism) in the public schools, the logical, practical result of this religious theory is that the strong continually do attempt to prey on the weak, which further justifies increasing government control and a concomitant loss of personal freedom. Either the Creator, through the creation of each individual, is the master planner, and thus has an important purpose (destiny) for the life of each individual on earth, which requires freedom to be fulfilled - or government, the substitute god, is the master planner and increasingly dictates, controls and rules over all areas of life, thereby minimizing individual freedom. As such, civil government, the substitute god, is and always has been the foremost adversary of a Creator God. In Christian cosmology, this makes government Satan's most important institutional workhorse. The nations rage and wage war against God. We're never told today that in 1892 the U.S. Supreme Court declared the United States a Christian nation, and that U.S. presidents were sworn into office with their hands on Deuteronomy 28.

Under evolutionary government, we have no protection under law. We have anarchy waiting to happen. How could we have protection under the law if law and lawyers (mini-gods as law givers) are evolving? The Constitution is of no value under evolution. How could it be? It is a 200-year old document which has not evolved. All men used to be equal under God. Nixon would have been prosecuted for Watergate 100 years ago. Clinton would have faced charges also. Then, we did not yet have a "divine right of kings," so to speak. Never mind that when the Constitution was adopted, out of a population of $3\frac{1}{2}$ million, there were 2 million Christians, whose religious beliefs - captured in Biblical law and the Constitution, which protected the individual - led to the greatest economic national prosperity in the history of the world. All this creation cause and effect is forgotten today. But, the lie of government (and its underlying religion of evolution) exposed is the reality that government, playing the role of god, is still a parasite. Government is a wonderful servant of free men, but a fearful all-consuming master when it becomes wrongfully involved in economics, i.e., wealth redistribution. Government is the guard, hired to protect the economic marketplace. It has no rightful role in economics whatsoever. Government consumes all wealth eventually, because it always finds work to do which consumes men's productivity. Also, it always creates class warfare through wealth redistribution, when it wrongfully becomes involved in economics.

The maximum distortion of reality comes at the pinnacle of the evolutionary spiral, where the false "lord of lords" is government, an economic parasite. The hard truth is that government cannot create anything (but misery). It can only steal wealth, through taxes and inflation, and then redistribute it. (Today, many see militias and gun ownership by free men as the last stand of economic and human protection against a thieving, immoral, unresponsive government.) Inflation is the government's corruption of the currency. Government-created laws have choked our economic society, sent industry abroad, cut us off from the land, frustrating real progress and meaningful human advancement. Many of the laws that are created favor special interest groups, creating monopolies and bureaucracies, which allow a few shrewd elite to prey on the many ignorant in the masses. Evolutionary big business, for example, hates competition and the free market. Big business runs in wolf packs, fixing prices, reaping government support and subsidies, seeking whomever and whatever they can devour. Labor unions used to do the same thing on the other side of the battle line. Conflict is the standard under evolution. Consumers, which all of us are, lose in the fight.

Under an evolutionary system, justice is sacrificed to power, just as truth is sacrificed to facts and deeds, and the short-term given priority over the long-term. Politics is power. Economics is power. Evolution recognizes power as right according to "survival of the fittest." Politics depends upon an economic base so evolutionary political powers go to war for economic reasons. Men's strength and power are thus drawn from external things. Money controls everything. The love of money (greed and selfishness) is the root of all evil. A perfect illustration of how money rules supreme in our political process and that law is what government chooses to enforce, is the fact that Jimmy Carter, in 1978, signed into law legislation requiring a balanced federal budget. This law has been ignored.

By contrast, under the creation model, power is given to men of character who can handle it, who turn right around and give it away, granting freedom to their fellow man. These men are statesmen, unlike the economic-lusting evolutionary politicians, whose desire to control others stems from insecurity and feelings of personal inadequacy.

Laws used to be just. Under the creation model, laws and justice are one and the same, and provide a stable, unchanging, reliable standard. Government's function is to enforce the Creator's law. Law protects the family. (Treason is first against the family, not the state.) Law protects the individual, because the individual has Creator-given rights, purpose and destiny. Law prevents men from imposing their will and ideas upon other men, with the use of force sanctioned only in cases of self-defense. Collective rights are based upon these individual rights, they do not supersede them. Realizing that a government ruler's only legitimate purpose was/is in this limited defense realm, in 1649, King Charles of England was brought to trial and executed for egregious violation of the Creator's law.

The building of political, economic and religious empires is impossible in the context of creation since all men are seen as equal under a Creator's law. Additionally, all men are equally in need of a Savior. There is an economic elite that has rightfully earned its elevated status by serving their fellow man in the free market. This aristocracy flows from a long-term perspective. The long-term view marks the true upper class of any society. Only slaves are equal economically.

It is impossible to hold to the theory of evolution and consistently believe in the free market, the development of individual human talents, the family, economic rights, human rights or trial by jury. Evolution is logically antagonistic to the best interest of man individually and collectively long-term. And yet, it is willfully embraced and defended by modern man. How has this occurred? Why is man so willing to defend a religious theory which leads him to the slaughter? The answer can be found in part in the public (government) schools, where it takes 12 years, and possibly four years more in college, to educate a man to act contrary to his and society's own best interest long-term, and then also to passionately defend the position.

We have two religious schools in this country - the public (government) schools and the Christian schools (which are popping up at the rate of three a day). The public schools submissively teach the religious theory of evolution/humanism. How could it be otherwise when the public schools are supported by funds (our taxes) provided by the evolutionary government? Thus, the financing of public education today, to the extent that it teaches the religious theory of evolution and promotes big government, is using taxpayers' money to ultimately finance their own suicide.

Government, the parasite, playing the role of god, can only self-destruct long-term. This is why mature civilizations fall when their governments are fully developed, just as ours is today.

As the education battle heats up (public schools versus the Christian schools), it should come as no surprise that there is increasing federal government harassment (stemming from the states, the Justice Department and the Department of Education) of the Christian schools. The Christian schools are teaching a theory of origin which is contrary to the self-interest of big government.

Education is and always has been religious. Education teaches the young the basic values and faith of a society. This type of instruction is of its very essence religious. Teachers, like all other men and women, also make religious assumptions about the nature of reality. Teachers usually teach what they have been taught.

This religious split on origin is also seen in our bookstores. We have the Christian bookstores, and we have the secular bookstores. One's underlying religion is creation, the other evolution. This separation also exists in music.

To the extent that man can be brainwashed into buying the theory of evolution, and thus taught to act contrary to his own self-interest long-term, he is playing directly into the hands of those who want to manipulate him, use and abuse him, and then throw him away. Have we already become a society of human slaves? We do pay taxes to a federal government which is intent upon creating social conflict through the redistribution of wealth, which minimizes our freedom through bureaucratic alphabet-agencies, congressional laws and judicial decisions, thereby limiting our human rights and thus our economic rights. Economic rights are always an extension of human rights, because it takes a mind to first think the thoughts and formulate the plans which create economic wealth. Also, without basic economic provision, we cease to exist.

We irresponsibly give our hard-earned productivity (our money) to banking institutions, which then use it to finance our own eventual unemployment. They accomplish this by first lending our funds abroad where low cost foreign workers manufacture products, which are then dumped back onto U.S. markets, throwing U.S. workers out of jobs. Not only were these foreign workers' manufacturing plants financed with our savings (economic suicide), but deposits in our financial institutions (inflationary in the first place through the fractional reserve system), also went to finance the implements of war (very profitable for the military/industrial complex) and the government-initiated war effort, which made the World War II destruction of our present-day economic competitors (Japan and Germany) possible. Enemies are created so someone else can profit. After a war, the parasitic, financial debt capitalists (international bankers) come into the war-torn countries and buy up property cheaply (using our dollars again), rebuild foreign plants and factories, and make a killing (financially and literally), all with the productivity/capital/money provided by the American working people, who naively first deposited their money in these "banks." U.S. taxpayers bailed out Soviet communism twice - after the Russian Revolution and again in 1941. In 1975, 78 percent of Chase Manhattan's earnings came from international lending.

All this, of course, is justified under evolution. John D. Rocke-feller had the nerve to tell his Sunday School class, "The growth of a large business is merely a survival of the fittest...the working out of a law of nature and the law of God."

Undoubtedly, America's financial banking and debt capitalistic system today, supported by big government, is to the economic wel-fare of the common man what abortion is to life. It just kills it. Would the average American be far better off, and act consistently with his own best self-interest long-term, if he never used a financial institution? Would not a typical American be better off under an Islamic banking system, which is far more Christian than the present system? Mohammed took his economics from Moses.

Again, why do men act so insanely? They have been edu-cated/indoctrinated/brainwashed into doing so. They have been taught to be "dumb" through years and years in the public schools.

Technical "factual" education in the United States used to be quite good - accounting, engineering, scientific research, math, read-ing and the like. However, it has broken down as the teaching of principles has ceased and outcome-based education has mushroomed. It is in the all important spiritual, and abstract areas of religion, phi-losophy, economics, history, literature, civics and social studies, where men are taught to be willing slaves. All of these areas today are clearly founded upon evolution and pagan, occult mysticism.

It is no accident that the father of American education, John Dewey, a confirmed atheist who praised Lenin, left this country and went to attempt to work his educational "miracles" under Stalin in the Soviet Union. Both educational systems, in the U.S. and the U.S.S.R., were essentially the same - evolutionary! Under evolution, men are encouraged not to think. After all, if there is no truth and everything is relative as it evolves, why think? John Dewey was a confirmed evolutionist who admired Thomas Henry Huxley, Dar-win's staunchest defender. Dewey taught, true to evolution, that man is an animal - pragmatic, without morals or conscience, and there-fore, void of evil. This is in direct contrast with the Biblical teaching of a sin (animal) nature within a spiritual being. John Dewey de-clared, "There is no god..." The foundations established by John D. Rockefeller and Andrew Carnegie financed the textbooks touting Dewey's evolutionary perspective.

The Doobie Brothers, in their smash hit, sang, "What a fool be-lieves he sees no wise man has the power to reason away." We Americans are played for real fools today. No wonder we're held in contempt by our government. Only fools act contrary to their own best self-interest and the best interest of society long-term. We are now a ship of fools on a reeling ship of state. The educational brainwashing process has been shrewd, clever and effective. The ruling evolutionists really do know that human nature is a constant and does not change as the evolutionists purport. The ruling evolutionists' planners have ruthlessly used man's foremost psychological barriers - pride, fear of the unknown and resistance to change - against him, to prevent him from seeing how his self-interest dovetails with creation.

Men are by nature proud. They hate to be wrong and in error. Stated differently, men hate to sin. Thus men, because they are proud, are reluctant to radically alter a position they presently hold. To do so is to admit that they were wrong and in error. This makes men feel foolish and embarrassed. It hurts their pride. After being taught the propaganda of the religion of evolution for 12 years in the public school system, it takes a good dose of humility for men to admit they have been played for suckers. Thus, pride is the primary barrier today to be overcome for men to reject the destructive religious theory of evolution. But this is to be expected. Pride is the worst of sins (Proverbs 6:16). It was Satan's first sin, according to Christian cosmology.

Are the public (government) schools today Satan's workshop and playground? If creationism is excluded from the public schools because it is an expression of the Christian religion, shouldn't evolution be excluded because it is an expression of atheistic communism, socialism and Nazism, which are all anti-religious religions?

Running in the same harness with pride is man's resistance to change. Men desire security. Fearing the unknown they are reluctant to change. This security need is basic, stemming from the ultimate in spiritual security, the anchor of an infinite sovereign, loving Creator, and in physical security, from the womb. In terms of these ultimate physical and spiritual securities, men are naturally drawn to family and God. Perhaps one of the primary reasons men are so unhappy today is that these basic security needs are violated as government planners attempt to make government the false mother and the false god, the source of security.

Men have to be educated to act against these security instincts. It takes awhile, but after 12 years of being taught that the religious theory of evolution is true, men, as would be expected, resist their true inclinations. They defend what they have been taught, even though it is contrary to their own self-interest and is destructive for society long-term.

To change the basic religious, evolutionary presupposition is a fearful thing, requiring men to reject and then restructure all they have learned throughout their carefully orchestrated lives. They first have to overcome their pride, fear of the unknown, and resistance to change. George Orwell's "1984" came in 1948, the date he originally intended for the title of that book. The programming of the American public began to pick up momentum nearly 50 years ago.

What about the churches? What about the religious leaders with all their rich, bureaucratic hierarchies, the evolutionary pinnacle of which are the National Council of Churches and the World Council of Churches? Consistent with the harmony of the elitist's theory of evolution, these organized, centralized, religious organizations have helped finance atheistic, Left Wing and/or communist, evolutionary, revolutionaries worldwide, and now promote the New World Order.

Organized, centralized, evolutionary, Western religion is little different today from that which existed in the Soviet Union. There, the Russian Orthodox Church was provided limousines and the fine life by the Soviet government. In the Soviet Union, the Council for Religious Affairs had the ultimate say as to which individuals were selected as bishops and priests. Today, in this country, the IRS wields the ultimate federal government hammer over religion.

Karl Marx, the father of communism observed, "religion is the opiate of the people." Institutionalized human religion, wherein man attempts to find or become god (evolution) and please him in some eternal sense, logically focuses on the eternal realm, the "Great Hereafter." This "opiate," this escape, mentally and thus functionally neutralizes man in time, which allows evolutionary elitists to do what they have always done best - rule and oppress (I Samuel 8). This is also the reason why all world religions have always been aggressively antagonistic to creationist Christianity. Christianity involves the Creator seeking after man, providing eternal salvation, and holding man accountable and responsible in time. The battle becomes one for dominion over the earth. This is the last thing evolutionary elitists want - involved, responsible, knowledgeable citizens. If man is individually accountable and responsible as a steward in time, he is concerned with current events. This thwarts and frustrates the purposes and plans of a ruling, evolutionary elite.

America's Christian churches are too often coffins. They are lukewarm institutions which have been spewed out by thinking men. They are effectively dead, having bowed to the sovereignty of government, rather than having held to the sovereignty of the "King of kings." As such, it should come as no surprise that these Sunday social clubs, these whitewashed tombstones, have little purpose or influence in society today. The all too effeminate American clergy, most being ignorant of economics, has thus missed the essence of man's Christian spiritual responsibility in time. Adam's responsibility in the garden was an economic issue. Israel's taking of the Promised Land had an economic base. The stewardship and development of talents in line with New Testament doctrines are ultimately economically grounded because the development and use of talents involves contracting, covenanting and personal interaction. Economics is, by definition, human action.

Just as governments cannot exist without an economic base - taxes - churches cannot exist without an economic base - tithes, gifts and offerings. While the real war is being fought in the real world over the real economic issue of who rules (dominion), the American clergy - the so-called leaders of the Christian soldiers, who have been given the responsibility of putting on the whole armor of God - are in fact no better than chess-playing warriors, if not the enemy. America's religious leaders have bought, in too many cases, the Greek and Manichaean idea of a separate and segregated spiritual and physical universe, thereby denying the reality of a Creator God who unified the spiritual and material realms. The American clergy, tiptoeing through the tulips of the spiritual realm, are heretics when compared to the religious leaders who helped build this great nation. Today's religious leaders' opium-type plans, conceived with a sound and fury signifying nothing, are being smashed as the evolutionary barbarians descend upon us. Sad to say, but too many ministers simply spew back out what they have been taught at seminaries which long ago became captured agents of evolutionary centralization.

Evolutionary religion is a man-directed attempt to attain eternal life by man's own efforts. Nearly all pagan religions are evolutionary, denying a Creator, and instead, assuming the ultimacy of space/time/matter. Creationist Christianity is the God-directed plan of providing eternal life through Jesus Christ's work on the cross, calling man to service in time. Christianity is the one "religion" in the history of the world which focuses upon the fate of a single man, Jesus Christ, at a point in time, as the central issue of the entire creation. Jesus Christ was/is the transitional bridge between man and God. He bridged heaven and earth, the infinite and the finite, eternity and time, spirit and matter, the perfect and the imperfect, the one and the many. It is no accident in today's New Age that everyone gets to be a god (or goddess) except Jesus Christ.

If, by contrast, evolution is true, there never was an original perfection. Therefore, there is no need for the restoration of that perfection made possible by Christ's work on the cross. Thus, the crucifixion of Jesus Christ was a waste. Evolution has no room for, or way of dealing with, love and self-sacrifice as epitomized by the historical act of Jesus Christ on the cross. For according to evolution, those individuals genetically predetermined toward love and self-sacrifice, which help the human species survive, should by now have been eliminated, given "natural selection" and the "survival of the fittest." However, their very elimination would unleash a flood of violence which would destroy the human race, not very evolutionary. Checkmate.

Evolution is, in fact, a spiral down, headed today for chaos where Satan destroys the world by fire, thereby thwarting the Creator's plan for the restoration of a perfect environment. As an alternative to chaos, men will opt for a new elitist, economic, political and religious world order; in other words, a global slave state, a phoenix rising from the ashes.

It is a timeless, proven truth that real progress in the human condition only comes through self-sacrifice, with an eye toward the future. Under evolution, it is impossible for man, the animal, to understand time or self-sacrifice. Thus, under evolution, progress is impossible. In fact, the opposite is true.

Evolution holds that man is an animal. True, man is the highest animal, the pinnacle of the factual universe. But as an animal primarily (and exclusively), once this evolutionary assumption is bought, mankind has opened himself up to being treated like one. The idea that man is a spiritual being, with an animal/physical nature, the highest earthly creature made by the Creator, is today hanging on by a thread in our society. It's important, therefore, that we now look at the devastating implications of our having adopted this evolutionary theory that man is an animal, as opposed to a spiritual being with an animal/physical nature. The working out of this evolutionary assumption is shocking.

The Human Evolutionary Animal

We have seen that societies and their governments, operating under evolution, move logically toward collectivism - whether democracy, socialism, communism or fascism. To prevent the full fury and ruthlessness of the doctrine of "survival of the fittest" from being manifest in society, governments act as master planners and regulate society. The tremendous wealth accumulated by the rapacious few, is redistributed by government to the hapless, victimized masses so these poor folks can survive economically. All the while, the parasitic government grows in size and power as it patrols the demilitarized zone between these warring classes, the producers and the consumers in the welfare state. Meanwhile, government-sanctioned bureaucrats build personal empires, based on seemingly limitless government finances, promoting the development of super egos among the scientists, social scientists, social workers, academicians and urban planners whose programs keep expanding but never function as planned.

A nation is a complex system. All complex systems function best when authority and responsibility are delegated to the lowest possible level of efficiency, that of the individual in the case of a nation. The Creator appoints each man as a manager (believer/priest/steward/king) who is provided with ethical guidelines (principles), impossible under evolution.

As the dependent folks, particularly those in the cities, feel increasing alienation, isolation and powerlessness in society, they either react with anger and violence (frustration externalized), or depression (frustration internalized). These folks are isolated in their neighborhoods and know little or nothing about how the system functions. They have not been taught. They cannot reason. They are effectively the true products of evolution - animals, or, as one Eastern Establishment liberal planner put it, "maggots in a flour sack."

Under evolution, since everything is relative and always evolving, everything is permitted. There are no standards under evolution whereby child molestation, cannibalism, incest, murder, rape, homosexuality and the like can be prohibited. Nor is there any protection of property rights. There are no absolute morals or ethics under relative evolution. Thus, there is no personal responsibility because responsibility is moral. The inner cities truly give us the animals who are the undesirable result of evolution. But such justifies the government.

Now, the question becomes, "What do the evolutionists at the top of the government-dominated evolutionary spiral do with their 'maggots in a flour sack' (the common people)?" Evolutionary, socialistic/fascist government has an inescapable problem. Whatever government taxes, there is less of. There is more of whatever government subsidizes. Government taxes the productive middle class and thus eliminates them, dropping them into the lower class, where eventually they wind up as members of the welfare state. Evolutionary government subsidizes the welfare class, allowing it to reproduce beyond its natural economic checkpoint, and so evolutionary government is continually plagued with overpopulation of the less productive members of society as a dominant problem in society. (Overpopulation was viewed as a problem in the dying Greek evolutionary culture, too.)

Because, under evolution, men are animals and thus cannot think, they cannot be creative, a situation which is most pronounced at the lower echelons of an evolutionary society. Without creative thinking and productive individuals, there is no real economic progress, so a society stagnates and overpopulation truly does become an issue which negatively impacts the environment. Next, the government is faced with the necessary elimination of all the excess animals (people) in the society. This was true in evolutionary ancient Egypt where the Hebrew slaves were expendable. It was true in evolutionary Nazi Germany where Hitler not only attempted to breed a super race, but also attempted to eliminate the undesirable animals (the Jews). It is and has been true in atheistic/evolutionary Soviet Russia, Communist China and Cambodia, ad nauseam, where millions have been slaughtered. How long until it will be true in the United States? War is traditionally the government's easy way out of complicated problems where the government's parasitic and unjust condition might be brought into question.

Abortion is already slaughtering many of our unborn - some estimates running as high as one out of every three conceptions. If the evolutionary model is false, and the creation model is true, with rampant abortion today, how many Albert Einsteins, Albert Schweitzers, Julius Irvings, Ernest Hemingways and Abraham Lincolns have been lost to this world? Under the creation model, God has a perfect plan for each individual which benefits other members of society. Are we any better now than the decadent ancient Greeks who put their imperfect babies in clay jars to die along the side of the road? The Greeks we so admire today were an aggressive, self-destructive, unloving bunch, reflecting the cynicism of their gods. A society always reflects the character, or lack thereof, of its god(s).

If men are animals, as logically is the case under the evolution model, how long can it be until we, like Hitler, in our science-oriented, technological, fact-dominated society, breed for evolutionary perfection - simultaneously eliminating, for the good of mankind, the downtrodden, the poor, the old, the racial minorities, the criminals, the troublemakers, the defective, and the weak, particularly as economic conditions become more difficult? Isn't this what primitive societies do with their undesirables? Isn't this consistent with the evolutionary doctrine of survival of the fittest? Will our civilization instead opt for drug therapy, shock treatment, psychological conditioning and/or subliminal advertising? How many geniuses will our evolutionary government eliminate in the process? Today's geniuses are yesterday's crackpots. An evolutionary government logically eliminates a genius at the crackpot stage. And yet, it has been the so-called crackpots throughout history who have eventually been seen as the true contributors long-term to the improvement of the human condition.

Scientists can measure IQ but they cannot measure creativity. Creativity is the product of self-discipline, of long, deep, consistent thinking, or desire which is unrelated to IQ. How many creative individuals have been (and will be) slaughtered if evolutionary governments continue to sweep the earth? This is another good argument for decentralized, local, people-controlled government, the preferred role for government under the creation model. Local individuals can fight City Hall a whole lot more effectively than they can Capitol Hill.

Here again we see the lie of government as the great benefactor in the evolution model. From a short-term perspective, government can, through the welfare state, provide the economic necessities of the lower class. But once the surplus is consumed, as it always is, and the middle class dies, and the economic/climatic conditions become unfavorable, the parasite (government) does what it has to do - it ruthlessly eliminates those who it earlier supported economically, either directly, or indirectly, through war. (One of the best ways to prevent a war is to refuse to finance it.) Governments don't redistribute wealth. They distribute poverty.

Given the god-like status of our fact-oriented, evolutionary scientists, supported by an evolutionary government; given the tremendous advances being made today in genetic research and quantum physics; and, further, given the impending collapse of our evolutionary economic and social order; how much longer will it be until the genetic techniques being applied to animals now are applied forcefully to human animals? How long until each of us has a number just like a cow at a cattle auction? (Social Security account number?) How long until we are under a required systematic breeding program, like that which is already in operation in Red China? How long until certain men are castrated and others are held for production as human studs? Who believes, given the government's ineptitude at planning in all other areas of life, that government can be trusted in the area of genetics?

Under evolution, man should logically attempt to breed up, as Hitler did, to attempt to produce a higher class of men, perhaps the ultimate "superman," the ultimate anti-Christ. Such would represent the epitome of the scientific/factual, genetic completion of the evolutionary spiral. Already, the scientific community is about ready to produce super animals, as we have entered the age of embryo engineering. In this animalistic fashion, an Arizona woman in 1982 gave birth to a baby girl whose male seed came from a scientific genius. Is this any different than the freezing of the semen of prize bulls which is later inseminated into cows? Gene manipulation, embryo transfer, and cloning are realities today in the production of animals, and human animals. If man is an animal, rather than a spiritual being with an animal nature, as under the creation model, how long will it be until such genetic techniques are applied wholesale to man - particularly when push comes to shove during tough economic times? How long until women (the weaker sex in a world of natural selection) have no say in whose baby they carry or whether they can bear children at all?

Do we trust the scientists and multinational corporations who are conducting the avant-garde experiments in these genetic research fields? We have no reason to trust them since in other areas corruption has clearly come with size and power. Men just can't seem to play the role of god without becoming corrupted. Genetech is hooked up with Monsanto. American Cyanamid owns 27 percent of Molecular Genetics. International Minerals and Chemical Corporation has linked up with Biogen. So, just like with solar energy, the evolutionary multinational debt capitalists are swallowing up the genetic research firms.

We are now seeing numerous groups call for equal rights for animals and plants. We have already witnessed the environmental and operant conditioning human experimentation conducted by B.F. Skinner, based upon stimulus/response, just like with Pavlov's dog. Natural selection among human animals is on the way. How many human animals will we need when robots become pervasive and computers coordinate their work? After all, truth and life itself will be what the government and its scientists say it is. Power under relative evolution will always determine truth, right and wrong, life and death. It's all relative, if evolution is true.

Animals cannot know truth. Truth exists in the timeless, abstract, thinking realm. Animals can know only facts. It takes a leap of faith (religion) for man, who can only know facts as an evolutionary human animal, to become a god and operate beyond good and evil, thereby knowing truth in the abstract realm. Government has made that leap of faith today, believing it has all the answers. It legislates accordingly. Thus, believing in the theory of evolution is understood as requiring faith. We can, therefore, classify evolution as a man-centered religion.

Evolution today has already polarized society into two powerful animalistic categories. One category is individual; the other, collective. The "macho man" epitomizes the individual at the top of an evolutionary spiral in the mode of survival of the fittest. The popularity of the likes of Charles Bronson, Sylvester Stallone and Clint Eastwood movies - the macho movies - as well as the heroes of professional sports (worshiped as idols), are the appropriate gods of the individualistic-oriented evolutionists.

The centralized federal government, multinational banks and corporations, religious, military, media and educational empires are the "collectivist" gods at the top of this other evolutionary spiral. The individual evolutionists, of course, are at war with the collectivist evolutionists. Conflict is always present with evolution. What both camps have in common is that other men, those beneath them in the spiral, are expendable. Sensing this, the masses are escaping into drugs (in many cases provided by the collectivist's Establishment, as discussed in the U.S. Labor Party's book, "Dope, Inc."), or into the escapist movies, television, or sports. On average, Americans watch seven hours of television a day.

Human rights and their attendant property (economic) rights become relative under evolution. After all, if all men evolved, then all men may be brothers somewhere back down the line, and so they should logically "share the wealth" (communism). Another evolutionary perspective, however, is clearly racist. If there are different origins for the human race, then certain races are obviously substandard - which ones, of course, to be determined by government where government is all-powerful.

As economic and climatic conditions become more harsh, racial lines will be more clearly drawn as society, consistent with this evolutionary logic, further discriminates against the economically dependent in society who cannot meet their own economic needs. "Might makes right" under evolution, and because the Whites have the population numbers in their favor, the minority groups in this country are headed for abuse. How many George Washington Carvers and Thomas Sowells will be victimized? By contrast, under the creation model, racism is never an issue for economic advancement. Men, in the free market, pay for the best goods and services available, at the lowest price, regardless of who produces them. Just look at the American public's preference for Japanese automobiles.

The Blacks particularly, and now Hispanics, are being played for suckers by the centralizing planners in this country. Having been freed from slavery by a wise Abraham Lincoln, too many Black minority groups have been conned into accepting the slavery of the dole, the economic dependency and slavery resulting from the government's welfare handout. Some Blacks have further been deceived into adopting the Muslim religion of the slave traders who ruthlessly abused their ancestors. For it was the Arab Muslims who composed nearly three-quarters of the world's slave trade in Black Africa. In the Old South, Black slaves looked to the plantation owner's white house for their welfare. Today, far too many Blacks look to the White House for their welfare.

Animals have no clothes. Pornography has flourished. Animals react instinctively. Emotionalism is rampant. They cannot reason. Animals react short-term to facts. They do not think in the abstract realm, long-term. They have no sense of time, no sense of history, and no sense of values. Animals live in the present and "do it now," "if it feels good." Animals cannot progress because progress demands self-discipline and sacrifice short-term for achievement and progress long-term. Such animals can and will be controlled by the technocrats who run the bureaucratic machinery of the oppressive, collectivist government social order.

There is no dignity for man under evolution, only slavery. Slavery used to be personal. It was abolished. Slavery today to the civil government is far more prevalent and deadly than personal slavery ever was, and it's getting worse as the evolutionary/humanistic cancer grows and spreads. Communism is forced slavery. Debt capitalism is voluntary slavery. Fascism is disguised slavery. Slaves cannot develop their Creator-given talents. The accurate perspective is not, "My country right or wrong." The correct perspective is, "My country when right, to be kept right; when wrong, to be put right." It's time for this country to be put right!

By glorious contrast, the future under the creation model can be fabulous. Men have the opportunity to be free and independent financially as never before, working at home. Already, the information processing and service sectors of the U.S. economy are engulfing approximately 75 percent of the work force. With advanced computer technology moving into the homes, upcoming audio/visual two-way communication, and with robots performing mindless tasks, more and more families could become autonomous, self-sustaining, creative, economic units. Men and women will be able to develop and market their complementary creative talents from the home, living wherever they choose, via computer satellite communications. No location will be remote. With the solar energy breakthroughs, families will permanently kick the utility and service station habit. The world will become one big economic electronic supermarket, with men buying and selling freely globally via computers. World harmony will exist as men barter and exchange their productivity directly - as debt capitalism, OPM, compound interest, socialism, communism and fascism all die. Banks will become safekeeping centers, brokerage and economic centers where men establish partnerships, joint ventures, and buy and sell stock, all the recording of which activity will be available on home computer. Education will move to the home via computer audio/visual instruction. The city will finally come to live in the rural country (the garden). Governments will finally compete in the free market for the citizenship of men and women, based upon governments providing the services desired by individuals. Politicians will finally learn that the key to maintaining power is to give it away, allowing men to be free.

Catch the vision of the future? Animals, as men are under evolution, have no vision. But, spiritual beings with animal natures under the creation model do. We are on the brink of the greatest disaster or the greatest opportunity in history, perhaps both in sequence. The choice of each individual will determine our collective destiny. Men must choose whom they will serve.

Science: Evolution's Ace in the Hole?

Now we come to the great stumbling block for credibility for the creation theory in the modern world, the great unknown (to the masses) on which evolution rests its case - science. All, or most of us, have been taught in the government-financed public schools, the government-financed and subsidized universities, and in the government-financed public television programs (PBS) that evolution is unquestionably the working basis of modern science, and thus the foundation of our wonderful technological society. But, is it really?

It's important that we distinguish between academic science and research science. It is not academic evolutionary scientists but research scientists - hard-working, practical men and women investigating the natural, scientific laws of the universe, based upon their faith that those laws exist - who have made our world a better place in which to live. The scientific method itself proceeds from an idea assumed as true (faith), verified or disproven through experimentation.

Science, before Darwin's evolution, primarily emphasized math, physics and chemistry. It can be well argued that all of our real material progress has been a product of physics and chemistry. But since Darwin, evolutionary academic science (theoretical science) has emphasized geology and biology. These academic so-called scientific pursuits operate in the evolutionary universe of chance when it comes to origin, and thus, by scientific definition, are not scientific. No research can either affirm or deny their evolutionary conjectures. There are no experimental methods in geology, paleontology, astrophysics or astronomy that are infallible. Such are impossible, in most cases. The scientific method is totally useless when it comes to proving evolutionary biology because that evolutionary experience, if it ever occurred, cannot be repeated. Besides, the scientific method, itself an experimental modality, is not infallible. It is subject to the perspective of the experimenter, the conditions under which the experiment is conducted, and the way the observations and conclusions are formulated. Heisenberg's indeterminacy principle established this.

It is true that the natural realm above the level of the atom, based in math, gives us a reliable, mechanical, scientific language. This is the arena in which real research scientists work best, not the spiritual arena. When scientists take a position on evolution or creation, they, too, are religious priests. In other words, they are guessing about origin. And, contrary to what the general public hears today, there is

a considerable war going on between scientific creationists and evolutionists, as to which origin religion is correct. Let's look at a few
eye-opening comments:

"Even Einstein couldn't come to grips with it. His general theory of relativity predicted the creation, but it was years before he
reluctantly accepted what his own equations showed." Robert Jas-
trow, Director of the Goddard Institute For Space Studies, a division
of NASA.

Astronomer Sir Fred Hoyle and Chandra Wickramasinghe challenged the basic foundations of the evolutionary theory in their book,
"Space Travelers: The Bringers Of Life!" They stated, "Once we
see that the probability of life originating at random is so utterly
minuscule as to make it absurd, it becomes sensible to think that the
favorable properties of physics on which life depends are in every
respect, deliberate, and it is almost inevitable that our own measure
of intelligence must reflect higher intelligence, even to the limit of
God."

An associate of Dr. Carl Sagan, Dr. William Provine of Cornell
University, on November 17, 1981 stated, "First, I agree with him
(Mr. Sunderland) that creationism should be taught along with evolu-
tionism from grade school through high school."

The senior paleontologist at the British Museum of Natural History, Dr. Colin Patterson, a respected evolutionary scientist for 50
years, speaking to over 50 classification specialists on November 5,
1981 at the American Museum of Natural History in New York
stated, "Then I woke up and realized that all my life I had been
duped into taking evolution as revealed truth in some way." Dr. Patterson also referred to evolution as, "Positively anti-knowledge," and
"story telling."

Dr. Patterson has also declared, "One morning I woke up and
something had happened in the night, and it struck me that I had
been working with this stuff for 20 years, and there was not one
thing I knew about it. It's quite a shock to learn that one can be
misled for so long. Either there was something wrong with me, or
there was something wrong with evolution theory."

The scientific evidence which reveals how badly we have been deceived by the evolution theory is available for curious minds. The comments which follow will be heavily weighted to the creationist scientific
perspective, to better give "equal time." This evidence is drawn primarily from three excellent sources: 1) One of the best books, discussing this creation/evolution issue is "The Creation-Evolution Contro-

versy," by Dr. R.L. Wysong (Inquiry Press, 4925 Jefferson Avenue, Midland, Michigan 48640, 1976). This work is, in its own way, what Josh McDowell's book, "Evidence That Demands A Verdict," is to Christian apologetics. (2) An excellent monthly newsletter on the creation/evolution issue is Bible Science Newsletter (2911 East 42nd Street, Minneapolis, Minnesota 55406). (3) One of the nation's leading think tanks on the subject of creation, is the Institute for Creation Research (2716 Madison Avenue, San Diego, California 92116).

M.P. Schutzenberger, a computer scientist, in a speech given at the Wistar Institute of Anatomy and Biology Symposium declared, "...we believe there is a considerable gap in the neo-Darwinian theory of evolution, and we believe this gap to be of such a nature that it cannot be bridged within the current conception of biology." Scientist M. Eden has computed that the probability of forming proteins and DNA for the smallest self-replicating entity, given astronomically large quantities of reagents and time, is $1^{167,626}$. To write this number would require 150 pages of solid zeros. Thus, the probability of DNA being formulated through evolution (chance) is negligible.

How about mutations leading to evolution? Mutations, as it turns out, have been shown to be almost always harmful and are evidence of degeneration, not evolution. Most mutations are buried within the genes or are corrected by DNA repair systems. Here, too, the mathematical probability that random mutations and natural selection ultimately produced complex systems from simpler life is infinitesimal.

The renowned scientist, Lord Zuckerman, who is not a creationist, has been unable to find any fossil traces of a transformation from an ape-like creature to man. (The atheistic philosopher, Jean Jacques Rousseau pushed this ape-man theory as far back as 1754, long before Darwin came on the scene.)

The Piltdown Man and the Nebraska Man, both hailed as "missing links," have both proven to be frauds. The only evidence that was used to reconstruct the entire Nebraska Man, a tooth, turned out to belong to an extinct pig. The Nebraska Man had been called an "authentic, genuine, impeccable" link, and aged at one million years. The Piltdown Man, even though a proven hoax, remained as the classic proof for evolution in textbooks nearly 40 years later. Along this same line, the Southwest Colorado Man was found to be an extinct Eocene horse. The Neanderthal Man was found in rock formations similar to those in which modern man has been found. The Neanderthal Man is now believed to have been fully human and crippled by osteoarthritis. Cro-Magnon Man is now conceded to have been fully human, too.

In the Paluxy riverbed, on the McFall farm outside Glen Rose, Texas, 24 Tyrannosaurus footprints have been found along side four human footprints. This was verified by a certified geologist, Dr. John Morris of Oklahoma University. (Dinosaur and human footprints together have been discovered at many locations.) According to evolution theory, these particular human and Tyrannosaurus footprints should have been separated by 70 million years.

The records of man date back to only about 3,000 B.C., and they reveal highly-developed and sophisticated civilizations, just the opposite of what we are taught under evolution, that primitives evolved. In fact, in these early civilizations are found remains of highly-developed societies that degenerated into a less complicated, more primitive lifestyle.

Using standard population computation methods, man's existence is shown to be only several thousand years. If an evolutionary history of just one million years is used in these computations, the earth's population could not fit into our entire universe.

One of the best books on the fossils is Dr. Duane T. Gish's "Evolution: The Fossils Say No!" The fossil skeleton that was held to be a link between birds and reptiles, Archaeopteryx, was found to be a true bird. All kinds of contradictions have also been discovered in the so-called evolutionary horse tree, with one of the most striking being that the Eohippus is almost identical to the African Hyrax. The Seymouria, the supposed evolutionary gap between the reptiles which followed the amphibians, even using evolutionary methods, is said to have existed 20 million years after the reptiles appeared. The link between snakes and lizards, Lanthanotus, was found alive in recent years in Sarawak, Malaysia. Dr. Clifford Burdick has scientifically substantiated that life on this earth has existed in modern forms since earliest times through his research involving spores. Finally, no evolutionary scientist has yet gotten around the scientific truism that life comes from like life. It seems that many scientists who believe otherwise simply have allowed their beliefs to arise out of evolutionary prejudices. E. Kellenberger declared, "Living things are enormously diverse in form, but form is remarkably constant within any given line of descent: pigs remain pigs and oak trees remain oak trees generation after generation." ("The Genetic Control of the Shape of the Virus," Scientific American, December, 1966).

The "micro" evolution argument is being challenged today. Micro-evolution says that development has taken place from a given state of complexity and order to an increased state of complexity and order. Yet, we have seen from studies with DNA, mutations and thermodynamics, that such net improvement is scientifically impossible.

There is natural variation because there is variation in all living things. This is the by-product of genetic variation, which is a result of the genetic variation potential of the species, and mutation. Neither of these, however, produce any true evolution in any species. Genetic variation potential produces horizontal variation only. And, as previously discussed, scientists have found mutations to be degenerative and harmful, threatening the very existence of the species.

Evolutionary scientists also have not been able to conquer the Second Law of Thermodynamics, the tendency for things in the natural order to run down. Our natural system, our universe, is like a wound-up clock, which is winding down. The question becomes, "Who wound it up in the first place? A Creator?" According to the Second Law of Thermodynamics, systems, over time, move toward greater disorder. The universe is moving toward a state of maximum entropy. At some point, all space will be the same temperature. All energy will have been uniformly distributed in the cosmos. There will be no life, no light and no warmth, just perpetual and irrevocable stagnation. There is no way of avoiding this destiny, according to the Second Law of Thermodynamics, which is the exact opposite of evolution. Natural change moves irrefutably toward decay. The matter and energy of the universe are defusing. The sun is burning out. The stars are dying. Heat is turning to cold everywhere in the cosmos. Matter is dissolving into radiation. Energy is being dissipated into empty space. If, as under evolution, the universe and matter are eternal, then by now, according to the laws of thermodynamics, the universe should be already a weak, useless energy field. But obviously it is not.

Scientists have attempted to venture into space to escape the limits of time, and the following implications of a Creator's judgment. However, there is one thing that evolution definitely requires, and that is lots and lots of time. An interesting evolutionary contradiction is that man, as an evolved animal, should not be able to think in terms of time, an abstract concept, unless he makes a "leap of faith," which he has done under the religion of evolution. The existence of linear time presupposes history, which further implies a judgment, and that man is responsible for how he uses his given time. Additionally, it is linear time plus Creator-given law that together produce patterns.

We are told how vast the universe is. And yet, at the University of Connecticut and MIT, scientists have shown, through Reimannian curved space astrophysics, that it takes only 15 years to reach the most distant stars, a far cry from what most of us have been taught in the evolutionary-biased public (government) schools. Now according to the physics of light, as we accelerate to the speed of light, time stops, and matter becomes infinite and fills the universe. This is particularly interesting in light of the fact that Jesus said in John 8:12, "I am the light of the world..." Also I John 1:5 declares, "God is light..."

The following is a small sampling of information that will help to paint a more realistic picture than the one we've been spoonfed.

Studies of rapidly decaying radioactive elements and pleochroic halos suggest that creation was accomplished quite quickly and completely. If the earth had cooled down slowly over hundreds of millions of years, as evolutionists suggest, polonium halos could not have possibly formed because all the polonium would have decayed soon after it was synthesized, and would have been extinct when crustal rocks formed. The very fact that pleochroic halos exist are evidence of the simultaneous creation of radioactivity and rocks.

When Dr. Henry Morris, creationist and author of "The Genesis Flood," spoke to oil industry geologists in Houston, Texas several years ago, he received a standing ovation upon completion. Practicing oil industry geologists recognized that Dr. Morris' work on creation fit with the real world of geology. Reality science is far different than the evolutionary, academic variety.

Oil has been produced from garbage in a few hours, suggesting that the oil found in the earth could have been made rapidly and recently. C-14 (Carbon 14) dating of oil has confirmed this young life for oil. Most convincing is the fact that the excessive pressure found within oil beds resulting in oil gushers, argues for trapped oil being less than 10,000 years old. Given the permeability of the rocks surrounding the oil beds, any pressure build up should have been dissipated and bled off into the surrounding rocks within a few thousand years. The fact that this has not occurred further supports the creation case for a young earth.

Robert Whitelaw, a nuclear consultant and Professor of Mechanical Engineering at Virginia Polytechnic Institute, has found that C-14 is not a valid method for dating the age of the earth. His conclusion is that the C-14 clock was turned on between 5,600 and 11,200 years ago, supporting evidence for a young earth, a far cry from the millions or billions of years that the evolutionists claim. Furthermore, C-14 dating has been found to be fairly reliable as a dating system only back to 4,500 years ago, the time of the global flood. This is also the time of the greatest fossilization. Archeologist J.R.

Jochmans has found evidence of the flood in 97 world cultures. If a water canopy existed above the earth before the global flood, which shielded out harmful radiation, and made it possible for men to live to over 900 years, it possibly also prevented it from raining, which would have significantly altered the rate of C-14 production.

Niagara Falls is calculated to be between 5,000 and 10,000 years old based upon the rate at which its edge wears away. Evolutionists tell us that the great canyons of the world "slowly" cut through hard rock over millions of years, causing their tremendous depth. What we find, however, is that the lower rocks in the Grand Canyon, for example, provide clear evidence of great heat and pressure, suggesting they were volcanic in origin. Furthermore, in the Grand Canyon, there is no evidence of "wall polish" which, if made "slowly" by the abrasive polishing agents in the waters of the Colorado River, would definitely be present. The probability is, in keeping with creationists' and catastrophic theory, that the Grand Canyon split open, for its elevation is higher than that of surrounding ground.

Evolutionists like to speak of uniformitarianism, that evolution took place slowly, smoothly and systematically over millions or billions of years. And yet, in addition to the above evidence, in March, 1982, bones of a land mammal were found in Antarctica. There have been sea shells found in the Himalayas of Tibet and huge boulders discovered on mountains in Vermont, weighing thousands of tons, that came from rock formations hundreds of miles away. All this suggests catastrophe, not uniformitarianism.

The age of the earth's magnetic field and its decay casts an important light on this evolution/creation controversy. The half-life of the earth's magnetic field has been computed to be 1,400 years. Calculating the rate of decay of the earth's magnetic field and extrapolating backwards just 20,000 years, we find that the earth has to be less than 10,000 years old. Going back just 20,000 years, scientists find that the Joule heat generated would liquify the earth. A NASA satellite's preliminary report showed a rapid decay of the earth's magnetic field. On a straight-line basis, the earth's magnetic field will be extinct in 3991 A.D. The decay is exponential. The earth's magnetic field is decaying faster than any other worldwide geophysical phenomenon.

The rotation of the earth is gradually slowing. If the earth had been slowing down uniformly for billions of years, its present spin would be zero. If we extrapolate backwards, we find that the earth's spin billions of years ago would have been so rapid that the centrifugal force would have pulled all the land masses toward the equator and extended them out to a height of over 40 miles. The oceans would have been displaced to the poles, and the shape of the earth would have been transformed from a globe to a "fat pancake."

The earth is slowly cooling from inside to outside, in keeping with Stefan's Law of Radiation. Lord Kelvin calculated that the earth could not be billions of years old based upon the existing temperature gradient in the earth, its rate of cooling, and the assumption that the initial state of the earth was white hot.

Robert V. Gentry, Professor of Physics at Columbia Union College, found that Precambrian granites, the "basement rocks" of the earth, were formed very rapidly, which rules out all the evolutionary explanations for our planet.

Meteoritic craters are all dated at only a few thousand years old.

If there were no plants or vegetation on the earth, and no oxygen in the atmosphere, and vegetation which covered the earth was suddenly created by God, the number of years needed to generate the present level of oxygen found in the atmosphere is 5,000 years.

Bristlecone pines can, according to scientists, live for thousands of years or even tens of thousands of years. And yet, all of them date to less than 6,000 years old.

The radioactive elements, uranium and thorium, are continually decaying to form helium. Based upon the present rate of helium formation, the earth is approximately 10,000 years old.

The old Mississippi River supports the creationists' perspective also. It dumps 300 million cubic yards of sediment into the Gulf of Mexico each year. If the Mississippi River was millions of years old, the Gulf of Mexico would have been filled up by now. By measuring the rate of growth of the Mississippi Delta (about 250 feet per year), the age of the Mississippi River is calculated at approximately 4,000 years.

Ocean sediment is only several thousand feet thick. Given that there are 28 billion tons of sediment added to the oceans each year, if this erosion process had been taking place for billions of years, as the evolutionists say, the continents would have been totally eroded away hundreds of times over and the layers of sediment on the ocean bottoms would be 100 miles thick. Further study of the nitrates and uranium found in the oceans, which do not break down or recycle like salt, suggests that, due to their small concentration, the oceans are only a few thousand years old. If the oceans were millions of years old, there would be far more uranium, sodium, nickel, magnesium, silicon, potassium, copper, gold, silver, mercury, lead, tin, aluminum, carbonate, sulfate, chlorine, calcium, lithium, titanium, chromium, manganese, iron, cobalt, zinc, rubidium, strontium, bismuth, thorium, antimony, tungsten, barium, molybdenum and bicarbonate concentrates than are found there presently.

Cosmic dust filters down to the earth from interplanetary space and enters the oceans at the rate of 14 million tons per year. The nickel content of this cosmic dust is more highly concentrated than that in earthly materials. If the earth was billions of years old, there should be 50 or more feet of this cosmic dust in the oceans' sediments. But, there is only enough cosmic dust on the earth, or the moon for that matter, to account for several thousand years of meteoritic dust influx.

It was long believed by space scientists that the moon was the same age as the earth. In fact, scientists were concerned that when men landed on the moon, they would sink into the moon dust. According to evolution theory, the moon is 5 to 10 billion years old. So, the astronauts should have had to contend with 20 to 60 miles of dust. But, the moon's surface, as many of us observed on television, was found to have only a few inches of dust at most, a real embarrassment for the evolutionists and a major victory for the creationists.

Why wasn't all this scientific, creationist information presented on PBS, on Carl Sagan's COSMOS? Who controls PBS? The federal government. With whose funds? The taxpayers, yours and mine, just like with the public schools and universities. Is it farfetched to suggest that the continual bombardment of the general public with the theory of evolution in the government-financed schools, the government-subsidized universities, and the government-sponsored and subsidized media is anything less than government acting consistent with its own self-interest? Could government possibly be selling us the religion of evolutionary origin in order to justify its enormous existence and centralization of power? Could it be that an engineered worldwide economic collapse, the unreal threat of nuclear terrorism or an alien invasion might be enough to break down the United States of America, the last free nation on the face of this earth, in order to consolidate it into a New World Order, fulfilling the ultimate of evolutionary, empire-building dreams, going as far back as the Tower of Babel and the Egyptian Empire?

What about our scientists? Why do we hear from so few of them regarding these matters? First of all, most scientists are not rich men. Their livelihood and economic well-being depends, in most cases, on the generosity of their sponsors. The National Science Foundation is an agency of the federal government, supported by our tax dollars. Most college and university scientific research projects are federally funded in whole or in part. Also, most private scientific research organizations are dependent upon multinational corporation and federal money, particularly where the military/industrial complex is concerned. Ernest Borek, in "The Code Of Life" (Columbia University Press, 1965), wrote: "The overwhelming portion of scientific activity is financed by our federal government..." As late as 1976, the Smithsonian Museum of Natural History allowed no exhibits which did not uphold evolution.

Scientists know which side their bread is buttered on. The real issue is money - economics! Money is the power that controls and manipulates everything visible in a fully-developed, evolutionary, economic empire, such as ours. And science is the most controlled area in our entire political/economic system.

The pyramid is the symbol of the international banking community, the money community. In ancient civilizations, such as the Mayan culture of central America, the kings, who were considered gods, were buried in pyramids. One great Mayan king was called the "lord of lords." This is exactly what the Bible calls Jesus Christ, along with "King of kings." The pharaohs, in Egypt were believed to be sun gods incarnate and were buried in the pyramids. Shelley called Ramses, one of the great Egyptian pharaohs, "king of kings" in one of his sonnets. We see the reality of evolutionary gods in the modern world even carried out through symbols from as long ago as the ancient Egyptian empire, i.e., the pyramid that is found on our Federal Reserve Note (U.S. dollar bill). Egypt made slaves of the Hebrews. Are God's children in the U.S., the New Israel, as our Founding Fathers called it, to be slaves also?

Science and technology cannot save us, as Colin Norman clearly argued in his book, "The God That Limps." The theory of evolution has about run out of rope and is gagging. Furthermore, science is running head-on into the same type of problems on the subatomic level that social scientists have run into with their disastrous collective dreams and schemes. While scientists are able to accurately predict activity in the physical universe beginning at the atomic level, the subatomic world is not so predictable. How the apparently random world of subatomic particles comes together and produces order that allows scientists to forecast the movement and behavior of the atom and larger matter is still a mystery. This is much like the action of a random distribution of free individuals in the social realm, coming together to accurately form a predictable bell-shaped curve.

Scientists are learning the great lesson of humility, that they are not all powerful or all knowing. Scientists, too, walk by faith and not by sight. They depend upon a design they do not fully understand. They operate with faith in the uniformity of nature and the natural order. They are, like all other men, incapable of perfect truth. They do have a vested self-interest in promoting the god-like status of science, however, not only to support their egos, but also to ensure the continuation of government and multinational corporation grants and subsidies on which they economically depend. But for this to occur, the public must be sold on the salvation of evolutionary science.

Ironically, the very base of science has been established, and still depends economically, upon the existence of a creationist Christian culture. Science depends upon excess capital (money), which allows scientific investigation to occur. Excess capital is the product of a culture operating under the creation model, long-term.

Science means knowledge; therefore, it is never complete because scientists are continually learning and discovering new scientific applications. This is progress, not evolution. The tremendous facts that science has given us proceed from an underlying faith in a universe that is knowable (thanks to a Creator). True progress does not come by way of the so-called circumstantial evidence of evolution which cannot be repeated. Rather, true progress - mistakenly called evolution - comes with the application of the scientific method, investigative doubt, and the discovery of laws which, in cause and effect manner, can then be utilized.

Down through the ages, men have always feared and worshipped what they did not understand. It is no different today. (Christian culture is the exception because it is uniquely reality-oriented. Christians are commanded to prove all things and hold fast to that which is good.) Today, scientists are held in awe. They are protected sacred cows, shielded from criticism and investigation by government, government-financed schools, universities, research centers and multinational corporations. Reality and scientific truth, like freedom, must come from the grassroots up. Thus, it has always been historically.

Hopefully, it has been clearly demonstrated by this point that man freely chooses which religious theory of origin he wants to live. under, the creation model or the evolution model. We are presently living under the evolution model. It has brought us nothing but mass misery (good times are an illusion of debt) with, of course, a few exceptions for those right up there at the top of the evolutionary order. Isn't it time we at least consider reestablishing the creation model as basic? After all, it was the creation model which first built and sustained this great nation. Human nature has not changed. So, we're not taking any real chances with the creation model. The prosperous results in the future can already be predicted from successful past history. All we have to lose are our chains. But, before we willingly drop those chains, we'll have to overcome our pride, fear of the unknown and resistance to change, and in the process, deprogram ourselves from the Machiavellian evolutionary conditioning with which we have been bombarded all of our deceived lives.

We haven't come close to scratching the surface of all the fields and areas of scientific investigation, which can potentially be discovered and applied for the benefit of all mankind. We are still in the early stages of the scientific technological revolution. We have not uncovered all the technology the federal government has developed and hidden from us. Science is reality-oriented. Christianity is reality-oriented. The two together are a natural, with economic prosperity the inevitable result. Our scientific dismay, just like our economic, political and social hopelessness, is a direct reflection of the bankrupt evolutionary theory which rules our scientific society today.

It is high time that free men again become responsible in all areas of their lives, first by getting their heads screwed on correctly religiously, with a workable creation theory of origin. Only evil can flourish when good men do nothing. A candle of light and truth drives out the darkness. We don't have to fight fire with fire. We can fight fire with water. Fighting fire with fire leads to revolution, which always results in a further centralization of power, the last thing we need. We need men and women to change their minds and approach life with a new optimistic and creative perspective. The future holds potentially tremendous scientific benefits. Within the upcoming trials and tribulations of the next 15 years lie the seeds for many glorious opportunities and breakthroughs, as our rigid institutions are forced to change or die. It is again time for men and women to draw comfort and strength from a living Creator, who is on their side and can give them what they seek, including breakthroughs in the scientific realm. With this mental decision once made, victory on this earth is just a breath away.

A Population Time Bomb?

Dr. David J. Rodabaugh, Associate Professor of Mathematics at the University of Missouri, has used several different mathematical models to show that evolutionary-based population figures for the earth are totally unreasonable. In fact, using the work of evolutionists Boyce, De Prima and May, Dr. Rodabaugh has concluded that the world's population essentially grows exponentially until it reaches equilibrium. As population nears equilibrium, growth slows.

Assuming that the earth's flood occurred 4,500 years ago, and the repopulation of the earth began with eight people, we are over half way to equilibrium.

Rodabaugh's work has been confirmed by studies with fish populations and various insects that naturally begin to level off at a certain density, even when there is plenty of food available. World population began slowing in 1977, even while life spans were increasing.

Holland is twice as densely populated as India. But India is marked by economic poverty, squalor and human misery, while Holland is relatively prosperous. India's population density is 400 people per square mile. India has more natural resources than Holland and a better growing climate, too. The logical conclusion is that the religion, philosophy, habits, motivational structure and attitudes of people are the primary determinants of human conditions, along with the following economic and political structure.

Dr. Colin G. Clark, in June of 1980, speaking to a college audience in Santa Paula, California, said, "Even at present levels of agricultural science, a properly cultivated world could support 10 times the present numbers on an American-style diet."

We have the technology and creativity, when harnessed with man's pursuit of his best self-interest long-term, to solve the world's problems. The solution begins with each individual being humble, empathetic, dutiful, responsible, long-term oriented, and accordingly free. Man's choice, on both the spiritual and natural level, is to grow or die.

SCIENTIFIC DISCIPLINES ESTABLISHED
BY CREATIONIST SCIENTISTS

DISCIPLINE	SCIENTIST
ANTISEPTIC SURGERY	JOSEPH LISTER (1827-1912)
BACTERIOLOGY	LOUIS PASTEUR (1822-1895)
CALCULUS	ISAAC NEWTON (1642-1727)
CELESTIAL MECHANICS	JOHANN KEPLER (1571-1630)
CHEMISTRY	ROBERT BOYLE (1627-1691)
COMPARATIVE ANATOMY	GEORGES CUVIER (1769-1832)
COMPUTER SCIENCE	CHARLES BABBAGE (1792-1871)
DIMENSIONAL ANALYSIS	LORD RAYLEIGH (1842-1919)
DYNAMICS	ISAAC NEWTON (1642-1727)
ELECTRONICS	JOHN AMBROSE FLEMING (1849-1945)
ELECTRODYNAMICS	JAMES CLARK MAXWELL (1831-1879)
ELECTRO-MAGNETICS	MICHAEL FARADAY (1791-1867)
ENERGETICS	LORD KELVIN (1824-1907)
ENTOMOLOGY OF LIVING INSECTS	HENRI FABRE (1823-1915)
FIELD THEORY	MICHAEL FARADAY (1791-1867)
FLUID MECHANICS	GEORGE STOKES (1819-1903)
GALACTIC ASTRONOMY	WILLIAM HERSCHEL (1738-1822)
GAS DYNAMICS	ROBERT BOYLE (1627-1691)
GENETICS	GREGOR MENDEL (1822-1884)
GLACIAL GEOLOGY	LOUIS AGASSIZ (1807-1873)
GYNECOLOGY	JAMES SIMPSON (1811-1870)
HYDRAULICS	LEONARDO DA VINCI (1452-1519)
HYDROGRAPHY	MATTHEW MAURY (1806-1873)
HYDROSTATICS	BLAISE PASCAL (1623-1662)
ICHTHYOLOGY	LOUIS AGASSIZ (1807-1873)
ISOTOPIC CHEMISTRY	WILLIAM RAMSAY (1852-1916)
MODEL ANALYSIS	LORD RAYLEIGH (1842-1919)
NATURAL HISTORY	JOHN RAY (1627-1705)

NON-EUCLIDEAN GEOMETRY	BERNHARD REIMANN (1826-1866)
OCEANOGRAPHY	MATTHEW MAURY (1806-1873)
OPTICAL MINERALOGY	DAVID BREWSTER (1781-1868)
PALEONTOLOGY	JOHN WOODWARD (1665-1728)
PATHOLOGY	RUDOLPH VIRCHOW (1821-1902)
PHYSICAL ASTRONOMY	JOHANN KEPLER (1571-1630)
REVERSIBLE THERMODYNAMICS	JAMES JOULE (1818-1889)
STATISTICAL THERMODYNAMICS	JAMES CLARK MAXWELL (1831-1879)
STRATIGRAPHY	NICHOLAS STENO (1631-1686)
SYSTEMATIC BIOLOGY	CAROLUS LINNAEUS (1707-1778)
THERMODYNAMICS	LORD KELVIN (1824-1907)
THERMOKINETICS	HUMPHREY DAVY (1778-1829)
VERTEBRATE PALEONTOLOGY	GEORGES CUVIER (1769-1832)

NOTABLE INVENTIONS, DISCOVERIES

OR DEVELOPMENTS BY CREATIONIST SCIENTISTS

CONTRIBUTION	SCIENTIST
ABSOLUTE TEMPERATURE SCALE	LORD KELVIN (1824-1907)
ACTUARIAL TABLES	CHARLES BABBAGE (1792-1871)
BAROMETER	BLAISE PASCAL (1623-1662)
BIOGENESIS LAW	LOUIS PASTEUR (1822-1895)
CALCULATING MACHINE	CHARLES BABBAGE (1792-1871)
CHLOROFORM	JAMES SIMPSON (1811-1870)
CLASSIFICATION SYSTEM	CAROLUS LINNAEUS (1707-1788)
DOUBLE STARS	WILLIAM HERSCHEL (1738-1822)
ELECTRIC GENERATOR	MICHAEL FARADAY (1791-1867)
ELECTRIC MOTOR	JOSEPH HENRY (1797-1878)
EPHEMERIS TABLES	JOHANN KEPLER (1571-1630)
FERMENTATION CONTROL	LOUIS PASTEUR (1822-1895)
GALVANOMETER	JOSEPH HENRY (1797-1878)
GLOBAL STAR CATALOG	JOHN HERSCHEL (1792-1878)
INERT GASES	WILLIAM RAMSAY (1852-1916)

KALEIDOSCOPE	DAVID BREWSTER (1781-1868)
LAW OF GRAVITY	ISAAC NEWTON (1642-1727)
MINE SAFETY LAMP	HUMPHREY DAVY (1778-1829)
PASTEURIZATION	LOUIS PASTEUR (1822-1895)
REFLECTING TELESCOPE	ISAAC NEWTON (1642-1727)
SCIENTIFIC METHOD	FRANCIS BACON (1561-1626)
SELF-INDUCTION	JOSEPH HENRY (1797-1878)
TELEGRAPH	SAMUEL F. B. MORSE (1791-1872)
THERMIONIC VALVE	AMBROSE FLEMING (1849-1945)
TRANS ATLANTIC CABLE	LORD KELVIN (1824-1907)
VACCINATION & IMMUNIZATION	LOUIS PASTEUR (1822-1895)

Source: Institute for Creation Research, 2100 Greenfield Drive, El Cajon, CA 92021

ENVIRONMENTAL JUDGMENT

In today's culturally conforming church, we do not hear many sermons preached from the Old Testament books of the prophets. The words of Jeremiah for example, are just too strong for today's "nod-to-God" Sunday Christians. The prophet speaks of God's judgment, of back-sliding believers reaping what they have sown. Disregard for law, political and economic injustice, and environmental abuse are the painful results of sin as described by the prophet.

By not rightfully dividing the Word of Truth and by ignoring the words of the prophet, the modern, secular, compromising church has not dealt with the sad fact that 93 cents of every dollar spent globally on Christianity today is spent in the United States. Of that amount, 40 cents of every dollar is spent on bricks and mortar - showplaces, buildings, crystal cathedrals and the like. Meanwhile, less than one-half of one cent of every dollar available to the church goes for missions, for recruiting soldiers for God's army.

Don't economics and Christian stewardship (works) boil down to nothing more than people and things, to labor and the resources of the land? Of course! People are more important than things, because people create, destroy, use, abuse, consume and determine the use of the resources of the earth. So, as people go, in a godly manner or an ungodly one, so goes the environment. Often God's blessing or judgment is revealed in the form of natural consequences. There is a direct link between environmental integrity and godliness, and environmental degradation following ungodliness. Godly men and women act as stewards of the earth, transforming the witchcraft-loving wilderness into a garden. Ungodliness leads to rape of the earth as humanistic, evolutionary man acts naturally as either a predator or a parasite. Even the secular press has had to come to grips with this reality. In first quarter, 1990, the U.N. Conference on Trade and Development began talking about a new class of displaced persons in the poor countries called "environmental refugees." To quote the U.N. report, "Growing human pressure on the natural environment has either rendered ecosystems more vulnerable or triggered off a self-reinforcing process of natural degradation, or both. As a result, more people are affected by natural catastrophes, such as landslides, cyclones, earthquakes and flood."

None of the countries plagued by "environmental refugees" are Christian nations. In fact, the world's 42 poorest countries, all of which are non-Christian, are becoming poorer, with economic growth rates lagging behind the population explosion. Further, as night follows day, environmental degradation has increased in these countries. The U.N. is confirming that government is always religion applied to economics. Religion always comes down to economics, just as on an individual level, faith comes down to works. Evolutionary, natural humanistic government bankrupts the environment as well as the economy.

Two quick examples of modern day environmental ungodliness come to mind - the situation in Ethiopia and the clear-cutting of the rain forests (jungles) of Brazil. Concerning Ethiopia, starvation among the people there inspired the song, "We Are the World." And yet, as global relief streamed to those impoverished people, the communist government of Ethiopia charged an outrageous tariff on the donated foodstuffs, and then diverted their use to their own dia-bolical means. The emergency foodstuffs were swapped for arms. Additionally, little American press was given to the fact that, in large part, the starvation of the people of Ethiopia was planned by the communist government as a means of eliminating internal opposition.

The impoverished masses of Ethiopia - uneducated, unskilled, ungodly, with no capital - were reproducing out of control and rap-idly turning the once-lush Ethiopian environment into a wasteland, a wilderness. Apart from Colin M. Turnbull's important book, "The Mountain People," little has been written about how magic, envy and environmental degradation among primitives have all been linked to-gether in Ethiopia.

While it is true that Third World inhabitants have an economic incentive to have many children in order to support agricultural labor and to provide for them in old age, it is also true that this short-term perspective - stemming from these motives, as well as lack of sexual restraint - puts an uncompromised burden on the environment, which leads to its devastation long-term. Eventually, the wasted environ-ment can no longer support the expanded population burden, much less the original numbers, and war, civil unrest, pestilence, disease, famine and natural catastrophes take their toll in the natural cycle. The natural man ends up reaping what he has sown in terms of na-ture and cycles, the fallout from his short-term view.

This is the reality the U.N. and the World Bank have had to come to grips with in Ethiopia today. The World Bank, in a compre-hensive study which received little press coverage, observed that it was effectively a Catch-22 to feed the starving masses of Ethiopia.

If the people of Ethiopia were fed, they would simply produce more children, whom they were unable to care for, leading to even further abject poverty, disease, degraded and impoverished human conditions, as well as accelerated environmental deterioration. On the other hand, if the people were not fed, they would starve. It was a lose-lose situation, according to the U.N. and the World Bank. Why? Because people are either the ultimate resource, or the ultimate predator or parasite. In Ethiopia, people are parasites and predators, not the Christian human resource necessary to turn the wilderness and desert into a garden. Clearly, Ethiopia needs Christian reconstructionist missionaries, for overpopulation is indeed a myth where a Christian world and life view exists and is applied.

Christianity requires short-term pain for long-term gain in the edification and progressive sanctification process. This is the obedience and discipline of discipleship. It is also a formula which is basic for success in the unbelieving world as well. God, in His mercy, causes the rain to fall on the good and evil alike. This is common grace. People who desire to prosper and to protect the environment have to first be willing to discipline themselves. This requires a long-term view of the future and a willingness to act in accordance with it, to forego short-term consumption and benefits (painful) for long-term objectives. This is called deferred gratification.

Have the people of Ethiopia shown a willingness to discipline themselves sexually, operate according to covenant and contract, husband their resources, save their seed corn to plant during the upcoming planting season, plan, learn skills, cooperate, and invest in and operate a free market where the balance of the one and the many can be maintained? No. So, reaping what they have sown, God's environmental judgment is upon them. While the Law-Word of God is life, the two-edged sword cuts both ways: the wages of sin are death. This is the difference between Holland and India today, between Christian America and the early America of the Indians, between South Korea and Ethiopia. Malthus is not the issue.

It is moral restraint and the long-term view which come only with a Christian culture that leads to sexual restraint, deferred gratification in economics, and resultant environmental blessing. These savings, where both human and natural resources are nourished for future development, provide the capital necessary to transform the earth from a wilderness into a garden. Again, man becomes the ultimate resource rather than an evolutionary predator or parasite.

In the case of the bulldozed Brazilian rain forests, the rich industrialized countries are at odds with the poor local people there. The Japanese, as the buyers of the land, exploit the region unmercifully, while West German and U.S. environmentalists try to bring pressure to bear on the Brazilian government to stop the slash-and-burn policy of the rich oxygen-producing rain forests of the Amazon, which are so critical to the environmental stability of the world. But the story which does not reach the newspapers of the American public is that the poor people of Brazil feel they have the right to try to make a better life for themselves. If that means slashing and burning the Amazon rain forests, so be it. It is their land, for the most part. It is their resource, and the people there need the money in the hyper-inflating Brazilian economy just to make ends meet. Actually, as the late Dr. Iben Browning demonstrated, grasslands produce more oxygen than jungles (rain forests). A garden is better environmentally than a wilderness.

UNICEF reports that more than 500,000 children died in 16 Third World countries in 1988 because the governments there cut back on social spending in order to pay debts to industrialized countries. Nearly one billion people are suffering because of these debts owed by the Third World. So, there is unresolved economic conflict between the Third World and the industrialized world. Who is correct? What is at issue here? The situation in Brazil, as in Ethiopia, is presently lose-lose.

A major problem and unaddressed issue is that of ungodly money, of compound interest and usury, something against which the Old Testament prophets railed with equal venom as against adultery, theft, murder and social injustice. Wealth is being transferred from Third World countries like Brazil to rich countries like the United States (a record $33 billion in 1988 alone) just to service debt on Third World loans. In order to meet this debt service, and in an attempt to keep up with Brazilian inflation, the locals in Brazil have to decimate their own environment. Eliminate ungodly loans, establish honest money, put into practice a biblical policy on lending which eliminates usury and compound interest, and the environmental problem diminishes. Invest instead in the developing Third World in the basic unit of economic development, the small family farm, where free energy from the sun through photosynthesis transforms energy into commodities which can be monetized, and a viable solution is found. Surpluses, over time, will then accumulate and the environment will get a rest.

Then there is the problem of absentee ownership of land, contrary to biblical economics. No man should own more land than he can restore to a garden. No man should own so much land that he violates the spirit of community. In Brazil particularly, the Japanese exploitation of the rain forest land is odious.

All this is nothing new. In Jeremiah 9:12-14, the prophet poses a question: "Why does the land perish and burn up like a wilderness, so that no one can pass through? And the Lord said, 'Because they have forsaken My law which I set before them, and have not obeyed My voice, nor walked according to it, but they have walked according to the imagination of their own heart and after the Baals, which their fathers taught them.'"

Evolutionary humanism and idol worship of things natural result in environmental judgment and bring economic suffering to a people. Human nature has not changed.

Do the words of Jeremiah 6 have application to environmentally degraded conditions in Ethiopia and Brazil? Absolutely. Should the words of this prophet convict rich, fat, backslidden and ungodly American clergymen and their flocks in this age? For sure. Climatological evidence informs us we have entered a difficult period extending to the year 2012.

Hosea, in Chapter 4:1-3, speaks directly to the state of a paper nation: "There is no truth or mercy or knowledge of God in the land. By swearing and lying, killing and stealing and committing adultery, they break all restraint with bloodshed after bloodshed. Therefore the land will mourn; and everyone who dwells there will waste away with the beasts of the field and the birds of the air; even the fish of the sea will be taken away." In the living energetic realm of the spirit, man's lawless actions negatively impact the earth.

Many patriotic American Christians readily quote 2 Chronicles 7:14 when they discuss God's condition for a national reprieve from judgment. What they should do first is quote 2 Chronicles 7:13: "When I shut up heaven and there is no rain, or command the locusts to devour the land, or send pestilence among My people, if My people who are called by My name will humble themselves, and pray and seek My face, and turn from their wicked ways, then I will hear from heaven, and will forgive their sin and heal their land."

Environmental judgment by God, causing economic hardship, is the forerunner of the godly humility, prayer and obedience necessary to ultimately heal the land.

REFLECTIONS ON THIRD-WORLD POPULATIONS, ENVIRONMENTAL DEGRADATION AND UNGODLINESS

The respected Scientific American of May, 1990 focused on "High Fertility in Sub-Saharan Africa," in an article written by John C. Caldwell and Pat Caldwell. The authors were exploring why, with a worldwide decline in birth rates over the past fifty years, the one exception was sub-Saharan Africa. The conclusions drawn were that in sub-Saharan Africa, religious and social beliefs promoted large families. The poverty, human misery and environmental degradation which accompany the population explosion there make it abundantly clear that sub-Saharan Africa is simply reaping the fruits (misery) of living according to a non-biblical model. Levels of income, education, health and urbanization are lower in this region than in other world regions. Ghana, the Ivory Coast, Kenya, Nigeria, Senegal, Tanzania and Zambia were some of the countries examined.

Quoting Scientific American, "The core of African society is its emphasis on ancestry and descent. In religious terms, this is usually reflected by a belief in the intervention of ancestral spirits in the affairs of the living. In social terms, the emphasis is reflected in the strength of ties based on the family of descent - the lineage.

"...The belief in the power of dead ancestors is continuous with the awe of living ancestors who will soon pass over through death and with the belief that both could effectively curse ungrateful descendants to whom they have granted the boon of life."

The women in the sub-Saharan region are subjected to hard lives. They bear at least four children and, more times than not, six. Plus, women and children perform nearly all of the agricultural labor in this agrarian, environmentally ravaged society. Further, 20 to 50 percent of wives are in polygamous marriages. Additionally, women are responsible for much of the economic support for themselves and their children.

The men in sub-Saharan Africa are effectively irresponsible since they regard their spiritual return from their fertility as their most important value. Put differently, sub-Saharan Africa lacks the responsible, long-term oriented, family-based patriarchs necessary to anchor the society, much less lead it out of economic squalor and environmental abuse. Men there are simply not tied to their lineage in a responsible, husbanding way.

"Husbands...usually provide only limited economic support for their children; nevertheless, they can expect both loyalty and, as children grow up, material support for the rest of their lives - not to mention the all-important burial and subsequent rites."

Here the men can have their cake and eat it, too. While they have the incentive naturally to be sexually active and irresponsible, these men have incredible power, stemming from a non-Christian religious belief system that does not link power with responsibility and accountability.

"A living father whose children do not provide for him can curse them with misfortune in reproduction and other aspects of life.

"Fathers are likely to receive much more from children than they spend on them. Furthermore, the return is likely to be just as great to fathers who neglect and mistreat their children and the children's mother as to those who spend lavishly on them."

As a result of this pagan injustice, fathers are likely to desert their families; hence in Nigeria, Ivory Coast, Sierra Leone and elsewhere, up to half of all dependent children live with persons other than their own biological parents. There is no Christian concept of the nuclear family, of the basic husband/wife unit, with the husband as head of the household. Furthermore, there's no private ownership of land. Therefore, the best investment these men can make is in producing other human beings. "The prosperous rural patriarch is the one who has many wives and children working in the field."

Another fallout of the loose-knit, ill-defined social and family structure is widespread sexual promiscuity. In cause-and-effect fashion, the people of sub-Saharan Africa are now subject to rampant venereal disease with AIDS being prevalent.

Today, as witchcraft-based environmentalism spreads like wildfire, both the developed and the underdeveloped world need to take to heart that neither individuals or collective society show their love for God unless they obey His laws. God's laws are an expression of His love for man. Put differently, God's laws are intended for man's individual and collective good, to maximize freedom, peace and harmony, love and light, and bring prosperity to both individuals and collective society. Man should want to obey them. To say one loves God but does not trust and love Him enough to obey Him is a contradiction. God tells us that if we love Him, we will keep His commandments. So when God's law is disobeyed, in the case of sub-Saharan Africa, the result is suffering. From man's perspective, man is reaping what he has sown. From God's perspective, judgment has occurred. The wages of sin are death. All those who hate (do not obey) God love death.

The deteriorating status of the world today is clear evidence that men still love darkness more than light, that men still prefer to be their own god, even if it brings them misery and judgment in time and eternity.

COLUMBUS AND THE NEW WORLD...ORDER

We memorized it as children: "In 1492, Columbus sailed the ocean blue" ...and discovered the New World. Now little more than 500 years later, with the European Economic Commonwealth (EEC) in place, the North American Free Trade Agreement (NAFTA) in operation and the General Agreement on Trade and Tariffs (GATT) coming on line, we are primed for the grand finale which began with Columbus' discovery of the New World - the bigger and better New World Order.

Before Columbus discovered the New World, we are told it was a vast wilderness, inhabited by tribes of Indians numbering about 10 million. The Indians lived in harmony with nature, with each tribe supporting all of its members. ...This is a fairy tale.

In 1991, the folks bringing us the New World Order successfully sponsored the movie, "Dances With Wolves." "Dances with Wolves" is a profoundly religious statement.

"Dances With Wolves" was nominated for 12 Academy Awards and won seven, including best picture and best director. The Writers Guild of America named "Dances With Wolves" as best screenplay of 1990.

The social ramifications of this extremely slick reel of Hollywood propaganda continue to roll as the reshaping of American opinion accelerates in dramatic fashion. The March 25, 1991 The Wall Street Journal, in the center front column featured: "A Century Later, Sioux Still Struggle, And Still Are Losing. But "Dances With Wolves" Has Brought New Pride - And Maybe Some Tourists." The March 25, 1991 issue of USA Today featured a major editorial page essay by Patricia Nelson Limerick, which headlined: "Hollywood's chance to get beyond the cliches of Western myth." Said Limerick, "For most of the 20th century, when Indians attacked the cavalry, the audience thought, 'Oh, no!' In "Dances With Wolves," when Indians attack the cavalry, the audience thinks, 'Thank heavens!'"

This 180-degree flip of American public opinion is a doublethink which boggles the mind. It is nothing less than revolutionary in nature. It marks the successful discrediting of the Christian basis upon which Western civilization in the United States stood. The natural has replaced the supernatural. A civilization cannot stand for long when its historical roots and values are undercut. "Dances With Wolves" accomplished this in one fell swoop of Kevin Costner's film-clipping tomahawk. No longer can John Wayne shoot once and four Indians fall.

Limerick went on to write, "The shift limbers up the thoughts and emotions. That flexibility, in turn, permits Americans to face the fact that this nation originated in invasion and conquest, and that shock waves from those events still rattle our world today."

Actor/director Kevin Costner is called a "Western historian." ...Limerick really gets into it: "Virtually every scene in "Dances With Wolves" reawakens us, as well, to the power of nature in the West..." The blue and gold clad Western U.S. Cavalry are referred to as white wretches."

Another piece which appeared in USA Today, penned by Susan Wloszczyna, headlined, "Wolves, the new leaders of the pack." "The Big Bad Wolf is extinct. Good wolves, start howling...Thanks to Kevin Costner - who put the endangered animal in star's clothing with his Oscar-winning "Dances With Wolves" - the formerly re-viled predator is getting its due."

"Dances With Wolves" ranks right up there as a social condi-tioner with "Network," "Patton," "Close Encounters" and "J.F.K." The cinematic capturing of the landscapes is breathtaking. The Sioux Indian tribe is depicted as clean, wise, considerate, compas-sionate, a group of "noble savages," who live in harmony with the earth in sophisticated sensitivity. By sharp contrast, the U.S. Army cavalry soldiers are depicted as vile, crass, brutal, stupid, filthy, wretched excuses for humanity, unjustly violent toward both their fellow white man and the Indians, and totally insensitive to their en-vironment. The buffalo hunters' greed and wanton slaughter of inno-cent buffalo just for their valuable hides left the audience solemn. A wolf is pictured as a smart, sensitive and shy creature, curious when it comes to man, an animal that is loyal and in the end sacrifices its life as an expression of this loyalty. All in all, it's a wonderfully spun story. But it is just that, a story, a movie myth, marked by half truths and outright lies.

Yes, there were greedy, butchering buffalo hunters who slaugh-tered animals mindlessly just for their hides. But there were also responsible buffalo hunters who were aghast at this practice by their fellow white man and railed against it. Yes, there were too many incidents of brutalization of the Indians by the white U.S. Cavalry, but these were not in the majority. The Indians initiated more than their fair share of massacres and often rightfully earned their reputation as "savages," as they were viewed by the majority of peaceful frontiersmen and pioneers who settled the West. How many wagon trains went out and attacked Indians unprovoked? Were the Indians' massacres and warring against peaceful, westward-traveling settlers any more justified than would be Americans today warring against and massacring Hispanics who come up from Mexico, or Vietnamese who came to this country from Vietnam? Of course not.

A main myth presented in the movie pertained to wolves. Wolves can be quite mean, and do kill just for the fun of it, but not for food. Wolves, long-time ranchers say, delight in preying on innocent livestock, often just for the joy of killing. Wolves are nature's most perfect killing machine and will kill off their own food supply, threatening their own survival. The spirit of wolves is also part and parcel of the Indian medicine man's black arts, particularly when he was involved with mind-altering drugs. Even the European legend of the "werewolf" has its basis in fact, depicting the uncivilized insane who roamed madly through the countryside at the time of the full moon, crying out like the bone-chilling howl of a wolf.

Of the approximately 10 million American Indians who lived on this vast continent prior to the arrival of the settlers, many regularly starved to death. There was no love or compassion shown for widows, orphans or strangers in the land of the American Indian. Such unfortunates were either appropriated as slaves, or in case of the old, including members of one's own family, often put out to die. What else could be done when tribes live off the land, which is exactly what "living in harmony with nature" is. There are unexpected food shortages, and someone has to be eliminated. "Survival of the fittest" is the natural evolutionary law of supply and demand. One accurate Hollywood depiction of this truth was Richard Harris' movie, "A Man Called Horse." Today, however, with man as a steward of nature, a Christian ethic brought by the settlers, 270 million Americans are able to live in this country and none have any reason to starve to death, providing the local churches and charities do their job.

Lewis and Clark's journals describe traveling through northwestern mountain valleys. There the smoke was so thick due to Indian campfires (air pollution) that they could not even see the mountains on either side of the valley. Further, it was not unusual for the Indians to burn entire forests or set fire to grass prairies to drive out game that were slaughtered wholesale as they fled the fire. At times, clouds of dust from the buffalo in the plains rose 10 miles in the air. The now fertile fields of Iowa, which feed the world, were once mosquito and vermin-infested swamps, effectively good for nothing, until they were terraced, drained, and the ground beneath tilled to handle runoff so the fertility of the soil could be utilized. Finally, Indian tribes did regularly massacre one another. This was not the case among white settlers in their communities.

It is important to keep in mind a basic economic principle, one proven evidentially, both in the present day and historically. People who live off the land live tribally - socialistically. Socialism (a collective) results in human poverty, environmental abuse, envy and a squelching of individual initiative and creativity. (See Colin Turnbull's "The Mountain People.") It also results in the lowest common denominator effect, tradition being favored over innovation, and the lack of a work ethic. Both the people and the environment in such sad situations lose long-term. This is true whether we investigate American Indian societies or the advance tribal socialism of the former Soviet Union and Eastern Europe, where basic human material needs go unmet, where civil rights do not exist, where millions have been murdered and abused, and where the environment has been devastated. It's also true in tribal Africa, Latin America, and in the South Pacific. Living "in harmony with nature" really means living in subjugation to nature. If nature turns niggardly, which it does, then both people and the environment suffer. Either there has to be a benevolent natural growing season, in which case the population expands beyond its natural limits (the limits of the land), or the limits of a tribe's land have to be expanded to take care of the population increase. This leads to tribal warfare. If expansion of tribal lands is not possible, then it's back to "survival of the fittest." The weak die, and the environment is savaged. The lack of savings, a long-term view, future orientation, capital formation, and technological development which goes with "living in harmony with nature," inescapably, time and time again, results in abuse of the environment and/or man. This does not even consider the fact that military history has repeatedly demonstrated that a people with a superior technology inevitably conquer and rule over those with an inferior technology. The development of technology is a function of savings, capital, creativity and a long-term view, of men being stewards of the earth and taking dominion, rather than living in subjection to nature, rather than so-called "living in harmony with nature." Environmental preservation, just like art, is a consistent product of excess capital and a long-term view. These are Christian virtues.

Now let's get down to the crux of this movie matter, which at its base is religious. As discussed above, there is no such thing as "living in harmony with nature." Nature on its own operates according to the "survival of the fittest." "Survival of the fittest" is conflict, the opposite of harmony. Nor is "Mother Nature" motherly. The characteristics of the natural earth are conflict, chance, cycles, scarcity and shortages resulting in poverty and death. None of these are motherly characteristics. Thus, peoples who live consistently under this tyranny of nature are subjected to this undesirable lifestyle.

The tribal American Indians lived in continuous conflict or fear of conflict, whether it was from the white man or his fellow red man. They also lived a chancy existence, dependent upon the whims of nature. In the case of "Dances With Wolves," the tribe's very survival depended upon the chance that "where the buffalo roam" would be close to them. They were subject to the cycles of nature, so much so that even their homes had to be relocated with the seasons. Shortages, scarcity and poverty, which were inescapably part of living under the tyranny of nature, continually threatened the American Indian. Death was a constant threat also, a result of nature's cruel "survival of the fittest" methodology.

There is yet another important religious tie. The myth of "Mother Earth" is basic to Wiccan and Druid, witchcraft and their feministic spirit of the earth, Gaia. The wood used by witches in making their magic wands and the like is the wood of the holly tree, in other words, "Hollywood." Further, natural, pagan, feminine deities ruled over the empires of old, the original "new world orders." Egypt and Babylon, for example, were both ruled by female goddesses. The East-West Journal of December 1990 featured a key article, "Return of the Goddess." So, this New World Order we've been promised is in the process of taking us full circle back to the slavery of ancient Egypt and Babylon, complete with their pagan rituals and religions, demonic feminine goddesses, ruled by a Luciferian elite who manage an army of bureaucrats. Thus, it is no accident that the radical feminist movement is finding its grounding in witchcraft and pagan goddesses. It is also no surprise that when we read the literature of these hardcore "Mother Earth" environmentalists, we find that they think the earth's population needs to be reduced from its present five billion-plus level, down to less than one billion. In other words, 80 percent of us have to be eliminated in order for man to again be able to "live in harmony with nature."

Now for the killing blow to the philosophical root of "Dances With Wolves." We were all taught in the public schools that before

Columbus came to America, there were only tribes of Indians living scattered across this continent. Their only disturbance for centuries were wayward Vikings who stumbled onto the place about 1000 A.D., then regrouped and sailed back home. But this, too, is an insidious lie. We were taught wrong. Would Americans believe the careful work of an emeritus professor of Harvard University, a man who was President of the Epigraphic Society, a man who is editor and co-author of eight volumes of decipherments of ancient manuscripts, a man whose book was presented to the White House in 1977 by the American Booksellers Association as one of the best 250 books published between 1973 and 1977 in the United States, a man whose work was published by none other than the prestigious Times Books - in other words, an impeccable Establishment figure? Would Americans believe such a man? Such a man is Dr. Barry Fell of Harvard University, who has authored three important books about the true history of early America. Dr. Fell's three books are "Saga America" (ISBN 0-8129-0847-3), "America B.C." (ISBN 0-671-67974-0), and "Bronze Age America" (ISBN 0-316-27771-1). Dr. Fell's chronological listing of dates and events which occurred in ancient and medieval American history, as it appears in "Saga America," explodes the myth of Indians as "Native Americans." Columbus was a Johnny-come-lately, and American Indians, too, were preceded by other American settlers.

Between 325 B.C. and 250 B.C. the Carthaginians and Phoenicians traded in America. Roman traders, mainly Iberians, also were active in America, trading between 400 and 100 B.C. Jews settled in Kentucky and Tennessee in 69 A.D., followed by a second wave of Hebrew refugees in 132 A.D. North African Christians came to America in 450 A.D. and Libyan science and mathematics flourished in the western portion of North America after 500 A.D. Christian Celts were found in the West, along with Islamic inscriptions, from 700 A.D. onward. Finally, in 1492, Columbus reached the Caribbean and "discovered" America. And as Dr. Fell notes, many of the early American so-called Indians were not red men, but white men, with blond hair and blue eyes.

There are no wild assertions in Dr. Barry Fell's work. There are academic documentation and photographic illustrations of physical evidence presenting the pre-Columbus history of America. Dr. Fell also documents how Old World ocean travellers settled in California and Nevada beginning in the third century B.C. He links the Pueblo Indian culture with the North African cultures. He plots the Norsemen's travels as far west as Colorado and British Columbia. Dr. Fell also describes how Thomas Jefferson had suspected a relationship between some American Indian and North African languages. All this is in "Saga America."

In "America B.C.," Dr. Fell examines European temple inscriptions from New England and the Midwest that date as far back as 800 B.C. In "Bronze Age America," Dr. Fell demonstrates that Bronze Age Norsemen reached North America thousands of years before the voyage of Columbus and built civilizations along the St. Lawrence River. Records were left behind by these Norsemen of their visits, their religious beliefs, a standard of measure for cloth and cordage, and an astronomical observatory for determining the Nordic calendar year. Wrote Dr. Fell, "Their (the Norsemen) presence in Canada also seems to explain the later appearance of Nordic peoples on the North American Plains. On the evidence of inscriptions and artifacts found there, some Nordics migrated west and intermarried with the Dakota tribes to form the Sioux nation." In other words, the Sioux Indian nation so exalted and glorified in the movie "Dances With Wolves" was really a descendent of the ancient Nordic peoples! So much for the myth of native Americans.

Other clear evidence of Christianity was found, too, in early America. In "America B.C.," on pages 326-328, in the epilogue, Dr. Fell presents epigraphs of the birth of Christ and their deciphering. The Ogam inscription found in West Virginia is the work of Irish monks of the sixth century A.D.

Another useful book on the subject of the true history of early America, is Orville L. Hope's "6000 Years of Seafaring." Hope includes in his documentation the work of Dr. Cyclone Covey of the Department of History at Wake Forest University. Professor Covey is author of "Calalus," an account of a Jewish colony that existed at the site of Tucson, Arizona, some 700 years before Columbus. (Dr. Covey is also the author of "Homeric Troy and The Sea Peoples.")

Hope, in "6000 Years of Seafaring," provides photographic evidence of the Old Stone Tower located in Newport, Rhode Island, which was built by Irish monks many years before the Norsemen came to America.

On page 17, Hope comments, "Practically every world map published in medieval Europe, showing North America, had a passage to the north around the continent. There was a good reason: Norsemen sailed the Northwest Passage before 1350, when it was ice-free for a short time in mid-summer. They left artifacts and housing foundations along the northern coasts of Canada, White Eskimos on Victoria Island, followed whales down the Pacific coast, hunted them in the gulf of California, and left blue-eyed descendants on the coast of Mexico among the Mayo and Yaqui Indians."

On page 103, Hope reports, "Brendan the Bold found the Promised Land in 550 A.D. He enjoyed a pleasant visit with monks already there, then returned to Ireland." On page 202 writes Hope, "Capt. Peter Wynne, a Welshman, was appointed to the Council of Jamestown by the London Company. In 1608, Capt. Wynne wrote a letter to his patron Sir John Egerton, York House, London. He stated that, 'Gentlemen have been up James River to the Falls. Near the Falls they met Indians who spoke Welsh. These Gentlemen desire me to accompany them on their next journey up stream, so that I may act as their interpreter.'" On page 204, "On May 15, 1819, the Public Advertiser, a newspaper in Louisville, Kentucky printed a story of Lieu. Joseph Roberts meeting a Welsh-speaking Indian in Washington, D.C." On page 207, "In 1804, the Lewis & Clark Expedition was sent up the Missouri River and then on to the Pacific by President Thomas Jefferson. They spent the first winter at a Mandan village which was farther up stream than the Mandan villages visited by Varrenes. William Clark was much impressed by some Mandan women's blue eyes and blonde hair." Also, on page 207, Hope describes how the Welsh under Owen ap Zuinch, in the 12th century, found their way up the Mississippi as far as the Ohio. On page 209, "Both legends and facts show that white people lived in the mountains of West Virginia long before Columbus. There are religious messages and astronomical information carved on stones in Irish Ogam and Tifinag scripts."

All of this makes us wonder if the purpose of public (government) education is the search for truth or simply indoctrination? Just what have we been taught in the public schools and why? Is there really a difference in what students are taught in the state schools in the United States and what was taught in the former Soviet Union? Are both effectively State Indoctrination Networks (SINs)? We know we and our children have been propagandized in American public (government) schools and universities when it comes to democracy, socialism, big government, money and economics. Now we know we've even been lied to about our own early history. What about science, health and religion? Given our current level of dis-education, how prepared can we be as we sail into the New World Order?

SECTION I
CONCLUSIONS

CONCLUSION I

It is remarkable in a nation professing to be 88 percent Christian that so little of the governmental and economic system is indeed Christian. And since government is always religion applied to economics in any society, it speaks to how adrift and disconnected the American public-at-large has become from its mooring. Unlike today's typical citizens, early Americans understood this important religious/economic interconnect. Remaining ignorant puts us at risk since those who are connected and conscious have the potential to intimidate and/or seduce those who are disconnected and unconscious. Given our current situation, it is no small wonder that Americans are scratching their heads in bewilderment. Effectively, a Luciferian religious perspective is running the nation today through behind-the-scenes witchcraft and astrology, and economically, through debt money which is promoting and has given rise to a federal bureaucratic beast, and is moving toward a New World Order politically.

Religion in America today is too often the opiate of the people, an escape from reality. The established Christian church, by and large, has few clues about how all this comes together. If it did, the nation would not be in such a sad state of affairs. Faith comes down to works. As a man believes, so he perceives, so he feels, so he thinks and so he acts. It is an inescapable process. But when the hyper-Calvinists on one end of the Christian spectrum live only on the cold, hard, legalistic foundation of biblical law, and the hyper-Charismatics at the other end of the Christian spectrum attempt to build a spiritual house without a foundation, the former lacks compassion and involvement and the latter collapses for lack of grounding. The remaining middle mass of Christianity is too often left to drift mindlessly, unconsciously, or traditionally, often procuring an eternal life and fire insurance policy - or worse yet, falling victim to the spiritual and mystical occult trend produced by Hollywood, the mass media's liberal atheistic propaganda, or the government public schools' agenda! In such a pagan, evolutionary, narrow, slanted environment, the elitists who belong to the Council on Foreign Relations, who permeate corporations, the military, the mass media and both major political parties, work their will. A few benefit handsomely at the expense of the many.

The New Agers do have some sense of the integration of these governmental, religious and economic factors, at least better than the church. But after all, the children of darkness are often wiser than the children of light. The danger is that if the light within is dark, how dark is that light indeed. Put differently, white magic is more dangerous that black magic. A lie that is 95 percent true is more captivating and more dangerous than one that is only 25 percent true. Satan comes disguised as an angel of light. The New Age is filled with dark light.

Satan's first mental attitude sin, was the sin of pride. It led to his first active sin: rebellion against God's lawful authority. This was also Eve's first combination of sins, and throughout biblical times to the present, are the sins whereby women, who are designed by God as receiving units primarily, burn themselves up and self-destruct in their desire to be dominant. On the other hand, men who become response-unable (irresponsible) cease to be gentle (gentlemen) and further flame this rebellion. This emasculates men.

Satan wanted to rule, to be his own god, to make his own laws, to determine right and wrong and good and evil, to be as the Most High. This is the same thing New Agers want to be, goddesses and gods. Thus, it is no accident that the "God is dead" hippie movement of the 1960s found its full flowering in the 1990s, as the hippies of the '60s came of age. The vacuum in the nation's belief system, left by the announced death of a Christian God, was filled by witchcraft as the Hollywood theater literally replaced the church, as illusion replaced reality. The growth of the environmental movement is witness to this as witchcraft attempts to ground out in the wilderness of Mother Earth.

The trap, the deception, is that the goddesses and gods of the New Age truly have no just way to balance the rights of the many (individuals) with the rights of the one (the collective majority). In other words, where does the sovereignty of one goddess end versus that of another goddess? The coexistence of two goddesses brings up the questions of limits. If there are limits, then by definition neither of them can be a goddess. Both cannot be sovereign because a sovereign is limitless. Moreover, if/when the New Agers slip into the pantheism of nature, where all are "one," they accordingly lose their identity. How can a goddess lack identity? Whoops! This error (sin) allows the centralized federal government to slip neatly into this void of conflict and serve as the master referee, The Big Mama (not Big Brother), building its bureaucratic empire in the process of moving toward a New World Order. The New Agers sense that the operative power behind the federal government as god stems from witchcraft and astrology in the spiritual/supernatural realm, and from taxes paid by American wage slaves from the economic realm. New

Agers lust for their own unearned power. Thus, many of them war with the federal government religiously, politically and economically.

Many New Agers even see that the centralized federal government is the enemy of their individuality as goddess and gods. They recognize that the federal government playing the role of god is the maximum distortion of reality. Why? Because the federal government is both a religious and economic parasite, dependent upon power which it draws from both the economic and religious realms in order to feed its bureaucracies. Bureaucracies have historically been the greatest institutional manifestation of human evil. When the government, the parasite, can no longer draw any more power from the supernatural realm, or extract more taxes from its citizens, it then consumes its host, "we the people," to whom it has lied in its role as master referee and Big Mama. But then again, Satan is a thief, liar and a murderer, too. Thus, the growth of the centralized federal government, particularly a New World Order beast, is a direct indication of man's error in separating himself from the God of creation and falling prey to Satan's trap.

In such an occult environment as exists today, Satan is able to use his supernatural power from his invisible realm (based in witchcraft and astrology), as well as his power from the visible world (money), activated through government, to work his will. The elite Luciferians even claim the high moral ground in their belief that Lucifer is the rightful first born son of God, who Jesus Christ wrongfully deposed. The Luciferian goal is to reestablish Lucifer to his place at the right hand of God the Father. This is to be accomplished through a global governmental, religious and economic New World Order.

There are two ways in which a society can be organized in its never-ending attempt to achieve the collective, the "one," from the top down or from the bottom up. A top-down organization, while it may succeed short-term, long-term becomes a curse for all those except the few at the top. Top-down structures certainly do not achieve the "greatest good for the greatest number," by playing king of the hill, by using force, which is what the evolutionary "survival of the fittest" turns out to be. This began in our nation with the Unitarian-backed U.S. Civil War, then continued on with the robber barons of the late 19th century. They eliminated the sovereignty of God in the early 20th century, by altering the theology of the seminaries from an emphasis on the sovereignty of God to a focus on the humanism of man and his free will. Next, the insider elitists established the nation's private debt fractional reserve banking system, owned by their big banks, and called it the Federal Reserve (1913). This, in turn, created the use and abuse of credit which eventually led to the Great Depression, which further centralized power in the hands of the federal government. Along the way, the direct election of senators, which gutted states rights, and an income tax (1913) were instituted. In addition, a couple of world wars, which are the ultimate in urban renewal, were fomented in order to create a more powerful central government also. Individual man progressively lost his sense of elected destiny under a Higher Power (God), which left him under the control of the highest earthly power, a collective, in the form of the centralized federal bureaucratic government. Individual Americans were thus stripped of their former biblical governmental, religious and economic power as kings/ambassadors, priests, and stewards, respectively. In its place, the federal government became god walking on earth, following Hegel.

The earth is now the lord's, the civil government's. Land, real property today, even if it's owned "free and clear" without debt, still is not truly free. There has to be a tribute paid, a tax, a tithe, rent if you will, every year by way of real estate taxes to the civil government.

The top-down system inevitably must use coercion (force) to enforce its will. Force, by its very execution, eliminates freedom of choice. Bureaucratic rules and regulation tie up freedom like a cat caught in the proverbial ball of twine. People, by their nature, being made in the image of God, resent man-made limitations on their freedom. This means the centralized government, which exercises coercion to enforce its will from the top down, must use intimidation and/or seduction if it is to avoid the direct use of force. Negotiation is out of the question. Negotiation assumes true equality, and is a lateral/horizontal activity, not a vertical one. Intimidation essentially says, "I'm O.K, you're not O.K, I'll take care of you." This leads to Big Mama, the modern version of the whore of Babylon, using intimidation and then force, as it did with the Branch Davidian's massacre in Waco, Texas. Then there is the more sly tactic of seduction, which convinces people to believe, "I'm not O.K. but you, the government, are O.K., so you take care of me." This appeals to the natural, fallen, womb-based needs for control, approval and security, which all of us have to combat if we are to mature. Intimidation or seduction in turn legitimizes theft, whereby government extracts wealth from the productive for its own power purposes, and/or through transfer payments to build a political base which sustains Big Mama. Thus, the fear of the lord (government) is established.

Wealth is either earned or unearned. Unearned wealth is theft unless it is gifted voluntarily, such as through inheritance, charities, the church or other voluntary organizations. Therefore, as the federal government sustains itself through unearned wealth and attempts to bring about a unified political, religious, and economic New World Order we come to the point of collapse, bringing chaos and destruction. This is "helter skelter" witchcraft style. A parasite cannot play the role of god to the point where it fully consumes the host, because in doing so, it destroys itself. Thus, the top-down attempt to form the collective does not work. It inescapably fails.

Just as a chain cannot be stronger than its weakest link, the "one," the collective, a society in total harmony, cannot be achieved unless the individual "many" component parts are strong, and with motivation, are willing to voluntarily be forged together into the "one." In other words, force does not work long-term. The use of force is the hallmark of philosophical and intellectual bankruptcy. A top-down attempt to produce the "one," the collective, is a bankrupt effort.

This leaves us with the only other option by which society can be formed, that is, from the bottom up. This attempt to achieve the "one," the collective, was what early America was all about. This caused not only power, but also responsibility and accountability, to fall on individuals. This is painful personally because it requires sacrifice and discipline (Christians are called to be disciples, disciplined). But because it is painful, most people will not enter this narrow gate. So, the "many" individuals opt for what comes naturally, the easy way, to attempt to form the collective from the top down, whereby someone takes care of them, such as the centralized federal government, Big Mama. But we know that the top-down approach collapses. We really have no option but the disciplined, responsible, accountable, individualistic approach to attempt to become a harmonious society and community. Thankfully, the individualistic approach does work, but it has been lost in the modern era, leaving us to crave individual heros.

Mankind will always strive to become as "one" because God is "One." The Trinity of the Christian Holy Bible consists co-equally of three "Individuals" who are simultaneously "One." Though we, mankind, have not reached that elevated state of perfection, we strive for it. Christians are commanded to become perfect as Christ was perfect. Jesus Christ claimed to be perfect when He as God became man, walking on earth and achieved that reality individually on earth, in history. Jesus Christ, by living a perfect life without error (sin), repaired the rift between heaven and earth, reunited the natural with the supernatural (Newtonian with quantum/chaotic physics). Jesus Christ accordingly has all the authority and power presently, and His kingdom is being progressively established over the face of the earth as time marches on. We move toward peace on earth, the kingdom of God on earth, "Thy kingdom come, thy will be done, on earth as it is in heaven." It is not a question of if every knee will bow and every tongue confess that Jesus is Lord, only a question of when.

The end product for Christians is very close to what New Agers seek on their own. Individuals/Christians reach their greatest point of sovereignty on earth as they are self-governing and creative under a hands-on sovereign God who is above and over all His creation, where each man sits under his own vine and fig tree. Each man rules over his own garden, so to speak. This is peaceably obtained primarily through a voluntary covenant which man enters with his family and local church, and through the contracts into which he voluntarily enters in the economic free marketplace. Covenants and contracts are governmental, religious and economic documents for use by individuals (masculine) and voluntary organizations. They achieve the "one," the collective, through voluntary association, from the bottom up.

This bottom-up approach to achieve freedom, peace, prosperity and relative equality on earth is a far cry from the top-down approach, with its conflict-based evolutionary lie which strips man of his spirituality as made in the image of God, and his humanistic link to the earth as formed from the dust of the earth. The evolutionary doctrine which has dominated this century has led to environmental degradation as well as the bloodiest century in the history of mankind. Both man's cities and his land are jungles - wildernesses. Therefore, this attempt to form the collective, the "one," via the top-down, king-of-the-hill, survival-of-the-fittest approach needs to be discarded once and for all. It needs to be replaced by bottom-up individualism. But man first must have hope for eternity, for something beyond the grave. Otherwise, why work, why sacrifice, why endure short-term pain? Why not instead eat, drink and be merry when all one has to look forward to is death? Such a "God is dead" philosophy creates the void into which civil government, the parasite, moves. It's one or the other, top down or bottom up. Man must choose who he will fear and serve, civil government or God.

Individualism forces man to deal with the Ultimate Individual, the real Superman, the personal, governmental, religious and economic implications of the person, life and work of Jesus Christ, and His Law-Word.

It is no accident that Jesus Christ is the only religious leader whose name is taken in vain as a cuss word. It is also no accident in the New Age that everyone gets to be a god or goddess except Jesus Christ. This is symptomatic of man's basic rebellion against his Creator. Man is deceived when he rebels against Jesus Christ's laws of love and liberty, which when rightfully understood and applied, resolve the conflict between individuals (the many) and collective society (the one), maximize the freedom of human action, provide the fewest limitations on the human will, balance out yin and yang, and maximize human peace, happiness and prosperity. Establishing this Higher Authority from above and outside of fallen, death-based Newtonian nature - of which man is inescapably a part - is what frees man from the tyranny of his fellow man, and the top-down coercive attempt to unsuccessfully form a harmonious collective society. Too often, this reality escapes the Christian church, with its "pie in the sky, by and by" mentality. In its rush to hand out eternal life and fire insurance policies, it gives defacto assent to hell on earth. The church misses the mark too often by sleeping in the unconsciousness of the traditions of men, by covering traditions with some type of pious religious blessing, by being legalistic to the core with merciless law, and by attempting to access and activate the power of the supernatural without the foundation of obedience to God's Law-Word, thereby sending Charismatics reeling off into witchcraft.

The New Agers, unlike lawless born-again Christians who use grace as an excuse to do their own thing, are more consistent. For the New Agers, doing one's own thing is a consistent expression of the lawlessness of their godhead. Such is harmonious with what a god and goddess would attempt to do. The Catch-22 however, is that, as discussed above, there are limits to mankind where his fellow man is concerned (the "many" versus the "one"), as well as limits to individual man. All of us have limited time, money, energy, knowledge and power. So, how can individuals be activated to bring about the collective good? By first being "born again" eternally, saved eternally out of a fallen, error-based human nature, through the work of the Holy Spirit, who makes Jesus Christ real to individual man as Lord and Savior. Next, we recognize that unity and the collective good are achieved by individualistic efforts from the bottom up, the working out of individual salvation with fear and trembling. This requires individual discipline, responsibility and accountability, functioning with humility and duty.

The individualistic principle is the "yang" principle, which is masculine, linear, cause and effect-based, directional and light. In this sense, we all (both male and female) are and must be masculine. We all have to work individually to achieve the collective. We have to work to become perfect as Jesus Christ was perfect. In other words, faith without works is dead, as James wrote in the New Testament of the Bible. Perhaps this is why God chose to present Himself as masculine, as Father, Son and Holy Spirit. It is consistent with the essence of His creation. When we voluntarily, through an act of covenant, become the collective (or the feminine - yin), we, through covenantal relationships, create families and churches, and through voluntary contractual relationships also interface with our fellow man in the economic marketplace. We act in the "masculine" (individually, many - yang) to become the "one" (feminine, the collective - yin). So ironically, while New Age, witchcraft-based, environmental feminists rail against the Holy Bible as being male biased, in fact, from the larger perspective of the spiritual/electromagnetic realm, from yang and yin, individual and collective, masculine and feminine, all of us, men and women alike, must begin with the masculine perspective as individuals to successfully reach the feminine collective. When we understand God's masculine perspective in this larger sense, we can harmonically understand why the yang Hertzian wave is the carrier for the yin non-Hertzian scalar wave, the masculine again grounding and carrying the feminine. And why regarding authority, males rule over females in families and churches (Stephen Goldberg's book, "Why Men Rule," is important in this regard), why justice proceeds mercy, and why the head grounds and balances out the heart. Both masculine and feminine are equal in a sense, but in terms of authority and direction, one is necessary to precede the other, the masculine being prior to the feminine. Even physiologically, males are the initiators and women are the receptors. What should be sought is an equitable relationship, the first voluntary collective being the family.

This work hopefully will be a starting point for making course corrections by both the Christian church and the New Agers, both of whom have a significant piece of God's overall puzzle, both of whom presently have lost their way like a ship off course. To sin is to err, to miss the mark. My fondest hope and prayer is that this work will help link past and present and future, provide generalistic insight in a world of specialists, and be a springboard toward helping mankind become all that God has created him to be, to hit the mark! Each of us, individually, will still come up against the Ultimate Stumbling Block, the Person, life and work of Jesus Christ, the God-man, who in history made all this possible. After the recognition of this reality, we must overcome a second stumbling stone, which requires swallowing our pride and dismissing our rebellion, so that we can become rightfully obedient to His Law-Word, so that we are then self-governing, creative, open to the leading of the Holy Spirit and grounded in the earth. Then the Holy Spirit can teach us all things and allow us to fulfill the destiny for which each of us was created. We can become crystal christs. The end result is life abundant, both during our time on earth, and eternally.

CONCLUSION II

The world as God intended it for us: "His Kingdom come, His will be done, on earth, as it is in heaven" is entirely possible today. The understanding and the systems, theoretically and practically, exist and are already in place to bring about a Christian world of peaceful prosperity. We no longer need to be deceived. We know what works and what we need to do to achieve it. We know how and why government is always religion applied to economics, and what it takes for this master equation of society to function in a godly manner. We know where we have gone wrong, and what to avoid. And, we know what is required of us.

We as individuals (masculine/yang) are each called upon to be humble, empathetic, responsible, and dutiful toward our fellow man, disciplined and accountable, with a long-term view. We know what is asked of us by way of covenant and contract in order to build a society (collective/yin) of voluntary associations so that we are blessed rather than cursed. We know that as we literally become sons of God - fully integrated spiritually, mentally, emotionally and physically - the earth revives and blossoms into a garden. It is only through dominion (masculine) and stewardship (feminine), working together, that we spiritually bring in the kingdom of God which supports us with manifest blessings. As we govern ourselves in this manner, our fellow man wins; we win; God, of course, always wins; and His creation, the earth, wins. It is a four-way win, a complete circle, four 90 degree turns. No one needs to lose. Cooperation replaces conflict. We are able individually to develop our talents, nourish our families, be creative, have joy and life abundantly here on earth. Our lives can be rich in our relationships in our churches and other organizations and we can enjoy the riches of truth, love, compassion, justice, mercy and material things. We have everything to gain, and nothing to lose but ourselves, the part of ourselves that is dying anyway, both in our time on earth and eternally. When we lose ourselves, we find ourselves. When we die, we live.

This brings us to the spiritual, governmental, economic and historical issue of who and what Jesus Christ is. The hard truth is that He is the spiritual, energetic, and physical reconnect between fallen earth and heaven, between a dying natural and an eternal supernatural, between the entropy of Newtonian physics and the bright new world of the quantum/chaotic/post-chaotic. There really never is something for nothing. Someone always has to pay the price. Jesus

Christ, the eternal living Light, the righteous, perfect son of God, humbled Himself to become man and restore eternal fellowship with His creation, which was lost in the death throes of time. In return, we owe Him praise, honor, glory, allegiance, and obedience. The burden He places on us, compared to the alternative, is light, and under His authority we experience the most abundant life possible. His system for the earth, His creation, transforms us into ambassadors, kings, priests and stewards. This is a far cry better than having some centralized federal government serve as god walking on earth as the supreme king, priest and steward. Our choice boils down to God or civil government.

Ultimately, we have to sacrifice our pride and rebellion, and be willing to humble ourselves under God's higher righteous authority. We're always under authority anyway. How much better God's than a centralized federal government that strips us of our freedom through excess regulation and subjective courts, steals and hinders our priesthood, and impoverishes us economically through burdensome taxation, a deteriorating currency and debt money. A bottom line truth for the New Agers in this regard is that the closest we can come to being as God is as sons of God. In this status, true supernatural power comes with righteous, godly obedience, and does not burn us up as witchcraft does, which also condemns us as lost for eternity. So in a very real sense, the New Agers need to learn what the evangelical Christians, reconstructionist Calvinists, and charismatics know about becoming sons of God. And the Christian church-at-large needs to learn all that the New Agers understand with regard to quantum/chaotic/post-chaotic/physics' supernatural application of science and technology to all areas of life, and particularly the New Agers' supernatural understanding of what it means to be made in the image of God.

The church knows far more about what it means for man to be formed from the dust of the earth, while the New Agers know far more about what it means for man to be made in the image of God. It is the pulling of these two together, ferreting out the lies and deceptions, that provides the answers for us becoming all that God intended us to be, individually and collectively. The economic systems are in place. Churches and families exist. The science and technology are with us. The understanding and techniques to prevent men from becoming emasculated and women from becoming used up, providing instead both equitable and correct authority relationships, are now evident. The tools of covenant and contract are widely used, and now can be better applied. The perception and the means to work "bottom up" individually (masculine-yang) to freely achieve the harmonious, voluntary organizations which are the feminine collective (yin) are now apparent. The link between the West and the East has been made, the conflict between men and women abstractly resolved. The need for a Savior and His law to escape the death trap of a fallen nature, which only brings conflict, chance, cycles, poverty and death is grasped. So, why not change, why not us, why not now? The crystal christ is within us all. God is no respecter of persons. His will is for us all to repent, alter our behavior, and be saved, not only eternally, but here on earth as well. Let us begin.

CONCLUSION III

A common unstated thread which runs throughout this book is that our inescapable subjective perception of reality best serves us when it is linked to God's objective truthful model. We cannot escape the fact that we are all religious. We know that energy creates matter, and so as living energy with personality, information and purpose, we are spirit before we are matter. In fact, less than one percent of us is congealed energy, what we call matter. But because we have imperfect knowledge, limited time, are not all powerful, or omnipresent, we all make assumptions about the nature of reality (presuppositions). We all make leaps of faith about what is ultimately true. These presuppositions about what we believe is true are our anchor points religiously that determine how we think, how we feel, and how we behave. We are best served when we begin with our point of faith, our assumptions about what is true, with the Creator, and then think His thoughts after him. By following His model in our lives, we fulfill His will, and also become crystal christs which manifests our destiny with the maximum blessings possible. We all win individually, and in the process, all win together.

Following the example of the ultimate Crystal Christ - Jesus Christ, who restored the original linking bridge between heaven and earth - we can also, as sons of God (crystal christs in him as it were), work to complete that process in our dominion and stewardship responsibilities. For this to occur, what we believe as true spiritually must flow down into our mentality, permeate our emotions, and be active in our physical being and actions. In other words, a change in religious values, thinking God's thoughts after him, leads to a change in thinking - which results in a change of heart (emotions), which in turn results in a change in behavior. Our religious values determine the attitudes, opinions, and beliefs which we hold, which in turn result in emotional responses and our subjective truth. Our personal, subjective truth leads to judgments about life. This results in choices which may lead to action or inaction, followed by behavior, which leads to results. This sequence is inescapable for all human beings.

Truth kills those who hide from it. The further we are removed from the truth of the way God's universe works, the more error/misery/sin/death we find ourselves in. Consistent with this perceptive, there are eight principles of truth that underpin His model which, when acted upon, bring us full blessings in life. These eight basic principles as discussed throughout this book are:

1. The principle of the one and the many. This is a reflection of the Christian Trinity, God being "One," and also "Many" simultaneously. The "One" is a collective, the "Many" are the individuals in the case of the Christian Trinity - Father, Son, and Holy Spirit, united yet separate. This is alternatively referred to on earth as unity amid diversity, the whole and its parts, inclusion and exclusion, and feminine and masculine respectively.

2. The principle of the "one." This is alternatively labeled the whole, the collective, the feminine, the universal, and unity. Mankind is always attempting to become the "one." The problem is, rather than taking into account his creaturehood, his "formed from the dust of the earth" nature as part of the fallen, cursed, entropic, Newtonian system, mankind instead wants to be immediately as God. (New Agers see themselves as gods and goddesses). Man attempts to jump instantaneously from his imperfect creature state to the "one," without using the transitional bridge provided by Jesus Christ, without working out his salvation with fear and trembling by obedience to God's Law/Word/Model, which these eight principles reflect. As the "one," mankind seeks to reestablish without work and pain the control, approval and security known in the womb, and avoid the pain and fear of loud noises, chaos, rejection, and abandonment which occur during the first three years of life. More importantly, he attempts to establish himself as the ultimate decider of right and wrong, replacing God's law with his own. As we have seen throughout this work, however, mankind must first start with the masculine (individualism), the "many," in order to achieve the "one" (feminine/collective), if he is to be successful. The "many" create the "one." Man must work individually, horizontally with contracts and with covenants, rather than rely upon top-down vertical bureaucracies to attempt to achieve the "one." The latter bring death. The solution for mankind is horizontal and bottom up, not vertical and top down, except for leadership which rises to the top (earned leadership). We cannot emphasize enough that the solution is masculine (individual) to achieve the feminine/one/whole/collective/unity, not a blind leap of faith or an ungrounded quantum jump to mythical god or goddess status from man's fallen, imperfect, entropic Newtonian state. We must also keep in mind that the masculine principle of individualism is not sex-based. All of us as individuals are masculine. The masculine requires short-term pain for long-term gain. The process of individual, then collective and environmental redemption begins, however, with men who become mature Christian gentlemen. Only men are labeled cowards. Men must lead in the dance of life.

3. In this third principle, <u>we must not do what comes naturally if we are to achieve our desired ends long term</u>. Stated differently, <u>we have to do the opposite of what naturally feels right or seems natural to us</u>. Our natural feeling state is distorted by our fallen, error prone, entropic Newtonian-based nature, which according to the Second Law of Thermodynamics, includes conflict, chance, cycles, and poverty in route to death. So, we must do the opposite of what seems natural for us if we are to overcome in this life. One example of this principle is, we have to give (serve) first if we want to get (receive). This is the only way to meet both our spiritual and physical needs for love and money, respectively. This is in line with the Second Great Commandment and The Golden Rule. Another example is, we must give love if we are to receive love as mature adults. So, if we do not operate in this manner, we remain as little children, not free, not prosperous, irresponsible, undisciplined and immature with some authority, usually a bureaucracy, ruling over us.

4. The principle of <u>paradox</u> is next. This is also called the simultaneous coexistence of apparent opposites, or TNT (Truth-In-Tension). In Eastern philosophy, this is known as yang - yin, which is masculine - feminine, individual - collective, light vector, directional cause and effect - dark, magnetic, chaotic matrix. This is also man - wo-man. These are different ends of the spectrum of creation. They are not opposites. The genius, the truth, comes in the ability to hold these apparent opposites in dialectic tension until the apparent conflict between them resolves itself. Again, this is a reflection of who and what God is in the form of the Christian Trinity, the "Many" and the "One." Anytime we are in conflict, we are out of touch with God's truth, and not at peace. It is His Law/Word/Model - His spiritual boundaries incorporated into our minds (knosis), which in turn flow down into and frame the emotions of our human hearts (epiknosis) - that bring about peace between these warring apparent opposites.

5. The fifth principle is that <u>there is a gap between the super-natural and the natural, between heaven and earth, between Creator and creation, between the quantum and Newtonian, between metaphysics and classic physics</u>. God created His creation, and is active in it. His creation reflects His nature. But there is a distinct moral and physical difference of essence between God and His creation. Accordingly, there is a very important and distinct difference between man seeing himself as a god or goddess, and man being made in the image of God, as elect sons of God, but still possessing a death-based physical nature. God as Spirit is perfect living light en-

ergy, righteous and living truth with personality, information and purpose. He is, in terms of the seven L's, love, light, life, liberty, law, laughter (joy) and a long term view (eternal). His creation, however, which is in the process of being restored and linked back up to the Creator, has been subject to the laws of sin and death, to the Second Law of Thermodynamics. The entropy of this earth-based system is marked by conflict, chance, cycles, poverty and death. These natural factors, in whole or in part, characterize all cultures built on earth-based religions. On a spiritual, historical, moral, religious and economic basis - when the pure and perfect living light Creator, Jesus Christ, became congealed energy (matter), and took on the form of man, walked on earth, was tempted to err, but instead perfectly obeyed God's Boundaries/Law/Word/Model - He restored the link between the supernatural and natural, between heaven and earth, between quantum and the Newtonium, between metaphysics and classic physics, between God and his creation. Jesus Christ crossed and repaired the Einsteinian relativity bridge.

6. The sixth principle is the master equation of collective human action in all societies for all time. It is, government is always religion applied to economics. This can take the form of the collective, such as the federal government which is, as the philosopher Hegel wrote, god walking on earth. Or, the principle may be instilled in individuals, who act as God's appointed sovereigns on earth. In the first case, a centralized federal government always is a religious and economic parasite which inescapably consumes its host, "we the people." Civil government draws its religious ideas about right and wrong, good and evil, moral and ethics from the religious realm and legislates these ideas into laws. It implements these laws in the arena of human action, which we call economics. The cost of this process is funded by the taxes paid by individuals who operate in the economic arena. This is the yin/collective/one/feminine/unity/whole application of how government is always religion applied to economics.

The yang/masculine/individualistic/diverse/many perspective is that individuals are called by God to be ambassadors, kings, priests and stewards. In this fashion, individuals are under God's authority as ambassadors; are self-governing on earth as kings; are individual believers - priests; are charged to fulfill their economic destiny on God's earth as stewards. Individuals operate to fulfill their mandate to become the "one" by following The Golden Rule/the Second Great Commandment, using covenants and contracts, obeying the Ten Commandments, and overall following God's supernatural laws of love and liberty. As such, these individuals/the masculine/the many, voluntarily achieve unity/the one/the collective. The masculine operating peacefully to achieve the feminine is what brings harmony and prosperity. And it begins with the initiators, gentle-men.

7. The seventh principle includes the four primary character traits an individual embodies in his own life and in his interaction with other people to achieve God's purposes on this earth. They are humility, empathy, responsibility and duty. Humility and empathy are abstract principles. Responsibility and duty are concrete principles. Humility and responsibility are personal, empathy and duty are others' oriented. Together, they link the "many" into the "one." These four principles are sheltered under the umbrella of love, of which the foremost applications are compassion and forgiveness. They are undergirded by both of the Golden Rules which speak to man's spiritual and physical nature: Spiritual - Do unto others as you would have them do unto you. Physical - Whoever has the gold (money) makes the rules.

8. The final principle has to do with man coming as close as possible to imitating God's eternal nature. By doing so, man always takes the long-term view. God is eternal, so the closest man can become to being God-like, is to take the long-term view. If we take every principle in the Bible, and flip it into the realm of time, the biblical principles require us to do the right thing long-term. The natural tendency of man is to follow the path of least resistance, which is to look for short-term gain with no pain. ("If it feels good, do it." "Trust your instincts.") The problem is, this leads to win-lose relationships short-term, and lose-lose relationships long-term, while God's way leads to win-win-win-win relationships - everyone all around wins, God, our fellow man, ourselves, and God's creation.

Life is not all that complicated. It is just that getting to the core of His truth requires us to slash through a hedge of thorns. The essence of these eight principles we see implemented daily in all cultures, in all races, and all languages, in all geographic locations throughout the world in the automobile traffic system (where it operates successfully). God's truth is truth whether we find it by way of specific election or common grace.

The world is searching for a New World Order. So is God. He desires to bring in His own New Age, His millennium, by godly individuals constructing it. As such, it begins with humble, empathetic, responsible, duty-bound, disciplined individuals, possessed of a long-term view, when their spirits, mentality, emotions and physical being and behavior emulate The Crystal Christ, the ultimate king, priest and steward, Jesus Christ. As we as individuals follow this process, letting, as Sheldrake put it, morphogenic information fields, righteous ones - literally the Spirit of God - lead us in all truth, then we as sons of God - individual crystal christs so to speak - will see the kingdom of God here on earth. Christ must be within us before we can effectively work toward restoring the earth to perfection.

For more information on R.E. McMaster, Jr.'s books, newsletter and other work, contact A. N. Inc. (International), P.O. Box 84901, Phoenix, Arizona 85071. Telephone (800) 528-0559.

INDEX OF SCRIPTURE REFERENCES

Old Testament

New Testament

INDEX

INDEX

INDEX

INDEX OF AUTHORS

INDEX OF AUTHORS